KITCHENER

Portrait of an Imperialist

BY

PHILIP MAGNUS

LONDON

JOHN MURRAY, ALBEMARLE STREET, W.1

First published October 1958
Reprinted November 1958

Printed in Great Britain by
Butler & Tanner Ltd., Frome and London, and
published by John Murray (Publishers) Ltd.

TO MY MOTHER

CONTENTS

	AUTHOR'S NOTE	xi
1.	IRELAND, 1850–1874	1
2.	PALESTINE AND CYPRUS, 1874–1880	13
3.	CONQUEST OF EGYPT, 1880–1884	30
4.	MAHDISM, 1884–1889	53
5.	COMMANDER-IN-CHIEF, 1889–1896	75
6.	THE SUDAN, 1896–1898	94
7.	KITCHENER OF KHARTOUM, 1898–1899	118
8.	RULER OF THE SUDAN, 1898–1900	138
9.	KRUGERISM, 1900–1901	160
10.	CONQUEST OF SOUTH AFRICA, 1901–1903	182
11.	THE QUARREL WITH CURZON, 1903–1905	204
12.	APOTHEOSIS, 1906–1910	227
13.	RULER OF EGYPT, 1910–1914	252
14.	SECRETARY FOR WAR, 1914	276
15.	RIDING THE WHIRLWIND, 1914–1915	299
16.	LOOS AND THE DARDANELLES, 1915	331
17.	ECLIPSE, 1915–1916	355
	INDEX	383

ILLUSTRATIONS

PAGE

Kitchener as a subaltern in the Royal Engineers [1] . . 66

Kitchener aged 35 [2] 66

Kitchener as Governor of Suakin, aged 38 [2] . . . 67

Kitchener as Commander-in-Chief of the Egyptian Army,
aged 46. 1896 [2] 67

Kitchener with his friend and A.D.C., Frank Maxwell, V.C. [3] 82

Kitchener Pasha [1] 83

First meeting between Kitchener and Boer envoys at Middelburg [3] 194

Kitchener at 22nd General Hospital, Pretoria, 14 June, 1900 [4] . 194

'Fallen Leader'. President Kruger [5] 195

'Laughing Cavalier'. Kitchener at Southampton on return
from South Africa 195
(*Photo. Cribb, Southsea*)

Lord Curzon of Kedleston, 1898 [5] 210

General Charles Gordon [5] 210

Kitchener at Simla [4] 211
With C.-in-C. Gwalior, Col. Hubert Hamilton and Capt. Victor
Brooke

Port Said, 1911 274
Khedive Abbas Hilmi II, King George V and Kitchener
(*Exclusive News Agency*)

Broome Park 275
(*Copyright 'Country Life'*)

Kitchener as Field-Marshal [1] 290

Recruiting Poster, 1914, designed by Alfred Leete . . 291
(*Imperial War Museum*)

ix

LIST OF ILLUSTRATIONS

PAGE

War Lord [1] 354

Kitchener in Gallipoli greeting French C.-in-C. [4] . . . 355

Kitchener with General Birdwood in Gallipoli [4] . . . 370

Kitchener with General Birdwood at Mudros [4] . . 370

Kitchener leaving the War Office before his journey to Russia,

June, 1916 [3] 371

IN TEXT

'Dreaming True' [6] 145

Eastward Ho ! [6] 193

A Waste of Good Material [6] 249

MAPS

Egypt and the Sudan 44–45

South Africa 161

By courtesy : [1] *Mansell Collection.* [2] *Illustrated London News.* [3] *Radio Times Hulton Picture Library.* [4] *From a photograph in the possession of the Family.* [5] *Gernsheim Collection.* [6] *The Proprietors of 'Punch'.*

AUTHOR'S NOTE

WHEN I undertook, in 1954, to write Kitchener's life, I found that he had left a large and miscellaneous mass of papers. They had been used by Sir George Arthur when he wrote his three-volume life of Kitchener which was published in 1920 ; and it was clear that Kitchener had been at pains from about his thirty-fourth year to preserve papers which he thought important.

Kitchener kept, for example, copies of all telegrams which he sent, and of all reports which he made, as well as all telegrams which he received, while he was establishing his reputation during the Nile expedition of 1884-5. And thirty years later, when he became Secretary of State for War in 1914, he took advantage of the fluid state of the contemporary distinction between private and public papers to lift many important secret letters and documents from the War Office.

On the other hand, when he was serving quietly in Zanzibar in 1886, and rather less quietly at Suakin a year later, Kitchener pre-served little ; and chance, rather than design, seems at all times to have determined the quantity of purely personal correspondence which he kept. He was notoriously careless with papers, and excep-tionally untidy ; and it is significant that, whereas Lady Salisbury, for example, preserved all the letters which she received from Kitchener, few of the many letters which Kitchener received from Lady Salisbury have survived.

Kitchener's handwriting is extraordinarily attractive. It is bold and clear, and almost as beautiful as the Prime Minister, Lord Palmers-ton's, which Gladstone described as the best he had ever seen. The letters, too, which Kitchener wrote to intimate friends, belied, at times, his reputation for taciturnity. His letters to Lady Salisbury, for example, were often surprisingly long-winded ; but every page is as legible as typescript.

Many of Kitchener's letters give an impression of breathlessness, owing to an almost total neglect of punctuation. He made a free use of dashes, but he followed no system ; and when he was really roused he would sometimes end one subject and start another without the aid of a fresh paragraph, a full stop, or even a capital letter. In those circumstances, when quoting his letters, I have inserted punctuation marks in order to help the reader.

All references to published and unpublished sources are given in footnotes. Where no reference is given the source is invariably Kitchener's unpublished private papers which belong to his great-nephew, Lord Kitchener. The only apparent exception is an occasional direct reference in the text to notes made by Kitchener's friend and favourite, Field-Marshal Lord Birdwood, which belong to the Field-Marshal's son, Lord Birdwood.

Apart from Kitchener's papers, the principal unpublished collections upon which I have drawn are those of the Prime Minister, Lord Salisbury, at Christ Church, Oxford (Salisbury Papers) ; those of Salisbury's son and grandson (Hatfield MSS.) ; those of St. John Brodrick, Lord Midleton ; those of Field-Marshal Lord Roberts of Kandahar ; those of General Sir Reginald Wingate ; and those of Kitchener's friend and solicitor, Arthur Renshaw.

I want to express my deep and warm gratitude to the whole Kitchener family, especially Lord Kitchener, Lady Broome and Miss Madge Kitchener. I owe a very great debt to Lord Kitchener for unstinted help and constant encouragement, as well as for his kindness in allowing me to keep all his family papers at my home in Shropshire while I was writing this book.

I am deeply grateful also to Lord Salisbury, K.G., P.C., for his kindness in allowing me to use the Salisbury Papers, and for his great courtesy in sending to me, and in allowing me to use, all the letters written to his mother, Lady Salisbury, by Kitchener, and by members of Kitchener's staff. That material has thrown as much light upon Kitchener's years as Commander-in-Chief in India between 1902 and 1909, and upon his quarrel with Curzon, as the Salisbury Papers have thrown upon Kitchener's character and conduct as Commander-in-Chief of the Egyptian Army, and as conqueror and ruler of the Sudan.

It is not possible to record the names of everyone who has responded generously to my inquiries ; but I would like particularly to thank Sir Ronald Wingate, Bt., C.M.G., who has been extremely kind and patient ; as well as Lord Birdwood, M.V.O. ; Mr. David James ; Dr. J. F. A. Mason, of Christ Church, Oxford ; the Dowager Lady Midleton ; and Lady Winifred Renshaw. They have all given me access, or facilitated my access to material of the greatest value.

I want also to record my gratitude to Lady Askwith, C.B.E. ; Colonel Robin Baily, C.B.E. ; Mr. L. R. Bradley (Director of the

Imperial War Museum) ; Lord David Cecil, C.H. ; Lady Chol-
mondeley ; Mr. Guy Cobbold, M.C. ; Sir Herbert Creedy, G.C.B.,
K.C.V.O. ; the late Lord Colum Crichton-Stuart ; Lady Gage ; the
late Mrs. (Florence) Cripps Marc ; the late Mrs. Frank Maxwell ; the
late Lord Mersey, P.C., C.M.G. ; Sir Harold Nicolson, K.C.V.O.,
C.M.G. ; the Secretary of the Palestine Exploration Fund ; Sir
Edward Playfair, K.C.B. (Permanent Under-Secretary at the War
Office) ; Lord Powis ; Major R. H. C. Probert ; Mr. E. K. Stopps
(Chief Registrar at the War Office) ; the late Marshal of the Royal
Air Force Lord Trenchard, G.C.B., O.M. ; Mrs. Twining ; and
Mr. D. H. Varley (Chief Librarian of the South African Public Library
in Cape Town). Last, but only because he would wish to be last, I
want to say how much indebted I am to my friend and publisher,
Mr. John G. Murray.

P. M.

Stokesay, Shropshire
1958

CHAPTER 1

IRELAND

1850–1874

HORATIO HERBERT KITCHENER was born on 24 June, 1850, at a shooting-lodge known as Gunsborough Villa, three and a half miles north-west of Listowel, in County Kerry, in the south of Ireland. His family had risen recently to gentility from small farming origins in Hampshire and, later, East Anglia, as a result of the enterprise shown by the boy's grandfather, William Kitchener (1768–1807), in leaving Lakenheath, near Mildenhall, Suffolk, to become a tea merchant in London.

The tea merchant's youngest son, Henry Horatio Kitchener, was born in London at 8, Bunhill Row, on 19 October, 1805, two days before the Battle of Trafalgar. He made the army his career, reached the rank of Lieutenant-Colonel, and became the father of the Field-Marshal.

Colonel Kitchener joined the 13th Light Dragoons and transferred, later, first to the 9th and finally to the 29th Foot. When he was a Captain, aged thirty-nine, he married on 24 July, 1845, Frances Ann, daughter by his third wife of the Rev. John Chevallier of Aspall Hall, Suffolk.

Mrs. Kitchener was twenty years younger than her husband, whom she accompanied to India. Their first child, a son, Henry Chevallier, was born in India on 5 October, 1846. The climate of India did not suit Mrs. Kitchener, and when her health became precarious her husband brought her home in 1847, and went on half-pay.

The second child, a daughter, Frances (Millie), was born in London in 1848. Colonel Kitchener tried throughout that year to obtain military employment at home, and resolved, when he failed, to start a new life in Ireland.

Colonel Kitchener sold his commission early in 1849 and moved his family to Ireland, where he looked round for a suitable property to buy. That country had just been decimated by the great potato famine of 1846–7, which caused about three-quarters of a million deaths and drove hundreds of thousands of survivors to emigrate. The population was reduced from some eight millions to some six and a half millions, and ruin had overtaken a high proportion of the less substantial Irish landlords, in consequence. Rents, during the famine, became difficult to collect, and bankrupt landlords were in no position to meet their liabilities under the Poor Law, or to carry out necessary improvements. In an attempt to resolve those difficulties, the Government passed the Encumbered Estates Act of 1849, with the object of facilitating the speedy transfer of estates from bankrupt owners to capitalists equipped with the means to manage them efficiently and to improve them. Vested interests were overridden accordingly, and power was taken to break trusts. The Act made possible the immediate unrestricted sale of any bankrupt estate on the petition of a landlord or of a creditor.

Speculators sprang forward to take advantage of that opportunity. They bought land cheaply in a glutted market, and proved even more ruthless than their predecessors had been in clearing wide areas for grazing and in evicting tenants who fell behind with their rent.

A large majority of the new landlords were native-born Irish capitalists, and Colonel Kitchener, who was an Englishman, was neither better nor worse than his fellows. He had no love for Ireland, but much for his family, and he was proud of his East Anglian connections. The name Horatio which he bore, and which he bestowed upon his famous son, was borrowed from the East Anglian hero, Lord Nelson.

Upon settling in Ireland, Colonel Kitchener quitted a profession which had lost almost all the popularity that it had earned during the long war against Napoleon. A liberal and secure age regarded the Army as an expensive incubus, and the disgraceful mismanagement of the war in the Crimea, which broke out in 1854, seemed to confirm the popular idea of the Army as an exclusive caste, and as a hotbed of patrician insolence. It was felt that Great Britain could safely rely upon her wooden ships, which often lasted for sixty years. They had been accumulated in such numbers, that before the advent of ironclads no foreign Power was in a position to outbuild or outclass Great Britain.

The Indian Mutiny, which closely followed the Crimean War, restored a measure of prestige to the Army without increasing its popularity. That was not regained until the 1870's, when a new mood of imperialism began to capture the imaginations of vast numbers of the newly-enfranchised British masses. That spirit, nursed by Disraeli, provided a response to the challenge posed by popular nationalist policies which were being pursued on the European continent.

2

During the late 1870's a prolonged agricultural and trade depression hit Great Britain. Railroads which opened up the American middle west, and tariff barriers which arose throughout the western world, were the principal causes. The great capitalist Powers could not have achieved upon a free world market the industrial strength and prosperity which they built up behind tariff walls. In consequence, the liberal dream of an age of universal peace, founded upon free trade and guaranteed by the Royal Navy, dissolved into air. Large sections of the most advanced and influential sections of the working class among the leading nations of mankind became dependent upon popular nationalist policies which plunged Europe into the catastrophe of 1914.

Even before the close of the nineteenth century those policies had precipitated a menacing growth of armaments which shook the foundations of the dominant liberal philosophy of the age. They seemed to portend a giddy race towards war or bankruptcy, and threatened the security of Great Britain. The outnumbered British masses were not subject to conscription and were beginning to lose their industrial lead. The wooden ships on which they had so confidently relied were already outmoded, and the naval arm, like much else within contemporary experience, became subject to a process of rapid and bewildering change. Ship-design, gunnery and armour took on the appearance of a series of dissolving views, and a subconscious sense of insecurity caused Great Britain to seek compensation for her increasing relative weakness in the Old World by consolidating her overseas strength and extending her imperial sway.

In a world-wide imperial policy, the Army as well as the Navy had a vital part to play ; and in a democratic age it was essential that the Army should secure an emotional hold over men's minds. Colourful leaders with impressive characters and commanding personalities were required ; and they arose to meet that need. None since the Duke of Wellington proved as colourful or as popular— none stamped the seal of his character and personality so deeply into the hearts of his countrymen—as the boy, Herbert Kitchener, who was born in a famine-stricken corner of Ireland within sight of the Shannon estuary on 24 June, 1850.

The boy's father, Colonel Kitchener, was still in the prime of life. He might have won distinction in the Crimea or in the suppression of the Indian Mutiny if his military career had not ended prematurely ;

3

but he never saw active service. He was a disappointed and frustrated man, noted for the foulness of his language ; and he became an eccentric martinet who ran his home as far as possible on army lines. His hour for breakfast was eight o'clock, and no servant would have dared to be even a few seconds late. Mrs. Kitchener, who invariably breakfasted in bed, was less fussy. But her husband insisted that, for reasons of discipline, her breakfast should be as punctual as his own. Accordingly, Mrs. Kitchener's maid was accustomed to wait, balancing the tray, outside the door of her mistress's room until the clock struck the hour, when she would march briskly forward at the sound of the first stroke.

Colonel Kitchener, who was proud, fearless and independent, brought up his children to regard themselves as members of a master race in a strange land. He had sufficient shrewdness and self-command to coax the best out of the native peasantry by whom he was surrounded, but its outlook and traditional way of life stirred his indignation and contempt.

Colonel Kitchener bought, early in 1850, under the terms of the Encumbered Estates Act, a bankrupt estate known as Ballygoghlan which was partly in Kerry and partly in Limerick. The village was deserted because the inhabitants had either perished during the famine or fled. The house, which was being made comfortable at the time when Herbert Kitchener was born, stood on a hill about twelve miles west of Gunsborough and two miles from the River Shannon. A year or two later Colonel Kitchener bought the finely-timbered Crotta House estate in Kerry as a second home. Crotta House was a mile from Kilflyn, where the household worshipped each Sunday in what was, in effect, a garrison church. The place is nine miles south of Listowel and about the same distance north of Tralee. Crotta House, which was grander than Ballygoghlan, had been built in three storeys for the Ponsonby family in the late seventeenth century. It enjoyed wonderful views over the broom-covered Kerry hills, but Ballygoghlan was the children's favourite home.

Colonel Kitchener improved his properties so well that he prospered. He bred and trained polo ponies, and became a recognized local authority on agricultural matters. He was especially proud of his success in setting up a brick factory and a pottery, and in reclaiming marsh land by means of an effective system of surface drainage. He cut out waste and delay by using slabs of local stone for drainage, instead of pipes or tiles.

4

Herbert's boyhood was passed against that background. He was the natural leader of his two younger brothers, Arthur, born in 1852, and Walter, born in 1858. A governess, Mrs. Sharpe, who joined the family in the autumn of 1858, recalled Herbert as a very pretty, fair boy, with golden hair, small pearly teeth, blue penetrating eyes and an angelic smile.

In comparison with the other children Herbert was exceptionally reserved. He was missed one day at luncheon and was found hiding under a bed with a badly crushed hand. A large piece of stone had fallen on it, but the boy seemed to prefer to suffer alone rather than to enlist adult aid and sympathy. It was noted also that, unlike the others, he preferred to say his prayers at night kneeling alone at the foot of his bed, instead of aloud to his mother or the governess.

Herbert's sensitiveness troubled his mother, who feared that his instincts were too much repressed. She found him weeping one day when a tree had been felled, holding in his hands four dead fledgelings which had fallen out of a nest on one of the upper branches. He would not be comforted until he had buried the birds himself with great care and deliberation, each in its separate grave.

Herbert was regarded as the most helpful of the children. He enjoyed cutting and packing the turf which was burnt in most of the rooms at Crotta and Ballygoghlan during the winter. Colonel Kitchener's steward maintained that Master Herbert packed the turf better than any peasant in the district. He appeared also to enjoy sorting potatoes when they were dug, and he never understood why his father laughed at him for undertaking menial tasks.

All the children possessed ponies, but Herbert lagged noticeably behind the rest in horsemanship. He made amends later, but he opposed, in consequence, his father's wish that he should join a cavalry regiment. He admired and feared his father, and had early resolved to join the Army; but he set his heart on the Royal Engineers.

The Kitchener children led an extremely simple country life without playfellows or expensive toys. They were a self-contained unit; they hardly ever quarrelled; and they developed a communal discipline to protect an exalted code of honour of which their father cordially approved. As a most rigid disciplinarian, Colonel Kitchener encouraged his children to govern their little commonwealth by inflicting punishments upon one another. The justice of those punishments was never questioned; they were endured with resignation; and although they were sometimes rather brutal, they

5

left no rancour behind. It is on record that after committing some minor offence against the family code, Herbert once submitted to being spread-eagled on the lawn in the attitude of a crucified man. He was found by his mother on his back in the hot sun, pinned effectively to the ground by his arms and legs, which were roped securely to croquet hoops.

Colonel Kitchener held strong views about a number of subjects, including education. He despised and detested schools. His children were educated by tutors, and Herbert's tutors, the Rev. William Raymond and the Rev. Allen Freeman, were not particularly successful. The boy's knowledge was tested from time to time by his first cousin, Francis Elliot Kitchener (1837-1915), who was a Fellow of Trinity College, Cambridge, from 1863 to 1868, subsequently an assistant master at Rugby, and finally Headmaster of the High School at Newcastle-under-Lyme. He complained that he had never known a boy more totally devoid of any groundwork of education.

Even at that tender age an aspect of Herbert's nature was exposed which was not apparent in any of his brothers. Although he disliked reading, he possessed a strong artistic sense ; and Francis Kitchener reported that the boy was quicker to appreciate the merits of a work of art, when they were explained to him, than he was to appreciate almost anything else.

In 1863 the Kitchener family experienced a period of tribulation. Mrs. Kitchener's health started rapidly to deteriorate, and one of her husband's more preposterous eccentricities may have contributed to that result. Colonel Kitchener detested blankets and held that they were unhealthy. He argued that newspapers were perfectly capable of keeping anybody warm ; and he always plumed himself upon his inventiveness. Accordingly, around the double bed in which he and Mrs. Kitchener slept, boards were erected to which sheets of newspaper, sewn together, were attached. Extra layers were added in the winter and removed during the summer, and the Colonel maintained that it was much easier to obtain the precise degree of warmth required with newspapers than it was with blankets. Colonel Kitchener would have preferred that he and his wife should sleep wrapped up in newspapers, but he hit upon the device of boards soon after his marriage because the rustling of paper prevented his wife from sleeping.

Colonel Kitchener adored his wife, and the children worshipped

6

their mother. As soon as it became clear that her lungs were seriously affected, the homes in Ireland were closed and sold at an extremely handsome profit. In 1864 the family migrated, first to Bex, and then to Montreux, in Switzerland, where it was hoped that medical treatment and pure mountain air might help Mrs. Kitchener to recover. But that hope was disappointed, and she died at Montreux in 1864.

Despite his masterful ways, Colonel Kitchener had always depended upon his wife. He married again two years later, Emma Green, who was his daughter's music mistress, and by her he had one daughter, Kawara, who was born in New Zealand in 1867. That marriage did not prove a happy one. He bought a property near Dunedin, New Zealand, with the proceeds of the sale of his Irish estates, and he visited New Zealand with his second wife, before settling at Dinan, in Brittany. In the meantime, Herbert and the two younger boys were left at school in Switzerland. They were sent first to a school near Geneva, and later to the Château du Grand Clos, at Rennaz, two miles from Villeneuve at the eastern end of the Lake of Geneva. They remained there from 1864 to 1867 in the care of the Chaplain of the English Church at Montreux, the Rev. J. Bennett.

In Switzerland Herbert acquired fluent French and rudimentary German, and some, at least, of his educational deficiencies were repaired. He discovered an aptitude for mathematics, but he and his brothers in later life could hardly bear to recall the bitter humiliation which they experienced when they first went to school and found that they knew virtually nothing. Among the cowed and unhappy Irish they had been accepted as natural leaders, and they had regarded themselves as such. But in France and in Switzerland they found that the valuation which they set upon themselves evoked ridicule. They were shy, and tongue-tied, and incapable of making friends easily ; and their pride received a severe and salutary shock.

As the most sensitive member of the family, Herbert made much the most vigorous response to that challenge. He worked so hard that he damaged his health, as he concentrated all his energies on qualifying himself for the entrance examination to Woolwich. When the time drew near he was coached by his cousin, Francis Kitchener, at Cambridge, and by a well-known Woolwich crammer, the Rev. George Frost, in London. At Frost's house at 28, Kensington Square, Herbert formed with Claude Conder, who was also being crammed, the first of those warm masculine friendships with which, throughout his life, he solaced a congenital loneliness.

In January, 1868, Kitchener passed into the Royal Military Academy at Woolwich. He was placed twenty-eighth in order of merit out of fifty-six successful candidates, and he made, on the whole, an indifferent impression. He was very tall, slim, and exceptionally good-looking ; but he played no games ; he had temporarily outgrown his strength ; and he was noted for an impulsiveness and naturalness which some of his fellows equated with bad form. He had not been moulded by a public school, and he was slow to learn the need for conformity. At the same time, he was attracted so strongly to the High Church ritualist movement that he studied Hebrew, in his spare time, with Claude Conder. He worked exceedingly hard in an effort to overcome the sense of inferiority which he had experienced when he first went to school in Switzerland, and he missed one entire term as a result of overtaxing his strength. When he passed out successfully in December, 1870, he joined his father at Dinan, in Brittany ; but there were no Christmas celebrations that year for the jubilant cadet.

That Christmas was the gloomiest which France had experienced for more than half a century. The Franco-Prussian War had broken out on 15 July, and one shattering disaster had followed another. On 2 September the Emperor Napoleon III had surrendered at Sedan ; two days later a republic had been proclaimed ; and on 27 October, by a miserable act of cowardice and treachery, Marshal Bazaine had capitulated at Metz. The last hope of France was a *levée en masse* of the adult male population ; and Lèon Gambetta escaped (7 October) in a balloon from the siege of Paris with the object of organizing a desperate struggle to the last man and the last round.

No better opportunity could have been presented to a military cadet, resident in France, eager to prove his courage, and to gain experience of his trade. Kitchener's father, who always regretted that he had seen no active service himself, encouraged his son, and his son's friend, Henry Dawson, to attach themselves to a field ambulance unit of the Second French Army of the Loire.

Kitchener and Dawson proceeded via Rennes to General Chanzy's headquarters at Laval, in the department of Mayenne. The army which they joined was composed of ill-trained and poorly equipped local levies, and it was heavily defeated (10 January, 1871) in a sanguinary three-days' battle around Le Mans. In that battle, and in the confused fighting which followed, Kitchener underwent his baptism of fire. He witnessed, without manifesting any visible

8

sign of emotion, the slaughter of large numbers of men and horses.

On one occasion Kitchener ascended with a French officer in a balloon. He wore no warm clothing, however, and he contracted a chill which developed into pneumonia and pleurisy. He was rescued, in a critical condition, by his father from an insanitary billet, and brought to England as soon as he was fit to travel.

First-hand experience of war is worth months and often years of training, and Kitchener's reputation was enhanced by the initiative which he had shown. His commission had, however, been issued while he was serving in France ; it was dated 4 January, 1871 ; and he was accordingly summoned to the Horse Guards to explain his escapade, and to endure a fiery rebuke at the hands of the formidable Commander-in-Chief, Field-Marshal H.R.H. the Duke of Cambridge. The Duke told Kitchener that, by attaching his miserably insignificant person to the army of one of the two warring great Powers, he had violated the policy of strict neutrality to which the Government of his country was committed. He threatened him with pains and penalties, including the loss of his commission. As the young man, abashed and shaken, prepared to take his leave, the Duke's eyes twinkled kindly and he stretched out his hand : " I am bound to say, boy," he remarked, " that in your place I should have done exactly the same."

Kitchener told his friends that he did not know, officially, that he had been commissioned, and that he had supposed that a resident in France at that time was as free to amuse himself by shooting Prussians as by shooting partridges. Everyone admired the pluck and zeal which he had displayed, but he had to wait forty-three years before he received (29 March, 1913), as a Field-Marshal, the commemorative medal for the campaign of 1870-1 which he had earned as a cadet.

Kitchener was posted to the School of Military Engineering at Chatham two days before the arrival of a new instructor in field-work, Captain R. H. Williams, with whom he quickly formed a close friendship. Williams ordered Kitchener to vacate his bedroom because it formed part of the quarters which had been allotted to the instructor. Kitchener, ' a very tall, very slight youth ', went at once to see Williams, whom he did not know, in order to protest. He spoke with such charming and disarming modesty that Williams arranged that Kitchener should continue to sleep in his quarters : ' In a week,' Williams noted, ' we understood one another, took our

daily exercise in company, sat next each other at mess, went to
evensong together, became inseparable.'

A glowing high-churchmanship helped to cement that intimacy,
and the friendship will serve to illustrate a significant aspect of
Kitchener's nature. Apart from one romantic attachment during
his middle thirties, he remained throughout his life a natural celibate.
He never married, and a great loneliness descended upon him which
was widely observed and regretted. But like a happy warrior he
turned his necessity and misfortune to glorious gain.

Kitchener's sexual instincts were wholly sublimated like those of a
Catholic priest. He found fulfilment in his work, admitted few
distractions, and thereby reaped an incalculable advantage in competition with his fellows. The key to his character, as one of his
A.D.C.s, Lord Edward Cecil, noted[1] many years later was a belief
'that he was defrauding the Almighty if he did not carry out his
task'. Kitchener placed the fulfilment of any task which he had
set himself, or which others had set him, ruthlessly before all else :
' Comfort, affections, personalities—all were quite inferior considerations . . . He preferred to be misunderstood rather than to be suspected of human feeling.'

Kitchener loathed any form of moral or mental undressing, and
he was a man of rare humility and simplicity. Whatever temptations
he may have experienced during a long career in the Orient, and
despite an increasing measure of intoxicating hero-worship to which
he was continuously exposed, he lived a life of inviolable purity
and self-control. He adhered inflexibly to an exalted moral code,
and he protected himself by constructing against the world a barricade
of impenetrable aloofness. That barricade was manned by a small
circle of intimate and understanding friends, from whom he won a
degree of affectionate devotion which few men are able to command.
In his unostentatious piety, in his few but fervent friendships and in
his love of art he found relief for the tensions of his mind.

At Chatham, for a time, Kitchener risked even mockery by his
resolute observance of quite minor Church festivals, fasts and vigils ;
and he astonished his father by displaying an unexpected passion for
porcelain. Colonel Kitchener often joked about his son's mania for
collecting bric-à-brac, but he would attend sales when asked to do
so, and he took scrupulous care of his son's treasures. Eccentric
himself, he always set the highest value upon independence of mind

[1] *Leisure of an Egyptian Official*, p. 184.

and strength of character ; and he soon came to regard his son's mildly improbable hobby as affording a substantial proof of both.

The militant phase of Kitchener's Anglo-Catholic enthusiasm was not of long duration ; but while it lasted he drew a number of like-minded officers and men around him in an effort to oppose the anti-ritualist agitation which led to the Public Worship Act of 1874. Williams noted that that Act provided 'just enough persecution to keep us all at white heat ', and Kitchener's religious enthusiasm was the main factor which caused him to apply successfully to be seconded for special duty in Palestine during the autumn of 1874.

After leaving the School of Military Engineering in April, 1873, Kitchener was selected to serve as A.D.C. to Brigadier-General George Greaves at the annual summer manœuvres of the Austrian Army. The subaltern's spirited bearing and rare good looks attracted the eye of the Emperor Francis Joseph, who more than once made Kitchener sit next to him at meals, and who gave him leave and facilities, when he asked for both, to investigate personally some new bridging equipment on the Danube.

Upon his return to England, Kitchener was posted to a mounted troop of Royal Engineers at Aldershot, a place which he detested. He worked hard, however, at the new science of field telegraphy, and his Commanding Officer, Lieutenant-Colonel K. E. Elphinstone, described[1] him (16 October, 1873) as ' A most zealous and promising officer—thoroughly acquainted with his special work, and performs his duties to my entire satisfaction.' At Aldershot, to which Williams was also posted, Kitchener was proud of having helped to increase an Anglo-Catholic congregation of thirty officers and men to a congregation of nearly one thousand.

Kitchener spent his summer leave in 1874 in Hanover, working to improve his German in order to study the books of German engineers. He had first conceived the impulsive idea of going out to the Gold Coast and of offering his sword to Sir Garnet Wolseley, who was campaigning there against the Ashanti ; but his father refused to provide him with funds, and warned him that he would make himself ridiculous. Kitchener had, however, another plan for escaping from the uncongenial regimental and social routine of Aldershot ; and at the suggestion of his friend, Claude Conder, he applied, in August, to be seconded for special service in Palestine under the aegis of the Palestine Exploration Fund.

[1] War Office Records.

The Fund had been formed in 1865 with an illustrious committee to prosecute scientific research in the Holy Land, which then formed part of the Turkish Empire. Its founders hoped to repel, with scientific aids, the onslaught which contemporary scientists were making upon the foundations of orthodox religion ; and the War Office seized that convenient opportunity to spy out the Palestine hinterland. In July, 1872, Kitchener's friend, Lieutenant Conder, R.E., was lent by the War Office to the Palestine Exploration Fund, and placed in command of a small expedition which was conducting a detailed survey of Palestine west of the River Jordan, on behalf of the Fund.

The fruits of that survey were a twenty-six sheet map of western Palestine from Dan to Beersheba which was published by the Ordnance Survey Department on a scale of one inch to a mile in 1880. The maps were accompanied by three volumes of ' memoirs ' which were compiled by Conder and Kitchener, edited, with additions, by E. N. Palmer and Sir Walter Besant, and published on behalf of the committee of the Fund between 1881 and 1883.

Conder had almost completed twenty out of the twenty-six sheets of his map, when on 23 June, 1874, his civilian assistant, Charles Tyrwhitt Drake, died of fever in Jerusalem. Conder immediately applied for Kitchener as Drake's successor, and Kitchener enlisted all his friends in support of his application. The military authorities were agreeable, and Disraeli's Government, which had come into power in February, 1874, was eager to pursue a forward policy in the Near East, and elsewhere. Kitchener was seconded, accordingly, on 2 November, 1874, for special service in Palestine ; and on 19 November he joined Conder in camp at El Dhoheriyeh, in the plain of Philistia. The party consisted of two subalterns, three corporals, and a native clerk.

CHAPTER 2

PALESTINE AND CYPRUS
1874–1880

KITCHENER in Palestine was as happy as a sand-boy. He infused such energy into the survey that the rate of progress quickly rose from about 76 to about 280 square miles a month. He calculated the cost, with characteristic frugality, at about one pound a square mile. He took innumerable photographs, and spent his spare time studying Arabic and Turkish.

At Christmas the party retired to Jerusalem, where Kitchener spent two and a half months arranging Conder's notes, conducting archaeological research on sacred sites and recovering from a severe attack of dysentery. He rejoined Conder, when his health was restored, at Beit Jibrin on 13 March, 1875.

The War Office wanted military information ; but it made every allowance for the fascination of the work of discovering and transcribing inscriptions, identifying biblical sites, and acquiring archaeological techniques. The honorary secretary of the Palestine Exploration Fund, Sir George Groves, discreetly reminded members at the annual general meeting on 10 June, 1875, that :

' Such archaeological results as are obtained in the course of exhausting labours in triangulation, must not be taken as part of the duties which the officers are sent out to execute, so much as additional proofs, if any were needed, of their zeal and ability. The real work for which Lieutenants Conder and Kitchener are responsible is the great map of Palestine.'

Kitchener found his feet in Palestine, and he impressed the eminent French archaeologist, C. Clermont-Ganneau, who met him on a number of occasions, as a tall, slim, vigorous boy who was capable of headstrong acts. Clermont-Ganneau described Kitchener as carefree and outspoken, with ' recesses of winsome freshness ' ; and he said that in comparison with Conder's preternatural seriousness, Kitchener's constant flow of high spirits made a delightful impression.

After completing the survey of western Palestine from Beersheba to Nazareth—more than four-fifths of the whole—the party travelled north, through Nablus and the Hebron hills, during June, 1875. That area was a hotbed of Moslem fanaticism, but no serious trouble

13

occurred until Safed was reached, in the high hills of upper Galilee, at four o'clock on the afternoon of 10 July.

The party had pitched its tents in an olive grove, when some Arabs approached and began to make disparaging remarks about Christ. A pistol, belonging to one of Conder's servants, had been hung upon the branch of an olive tree. It was missed, and when inquiries were made, the servant was violently abused by a well-dressed, turbaned and insolent Arab. Conder turned fiercely on the Arab, who retorted by picking up two or three large stones which he hurled at Conder's servant.

When Conder advanced to the rescue of his man, the Arab sprang at his throat. Conder knocked him down with a blow to the chin, and his servants picked up a knife which the Arab had drawn. They then bound the Arab's arms and legs with ropes.

On arriving at any place, Conder invariably sent to the local Turkish commander, and to the chief native resident, a messenger carrying the Sultan of Turkey's imperial order that every courtesy and assistance should be offered to the English survey party. That order had always resulted in the prompt arrival of a deputation to inquire what help was needed. Conder was expecting such an official visit at any moment, and he decided to retain his prisoner until the Turkish soldiers should arrive.

The prisoner bellowed so lustily that a crowd of over two hundred quickly assembled ; its mood was ugly, and Conder prudently ordered that the prisoner should at once be unbound and set free. The prisoner responded by inviting his friends to cut the Christians' throats ; and the entire party, which consisted of five Englishmen and ten native servants, was immediately subjected to a fierce fusillade of stones.

Conder and Kitchener succeeded, by their intrepid bearing, in causing a momentary lull in that storm, but not before Kitchener's left thigh had been painfully bruised by an enormous stone. Conder ordered all the native servants into the tents in order to avoid further provocation, but they were too much excited to obey. The Arabs, in the meantime, continued to shout, and to heap every species of obscene and blasphemous epithet upon the Christian religion in general, and, in particular, upon the members of the survey party.

At that moment the mob was reinforced by a number of armed men, and Conder and Kitchener, who had been facing it unarmed, a few paces in advance of their men, were immediately surrounded. The handle of a battle-axe was thrust into Conder's side, and Conder told

14

his assailants that they were mad. He warned them that they would all be hanged if they dared to lay hands upon an Englishman. While the mob hesitated, an Arab elbowed his way to the front and dealt Conder a violent blow on the head with a large club, causing two wounds and covering his face with blood. A second blow, directed with full force at the top of his head, would certainly have proved fatal if he had not butted his assailant in the chest. The club struck Conder's neck, causing a great swelling and an injury from which he never wholly recovered. He fell, but scrambled to his feet again, and hit his assailant in the face with the handle of his hunting-crop. As he did so, the whip flew out of his hand, and left him entirely defenceless.

Conder's report [1] continued :

' I must inevitably have been murdered but for the cool and prompt assistance of Lieutenant Kitchener, who managed to get to me and engaged one of the club-men, covering my retreat. A blow descending on the top of his head, he parried it with a cane, which was broken by the force of the blow. His escape is unaccountable.

' Having retired a few paces from the thick of the fray, I saw the Arabs were gradually surrounding us, stealing behind trees and through vineyards ; and I well understood that in such a case, unless the soldiers arrived at once, we must all die. Many of the servants had, indeed, given up hope, though no one fled. I gave the order to leave the tents and fly round the hill.

' Lieutenant Kitchener was the last to obey this order, being engaged in front. He retreated to his tent, and whilst running he was fired at, and heard the bullet whistle by his head. . . .'

The party ran some distance up the hillside before it stopped to recover its breath, to inspect its wounds, and to consult. Kitchener's resolute bearing had played a vital part in assisting that escape and in discouraging the pursuit, by planting just enough doubt in the minds of the Arabs about the enormity and probable consequences of the massacre which they were on the brink of perpetrating. After a few minutes' rest the party, which had outpaced its pursuers, climbed to the brow of the hill in order to reconnoitre the scene. From the summit it beheld with inexpressible relief the arrival of a posse of Turkish soldiers, accompanied by a British consular agent, Marcus Cigal :

' I am informed,' Conder continued, ' that all offensive weapons

[1] Archives of the Palestine Exploration Fund.

were immediately concealed ; the stoning and blasphemous language ceased at once ; and not an individual of the crowd remained.'

After detailing the casualties suffered by individual members of the party—Kitchener suffered from a ' bruise covering all his left thigh, and another on his arm. Both still very painful '—Conder collapsed from fever and from the after-effects of his injuries. His unfinished report, accordingly, addressed from Haifa on 14 July, 1875, to the British Consul-General at Beyrout, was signed by Kitchener, who sent a copy, with a covering letter addressed from Mount Carmel on 15 July, 1875, to the committee of the Palestine Exploration Fund :

' Being placed in command of the expedition,' the twenty-five-year-old subaltern began, ' owing to the temporary illness of Lieutenant Conder, I write by his wish to inform the committee that the survey is at present entirely suspended in consequence of two causes—the first being a murderous and unprovoked attack on the party by Moslem inhabitants of Safed (particulars enclosed) : the second, the gradual spread of cholera over the North of Palestine. Lieutenant Conder and myself consider, under these circumstances, that we cannot take the responsibility of conducting the party again into the field till a very severe punishment has been awarded to the inhabitants of Safed, and until the steady advance of cholera is checked. I feel certain that neither of these obstacles will be removed under two or three months. . . .'

No report could have been more lucid or succinct. Kitchener was the man on the spot, full of pluck and assurance, and thrilled by the limelight which beat upon him. In a covering note to Walter Besant he wrote :[1] ' You will see an account enclosed of the great and glorious battle of Safed. We are very glad to be so well out of it. Conder thinks it would be a good thing for justice out here if it got mentioned in the English papers.' Kitchener was confident that his country's honour was safe in his hands, and he informed the commitee of the Palestine Exploration Fund that Conder was in communication with the Ambassador at Constantinople and with the Consul-General at Beyrout, and that he had himself reported the facts to the Deputy Adjutant-General, Royal Engineers.

The survey was, accordingly, suspended, while Sir Henry Elliot, the British Ambassador at Constantinople, made arrangements with the Turkish authorities for bringing the Safed rioters to justice. After

[1] Archives of the Palestine Exploration Fund.

some delay, a number of delinquents were arrested, and a special commission which included Noel Temple Moore, the British Consul at Jerusalem, and Colonel Rushdi Bey, the Turkish police chief for Syria, assembled at Acre for the trial.

The trial lasted from 11 to 28 September, 1875, and Conder and Kitchener, who were present during most of that time, were scandalized by the lightness of the sentences imposed. Eight persons were sentenced to two months', six to three months', and two to twelve months' imprisonment. £112 10s. was awarded in damages in the form of a collective fine upon the town of Safed. In response to vigorous British protests, one extra month's imprisonment was added to each of the fourteen shorter sentences, and six months to each of the two twelve-months' terms. The fine was eventually increased to £340.

Conder and Kitchener left Palestine for England on 1 October, 1875. Both were sick with fever and both were granted leave. Kitchener, who had grown a tremendous beard of which, for a time, he was inordinately vain, spent Christmas at his father's house at Dinan. He put into shape there his maiden literary effort, *Photographs of Biblical Sites* by Lieutenant Kitchener, R.E., F.R.G.S. It cost one guinea and was poor value at that price. Walter Besant handled the arrangements for its publication by Edward Stanford, on behalf of the Fund, during the spring of 1876; and Kitchener admitted that he felt ' the fever of an author, or rather perhaps authoress, at the production of a first born '. The book was handsomely bound, but it contained only twelve photographs mounted on tinted boards. Kitchener complained[1] about the ' enormous commission ' given to the publisher, and suggested that, if the publisher had been less grasping, the book could have been produced more cheaply with a larger number of photographs and more descriptive matter. He told Besant that he was ' utterly disheartened and disgusted ' and that he objected to the way in which his descriptive matter had been slashed.

Kitchener expected to return to Palestine early in 1876. He told Besant (22 December, 1875) that Europe was ' not worth living in ' ; and he was dismayed to find that he was required to spend another twelve months in London in order to give Conder's health a chance to improve. The Fund's quarterly report for January, 1876, stated that ' the materials brought home by Lieutenants Conder and Kitchener are of far greater importance than was expected ' ; and

[1] Ibid.

for a year the two officers worked together on the map, and on the
' memoirs' which were to accompany it, in a rented office in
Kensington.

Despite that delay, Conder's health failed to improve, and Kitchener
was therefore appointed to succeed him in command of the survey.
He was paid at the rate which Conder had formerly received (£37 10s.
a month). Conder was left working in London upon the map, while
Kitchener left for Egypt in January, 1877. Kitchener's orders were
to procure horses and servants in Damascus, and to proceed thence, via
Beyrout and the coast road, to Haifa, where he was to meet his staff.

After executing those orders, Kitchener resumed his survey of
Galilee on 27 February, 1877. He was confident, resolute, energetic
and gay, despite the imminent threat of a major war and of civil
disturbance in Palestine. He reported [1] cheerfully on 30 March, 1877,
that ' the Druses are giving a lot of trouble, cutting people's throats
on the road to Damascus '.

War broke out between Turkey and Russia on 24 April, 1877,
but a month later Kitchener was able to report (25 May) that he had
found ' the authorities in the country most active and obliging in
helping the work as far as they can. I have had no serious difficulty
with the natives. The health of the whole expedition has been excellent.' He described his return on 11 April to Safed :

' The Governor, Kadi, and H.B.M. Consular Agent, with twenty-
two followers, came out about an hour and a half on the road to meet
me. We rode into the town in quite a triumphal procession. After
coffee with the Governor, I pitched camp, and then the Governor came
and called. After him, the British Agent, and then the Kadi, with
all the members of the Mejlis. Nothing could be more civil and
obliging than everybody was.'

No experience could have been more formative and fruitful for a
young subaltern than that of negotiating—on terms which his charm
and spirited bearing rendered virtually equal—with governors, consuls and similar notables. Unlike Conder, Kitchener never hesitated
to press his views about political matters. He repeatedly recommended, for example, that a British consulate should be re-established
in Haifa, and that the Foreign Office should be asked to review the
whole question of the consular establishment in north Palestine. He
also insisted that the last instalment (£60) of the fine which had
been imposed upon the town of Safed should be remitted.

[1] Archives of the Palestine Exploration Fund.

Kitchener displayed initiative and judgement in circumstances of exceptional difficulty. The outbreak of war made it essential that the survey should be completed within the shortest possible time ; but the quality of the work was maintained. As the Russian armies advanced on Constantinople, the British Prime Minister, Disraeli, supported by the Queen, high finance, and what was left of the rough, happy, ignorant mass of ' Merry England ', identified British imperial interests with the task of maintaining Turkish territorial integrity. He did his utmost to foment an hysterical wave of anti-Russian sentiment, which found expression in the popular music-hall refrain :

We don't want to fight, but, by Jingo, if we do,
We've got the ships; we've got the men; we've got the money too!

Gladstone, the Liberal Opposition leader, on the other hand, deriving his support from intellectuals, Nonconformists and hosts of strait-laced but God-fearing and upright men and women, declared publicly that the Government of Turkey was ' incorrigible in sin ' and ' impotent for reformation '. He called for the expulsion of the Turks ' bag and baggage ' from Europe, described the Russian Emperor as a ' Christian gentleman ', and urged him to give effect to the will of God by sounding ' the knell of Turkish tyranny '.

Against that stormy background Kitchener worked for a minimum of twelve hours a day. He completed the survey of Galilee on 10 July, 1877, and then paused for four weeks' rest in the Lebanon, while the Consul-General at Beyrout arranged for the country around Banias to be scoured by Turkish troops in consequence of false reports that Kitchener had been attacked and wounded by Bedouin tribesmen. Kitchener, who had, in fact, been on a hunting expedition with the Governor of Acre, was not in the least displeased to find that a legend was beginning to form itself around his name. He may have reflected that only some fourteen years had passed since a similar legend had begun to form itself around the personality of another subaltern of engineers, ' Chinese ' Gordon.

On 23 August, 1877, Kitchener again took the field. He led his party into the desert around Beersheba, and told them that they would be expected to work twelve hours a day, for seven days a week, until their task was completed. Their response was so wholehearted that the survey of western Palestine was completed on 28 September, 1877.

The committee of the Palestine Exploration Fund had already on 17 July expressed its ' high sense of Lieutenant Kitchener's ability and zeal '. The annual meeting was informed that he had ' conducted the work for six months without any accidents during a period of suspicion and excitement. His reports, which are in the hands of the General Committee, are careful and intelligent, and his monthly accounts show due regard for economy. He has hitherto managed to conduct the survey for a monthly sum less than that which the Committee gave him as a maximum.'

On 5 October, 1877, a letter signed by W. Hepworth Dixon, the chairman of the Fund's executive committee, appeared in the principal morning newspapers throughout Great Britain. It announced the completion, by Lieutenant Kitchener, R.E., of the scientific survey of western Palestine :

'Lieutenant Kitchener is now riding over the district already surveyed, in order to clear up on the spot certain small difficulties which have arisen in laying down the work at home. We expect the party back in England by the end of the year.'

When he quit Palestine at the end of November, 1877, Kitchener reported that he had personally triangulated and surveyed 1,340 square miles, and revised 1,700 square miles of Conder's work ; that he had examined and described 816 ruins ; completed the line of levels between the Mediterranean and Lake Galilee; and written special reports about the water supply of every village. He added that he had investigated 'all known' archaeological and geological points of interest ; and that he had collected 3,850 names, made 29 special plans, and taken many photographs.

The mood of the population was becoming dangerous during the final weeks, and Kitchener reported that at Nablus, on 1 November, he had been compelled to have a number of boys tied to posts and publicly flogged for throwing stones. On the other hand, he noted that people had, on the whole, remained extraordinarily civil and obliging. On one occasion, for example, at Amwas, a mob had informed him, in front of his Turkish escort, that it longed for England to annex Palestine and to introduce a just Government : 'Nothing that I could say would induce them to believe that England had no intention of doing anything of the sort.'

After sending his staff home on 22 November, 1877, Kitchener sailed four days later for Constantinople. He carried letters of introduction and was taken to see the sights by high-ranking Turkish officers who showed him many kindnesses before he left on 12 December, armed with passes and further letters of recommendation, for Adrianople, Sofia and the front at Kamerleh. At

Tatar Bazardjik he was mildly startled by the sight of Bulgarian corpses dangling from almost every lamp-post ; but he shared the Turkish loathing for the Bulgarians, whom he described in an article [1] which he contributed to *Blackwood's Magazine* (February, 1878) as physically and morally ' a most despicable race '. He wrote : ' If some of those who agitated about the Bulgarian atrocities really saw and talked to the people, they would, I feel sure, modify their opinions.'

It is unlikely that Gladstone, who was the principal agitator against ' the Bulgarian horrors ', would have modified his views in deference to those of Lieutenant Kitchener, R.E. ; or that he would have shared Kitchener's gay and boyish enthusiasm for the martial qualities of the Turks. Kitchener reached the front partly on horseback and partly by disguising himself as a wounded Turk and securing a place on a Red Crescent ambulance cart. He noted that on the way he met many frost-bitten Arab conscripts to whom he spoke in Arabic. They told him that they hated the war and longed to return to ' the beautiful gardens of Jaffa, where there was always a warm sun, and oranges and tomatoes for all, however poor '.

At the front Kitchener attached himself to Valentine Baker Pasha (1827–87), who had formerly commanded the 10th Hussars. He had, however, taken service in the Turkish Army as a divisional commander after serving a term of twelve months' imprisonment and being dismissed from the British Army in the summer of 1875 for an indecent assault upon a young woman in a train. Kitchener climbed with Baker to a Turkish redoubt on the summit of a 6,200-foot mountain :

' The sun threw a rosy tinge over all, making the most perfect scene imaginable. There were the Russians, just below us in their trenches. We could see them relieving guard, and they could easily have been picked off with a rifle. . . . The whole positions both of the Turks and the Russians were laid out below us as on a map.'

On Christmas Day, 1877, Kitchener left the front for Constantinople, travelling for a part of the way concealed under the seat of a first-class railway carriage on a troop train bound for Adrianople. He was, of course, in mufti and his presence was discovered after a time; but his papers were in order, and they included a warm letter of recommendation from Mehemet Ali Pasha, who had recently been dismissed from his post of Commander-in-Chief, and who had shown Kitchener

[1] A Visit to Sophia and the Heights of Kamerleh—Christmas, 1877.

kindness in Constantinople. In those circumstances, Kitchener's companions merely laughed, and treated him with all friendliness after brushing him into an appearance of greater comparative respectability.

Kitchener returned to England in January, 1878, to his family's considerable relief : ' You have no idea ', his favourite brother, Walter, wrote (January, 1878) to his young wife, ' what a fellow Herbert is. I don't think there *is* anyone a bit like him. Talking to him does one good. . . . It changes one altogether and leaves one full of determination.' Kitchener went to stay with his father in a flat in Victoria Street, London, and Walter was amazed [1] (4 June, 1878) to find his brother sitting there, bearded and cross-legged like an Oriental, ' in a room fitted up entirely in Eastern fashion '. There were cushions instead of chairs, and a smell of incense ; and Kitchener gravely dispensed an exotic brand of tea.

Throughout the spring and early summer of 1878 Kitchener worked with Conder on the map of Palestine and on the accompanying descriptive material ; and he crossed to Dublin on 16 August in order to speak about the survey of Galilee at the annual meeting of the British Association for the Advancement of Science. He made an appeal for the preservation of the synagogue at Capernaum, which he described as his most important archaeological discovery; and he was warmly praised by his chairman and fellow-sapper, Major Charles Wilson, C.B., F.R.S.

On 10 September, Kitchener handed over his completed work to the committee of the Palestine Exploration Fund, which resolved, formally, that it was impossible to praise too highly his energy, tact, and scrupulous attention to economy. It was unanimously decided that his merits should be brought to the notice of the Deputy Adjutant-General, Royal Engineers, with a request that they should be brought to the personal notice of the Commander-in-Chief, Field-Marshal H.R.H. the Duke of Cambridge.

On the same day (10 September) the committee of the Fund congratulated Kitchener ' on his appointment to the very important work of a similar nature which has been entrusted to him by the Secretary of State for Foreign Affairs '. That work lay in Cyprus, to which Kitchener was posted on 3 September, with orders to survey and triangulate the island.

Kitchener owed that appointment to the influence of a distant

[1] Letter in the possession of Miss Madge Kitchener.

cousin, Thomas Cobbold, who had once been in the Diplomatic
Service and who was at that time a banker and brewer in Ipswich,
which he represented in the House of Commons. Kitchener wrote [1]
(11 September) to thank Cobbold very warmly for having procured
for him that ' most delightful appointment. . . . It is exactly what I
like, and will be a great advance to me professionally. . . . I expect
I shall take $2\frac{1}{2}$ to 3 years to finish.'

Walter Kitchener told [2] his wife (3 September) that ' Herbert is
going out *in charge* of a party to survey Cyprus. It is a splendid
appointment . . . but the great thing is that he is employed directly
through the Foreign Office, making his reports to Lord Salisbury, and
of course bringing out the map under his own name.' Walter
Kitchener explained that that was ' a most unusual way of doing
such a thing ', and that it had been adopted because the Intelligence
and Ordnance Survey branches of the War Office had been unable to
decide which had the prior claim upon Kitchener's services.

Kitchener had a personal reason for wishing to escape from England
at that time ; his domestic background had become unhappy as a
result of a dispute which soon led to a judicial separation between
his father and his stepmother. The home at Dinan was closed and
Kitchener returned with relief to the Mediterranean after his well-
meant efforts to effect a reconciliation had failed. He removed his
beard in London, and landed in Cyprus on 15 September, 1878. He
did not spend another winter in England until 1914.

Cyprus had been transferred to Great Britain earlier that year by
Turkey at the Congress of Berlin, when Disraeli obtained ' peace with
honour ' after abandoning the stand which he had made for the maintenance of Turkish territorial integrity. Kitchener strongly approved
of the acquisition of the island, and an article entitled ' Notes from
Cyprus ', which he contributed anonymously to *Blackwood's Magazine*
(August, 1879), expressed some aspects of his imperialist ideal. He
invoked ' the hand of the capitalist' to transform Cyprus from a
barren waste to its ancient fruitfulness, and he suggested that the
War Office had had its eye on that island for some time. He considered that Palestine might have served equally well as a base from
which to extend British influence over Asia Minor, but ' we know
the advantage of a sea-girt shore '. He added :

' No complication of holy sites and sentimental interests, no religious

[1] Letter in the possession of Mr. Guy F. Cobbold.
[2] Letter in the possession of Miss Madge Kitchener.

task of sending the Jew back and placing a King on the throne of Judah tend to embarrass our occupation of the island.'

Kitchener pleaded for the raising of a Turkish regiment in Cyprus which should be used as a training school for Turkish officers. Those officers required to be taught what reforms were needed in the Turkish Army in case of a general war. They could subsequently be used ' to raise troops among the many warlike tribes of Syria and Asia Minor, who would follow an English leader to the death. By thus employing Cyprus we should make its possession politically of the vastest importance, and we should really possess the key of the East.'

Several views of British imperialism were current in its heyday during Kitchener's lifetime, and there was confusion in regard to the meaning of the word. Some regarded it with horror as a cloak for barefaced exploitation ; while others hailed it with exultation as the religious mission of a great people elected by God.

Kitchener believed in the reality of the white man's burden. He considered that a reluctance to shoulder it would have constituted a cowardly betrayal of a missionary duty which God, or providence, had imposed upon the British race. The poet Virgil had exhorted Augustus Caesar to acknowledge a similar duty to rule backward races and to lead them kindly and firmly towards the goal of participation in a fuller and richer life.

The roots of imperialism are buried deep in human nature. Persians, Greeks, Romans ; Christians, Moslems, Marxists ; Arabs, Spaniards, Turks, Frenchmen, Englishmen, Germans, Russians and Americans have all responded in varying ways to broadly similar challenges in different ages. They have all taken a hand in the lordly task of fertilizing stagnant cultures and bringing a wide area of the earth's surface within the influence of their interests and ideals. In so doing their motives have been mixed. National advantage and personal ambition have in different degrees joined hands with the highest ideals of duty, self-sacrifice, integrity, justice and efficiency.

Kitchener, as a realist, understood better than many of his contemporaries the strength of the economic motive by which, in one of its principal aspects, British imperialism was inspired. Great Britain was steadily losing the lead which she had gained over her rivals during the early decades of the industrial revolution ; and the growing wealth, population and armaments of other great Powers threatened her supremacy and security. The once-despised overseas empire offered a means of restoring the balance.

That was Kitchener's creed, and unlike Rudyard Kipling, the laureate of empire, Kitchener felt no need to rationalize it. He cherished no illusions, and found it hard to endure illusions in others. He had little knowledge of history and relied much, like a Hebrew prophet, upon his intuitions, as he strove to do his duty as he saw it. The British public persisted, nevertheless, in reading into his actions a wisdom which transcended reason, and in investing his personality with a haze of poetry and romance.

The imperialist creed could never have subdued the minds and hearts of a majority of the British race unless it had embraced ethical motives also of the deepest potency, in which there was no conscious element of hypocrisy. There have been few, if any, more exalted forms of imperialism than the British. It involved exploitation, but it inculcated many great virtues which recalled those reverenced of old by the Romans upon whose history the British upper-middle class was educated in the public schools. Those virtues, sweetened by nineteen hundred years of Christian teaching, relieved British imperialism of some of the poison inherent in any theory of racial or cultural superiority by excluding much of its arrogance.

British imperialism was dependent upon a willing and united acceptance of responsibility on the one side, and of subordination on the other. Those conditions were sufficiently well satisfied during Kitchener's lifetime to permit a splendid achievement. That was his good fortune, for the tempest in which he perished destroyed the conditions which made that achievement possible.

Kitchener regarded British imperialism as the creed of a nation, and not of any party or class. And the subject Oriental races, on the whole, accepted their inferior position as natural and inevitable, before 1914. Thereafter a great change was apparent. British power and predominance were subjected to a continuous process of relative decline ; and the British democracy, after the concession of universal suffrage, took a different view of the imperial responsibilities which it had inherited. At the same time, the subject races, impatient of tutelage, came to regard any kind of subordination as an affront.

Undermined in that way, the tide of British imperialism receded ; and a new generation arose which forgot Kitchener. But a generation after his death new forms of imperialism arose also, in which Great Britain had almost no part left to play. Soviet Russian imperialism, based upon brute force, employed methods and professed a totalitarian creed which shocked the conscience of the British race.

American imperialism, resting upon an unprecedented industrial efficiency and prosperity, based itself upon a discreet and generous distribution of economic and military aid on a scale which ruled out the possibility of effective British competition.

All that was in the future when Kitchener left England for Cyprus. He felt then, as imperialists of many nations have felt throughout the ages, that his country had a duty to encourage by every means the growth of civilized institutions in those parts of the world in which divine providence had given it a preponderating interest. There was no chance, without such encouragement, of a spontaneous development of a Western pattern of thought and conduct. The task of evoking that response was termed the white man's burden, and that burden rested primarily upon British shoulders at the close of the nineteenth century. No pair of broad shoulders were better fitted to bear their full share of it than those of the slim, handsome young subaltern, who stood 6 feet 2 inches in his socks, when he reached Nicosia on 15 September, 1878.

The newly-acquired island was intended to serve as a base from which the single-handed guarantee of the future territorial integrity of Turkey-in-Asia, which Disraeli had given at Berlin, could be implemented. But it also became a useful springboard from which a fresh British advance could be launched at any time into Egypt, Palestine or the mainland of Asia Minor. Kitchener eagerly awaited such an advance, but his first months in Cyprus were unhappy and frustrating because he came into direct collision with the High Commissioner, Major-General Sir Garnet Wolseley.[1]

Wolseley disliked the arrangement under which Kitchener was employed by the Foreign Office. He thought it unsuitable, and he listened with unconcealed impatience to Kitchener's boyish and enthusiastic account of what the Foreign Office required. Kitchener said that his map would be published under his own name after about three years' work ; that it would be a model of its kind ; and that future scholars and archaeologists would be placed permanently in his debt.

Wolseley observed crisply that his ideas extended less far. He said that he needed only a rough survey for revenue purposes, which could be pieced together anonymously within a few weeks or months ; and that he was not concerned with the needs of scholars or archaeo-

---

[1] Field-Marshal Viscount Wolseley, K.P., P.C., G.C.B., O.M., G.C.M.G. (1833-1913).

logists. When Kitchener protested, Wolseley curtly informed him
that he ruled in Cyprus and that his orders would be obeyed.

Kitchener incurred Wolseley's wrath by writing to ask the Foreign
Office for instructions ; but Wolseley wrote to Lord Salisbury and,
after some delay, obtained permission to vary the terms upon which
Kitchener was employed. Salisbury told [1] Wolseley (29 November,
1878) that 'The requisitions of Lieutenant Kitchener and his survey
staff, which you have generally accepted, have created some consternation at the Treasury. . . . I myself entertain some doubt whether
a scientific survey on so elaborate a scale, however desirable, is
really necessary for revenue purposes which you have primarily in
view. . . .' He reminded Wolseley that as soon as the land survey
was finished, 'there will be no difficulty in going forward with the
Maltese colonization, which it is very important to encourage, both
for the sake of developing the island, and to prevent the development
of a Graecia Irridenta'.

That prudent colonization plan was not, in the end, implemented,
because Disraeli fell from power too soon. But Wolseley was
entitled, under the terms of an annexe to the Anglo-Turkish Convention which had transferred Cyprus to Great Britian, to expropriate,
on payment of compensation, all uncultivated land which had in the
past yielded revenue. He intended to settle Maltese upon such land ;
and for that reason he wanted a rough survey from Kitchener as quickly
as possible ; and he was infuriated by Kitchener's continued insistence
upon the need for a proper scientific survey. Wolseley repeatedly told
Lord Salisbury that he needed common land surveyors, not scientific
engineers with exalted ideas, and he obtained from Salisbury a ruling
that Kitchener's expenses should be defrayed from the revenues of
Cyprus instead of being borne upon the Foreign Office vote. After
obtaining that adjustment Wolseley successfully demanded [2] (5
February, 1879) that Kitchener 'should devote all his time, and the
time of his party, to a revenue survey. The scientific work he is
employed upon may safely be postponed. It is of no immediate
practical value to us. . . . My proposition would therefore be to
place Mr. Kitchener at the head of the revenue survey work, and to
hand him over as many intelligent natives as I could find to be taught
the simple art of land measurement.'

When Salisbury accepted that request, Kitchener exhausted the

[1] Salisbury Papers, 24.
[2] Ibid., 20.

27

last remnants of Wolseley's patience by expressing openly his extreme mortification and surprise. Six years passed before Wolseley forgave him, but Kitchener accepted the advice of friends not to apply immediately for a posting elsewhere, lest Wolseley should equate such action with outright insubordination. Kitchener was immensely relieved when in April, 1879, Wolseley accepted the command in South Africa ; and he then wrote immediately to Colonel Charles Wilson, R.E., who had started the survey of Palestine in 1864, and who was now serving as Consul-General in Anatolia. He told Wilson that he was extremely discontented in Cyprus and asked if employment could be found for him in Anatolia.

At Berlin, during the previous year, Disraeli had devised a characteristically imaginative plan for establishing through peaceful penetration an informal British protectorate over the whole of Asia Minor. He guaranteed its territorial integrity in return for a worthless pledge by the Sultan of Turkey that administrative reforms would be instituted. Lord Salisbury, accordingly, began to infiltrate British military officers into Anatolia as soon as the treaty was signed.

Those officers, with Colonel Wilson at their head, were seconded officially to the Consular Service, with orders to supervise the reforms, and to help to organize Turkish defences against any possible renewed threat of Russian aggression. Their unavowed duty was to spread British influence and to spy out the land. Wilson, who had taken up his post in April, 1879, liked Kitchener and thought highly of his work. He was amused by the bold stand which the subaltern had taken against Wolseley, and he invited Kitchener accordingly to Anatolia. He posted him (26 June, 1879) as Military Vice-Consul at Kastamanu, in northern Anatolia, where he remained for eight months.

Kitchener greatly enjoyed that work, and although his reports to Sir Henry Layard, the new Ambassador in Constantinople, constitute [1] a damning and almost wholly unrelieved indictment of Turkish cruelty, oppression and misrule, he found individual Turks extremely congenial and made many friends. He was only tempted to return to Cyprus when Major-General Sir Robert Biddulph,[2] who succeeded Wolseley as High Commissioner, offered him a doubled salary and a better status.

Biddulph took a different view from that of Wolseley about the

---

[1] *Parliamentary Papers, Turkey*, Nos. 4 and 23 (1880).

[2] General Sir Robert Biddulph, G.C.B., G.C.M.G. (1835–1918).

value of a proper scientific survey of the island ; and at the end of 1879 he persuaded Lord Salisbury to consent to its renewal. He then offered Kitchener the post of Director of Survey for Cyprus at an annual salary of £672, as well as responsibility for conducting the work of land registration, assessment and sales, for which he was paid an almost similar amount. Kitchener returned, accordingly, to Cyprus on 15 March, 1880, but he wrote[1] a fortnight later (29 March) to Walter Besant to express his fear that he had made a mistake in giving up ' the diplomatic line '. He had, in fact, been fortunate, for at the British general election of April, 1880, Disraeli was unexpectedly ousted by Gladstone, and the new Government promptly withdrew all the military vice-consuls from Asia Minor. The British bulldog ceased to nose the body of Anatolia, and sank its teeth, a year later, into Egypt.

[1] Archives of the Palestine Exploration Fund.

CHAPTER 3

CONQUEST OF EGYPT

1880-1884

KITCHENER was much happier during his second period of duty in Cyprus, although he became increasingly afraid of prejudicing his career through failing to see active service. He enjoyed his scientific survey work best, but he was proud also of his reorganization of the Cyprus land registry. After he had left the island he told [1] (5 March, 1885) an acquaintance that the system established in Cyprus—' a registration of titles, and a complete system of immediate transfer of property without the aid of the conveyancer ' —ought to be applied in England also ; and he noted that he had advocated similar reforms while he was in Anatolia, where ' it is not too much to say that the capability of English administrators to govern oriental races has now been recognized '. As a natural autocrat, Kitchener could not resist adding that Gladstone's action in forcing ' elective self-government' upon the Cypriots before they were prepared for it had been ' disastrous to the results achieved by the energetic and hard-working officials to whom the material progress made by Cyprus is due '.

Kitchener shared a house in Nicosia with Lord John Kennedy, a horsy, daredevil boy, who was a subaltern in the Royal Scots. They kept a bear-cub, which Kitchener had brought from Anatolia, as a pet ; and Kitchener was at pains to cultivate for the first time the long, bushy moustache which presently became famous.

Kitchener in Cyprus was a colourful figure, and he formed lasting friendships with two British visitors to the island, of which later he made full use. He met in Cyprus for the first time Pandeli Ralli (1845-1928), a wealthy bachelor member of the Anglo-Greek community in London, and a Liberal Member of Parliament, who was cruising in the Mediterranean in his yacht ; and Sir Samuel Baker (1821-93), the famous explorer. He told Ralli that the scientific survey of Cyprus was more difficult than that of Palestine ; and that the mountainous south-western portion presented formidable difficulties. The inhabitants were frequently suspicious, and on one occasion [2] (6 December, 1881) shots were fired at Kitchener by an escaped convict near Pissouri.

[1] Letter to Trelawney Saunders.   [2] cf. *Cyprus Herald*, 7 and 14 Dec., 1881.

Kitchener became a first-class horseman in Cyprus, and he won a number of cups for racing on the flat and over the sticks. He rode his own horses and served as a whip to the local hunt. He also organized archaeological excavations, and he became [1] (15 June, 1882) Curator and Honorary Secretary of the Cyprus Museum as soon as it was founded. He was annoyed, early in 1881, when Biddulph forbade him to accept an offer from the trustees of the British Museum to take charge of an archaeological expedition to Assyria and Babylonia.

Kitchener impulsively tried to persuade the trustees to approach the Foreign Office with a request that he should be appointed British Consul at Mosul. He assured them that consular duties could be combined satisfactorily with archaeology and with intelligence work ; but the trustees answered (17 March, 1881) that his proposal was quite impossible. Biddulph had good reason for describing [2] Kitchener (July, 1882) as 'rather impulsive and does not always foresee results'. His 'general ability' was stated to be 'very good' and his 'professional acquirements' to be 'good'. He was 'a well-informed officer of active habits'.

After applying vainly to Wolseley for secondment to South Africa, Kitchener's hopes became centred upon Egypt. In that country, which still formed part of the moribund Turkish Empire, the structure of society was on the brink of collapse. The Suez Canal, constructed with the aid of French capital and Egyptian labour, had been opened in 1869. It formed a vital artery in British imperial strategy, and Disraeli, with Rothschild's help, had secured a large slice of the company's shares for Great Britain by a brilliant *coup* in 1875. Egypt was being rapidly opened up to European enterprise with the aid of loans advanced at rates of around seven per cent by Rothschild and others ; but wild extravagance and incompetent administration caused the Egyptian Government to default on its liabilities.

Under strong pressure from European banks and bondholders, the British and French governments, in the autumn of 1879, imposed upon Egypt a system of dual financial control. The country was run on the lines of an estate in bankruptcy, and a severe cut in military establishments and expenditure provoked a mutiny of the ill-trained and badly-disciplined Egyptian Army.

Colonel Arabi constituted himself the mouthpiece of those discontented Egyptian officers who found themselves either placed on

---

[1] cf. *Cyprus, An Independent Newspaper*, 24 June, 1882.
[2] War Office Records.

CONQUEST OF EGYPT, 1880–1884

half-pay or left with greatly reduced prospects of promotion. Arabi compelled the Khedive, Ismail, to appoint him as Minister for War ; and he set up what was virtually a nationalist military dictatorship in opposition to the European financiers. A ferment of indignation convulsed Great Britain when, on 11 June, 1882, a large-scale nationalist riot occurred in Alexandria. On that day Sir Charles Cookson, the British Consul, was hustled and insulted, and at least fifty Europeans were massacred.

On the forts protecting Alexandria the nationalists started to mount guns, which were evidently intended as a threat to the Royal Navy. Kitchener telegraphed in all directions in an effort to secure employment in any expedition which might be sent to restore order in Egypt. The climate of European opinion at that time made it virtually unthinkable that Egypt should be permitted to default ; and the British Prime Minister, Gladstone, was profoundly disturbed. He regarded war as a product of imperialism which he equated with jingoism, and he loathed all three. He had, however, incurred odium during August of the previous year, 1881, by meekly conceding independence to the Boers in South Africa, after a humiliating British reverse at Majuba. He tried now, without success, to induce other European nations to join in restoring order in Egypt, while powerful British and French naval squadrons awaited orders from their admiralties at the entrance to the harbour of Alexandria.

At the last moment the French squadron withdrew. The Republic was rocked by a sudden political crisis, caused by fear lest Bismarck might have a sinister motive in encouraging France to commit herself in Egypt at a time when large French forces were already committed in Tunisia and Algeria. The French Government had a traditional interest in Egypt ; its outlook was far more imperialistic than that of the British Government under Gladstone ; but a panic fear of German intentions threw Gambetta from power. The French squadron, accordingly, sailed away from Alexandria, and the British were left on their own.

Kitchener's excited telegrams had elicited no firm offer of employment. He was consumed by ambition and resolute not to repeat his father's mistake of seeing no active service. There were no other means by which promotion could be obtained. Since the Indian Mutiny, opportunities of active service had been so limited and infrequent that officers invariably tumbled over one another in their frantic efforts to have themselves seconded for service in the few little

32

frontier wars which occurred. Kitchener possessed relatively little influence ; but his fluent knowledge of Arabic was extremely rare among British officers at that time, and he was determined to turn it to profit in Egypt if he could. Accordingly, in desperation, he asked for and obtained a week's sick leave which it was assumed he would spend in Cyprus. Instead, on 2 July, 1882, he took ship from Limassol to Alexandria, where he reported to Lieutenant-Colonel A. B. Tulloch, Military Liaison Officer with Admiral Sir Beauchamp Seymour (Lord Alcester), who commanded the Mediterranean Fleet.

Kitchener found a berth on one of the steamers in the harbour on which British residents had been advised to seek refuge. Pleading that he spoke Arabic like a native, Kitchener persuaded Tulloch to take him on a reconnaissance ashore. The two officers, after disguising themselves as greasy Levantines, were rowed ashore by night. Their task was to inspect the Egyptian defences and to spy out Colonel Arabi's dispositions.

Tulloch and Kitchener took tickets at the railway station for Zagazig. They travelled some distance along the line before they slipped off the train. They made notes and sketches before they returned to an agreed rendezvous where they were picked up by a boat and rowed to the Admiral's flagship during the early hours of 7 July, 1882.

After that adventure Kitchener could not endure the thought of returning immediately to Cyprus. He secured a conditional promise of employment on the Intelligence Staff if Sir Robert Biddulph would release him ; and Tulloch persuaded the Admiral to cable a request to Cyprus for an extension of Kitchener's leave. As Kitchener had anticipated, that request was promptly refused ; but by a calculated act of indiscipline, he concealed himself on a refugee steamer until the regular weekly mail for Cyprus had departed. He then returned to the flagship and was formally notified by Tulloch of the adverse result of the Admiral's application. He began at once hypocritically to bemoan his equivocal and embarrassing situation, and it is impossible not to sympathize with Kitchener, although that act might have blasted his career.

It seemed unlikely that even a Liberal British Government would dare to incur the obloquy of withdrawal. Gladstone was appalled equally by the threat which Colonel Arabi represented to financial morality by seeking to repudiate his country's lawfully-incurred indebtedness to foreign bondholders, and to political morality by seeking to establish an arbitrary tyranny. He became intensely excited

33

and declared that Colonel Arabi was 'the greatest villain alive'. Sir Beauchamp Seymour, accordingly, was ordered to deliver an ultimatum requiring that all work on the fortifications of Alexandria should cease within twelve hours.

That ultimatum was presented on 6 July to the commander of the garrison at Alexandria. The commander replied that all work had ceased ; but three days later new guns were mounted. At daybreak on 10 July Sir Beauchamp announced that he would bombard Alexandria unless the forts protecting the harbour were surrendered within twenty-four hours. No offer of surrender was received, and at dawn on 11 July the British fleet opened fire. The guns which Arabi had mounted were silenced after a bombardment lasting ten and a half hours ; and in the rioting and anarchy which followed the city was reduced to a flaming and smoking ruin.

Kitchener witnessed every phase of the bombardment from Sir Beauchamp Seymour's flagship. His request for permission to go ashore was refused on the ground that he was present in mufti, on leave, and without orders. On the same grounds his application for the Egyptian medal of 1882 was refused by Wolseley, early in 1884, despite the fact that before being present at the bombardment he had carried out intelligence work ashore.

When Kitchener returned to Limassol on 30 July, 1882, he was asked to explain his absence from duty without leave. Sir Robert Biddulph took a generous and gentlemanly view of the matter ; but a coolness, which hurt Kitchener very much, came over his relations with his chief. He wrote to Biddulph on 2 August, 1882 :

'My Dear General,
    'I have been very much pained ever since my return at the view you took of my absence in Alexandria.
    'I think it my duty to let you know how extremely anxious I am to see service in Egypt. At the same time I feel fully the claims you have on my services with regard to the Survey.
    'A proposal was made to me to help on the Intelligence Staff, and should a more definite appointment be offered, I cannot help feeling that my remaining here in a civil capacity, while military service was offered me, might be used against me in my future career.
    'My greatest ambition, up to the present, has been to finish the map of Cyprus, and there is nothing I should so regret as not being

able to do so after three years' work. But at the same time I feel sure that you will agree with me that a soldier's first duty is to serve his country in the field when an opportunity is offered him, and not to remain at his ease while others are fighting. I hope, therefore, that you will not consider it necessary to keep me in the Island if I can make arrangements which would meet with your approval for carrying on my duties so that there will be no hitch until Grant comes back.

'Of course I would gladly relinquish all my pay to those doing my work, and I would leave my resignation in your hands to be used as you thought fit, at the same time guaranteeing to return in order to complete my work as soon as military operations would allow.

'I have not thought fit to make any application, but should my services be asked for, I implore you not to oppose my going, as such a course would absolutely capsize all my hopes in the service for the future.'

When Kitchener wrote that letter, a British army commanded by Sir Garnet Wolseley was on its way to restore order in Egypt. The main body began to disembark at Ismailia on 21 August, 1882, and within a month the highest British hopes had been realized. The enemy was brought to battle on 13 September and destroyed at Tel-el-Kebir. British losses in killed and wounded amounted to 459, while no less than two thousand Egyptian corpses were counted. Broken and bankrupt, Egypt lay at England's feet.

Colonel Arabi fled to the Citadel at Cairo, where he surrendered on the following day after a brilliant and spirited dash by British cavalry. Kitchener's friend, Colonel Sir Charles Wilson, served as advocate-general to the court which tried him on 4 December, 1882. Arabi pleaded guilty to a charge of rebellion against the Khedive, and was sentenced to be hanged. That sentence was commuted immediately to one of banishment for life.[1]

The British occupation was intended to be brief; and the Sultan of Turkey, who was powerless to resist or even to resent the British action, was retained as Egypt's nominal suzerain. In the meantime, such parts of the old Egyptian Army as had escaped destruction were disbanded by the conquerors' decree on 20 September, 1882. Force is, however, the bedrock upon which government and society rest, and it was obvious that the first step in the regeneration of Egypt

[1] Arabi was exiled to Ceylon, and permitted to return to Egypt in 1901.

would have to be the formation of a new Egyptian army to preserve internal order and to protect the frontiers. Accordingly, Major-General Sir Evelyn Wood, V.C.,[1] was appointed to be the first British Sirdar, or Commander-in-Chief, of the armed forces of Egypt.

The new Egyptian army consisted of six thousand conscripts ; and Kitchener was included among the twenty-six British officers who were selected to train it on European lines. Sir Evelyn Wood cabled (28 December, 1882) to offer Kitchener a two years' engagement in the acting rank of Major. Kitchener, who reckoned that one year's work remained to be done on the Cyprus survey, had shrewdly reached a private understanding with Sir Evelyn's A.D.C.

Kitchener had arranged that he should refuse the offer out of loyalty to Biddulph, but that it should be at once repeated. He calculated, rightly, that Biddulph would be greatly mollified in that way, and that he would not wish to stand in the way of an officer employed on civilian duties who was seeking a chance of active service. To Wood's first telegram, accordingly, Kitchener replied, ' Very sorry—present work will not permit me to leave Cyprus for one year.'

Biddulph urged Kitchener to accept at once, after Wood had cabled a second time (30 December) : ' Write your plans, as we wanted you for second-in-command cavalry regiment.' Kitchener's posting was dated 21 February, 1883, and he left Larnaca for Alexandria ten days earlier. He received, shortly afterwards, elaborate letters of fare-well and appreciation from the Greek and Turkish communities of Cyprus.

The letter from the Greeks (4 March, 1883), which was signed by the Archbishop and fifteen others, stated [2] : ' You have always shown the greatest courtesy to those who had to come to your office, and whenever your duty allowed, you rendered much assistance to those who had complicated land cases. The formation of the Cyprus Museum for the preservation of the antiquities of the island is greatly due to your efforts.'

Kitchener, who became a Major in the Egyptian Army, was promoted to Captain in the British Army on 4 January, 1883. He was dismayed to find that he was viewed with much disfavour by Lord Wolseley, who had left Egypt with a peerage and a grant of thirty thousand pounds, after his victory at Tel-el-Kebir, to become Adjutant-General at the War Office. Wolseley demanded an explan-

---

[1] Field-Marshal Sir Evelyn Wood, V.C., G.C.B., G.C.M.G. (1838-1913).

[2] *Cyprus Herald*, 16 April, 1883.

ation of the long delay in producing the Cyprus map, about which
so much fuss had been made ; and although a satisfactory explanation
was made by Biddulph, Kitchener's father wrote [1] as late as 7 November, 1884, to Walter Besant :

' With my old military notions, I've no inclination to rush into
print, but Wolseley and Herbert having come to loggerheads as
to how the Cyprus map should be brought out, and as I know W.
doesn't forgive or forget—he having refused Herbert the medal,
although he was under military command on board the flagship
at Alexandria—and since in two cases I have seen he has not forgotten
their disagreement, I think it not unlikely that, when the time
comes, Herbert may not get all he deserves . . .'

The Colonel suggested, accordingly, that Besant should start a
campaign in the Press, praising the decision of the Foreign Office to
publish the map of Cyprus in the detailed and scholarly way which
Kitchener favoured, and in regard to which Lord Wolseley had shown
himself to be indifferent. But Besant, happily, poured cold water
upon that dangerous and imprudent suggestion. The map was finally
published by Edward Stanford in April, 1885, with a statement that
it had been ' executed by command of His Excellency Major-General
Sir Robert Biddulph, K.C.M.G., C.B., R.A., High Commissioner,
under the direction of Captain H. H. Kitchener, R.E., Director of
Survey, assisted by Lieutenant S. C. N. Grant, R.E.'

Kitchener's map showed all the usual features, as well as a number
of special ones which enhanced the growing reputation of the former
Director of Survey for Cyprus. It provided block plans of the
principal towns and villages, distinguished between Christian and
Moslem villages, and gave Greek as well as Turkish place-names.
Aqueducts, springs, wells, monasteries and ruins were clearly marked,
and all known ancient sites were identified.

Ruthless and unconcealed ambition made Kitchener unpopular
in Cairo. He preferred to spend his annual leave in the East, instead
of in England, in order to improve his professional qualifications ;
and he neglected entirely to pay court to the women who ruled the
narrow, close-knit English society during the early days of the occupation. Masculine envy and feminine pique combined to provoke an
outbreak of ill-natured mockery when Kitchener designed a flashy
light-blue uniform for his regiment of Egyptian cavalry.

[1] Archives of the Palestine Exploration Fund.

37

Nevertheless, Kitchener proved himself to be an inspired leader and trainer of men. He impressed profoundly his commanding officer, Lieut.-Colonel Taylor, 19th Hussars ; and within a few weeks he was regarded as the most determined and efficient officer in the Egyptian Army, which was, at that time, the laughing-stock of every soldier in Europe. British officers of the regular and Indian armies made no effort to conceal the contempt which they felt for Sir Evelyn Wood's experiment. They argued that centuries of subservience had destroyed the spirit of a race which might be vain, but never proud ; cruel, but never fierce ; treacherous, but never warlike ; cringing, but never disciplined ; apathetic, but never resolute to conquer or to die. Despite that bad reputation, however, the new Egyptian Army was tirelessly trained by its devoted band of British officers, between whom and the men they commanded an extraordinarily strong bond of trust and sympathy arose.

Two months' leave were due to Kitchener in November, 1883 ; and he volunteered to spend them in assisting Professor Edward Hull, F.R.S., who held the Chair of Geology at the Royal College of Science, to conduct, on behalf of the Palestine Exploration Fund, a survey of the Arabah valley from the southernmost point of the Dead Sea to Aqaba on the Red Sea, at the head of the Aqaba Gulf. Sir Charles Wilson, who was serving in the War Office as Military Adviser on Egyptian Affairs, had suggested Kitchener's name ; and Walter Besant, on behalf of the Fund, asked Claude Conder to advise Kitchener about the best method of linking the new expedition with the former Palestine survey. But Conder refused to help. He wrote [1] (11 October, 1883) to Walter Besant :

' In 1877 I worked very hard to equip the expedition which Kitchener took out. My reward then, and in 1879, was that he appropriated my discoveries and gave out a great deal of my work as his own ; that he told people he had " slipped into my shoes ", and made my brother-officers believe that he was the explorer of the greater part of Palestine.

' He may now help himself.'

Great credit had, in fact, been given to Conder for the leading part which he took in the work of the Palestine survey, but Kitchener, who was extremely ambitious, would have been less than human if

[1] Archives of the Palestine Exploration Fund.

38

he had not been delighted to succeed to the command after Conder had been rendered permanently unfit by the head injury which he sustained at Safed. A commander in the field cannot afford to be deflected from his goal by grief for the loss of comrades ; and the breach between the friends was never healed.

Kitchener and Professor Hull left Suez for the Arabah valley on 10 November, 1883. Their journey was much too hurried to achieve any useful results, and Kitchener regarded the Professor as an incubus, because he was so unduly fearful of adventuring into little-known regions. Hull spoke much about the murder by Arabs of Professor E. H. Palmer and two British officers while they had been engaged on a similar expedition in August, 1882. Kitchener discovered that they had been murdered after a false report had been received that the British had been annihilated in Egypt ; and he was at times a little malicious in playing upon the Professor's fears. He took a strong dislike to Hull, but he enjoyed visiting Petra and climbing Mount Sinai (10 December, 1883).

On Christmas Eve, 1883, Kitchener received a letter at Tell abu Hareirah, on the Dead Sea, from the Sirdar, Sir Evelyn Wood. It contained news of a military disaster in the Sudan, and expressed fears for the safety of the expedition if the Arabs became unduly excited.

After a week's hesitation, Kitchener decided to return to Cairo by the shortest route across a waterless and trackless desert. The Professor, who regarded that ride as a most risky undertaking, advised strongly against it ; but Kitchener laughed at him. Leaving the Professor, with the rest of the party, to make their way quietly to Gaza, Kitchener, accompanied only by the four bearers of the Sirdar's letter, set out on his two-hundred-miles ride to Ismailia. He was greatly troubled by sandstorms as well as by the glare of the desert sun, and his eyesight, in consequence, became permanently impaired. He developed a slight squint and suffered severe occasional headache ; but he arrived safely at Ismailia, where he made fun of the Professor, and light of a remarkable feat of personal endurance.

After a month's strenuous round of military exercises and training, Kitchener was ordered south on active service. Marvellous and exciting events were taking place in the Sudan, where a false prophet had arisen ; and chances of promotion danced before men's eyes. Kitchener found time, nevertheless, to fret lest his reputation might suffer on account of the negative results of the expedition to the Arabah valley. He wrote [1] to Besant on 1 March, 1884 :

' I hope the Committee will be satisfied with the work done. 3,000 square miles is not a bad total for 2 months . . . Remember me to all friends and to Sir Charles Wilson if you see him. I should much like to know what *his* opinion of the work is, considering *the time and the way we were travelling.*'

In April, 1884, Kitchener complained [1] that he was ' awfully astonished at not having heard anything pleasant '. He asked Besant if the Palestine Exploration Fund proposed to pay him anything, ' as Sir Charles Wilson . . . certainly said they would, and I should certainly not have given up my leave for nothing, and worked like a slave into the bargain '. He added that he was very sorry that his work was not considered satisfactory : ' All I can say is, I did my best, but I had no time to write a good report.'

Kitchener had had no time to polish his report on the Arabah valley expedition because he had had a much more important one to write. He left Cairo by train on 8 February, 1884, with orders to proceed to Qena, and to report on the state of the roads between Qena, on the Nile, and Quseir, on the Red Sea—the places in upper Egypt where the river approaches most nearly to the coast.

Kitchener composed two admirable reports, about the state of the roads and about the character and outlook of the local tribes. He suggested ways of raising an Arab force for service in the Sudan, and Sir Charles Wilson was greatly impressed. He told Kitchener (6 April, 1884) in a private letter : ' Lord Granville and the Foreign Office are much pleased with the way in which you did your work, and Lord Wolseley was also much taken with your reports '. Wilson added that Kitchener was not to worry about the negative results of the Arabah valley expedition : ' Your work is extremely valuable . . . I take all the blame on myself for any miscarriage in the expedition, and must confess that I am terribly disappointed in Hull as an explorer ; he seems to have been very nervous throughout . . . I am afraid you must have had an unpleasant time, but your work has decidedly added to your reputation as a surveyor and explorer.'

The committee of the Palestine Exploration Fund voted Kitchener an honorarium of fifty guineas, and as late as 1 July, 1884, at a moment

[1] Archives of the Palestine Exploration Fund.

when he was employed on special service of a peculiarly difficult
and dangerous kind, which made his name, Kitchener begged Besant
not to forget to write to the War Office in order to ensure that that
award should be duly recorded on his personal file.

Kitchener's attention in the meantime was centred on the Sudan,
where an extraordinary complication had arisen. That country had
been under Egyptian rule for sixty years, but a revolt had started in
1881, under a cloak of religion, which was no mere convulsive gesture
of despair on the part of an oppressed peasantry. It was, in essence,
a nationalist rising of powerful tribes against the alien and incompetent
Turco-Egyptian administration.

In August, 1881, Mohammed Ahmed, the son of a boat-builder and
the possessor of a magnetic personality, proclaimed himself to be the
Mahdi, or the Messiah. His movement quickly assumed the strength
of a tornado and within a year most of the Sudan was subject to his
control.

The exotic glare on the upper Nile fascinated late-Victorian England.
The rich and little-known Sudanese hinterland of Egypt offered a
tempting field of adventure ; and the dramatic appearance of a
false Messiah exercising despotic authority over a gigantic territory,
and claiming supernatural powers at a time when the controversy
between science and religion was at its height, posed a romantic challenge. Egyptian garrisons and an Egyptian civil population were
scattered throughout the Sudan ; but Gladstone's Government, which
disclaimed any interest in that country, was extremely reluctant to
admit that its occupation of Egypt had involved it in responsibility
for their safety.

While the British Foreign Office sought to evade responsibility,
the British-controlled Egyptian Government engaged the services of
a retired officer of the Indian Army, Colonel Hicks, and sent him to
Khartoum to consolidate Egyptian positions. Hicks, who thought
himself lucky to be employed at all, was appointed Commander-in-
Chief in the Sudan and despatched into the Kordofan desert to meet
the Mahdi. His army consisted of 7,000 infantry and 1,000 cavalry,
with artillery support and transport auxiliaries. The encounter took
place on 6 November, 1883, in thick bush not far from El Obeid,
the second city of the Sudan. Hicks and his army were annihilated,
and news of that disaster was brought to Kitchener and Professor Hull
on the shore of the Dead Sea on Christmas Eve, 1883.

Less than a month later, on 18 January, 1884, the British Government instructed the Egyptian Government to evacuate the Sudan and to withdraw all Egyptian garrisons and civilians. Two possible escape routes existed—by way of Berber, Suakin and the Red Sea ; or down the Nile River. The British Government tacitly acknowledged at last that it shared some responsibility for the successful conduct of that hazardous operation ; and, spurred by newspaper pressure, it despatched to Cairo a Major-General of Engineers, Charles Gordon, C.B., aged fifty-one, with orders to report on the military situation, the safety of Europeans in Khartoum, the best means of effecting a withdrawal, and to undertake ' such other duties as may be entrusted to you by Sir E. Baring '.

Sir Evelyn Baring (Earl of Cromer) had once been the finance member of the Viceroy of India's Council. From 1883 to 1907 he was the virtual ruler of Egypt, and he completely transformed that country while holding the modest title of British Agent and Consul-General. Baring acquiesced in the decision to send Gordon to Khartoum, and he acceded to Gordon's request that he should be made Governor-General of the Sudan. Gordon had served once under the Khedive in that capacity from 1877 to 1879, and it was difficult to resist his argument that the tribes would be easier to handle if he were called Governor-General again.

In England every schoolboy's heart beat faster at the thought of Gordon speeding to his lonely post of danger ; for Gordon had cast an extraordinary spell over his contemporaries. Sword in hand and Bible in pocket, he had enjoyed a career of spectacular warfare in Russia, China, India and Africa. Fearless, erratic, brilliant, perverse, he seemed to bear a charmed life. It ought to have been foreseen that such a hero would be quick to find excuses to avoid the necessity for executing an inglorious retreat.

Gordon took with him to Khartoum, Lieutenant-Colonel Herbert Stewart of the 11th Hussars. Stewart had become intimate with Kitchener while they were both serving as military vice-consuls in Anatolia. With his knowledge of Arabic and love of the Arab way of life, Kitchener yearned to follow Stewart into the limelight, and to emulate the gift which his fellow-sapper, General Gordon, possessed, of attracting glamour and romance around his name.

In March, 1884, the Mahdi's forces began closely to invest Khartoum ; and it became urgently necessary in consequence to consider means of opening communications. Kitchener eagerly volunteered for that work, and was at once ordered to go to Berber in the Sudan, and to open the road between Berber on the Nile and Suakin on the Red Sea. He was to report daily to Sir Evelyn Wood, and to spare no expense in seeking to communicate by messenger with Gordon. He was to execute any orders which Gordon might give him, and to report about the attitudes of all tribes in the regions of Suakin, Dongola and Khartoum.

That important assignment put Kitchener into the lead. It made him the eyes and ears of the Sirdar, and enabled him to act as the herald of any expedition which might be despatched to rescue Gordon or to conquer the Sudan. Kitchener took with him, as assistant, Major Leslie Rundle, [1] and they found it impossible to reach Berber. That place surrendered to the Mahdi's forces on 20 May, 1884, and Kitchener expressed the view that a strong force of British regular troops would be needed whenever the Government made up its mind to overthrow the Mahdi.

The Egyptian Government's writ hardly extended south of Aswan, on the upper Nile, so that Kitchener's orders had presently to be changed. He remained for two months at Aswan, obtaining and transmitting information, and organizing his 1,500 irregulars, most of whom belonged to the Ababda tribe, into a disciplined body which he christened the Abbada Frontier Force. He mounted them on dromedaries and asked permission to lead them in an assault upon Abu Hamed. That spirited proposition was rejected, but it enhanced Kitchener's prestige.

Early in June, Kitchener moved to Korosko, only 40 miles north of the Sudanese border. He left Rundle there while he personally reconnoitred the country between it and the Red Sea. He reported that all was fairly quiet, and on the day of his return (30 June, 1884) he wrote [2] to Walter Besant :

'Just got back from 17 days' desert ride and rather exciting hunt of one of the Mahdi's emirs. I got within a day of him with 200 men, and he had only 50 ! I was told he was most fanatical, and that nothing would induce him to go back—that he had declared to die or advance—and, after all, the brute bolted into a country I could not follow him in. All my splendid arrangements for surrounding him collapsed ! '

[1] General Sir Leslie Rundle, G.C.B., G.C.M.G., G.C.V.O., D.S.O. (1856–1934).
[2] Archives of the Palestine Exploration Fund.

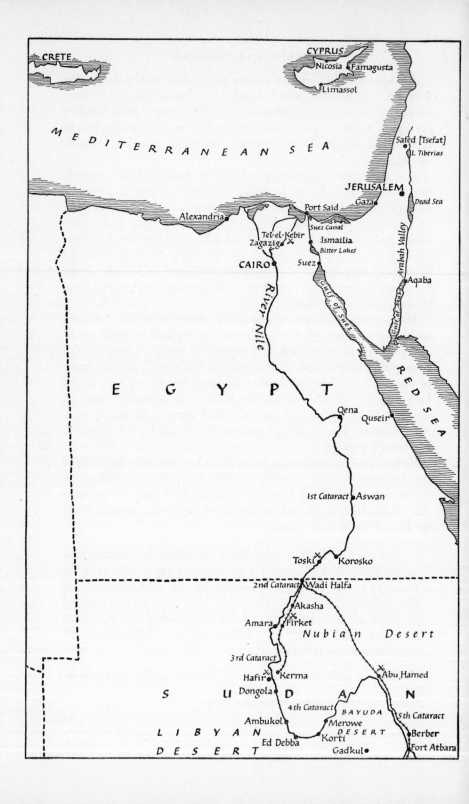

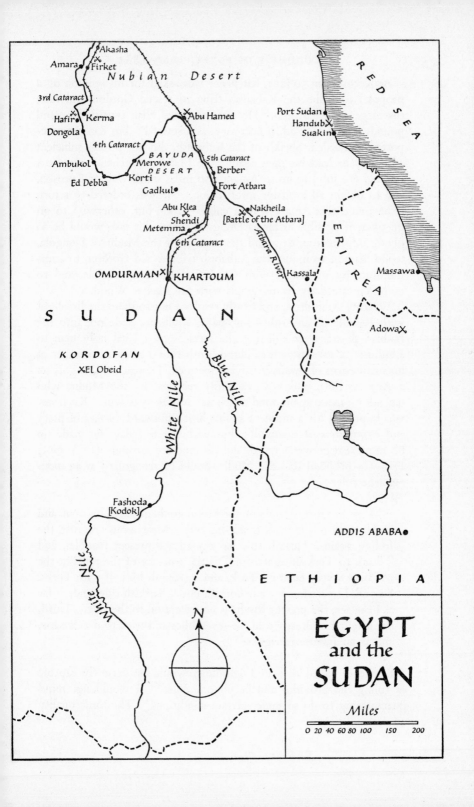

Akasha
Amara
Firket
Nubian Desert
3rd Cataract
Hafir
Kerma
Dongola
4th Cataract
Ambukol
BAYUDA
Merowe
DESERT
Korti
Ed Debba
Gadkul
Abu Hamed
5th Cataract
Berber
Fort Atbara
Abu Klea
Shendi
Metemma
Nakheila
[Battle of the Atbara]
6th Cataract
OMDURMAN
KHARTOUM
Atbara River
Kassala
S U D A N
K O R D O F A N
El Obeid
White Nile
Blue Nile
Fashoda
[Kodok]
White Nile
Port Sudan
Handub
Suakin
R E D S E A
E R I T R E A
Massawa
Adowa
ADDIS ABABA
E T H I O P I A
N

EGYPT
and the
SUDAN

Miles

0 20 40 60 80 100   150   200

At Korosko on 30 June, Kitchener was asked for his opinion on a proposal to bribe the Kababish tribe to rescue Gordon and raise the siege of Khartoum. He was informed that twenty thousand pounds would be paid, if necessary, as a reward ; but Kitchener reported that Saleh, Sheikh of the Kababish, did not possess sufficient authority to lead his men against the Mahdi. Kitchener was next ordered (19 July) to go to Amara, 170 miles south-west of Korosko, and to obtain all available information. He was ordered to return if he found that Amara was in enemy hands, but, otherwise, to go up-river, if possible as far as Dongola, where his task would be to obtain information, to sound the attitude of the Mudir of Dongola, to do his best to induce the Kababish tribe to aid Gordon, to communicate by messenger with Gordon as often as possible, and to communicate daily by telegraph with Sir Evelyn Wood.

Wearing Arab dress, and firmly resolved not to share the limelight with Rundle or any other European, Kitchener rode out into the Nubian desert, after enlisting the services of a local holy man to administer a solemn oath of blood-brotherhood to every member of his small escort of twenty Ababda tribesmen. He reached Dongola on 2 August, 1884, and was graciously received by the Mudir, who had not yet made up his mind which side was likely to win. Kitchener was impressed for a moment by his host's outward display of piety and expressions of goodwill ; but within a few days he made up his mind that he was a rascal, and he reported strongly (19 August) against a proposal that the Mudir should be recognized as an independent ruler :

' I am decidedly of opinion the Mudir could not hold his own, and trade could not flourish under his rule. My reasons are, first, the feeling against Turkish rule has caused the present troubles, and " death to Turkish oppression " is the war-cry of the rebels ; the Mudir is a very fanatical Turk, and surrounds himself with Turks. Second, I never knew trade flourish under Turkish rule, and, as far as I can see, the present Mudir is no exception to the rule. Third, the Mudir has already told me several lies and tried to deceive me, and is an intense intriguer.'

Kitchener added that an Englishman would be perfectly capable of ruling the province and keeping it quiet : ' I would not mind guaranteeing to do so under certain conditions.' The tonic quality of Kitchener's reports was relished in Cairo where the authorities were desperately worried by the British Government's long delay in making up its mind about a relief expedition to Khartoum. As late as 30 July, 1884, Gladstone circulated a memorandum to his Cabinet in which he argued that no expedition was needed. On 5 August, however, under irresistible pressure, he demanded from the House of Commons a vote of credit of £300,000.

Three days later, on 8 August, 1884, Lord Hartington, the Secretary for War, instructed Sir Frederick Stephenson, the commander of the British occupation forces in Egypt, to take preliminary steps for an advance southwards. Hartington felt it necessary to state at the same time that ' Her Majesty's Government are not at present convinced that it will be impossible for General Gordon, acting on the instructions which he has received, to secure the withdrawal from Khartoum, either by the employment of force, or by pacific means, of the Egyptian garrisons, and of such of the inhabitants as may desire to leave.'

Lord Wolseley arrived in Cairo on 10 September, 1884, to command the relief expedition. He asked at once for additional troops, and Hartington, in complying with that request, again felt obliged to state (17 September) : ' Her Majesty's Government desire to remind you that no decision has yet been arrived at to send any portion of the force under your command beyond Dongola . . . You are fully aware of the views of Her Majesty's Government on the subject, and know how averse they are to undertake any warlike expedition not called for by absolute necessity.'

Gordon's necessity was absolute and urgent ; Kitchener felt, as all soldiers and many others must have felt also, that Gladstone's Government was strangely blind to the code of honour which held Gordon chained to his post of danger. Gordon could, at any moment, have abandoned Khartoum and its forty thousand inhabitants, and slipped northwards through the Mahdi's lines to safety with a few companions. He could never have hoped to succeed, however, in withdrawing all those for whom he was bound to feel responsible. In his journal (21 September, 1884) Gordon recorded the receipt of a note addressed by Kitchener to Colonel Stewart :

' Can I do anything for you or General Gordon? I should be awfully glad if you will let me know. The relief expedition is evidently coming up this way, but whether they will go by Berber

47

or attempt the desert road from here, I do not know. The Mahdi is in a bad way . . .'

No date was recorded, but two days later (23 September) Gordon noted the receipt of another letter addressed to him by Kitchener from Ed Debba (Debbeh), a few miles up-river from Dongola and dated 31 August, 1884. It asked Gordon to say 'exactly' when he expected to be in difficulties 'as to provisions and ammunition'. Kitchener had added : 'I think an expedition will be sent across from here to Khartoum, while another goes with steamers to Berber. A few words about what you wish done would be very acceptable.'

Few letters trickled through, in either direction, of the large number which were despatched, although the messengers were invariably well rewarded. Gordon was in a highly-strung condition, and he commented acidly in his journal : 'It is as if a man on the bank, having seen his friend in the river already bobbed down two or three times, hails, "I say, old fellow, let me know when we are to throw you the life buoy ; I know you have bobbed down two or three times, but it is a pity to throw you the life buoy until you really are *in extremis*, and I want to know *exactly*, for I am a man brought up in a school of exactitude . . ." . . .'

On 24 September, after re-reading Kitchener's note to Stewart, Gordon again recorded his mood of frustration :

'I altogether *decline* the imputation that the projected expedition has come to *relieve me*. It has *come to* SAVE OUR NATIONAL HONOUR *in extricating the garrisons etc., from a position our action in Egypt has placed these garrisons. I was relief expedition No. 1.* They are *relief expedition No. 2.* As for myself, I could make good my retreat at any moment, if I wished . . . We the *first* and they the *second* expeditions are equally engaged for the honour of England . . . I am not the *rescued lamb*, and I will not be.'

That was not the Government's view. Gladstone considered that Gordon could and should make good his own retreat ; and it had been stated on many occasions that the primary object of Lord Wolseley's expedition was to bring away General Gordon. Once that object had been attained no further offensive operations of any kind were contemplated. Furthermore, whatever Gordon might choose to write in moments of exasperation, he had an extremely high

48

opinion of Kitchener. Gordon noted, for example, on 26 November, 1884 :

'I like Baker's [1] description of Kitchener—"the man I have always placed my hopes upon, Major Kitchener, R.E., who is one of the few *very superior* British officers, with a cool head and a hard constitution, combined with untiring energy . . ." . . . Whoever comes up here had better appoint Major Kitchener Governor-General, for it is certain, after what has passed, *I am impossible.* (What a comfort !)'

Gordon noted the next day : 'If Kitchener would take the place, he would be the best man to put in as Governor-General.'

In the meantime the Sirdar had telegraphed to Kitchener on 4 August :

' The most important work for you, after arranging to communicate with Gordon, and for a meeting with Sheikh Saleh of the Kababish, is to find out all you can as to all the routes leading from Dongola and from Ed Debba to Khartoum, and also from Ambukol to Shendi. The information required is that usually compiled in all reconnaissance reports, it being, of course, understood that as you will not be able to traverse the routes yourself, you must be dependent on what you hear.'

Ambukol was a short distance up-river from Ed Debba, and Shendi, less than 100 miles from Khartoum, was distant some 140 miles across the Bayuda Steppe, round the great bend of the Nile. Kitchener disguised himself as a prowling Arab and personally reconnoitred a substantial portion of the routes specified by the Sirdar. He reported fully, and expressed the view that the route from Ed Debba across the desert to Khartoum was likely to prove the most suitable for the expedition. He made Ed Debba his headquarters from 8 August, 1884.

Kitchener had already assumed the local unpaid rank of Lieutenant-Colonel because he found it useful in his work. He was delighted to be informed by the Sirdar (30 August) that he had been recommended for a brevet majority in the British Army. That award was gazetted

[1] Sir Samuel Baker, F.R.S., had served as Governor of the Equatorial provinces of the Nile under the Khedive from 1869 to 1873.

on 4 October, but Kitchener had to remind the Sirdar to address him as Colonel, and he begged (5 September) that his local rank should be made definite in orders: ' I am afraid of denouement destroying all my influence here. I could not work with local force under rank I have assumed.'

Wolseley was informed about Kitchener's brevet promotion almost as soon as he landed in Egypt to lead the relief expedition to Khartoum. He dismissed the matter with a good-humoured chuckle, although almost his last action before leaving the War Office had been a refusal to allow that promotion. He had been mindful of past disagreements, but his attitude of hostility changed to friendliness overnight when he learned details about Kitchener's most recent activities. The light in which those services were viewed officially can best be gauged by quoting from two documents which were added at that time to Kitchener's personal file at the War Office.

On 28 June, 1884, Kitchener's commanding officer, Lieutenant-Colonel Taylor, 19th Hussars, reported : [1]

' It would be impossible for me to speak too highly of the assistance which this officer has given me. The facility with which he mastered the details of cavalry drill, and his capacity for imparting instruction, are remarkable. His energy is untiring. As a second-in-command he has left nothing to be desired, and he has at all times given me his most cordial support.'

Kitchener's specific qualities were described in glowing terms. His ' general ability ' was ' remarkable ' ; his ' general professional acquirements ' were ' thorough ' ; his ' self-reliance ' was ' unfailing ' ; his ' readiness and resource ' were ' unbounded ' ; his ' judgment and tact ' were ' sound and great ' ; his ' temperament ' was ' cool '. He had ' not yet practised ' outpost or patrol duty, but his ' capacity for command ', ' reconnaissance ', ' horsemanship ', and ' application of drill to the circumstances of the moment ' were all ' very good '. It only remained for Sir Evelyn Wood, as Sirdar of the Egyptian Army, to add : ' This is an excellent officer in every respect—a good Arabic linguist—a fine horseman—great determination and courage. He is now pressing me every day to be allowed to cross the Korosko desert, with some Arabs. I have the highest opinion of him.'

Ten weeks later (1 September, 1884) Lieutenant-General Sir Frederick Stephenson, Commander-in-Chief of the British Army

[1] War Office Records.

of Occupation in Egypt, wrote [1] to the Military Secretary at the War
Office in London :

'I have the honour to request that you will bring to the notice
of H.R.H. the Field-Marshal commanding-in-chief [2] the very
valuable services recently performed by Captain Kitchener, R.E.,
now serving with the rank of Major in the Egyptian Army.

'Major Kitchener, owing to his knowledge of Arabic, and intimate acquaintance with the habits of the Bedouins, over whom he
exercises great influence, was appointed to the command of about
1,500 of those men for the purpose of watching the South frontier
of Egypt from Korosko to the Red Sea—a distance of about 200
miles, and also of patrolling to the front and obtaining such information as he could of the movements of the hostile tribes in
the neighbourhood of Abu Hamed.

'This duty, involving to some extent the security of the active
frontier, as well as of the British and Egyptian troops at Assouan,
has been performed to my entire satisfaction, and with very great
tact, energy, and self-devotion.

'It required the exercise of those qualities in a high degree ;
and I know of no other officer in the Egyptian Army—there is
certainly none in the English—capable of performing it so well.

'It was necessary, subsequently, to obtain information of what
was going on at Dongola, of the feelings of the natives towards
ourselves, as well as towards the Egyptian Government, and
especially as regards the disposition of the Mudir, [3] as to whose
loyalty very great doubts were then entertained.

'The Egyptian Government had warned us of the inexpediency
of sending an English officer to Dongola for that purpose ; but
when an Egyptian officer volunteered for this duty, he made it a
condition that he should be accompanied by a force of 1,200 men
and receive a reward of £10,000—so great was the risk which was
considered by many as likely to be incurred.

'Major Kitchener then offered his services, and went at once to
Dongola accompanied by an escort of Bedouins.

'His expedition has resulted in complete success. Valuable
information was obtained which has been furnished since almost
daily, and is of growing importance.

[1] War Office Records.　　　　　[2] The Duke of Cambridge.
[3] The native ruler of the province of Dongola.

' Major Kitchener has, since then, advanced as far as Debbeh, and even beyond.

' I consider the services performed by Major Kitchener, of which I have merely given a rough sketch—performed single-handed, as it were, and far removed from any possibility of support—as of the greatest value to the security of Egypt, and to Her Majesty's forces now protecting it.

' These services have been carried out in an adventurous spirit, and with great intelligence and a high sense of duty, and I trust His Royal Highness will not consider that I view them too highly when I trust that they will meet with his favourable consideration with a view to Major Kitchener's promotion.'

CHAPTER 4

MAHDISM

1884–1889

THE almost effortless conquest of Egypt had lifted British military prestige to a height which it had not known since Waterloo. Kitchener revelled in that knowledge as much as he revelled in the Egyptian sunshine, and in the thought that at the age of thirty-four he was starred officially, in London as well as in Cairo, for rapid promotion. He was therefore the more unwilling to return from Ed Debba to Korosko, and to abandon the limelight which continuously played upon him.

Kitchener wanted, if possible, to enter Khartoum in advance of the leading elements of Wolseley's relief expedition. But he knew that he ought to return to Korosko, where Leslie Rundle was having trouble with the Ababda Frontier Force. Its leaders refused to march southwards, alleging that the season was unsuitable and the pay inadequate ; and Rundle, who was furiously jealous of Kitchener, repeatedly begged him to return : ' I have always ', Rundle telegraphed, early in September, ' distinctly given you to understand that I decline to take the responsibility of this work off your hands, although perfectly willing to work under your orders. You cannot control this work from the end of a telegraph wire . . . Do you intend returning ? If so, when ? Surely any intelligent officer could do your present work . . .'

Kitchener told Rundle that he would return in due course ; and he asked the Sirdar to decide the matter. He pointed out to Sir Evelyn Wood that he was still reconnoitring possible routes to Khartoum, and that his presence at Ed Debba, which he was fortifying, was having a tonic effect upon the natives.

Sir Evelyn, who had been placed under Wolseley's orders and given command of the line of communication troops, took no action to recall Kitchener to Korosko. Kitchener's reports were far too valuable, and Rundle was left to cope with his difficulties as best he could, while the relief expedition pursued its leisurely progress up the Nile. On 31 August, 1884, Sir Evelyn Baring sent Kitchener a private and confidential telegram :

' Time question for Gordon's relief now so serious that I should be

53

obliged if you would telegraph me, for my personal information, if there is any feasible means of helping Gordon by irregular and native Dongola forces ; if any such forces are available ; and how many ; and what direction could they take ; and could they recapture Berber ? Also your opinion as to most rapid means of relieving Gordon. Keep this confidential, I beg.'

Kitchener replied the same day :

> ' There is no doubt Gordon means he can hold out until middle of November . . . From his conversation with my messenger I think he will hold out longer, and when English troops appear, everything will be easier for him. The Dongola forces are all bashibazouks mounted on camels, and regular black infantry. When English troops arrive here, they may be pushed on by Mudir, but I doubt their going far. For instance, Mudir the other day ordered force to go to Merowe. They refused on grounds of pay. I said I would advance pay, but they still declined to go, and have not gone.
>
> ' I therefore think there is no feasible means of helping Gordon, except by English troops.
>
> ' If gunboats come over cataract, Berber can be very easily taken. I think it possible Mudir might do it with his troops, supported by gunboats.
>
> ' From all accounts Mahdi's forces are much dispirited, and Mahdi is asked for reinforcements in every direction, which he is unable to send. On arrival of English troops here he will be deserted by many.
>
> ' I do not think a large expedition would be necessary from here. A flying column to Khartoum composed of a strong force of cavalry and artillery and some infantry on camels or on foot—altogether about 4,000—could, I believe, relieve Khartoum in less than the time required. If Gordon knows expedition is coming up, he will hold out, never fear, and will co-operate.
>
> ' Gunboats should be sent to Berber which can be taken easily, as it is quite open to the river and they have no cannon.
>
> ' My opinion is, decidedly, send up your troops. There is no difficulty, and one good fight close to Khartoum will see the matter through.'

Kitchener continued during September to keep a close watch on the Mudir of Dongola. The Mahdi had nominated one of his followers to replace the Mudir, but the Mudir defeated and killed his rival at Korti on 10 September. The Sirdar at that time was sailing up the Nile, and Kitchener could obtain no reply to his telegrams requesting permission to join the Mudir. He joined him, therefore without orders, at Ambukol ; and after visiting the scene of the Mudir's victory at Korti, accompanied him up-river to Merowe, which he proceeded to put into a state of defence.

Kitchener carried a bottle of poison with him for use in case he was captured. He had been present, by chance, at the execution of a spy whom the Mudir had taken, and had been horrified by the tortures inflicted upon the unfortunate man. On one occasion during that journey Kitchener's disguise was so perfect that he was himself taken for a spy by the Mudir's men and arrested. He was confined in a tent with two genuine spies, who had previously refused to talk, and who accepted Kitchener as a comrade. He had difficulty in convincing the guards of his identity, after he had secured the information he wanted.

Kitchener returned to Ed Debba on 22 September, and learned there that his friend, Colonel Stewart, accompanied by the British and French consuls, had left Khartoum by steamer on 10 September, and were risking the passage down the Nile. Gordon's purpose in sending Stewart away was to make the outside world aware, beyond all possibility of doubt, of the straits to which he had been reduced. Kitchener sent a trusted messenger immediately to intercept Stewart at Berber, and to warn him to leave the steamer there, and to take the desert route from Berber to Dongola, instead of attempting to pass by steamer through the territory of two hostile tribes ; but that messenger never reached Stewart.

Stewart's steamer passed Berber and Abu Hamed without incident, and came successfully on 18 September to the beginning of the Fourth Cataract, about 70 miles above Merowe. There it struck a rock in mid-stream, and Stewart, disregarding his companions' fears, responded to friendly overtures made to him by natives on the bank. He spiked his gun, cast his ammunition overboard, and went ashore with his party.

Stewart was promised a supply of camels, and was taken with his friends to a nearby dwelling of the local sheikh. He was offered dates and coffee while the camels were being collected. As the party sat down to eat and drink it was surprised by soldiers, and every

55

member of it was murdered with swords. The steamer was then looted at leisure.

Before news of that event reached Ed Debba, Kitchener was notified (24 September) that his name had appeared in orders ' as D.A.A.G. to serve in the intelligence department' of the relief expedition under Colonel Sir Charles Wilson, who was due to leave Cairo on 25 September for Dongola. Until Sir Charles reached Wadi Halfa on his way to Dongola, Kitchener was ordered to report daily to Major-General Sir Redvers Buller, V.C.,[1] Lord Wolseley's Chief of Staff, giving ' full details of all you know and hear as to position of affairs at Khartoum, Berber, in your neighbourhood, and among tribes', and to keep in touch with Gordon. Buller added :

'You will not leave Ed Debba without my permission, as Lord Wolseley must have a reliable officer there. He does not approve of your going to Berber.'

Kitchener had asked leave to go to Berber himself, in order to meet Stewart and to escort his party across the desert ; and he resented the rejection of that request. In the daily reports which he dispatched before Wilson's arrival he irritated Buller by repeatedly begging for native troops, ' or, better, an English steamer ', to be sent to Stewart's aid. Buller wired (1 October) : ' It will be some time before we can do anything of that sort on account of difficulty of supply.' Three days later, on 4 October, 1884, Kitchener informed Buller that Stewart and his party had been massacred.

Kitchener had been extremely fond of Stewart, and he told his friends that Stewart was the finest soldier he had ever met. He clung desperately for some days to the hope that his friend might, after all, have been taken prisoner, and that a rescue might still be possible. The anguish which he felt betrayed him into permitting a shrill note to creep into two of his telegrams, of which later, he was, without any just cause, much ashamed.

On 6 October Kitchener wired to Sir Redvers Buller : ' What I want is two telegrams from Lord Wolseley.' Kitchener asked for an order giving him *carte blanche* to quit his post for the purpose of rescuing any possible survivors of Stewart's party, by diplomacy, if possible, or, if necessary, by a surprise assault. He said that he could obtain troops and guns in Dongola and Ambukol, and he asked

[1] General the Rt. Hon. Sir Redvers Buller, V.C., P.C., G.C.B., G.C.M.G., (1839-1908).

only for the loan of one British officer. He asked for a second order placing the Mudir of Dongola under his command.

Kitchener's request for leave to quit his post was rejected on 8 October by Brigadier-General Sir Herbert Stewart, who was no relation of the murdered colonel. Kitchener was informed that the Mudir of Dongola had been asked to procure the release of any prisoners by the use of force or bribery. On 9 October Kitchener telegraphed to Sir Herbert : ' The great necessity is rapidity of action. If it were possible to relieve me by sending another officer in steamer here, I would promise to do nothing rash. Please ask General Wood if I cannot be trusted in this respect.'

When Sir Charles Wilson arrived at Dongola a few days later, Sir Redvers Buller and Sir Herbert Stewart complained to him about the insubordinate tone of Kitchener's telegrams. Wilson held, rightly, that the telegrams did Kitchener honour ; but he asked Kitchener for a précis of all the telegrams which he had sent. In forwarding that précis, Kitchener wrote (October, undated) :

' My Dear Sir Charles,
' In forwarding the précis you desire . . . I feel that it is very likely that the matter may form the subject of further remarks on, and criticisms of, my conduct.
' I hope, in reading the telegrams, you will remember that I was all alone without a soul to speak to or discuss the matter with. I assure you I was animated throughout with only one view— how to give help to Stewart, who was a friend of mine, and the party that were with him.
' Many nights I have hardly slept at all with thinking over what could be done ; and in the mornings I was so certain something would be done that it may have affected the tone of my telegrams, as it did in one case—viz. the 6th Oct.
' I can only say I did my best according to my lights, and that I would not go through that 8 days again, from 2nd to 10th Oct., for a fortune.
' In these few remarks I leave the question of my conduct confidently in your hands.'

Wilson stood loyally by his subordinate, as Kitchener a few weeks later stood loyally by his chief when Wilson was placed in a situation of far greater embarrassment. All jealous mutterings about

Kitchener's wish to fight a private war died down ; and Wilson obtained special permission for Kitchener to wear an Arab headdress instead of a regulation army helmet.

Desert intelligence and reconnaissance kept Kitchener fully occupied ; but he also assembled a large supply depot at Ed Debba and constructed many telegraph lines. He prepared maps, collected camels, and marked suitable sites for camps and hospitals ; and when he was seconded formally, early in November, from the Egyptian Army for service with Wolseley's expeditionary force, his name was headlined in most of the principal newspapers in England. A typical comment appeared in a leading article in the *Western Morning News* (5 November, 1884) :

' But for the investigations and intrepid daring of this gallant young officer, Lord Wolseley could have sent no satisfactory reply to the anxious inquiries which have been made by the Government. Major Kitchener has been the pioneer of the expedition. He went alone into a district where it was not known whether he would meet friends or foes, carrying his life in his hand . . . Every war brings it heroes ; and when the military operations in the Sudan are over, the name and deeds of Major Kitchener will be remembered.'

That was the music that Kitchener wanted to hear, and his father, who was often, until his death in August, 1894, to be found at the Oriental Club in Hanover Square, stirred up friends and acquaintances to swell the chorus. Sir Samuel Baker, for example, wrote frequently to Kitchener. He had already told him (10 August, 1884) :

' I am delighted to see that you are leading . . . You have been doing excellent service, and in letters to *The Times* and other papers I have endeavoured to draw attention to the fact of the energy you have displayed in the desert journeys at this hottest season . . . There is a splendid field open to you, as you are *alone* ; and you will have much more influence over the people than you would have with an English companion.'

On 9 October, Baker wrote : ' You have done better than all the others, and are thoroughly appreciated by the British public as the one who has led the way.'

On 6 November, 1884, Wilson explained to Kitchener that the British Government wanted 'to settle the Sudan question, if possible, without bloodshed'. It considered that a mere threat might be sufficient to cause the Mahdi to abandon the siege of Khartoum ; and Wilson warned Kitchener accordingly to make full use of the services of the Mudir of Dongola : 'I have no doubt the Mudir has not been running straight, but I think he will be better now. He has been made a K.C.M.G., and is aware that his interests are ours.'

Kitchener protested hotly (8 November) that the Mudir of Dongola was 'exploiting the English and filling his pockets' ; and that he was a fanatical enemy of the British Empire and of Christianity. Wilson replied patiently (13 November) : 'We are not trusting him in any way, but are working independently, and whatever assistance he renders is so much to the good, whether as regards supplies or pushing on in front of us. If he can get the tribes in by threatening them with our approach, so much the better.'

Wolseley had based his operational plan upon that broad policy which Kitchener regarded as fatuous. Infantry had been transported up the Nile in steamers from Wadi Halfa, accompanied by cavalry and supplies on the banks ; and that river column was not scheduled to reach Khartoum until the spring of 1885. If Gordon's need became critical before the spring, it had been arranged that a desert column, mounted on camels, should cross the Bayuda Steppe from Korti to Metemma, where it would meet steamers which Gordon would send down-river from Khartoum.

On 17 November, Wolseley received from Gordon a note dated 4 November which stated that Khartoum could hold out 'with ease' for forty days, but that it would be 'difficult', thereafter, to maintain the defence. The desert column, accordingly, was immediately ordered to advance from Korti to Metemma under the command of Sir Herbert Stewart. It was composed of units of crack regiments, and it contained so many officers bearing famous names that in some quarters it was jealously described as a social stunt. Kitchener was ordered to accompany it as intelligence officer.

Unfortunately, the desert column's transport arrangements proved to be chaotic as a result of a muddle for which Sir Charles Wilson was blamed. He had ordered Kitchener, as well as the Mudir of Dongola and others, to stop purchasing camels on 11 October, before a sufficient number had been collected to carry 3,100 officers and men across the Bayuda Steppe in one rush. The column had, therefore, to move in two parts, and even the first part was not ready to leave Korti until 30 December. It had to halt half-way at Gadkul in order to form an intermediate depot.

Kitchener accompanied Sir Herbert Stewart to Gadkul, and remained there, while Sir Herbert, with the unloaded camels, returned to Korti to fetch the remainder of his force and supplies. Stewart returned on 12 January, 1885, accompanied by Wilson. Kitchener, to his dismay, was then ordered back to Korti. On 14 January, Stewart resumed his advance on Metemma, and ran into strong opposition four days later. He won a decisive victory on 17 January at Abu Klea, but was mortally wounded on the following day in the course of a successful attempt to reach the bank of the Nile a short distance above Metemma.

The next most senior officer (Colonel F. G. Burnaby, who had been designated to act as commandant at Metemma) having been killed on the previous day, the command devolved upon Colonel Sir Charles Wilson. Sir Charles was a well-known scholar and a Fellow of the Royal Society. He was a distinguished member of the Corps of Royal Engineers, but he had never commanded troops in action before, and he felt somewhat out of his element. After consulting Sir Herbert Stewart, who did not die of his wound until 16 February, Sir Charles entered the square and ordered Lieutenant-Colonel the Hon. E. E. T. Boscawen, Coldstream Guards, to take executive command.

On reaching the Nile, Wilson intercepted (21 January, 1885) four steamers bearing letters from Gordon, dated 14 December, which stated that Khartoum could only hold out for a few more days. Nevertheless, Sir Charles hesitated for three fateful days before starting for Khartoum.

For that delay the gallant but unhappy officer was condemned unanimously by military opinion. He protested to Lord Wolseley that the steamers needed repair and protection against bullets ; and that it was necessary to reconnoitre south and north before splitting his force in obedience to his orders. Wolseley felt obliged to dismiss those excuses, and it has to be admitted that Wilson, on that occasion, failed to meet the demands of the critical situation which confronted him.

Wilson started for Khartoum on the morning of 24 January. Little opposition was encountered, and on the morning of 28 January he came within sight of the town. He sailed on to the junction of the Blue and White Niles, and was saluted by a heavy fire of muskets and concealed guns from both banks. Swarms of dervishes appeared, gathered under banners, and there was no flag over the palace. Khartoum had fallen two days earlier, on 26 January ; six hours of massacre had followed ; General Gordon was dead.

The skill and courage which Wilson showed in withdrawing his steamers from the jaws of death after hours of severe fighting, and at the cost of many casualties, did much to retrieve his reputation. There was more heavy fighting on 31 January when one of the steamers grounded and could not be refloated. On 4 February, 1885, Wilson reunited his force, which started two days later on the return march across the desert to Korti.

The news that Khartoum had fallen reverberated throughout the world ; it reached London on 5 February, and plunged the nation and empire into mourning. On Gladstone's unbowed but by no means blameless head a cataract of ridicule, hatred and contempt descended ; and a mood of hysteria which lasted for about three weeks, drew crowds every day to Downing Street in the hope that they might have a chance to hoot and jeer at the Prime Minister. Kitchener heard the news at Gadkul where, as intelligence officer, he was accompanying Sir Redvers Buller across the Bayuda Steppe. Buller had been sent to succeed Wilson in command of the desert column.

Kitchener reached Gadkul on 11 February, 1885, and found all ranks plunged in bitterness and gloom. A revised plan, formed before the news of the disaster was known, enjoined Buller to march to Berber to meet the river column. Reinforcements were to have been sent by sea from England to disembark at Suakin, and to march from Suakin to Berber. The whole of that plan was, of course, abandoned, after a series of bewildering and contradictory orders. By a strange irony, despite the elementary failure to provide the desert column at Korti with an adequate supply of camels, arrangements had been made to ship an entire railway to Suakin, to be laid to Berber ; and ten thousand umbrellas had been ordered from a London firm to give shade in the desert to the troops.

The morale of the desert column was low when Buller, threatened by the advance of a large dervish army, ordered a general retreat upon Korti. The withdrawal was harassed by the enemy, and some of the most advanced British units, which had been surrounded, were only saved by a bold diversionary manœuvre on the part of Sir Evelyn

61

Wood. Wood, who had succeeded Buller as Wolseley's Chief of Staff, left Korti with all the soldiers he could collect at short notice to assist the withdrawal.

In an effort to hamper the pursuit, Kitchener begged Buller to agree to the filling-in of desert wells. Buller objected that the usages of war forbade such action ; but the peril was great and it seemed essential to deprive the enemy of water. Kitchener at last extracted from Buller a reluctant assent to the filling-in of the principal well at Abu Klea. Seizing his advantage, Kitchener turned to a group of his brother-officers, asking each to destroy the principal well which he could find, and adding gaily, " I'll go and see about the rest."

Early in March, 1885, exhausted and in disorder, the desert column straggled back to Korti, in the knowledge that its sacrifices and labours had been in vain. The catastrophe gave rise to endless recriminations, which could not obscure the essential fact that the expedition had been launched irresolutely and too late.

Whatever reputations were blasted, Kitchener's reputation was made. His promotion to a brevet lieutenant-colonelcy was gazetted on 15 June, 1885, and he was highly commended for his services by Lord Wolseley. On 10 April, Sir Charles Wilson poured his heart out to Kitchener. He complained that he had been made responsible by the public for the Government's policy of ' scuttling ' out of the Sudan, ' as well as for Gordon's murder and the fall of Khartoum . . . As regards Gordon, I must leave it to time. I cannot say to the public, " If Stewart had been allowed to carry out the original plan and march straight to Metemma, there would have been no desert fight and Khartoum would have been saved " ; nor can I talk about contradictory orders relating to the purchase of camels which upset the transport ; nor again, that everyone, knowing in November that Gordon could only hold out until Xmas day, no special efforts were made to perfect the desert column and transport ; nor that the force which reached the Nile was too weak and composed of too many different regiments to attempt any important enterprise.'

Lord Wolseley was equally bitter. He sent Kitchener a warm and friendly letter on 30 January, 1886, expressing his opinion of Gladstone, who was then in process of forming his third administration :

' God must be very angry with England when he sends back Mr. Gladstone to us as First Minister. The prospect of having such an unprincipled man directing our affairs at this moment is indeed sad, and causes even the most light of heart to look grave at present.

' Nothing is talked of or cared for at this moment but this appalling calamity that has fallen upon England.

' The more frequently you can find time to write me, the more agreeable it will be to, very sincerely yours . . .'

The bitterest letter of all, however, was the one which Kitchener valued most. It was addressed to him by General Gordon : dated 26 November, 1884 ; and delivered at Korti on 25 February, 1885. Kitchener found the letter awaiting him when he returned with the defeated desert column ; its ostensible purpose was a request that he should convey Gordon's thanks to the King of the Belgians for a kind message ; but its interest lay, characteristically, in the postscript :

' There will be no peace between me and Gladstone's Government . . . Neither will I accept anything whatsoever from them. And I will not let them pay my expenses. I will get the King of the Belgians to do so, and I will never set foot in England again . . .

' If you would take up the post of Governor-General . . . it would be well for the people, and you would have no difficulty that you could not master.'

In sending that letter to his father for safe keeping, Kitchener wrote : ' I enclose a letter from Gordon which came down on his steamer. It is the best reward I shall get for a good many months' hard work ; so please keep it most carefully for me. I feel that, now he is dead, the heart and soul of the expedition is gone.'

Nevertheless, Kitchener believed for a few weeks that even Gladstone would not dare to repudiate the policy which he announced, with the most extreme repugnance, to the House of Commons on 19 February, 1885, in a feeble and unconvincing speech. Gladstone declared that the Mahdi would have to be destroyed, and that a civilized government would be established in Khartoum. An unprecedented explosion of popular emotion had wrung from Gladstone that compromise with what he termed ' the fiend of jingoism ' ; but he could not be induced to speak one word in praise of Gordon, or of the army which had striven to rescue him in vain.

Reinforcements were dispatched to Suakin, on the Red Sea coast, and Kitchener told Sir Samuel Baker that the issue confronting England in the Sudan lay between ' anarchy—a return to savagedom and great danger to Egypt . . . or the development of an enormous trade in central Africa, under a good government '. But throughout March, 1885, it was rumoured everywhere that Gladstone, under Radical pressure, was seeking a means of withdrawing altogether from the Sudan.

On 20 March, the control of Egyptian finance was vested in a board on which Great Britain, France, Russia, Germany, Austria and Italy enjoyed equal representation. A loan of nine million pounds was made to Egypt by those Powers, and Great Britain's position was crippled in consequence. The French, who had never ceased to regret the position they had lost in Cairo, voted invariably with the Russians. Any British proposal, therefore, was liable to be defeated on the board, unless the Germans and Austrians, who also worked in harness, could be induced to support it ; and successive British Foreign Secretaries had constantly to purchase German support with scraps of Africa at the height of the colonial scramble.

Gladstone concluded that unhappy settlement from exalted motives ; but he thereby impaired European stability and helped to keep France and England apart for nineteen years. He told his constituents at Midlothian (17 September, 1885) that the humiliations and inconveniences which Great Britain was called upon to suffer in Egypt should all be regarded as part of a divine retribution for the crime which he had committed when he had ordered the invasion of that country.

On 30 March, 1885, an incident in Afghanistan gave Gladstone the excuse which he urgently desired for reversing his declared policy of crushing the Mahdi in the Sudan. It appeared to the Russians that while British attention was concentrated in the valley of the Nile, the time might be favourable for an advance in the valley of the Oxus. Accordingly, the Russians staged an experimental but sanguinary affray at the village of Pendjeh, a few miles on the Afghan side of the Russo-Afghan border.

The Afghans, who had suffered much worse things at Disraeli's hands, were not unduly perturbed. But the Government of India was alarmed, and a wave of anti-Russian sentiment convulsed Great Britain and caused a panic on the Stock Exchange. Public opinion was tense and highly strung ; and a flood of newspaper articles and political speeches described Pendjeh, of which no one had ever heard before, as the Gateway of India.

Gladstone considered that God had inspired that crisis in order to relieve his conscience of the guilt and burden of having to conquer the Sudan. He astonished the world by demanding a vote of eleven million pounds from the House of Commons, and by announcing that all the forces of the Empire would be concentrated immediately in readiness to repel Russian aggression. He told the Commons on 21 April, 1885, that there could now be no question of permitting Lord Wolseley to undertake further operations in the Sudan. Circumstances had entirely changed : 'It is a paramount duty incumbent upon us to hold our forces in the Sudan available for service wherever the call of duty or honour may summon them in the service of the British Empire.'

In face of that unexpectedly resolute attitude, the Russians drew back, and the incident at Pendjeh was submitted to arbitration. It had, however, served its purpose, and neither the frantic protests of Queen Victoria, nor the fall (9 June) of the Liberal Government, nor the death (20 June) of the Mahdi from smallpox at Omdurman, availed to prevent what Kitchener and the Army termed the policy of scuttle in the Sudan.

Kitchener, who always regarded Gordon's death as a stain upon his country's honour, was sickened by that policy. He was given a roving commission by Wolseley on 23 March to organize a chain of desert intelligence posts ; but he felt little enthusiasm for the assignment. He felt even less enthusiasm for the post-mortem atmosphere at headquarters, and he became impatient when Wilson asked him (15 April) for full details about the Mudir of Dongola's management of 'that camel transaction at Korti', and about all messengers dispatched to Khartoum.

Wolseley asked Kitchener to prepare a report on the fall of Khartoum, which is the only authentic account. It was finished in August, and Kitchener concluded : 'In my opinion, Khartoum fell from sudden assault when the garrison were too exhausted by privations to make proper resistance.' He rejected utterly Gladstone's suggestion that the fall of the town had been caused by treachery which might, of course, have occurred at any time—instead of by muddle, starvation and delay.

On 7 April, 1885, Kitchener wrote moodily to Wilson : 'Since Gordon's death, I personally have very little interest in the Sudan and its future.' Kitchener knew then that Sir Evelyn Baring was advocating caution, on economic grounds, and that little chance remained of a forward policy ; but an attitude of such total detachment was out of harmony with Kitchener's character ; and it is probable that a recent double tragedy, coming on top of Gordon's death, had provided him with a private motive for expressing it.

In Cairo, during 1883, Kitchener had seen much of Sir Samuel Baker's brother, Valentine Baker Pasha, who had entertained him in Bulgaria in December, 1877. Through the good offices of his former friend, the Prince of Wales, Valentine Baker was in process of being rehabilitated after his disgrace and imprisonment in 1875. He had been persuaded to resign his commission as a lieutenant-general in the Turkish Army by the prospect of being appointed to command the new Egyptian Army immediately after the British conquest of Egypt. But strong opposition arose in England, and the British Government let him down very badly by refusing, at the last moment, to appoint him. Sir Evelyn Wood became Sirdar instead of Valentine Baker, who had to be content with the command—for which he was unsuited—of the Egyptian police.

Baker had two daughters, and the elder, (Mary) Hermione, fell in love with Kitchener in 1883, with a rare degree of passionate intensity. She was aged only sixteen, and Kitchener was then thirty-three, so that a formal engagement might have been considered premature. It is impossible, moreover, to know to what extent Kitchener may have responded to the young girl's fervent adoration.

Hermione Baker, was, by all accounts, an extraordinarily beautiful and attractive child. She died, aged eighteen, on 21 January, 1885, of typhoid fever in Cairo while Kitchener was at Korti ; and her mother, who had nursed her, died a month later of the same disease. No correspondence has survived, but it is certain[1] that the families of both Valentine and Sir Samuel Baker took it for granted in 1884 that Kitchener would marry Hermione during the following year. It is certain[1] also that Kitchener wore at times for many years under his shirt a gold locket given to him by Valentine Baker which contained a miniature portrait of Hermione.

The possibility cannot be excluded that Kitchener loved the girl with an ardour equal to her own. It is perhaps more likely that he wished to marry and was pleased and flattered ; and that he would have come to love her. He was always preternaturally reserved. Valentine Baker himself died in November, 1887. That is all that is known of that unique romantic episode in Kitchener's career.

*   *   *

[1] Private family information.

Kitchener as a subaltern in the Royal Engineers

Kitchener aged 35

Kitchener as Governor of Suakin, aged 38
Kitchener as Commander-in-Chief of the Egyptian Army, aged 46. 1896

Ambition was the passion which warmed Kitchener's life ; and after it had become evident that nothing further would be attempted in the Sudan, he resigned his commission in the Egyptian Army and sailed (3 July, 1885) for England in order to enjoy some leave and to push his career. Before Kitchener left Egypt, Wolseley's intelligence staff recorded its unanimous conviction that the reconquest of the Sudan would have to be undertaken within the next ten years.

In England, a growing reputation made Kitchener a welcome guest in many influential country homes. In August, 1885, he visited Taplow Court, near Maidenhead, where he met William Grenfell, the future Lord Desborough. Kitchener was asked to stay there by Desborough's younger brother, Major H. M. Grenfell, 10th Hussars, with whom he had served in Egypt ; and Lord Desborough never forgot his first impression of Kitchener in 1885 : ' He was a most striking figure, tall and spare, with the most wonderful piercing bright blue eyes, set very far apart.' [1] Lord Desborough noted also the strange atmosphere of loneliness which appeared to surround Kitchener.

Kitchener, later, became much attached to Lord Desborough's younger sons, Julian and Billy, who were killed in the First World War. Julian, in particular, was devoted to Kitchener, and his early impressions of Kitchener were fuller and more revealing than his father's. The boy who was Kitchener's page at the coronation of King Edward VII, on 9 August, 1902, wrote them down at his father's request during the autumn of 1902, when he was aged only fourteen, and the sketch is delightfully vivid :

' The first time I saw Lord Kitchener was before the South African War. I had come home for the holidays and the first morning I got up before breakfast and on going downstairs found a gentleman whom I did not know at all. He asked me to come for a walk, and we went for over an hour. He found out that I was going to be a soldier and asked me what regiment I was going in for, and how I was getting on at school, and a great many other questions ; he told me a great many things about the army, and yet he never mentioned himself at all, and I had not the least idea who he was. I enjoyed the walk very much indeed . . .

' He looked a soldier from head to foot, and there was something

[1] cf. an address delivered by Lord Desborough at a Memorial Service to Kitchener at the Canadian Red Cross Hospital at Cliveden on 11 June, 1916.

about his manner that showed that he was no ordinary man, and yet he said nothing about himself or his own doings . . . I should think it would be impossible to find features on which self-restraint and tremendous will are more clearly marked.

' When I asked him about South Africa, he told me without the slightest " swagger " or self-praise ; in fact I think modesty is one of his greatest qualities . . . He said that he wondered what the Boers would think of our life over here in the summer, going lazily on the river in boats, and lounging about all day ; and he said that they " did not look at life that way ". Whatever was going on he seemed to pay the greatest attention to it, even if it was not of the slightest importance.

' He saw me catch a pike once which got into a deep bed of weeds and took a very long time to land, and proposed that we should get up early next morning and see if we could have any luck . . . He was dressed before the time, and came into my room while I was still in bed. We managed to land two nice fish that morning and Lord Kitchener seemed very pleased ; while he could not help laughing as he just slipped the landing-net under the biggest we had yet seen, and it gave a sharp turn, made a frantic rush, and broke the line . . .'

Kitchener told the boy that there were two things he hated—public dinners and being photographed. And the boy concluded that it would be hard to find another man ' so modest, so interested, and so clever and amusing '. Lord Desborough liked to set that sketch by a gifted and candid schoolboy beside the stern portrait of popular imagination. Kitchener relished his friendship with the Desboroughs, and he was godfather to Lord Desborough's younger daughter, Imogen.

During that period of leave, much of which was spent in a furnished flat which he rented in Queen Anne's Gate, Kitchener laid the foundations of a lifelong friendship with Pandeli Ralli, known to his friends as Pandeli Tom, whom he had first met in Cyprus. Ralli and Kitchener had been equally devoted to Herbert Stewart, who had been murdered in the Sudan in October, 1884, on his way down-river from Khartoum ; and Ralli's London house, 17, Belgrave Square, was often, in later years, Kitchener's social headquarters. Ralli's sister, Janie, had married (1868) the Hon. Sir Richard Moreton, who was H.M.'s Marshal of Ceremonies from 1887 to 1913 ; and Lady

Moreton was Lady of the Bedchamber to H.R.H. the Duchess of Albany. Such contacts in that age were useful to a rising and ambitious soldier.

Kitchener had not passed through the Staff College, but he had applied, through Sir Redvers Buller, for a staff appointment in consideration of his services on the intelligence staff of the Nile expedition. He renewed that application after hearing that he was likely to be posted to Dublin for routine duties in his rank of Lieutenant-Colonel; and after pulling every string within his reach he secured (6 November, 1885) an appointment as the British member of the Zanzibar Boundary Commission. His basic pay of eighteen shillings a day as a Lieutenant-Colonel of Engineers at home was supplemented by an annual salary of one thousand pounds, plus travelling expenses, and a subsistence allowance of one guinea a day.

Zanzibar was an independent island off the east coast of Africa; and it was in process of dismemberment as the work of carving up the continent between the interested Powers went forward after the close of the great age of African exploration. Sir James Kirk, the British Consul-General in Zanzibar, wanted to see a British protectorate proclaimed, and the Germans were trying to thwart him. The limited object of the boundary commission was to conduct an impartial inquiry into the claims of the Sultan of Zanzibar to exercise sovereignty over certain disputed territories on the mainland, opposite his islands.

The German East Africa Company had already signed a number of treaties with small local potentates on the mainland; and Kitchener, who landed in Zanzibar on 29 November, took an instant dislike to his German colleague. He had two colleagues—a Frenchman and a German—and the German Ambassador in London complained to the Foreign Secretary, Lord Rosebery (24 March, 1886), that Kitchener was not carrying out his duties impartially and that he and his French colleague had ganged up against the German. Rosebery, in consequence, sent Kitchener a private warning: 'It seems to me', he wrote (27 March), 'that you have steered your course with skill and impartiality in circumstances of difficulty. But I think it well to give you a hint that at Berlin they think you lean a little towards the French Commissioner.'

With his fellow-commissioners, Kitchener explored the mainland coast and questioned many native notables about past payments of taxes, customs, tribute and homage to the Sultan of Zanzibar. He

69

strongly urged the Foreign Office to secure as quickly as possible the great mainland port of Mombasa; and he wrote constantly to Lord Wolseley, who had resumed his post as Adjutant-General at the War Office, about his difficulties and about British strategic needs. He formed the view that the Sultan's sovereignty extended for ten miles into the interior along a wide stretch of the African mainland.

The Frenchman agreed with Kitchener, but the German dissented, and the three governments, over the heads of their representatives, settled for sovereignty over a shorter coastal strip three miles in depth. In that way an appearance of unanimity was presented to the world; and Kitchener, who was rewarded with a C.M.G., was ordered to proceed immediately to Suakin, the last British outpost in the Sudan, in order to take up an appointment as Governor of the Eastern Sudan and the Red Sea Littoral with the acting rank of Colonel. He was not involved in later negotiations which led, in 1890, to the proclamation of a British protectorate over Zanzibar.

Kitchener reached Suakin on 1 September, 1886, and he found that his sonorous title was misleading. His writ extended only for a radius of a few miles, and he was hemmed in, along the coast as well as inland, by powerful and hostile tribes, which were held in the grip of Mahdism. They acknowledged allegiance to the Mahdi's successor, the Khalifa Abdullahi, who was a debauched and brutal but a capable and formidable despot.

Kitchener resolved at the outset that the tribes should learn to fear him; and he was tempted to pursue a forward policy. Sir Evelyn Baring for example, complained[1] (15 January, 1887) to Lord Salisbury that Kitchener had issued a proclamation in which he spoke of the need to establish 'a simple firm government in the Sudan, which should do justice to all'. When asked for an explanation, Kitchener said that he had been considering the use of subsidies, not of force; and the Sirdar, at Baring's request, sent him some general instructions to guide his conduct.

After their experience of the Nile expedition, the British and Egyptian governments were morbidly fearful of becoming entangled by another soldier like Gordon in fresh military adventures. They held that peace could best be secured at Suakin by opening up trade with the interior. Kitchener was determined not to forfeit the confidence of the civil authorities, on whom his future depended; but he wanted to acquire glory, if possible; and he was convinced

[1] Salisbury Papers, 52.

that it was imperative to stamp out all trade with the interior. It was common knowledge that the Khalifa was preparing to invade Egypt, and Kitchener repeatedly warned Baring that under cover of a plea for legitimate trade, the Mahdists were seeking to obtain money with which to buy arms for use against Egypt.

Baring retorted that the Mahdists in the Sudan constituted a small minority which was tyrannizing over the apathetic mass of the population to whom Kitchener's ban on trade was causing great and unnecessary suffering. But he, nevertheless, allowed Kitchener entire latitude and discretion. Baring's view was supported by some British newspapers, and the *Pall Mall Gazette* fiercely attacked Kitchener's policy ; but the soldiers were unanimously on Kitchener's side. Lord Wolseley, for example, congratulated Kitchener warmly (3 September, 1888) upon having ignored ' the narrow tradesmen's point of view ', and upon having concentrated upon ' the main questions which concern us as a nation '.

Kitchener, who was hardly on speaking terms with his civilian assistant, adhered inflexibly to the stern policy in which he trusted ; and by the autumn of 1887 the tribes bordering Suakin appeared so cowed that two battalions were withdrawn from the garrison. As a result, Osman Digna, one of the ablest of the Khalifa's lieutenants, seized his opportunity to harry that last British outpost in the Sudan.

From Handub, 15 miles north of Suakin, Osman Digna openly threatened the fortifications which Kitchener had constructed around the port and town. Kitchener begged the new Sirdar, Sir Francis Grenfell,[1] for permission to attack the enemy, but Grenfell feared that, if the attack failed, Suakin might be besieged and that a relief expedition might then become necessary. He therefore ordered Kitchener to confine his activities to reconnaissance, and not to commit any part of his regular garrison.

Kitchener construed that order in his own way. He collected a strong force of irregular troops and led them out of Suakin with the object of storming Handub. He coolly turned a blind eye on the presence of many of his native regulars, who had paraded, with his knowledge and consent, dressed as irregulars.

That mixed force stormed Handub on 17 January, 1888 ; but Kitchener's irregulars were ill disciplined. They dispersed in order to loot, and while thus engaged were attacked by enemy reinforcements and driven back in disarray to Suakin. Kitchener, who had

[1] Field-Marshal Lord Grenfell, P.G., G.C.B., G.C.M.G. (1841-1925).

remained with a small force of mounted regulars in support, stood his ground under heavy fire. Although severely wounded by a bullet in the neck and lower jaw, he continued to direct the fight; and in great pain and almost speechless, after covering the retreat, he brought his force back to the fortifications of Suakin.

A number of Kitchener's regular soldiers were killed in that affair, and their loss had, of course, to be reported when the battalion strength returns were sent to Cairo. Kitchener himself had to be taken to Cairo immediately for the treatment of his wound, which was described as a 'comminuted fracture of the right lower jaw'. His sister, Mrs. Parker, came out from England to nurse him. Sir Francis Grenfell, who had forbidden Kitchener to employ regular troops, remarked, laughingly, when he visited him in hospital, that he deserved to be tried by court-martial. But he added, with truth, that great enthusiasm had been aroused in England, and he congratulated him warmly on his spirited conduct.

The British Radical Press suggested that if Kitchener had been less aggressive, the Red Sea coast would have enjoyed peace, and trade would have flourished. In many influential quarters, however, the affair was interpreted as a welcome sign that Gordon's death would presently be avenged. Kitchener received telegrams of congratulation from the Duke of Cambridge as well as from the Secretary for War; and he was promoted (11 April) to the brevet rank of Colonel.

Queen Victoria, who asked repeatedly for news of Kitchener's health, appointed him immediately to be one of her aides-de-camp. The Khedive of Egypt made Kitchener a Pasha, and Lord Salisbury wrote[1] (20 January, 1888) to Sir Evelyn Baring: 'I was very much grieved to hear of Kitchener's wound. Though I do not think I have ever met him, I have been familiar with his name for many years, and feel as if I knew him well. He is a very gallant and efficient officer—though a headstrong subordinate.'

On 19 February, Sir Francis Grenfell reported[2] that Kitchener was 'an admirable officer', who had 'under great difficulties' filled his position 'with credit'. He was stated to be 'very smart' and in possession of 'all' the necessary qualities for command, for which his capacity was 'very great'.

Kitchener returned to Suakin on 15 March, 1888, before his wound had completely healed; and his sister, whom he took with him as

[1] Salisbury Papers, 55. [2] War Office Records.

nurse and hostess to Government House, was impressed by the amount of ceremony which he had established. He had always hitherto expressed a quizzical dislike of music ; but he now dined every evening at a late hour to the accompaniment of martial airs rendered in quick time, and without intermission, by a large native military band.

Immediately after his return to Suakin, Kitchener was dismayed to receive through Reuter the report of a statement, made by Salisbury in the House of Lords, that ' Egypt is only justified in holding Suakin to prevent the slave trade '. Kitchener did not scruple or hesitate to suppress that statement at once, and he explained[1] his reason to Baring on 23 March : ' I have not allowed the paragraph of Reuter's to circulate in the town, as you can easily realize that the 7,000 inhabitants of this place would not become more loyal or trustworthy if the idea was forced upon them that their future depended upon the continuance of the humanitarian policy of England in the suppression of the slave trade.'

Kitchener warned Baring that, if Suakin were abandoned, it would be impossible to preserve the loyalty of the tribes between the Suakin–Berber road and the Egyptian frontier, or to prevent the importation of arms and ammunition along three hundred miles of coastline : ' This supply would greatly help any attack on the Egyptian frontier, and would perhaps so strengthen an invading army as to overtax the resources of Egypt to resist it.' Kitchener added that, without a garrison at Suakin, it might be difficult to counter Mahdist propaganda among the tribes of the Hedjaz, who were being urged to rise against the Turks.

Early in June, 1888, Kitchener returned on leave to England, where he stayed at Hatfield with Lord Salisbury. The Prime Minister then told him that he was to be appointed Adjutant-General of the Egyptian Army. Kitchener took up that post on 13 September, when he returned to Cairo ; and although the popularity which he had acquired in England was not reflected in the minds of his jealous brother-officers in Egypt, Baring sent[2] Salisbury (15 January, 1889) an extremely generous appreciation of Kitchener's work at Suakin :

' As regards the opening of trade . . . I am inclined to think that, judged by the light of subsequent events, Colonel Kitchener's view of the situation a year ago was more correct than my own.'

[1] Salisbury Papers, 53.
[2] *Parliamentary Papers, Egypt*, No. 1 (1889), 35.

Baring added that Kitchener was ' a very gallant soldier ' who had ' often risked and, at least on one occasion, very nearly lost his life in the performance of his military duties ' ; that his civil administration had been a task of ' very exceptional difficulty ' which he had performed, on the whole, extremely well ; and that ' no one possessed so much influence with the heads of tribes as Colonel Kitchener '.

CHAPTER 5

COMMANDER-IN-CHIEF
1889–1896

KITCHENER had stirred up a ferment around Suakin, which was besieged, soon after he returned to Cairo, by Osman Digna. While Kitchener had been on leave in England, Baring had lifted, as an experiment, Kitchener's ban on trade at Suakin ; and Kitchener complained that Osman Digna would not have been able to maintain his positions if he had not been enabled, in that way, to draw almost unlimited supplies from the town. Baring admitted that Kitchener was probably right, and he sent him to Suakin with Grenfell to organize the defence.

Baring grumbled,[1] nevertheless (8 December, 1888), to Lord Salisbury that it was difficult to trust even the best of soldiers, because they were all avid of glory : ' Grenfell is cool-headed and sensible enough but he is rather liable to be influenced by his subordinates.' Baring said that he had recently discovered that Kitchener exercised great influence with Grenfell : ' Kitchener possesses many good qualities, but he is headstrong and wanting in judgement. He has been talking very wildly . . . He expressed in extreme form " the maximum amount of glory " policy, and he went to Suakin fully determined to do all in his power to extend the operations.'

On 20 December, 1888, Kitchener took part in a spirited and victorious engagement outside the walls of Suakin. Grenfell reported that Kitchener had led his Sudanese brigade ' to the attack with coolness and gallantry ', and that he had ' well-sustained his previous reputation '. After Grenfell's departure, Kitchener remained at Suakin until Osman Digna ceased to threaten the town ; and despite Baring's forebodings, Kitchener obeyed scrupulously his orders to remain strictly on the defensive.

At the end of January, 1889, Kitchener returned to a fine house which had been made ready for him in Cairo ; and he found himself in his element as Adjutant-General. His filing system was chaotic, but he carried everything in his head and was never at a loss so long as he was not called upon to deal with imponderables. He spent most of his evenings at home, working prodigiously hard, undistracted by domestic or social ties. He had few friends and he continued to be

[1] Salisbury Papers, 53.

unpopular with his brother-officers ; but he studied his chiefs carefully and felt sufficiently secure, within a few months, to invite influential friends in England to come out and visit him. He invited Lord and Lady Cranborne (9 November, 1889), and he told[1] Lord Cranborne, the Prime Minister's son, that ' the Egyptian question requires to be studied on the spot . . . I have lots of rooms in my house, so if you would like to bring anyone with you, please do so.'

During the spring of 1889 the Khalifa was ready at last to invade Egypt. He dispatched a brave and fanatical lieutenant, the Emir Wad el Negumi, down the Nile with an arm some 13,000 strong, and with orders to isolate Wadi Halfa by striking through the western desert to a point on the Nile 25 miles north of Aswan.

At Toski, a short distance inside the Egyptian frontier, Wad el Negumi was brought to battle by Sir Francis Grenfell and killed on 3 August, 1889. Ten thousand dervishes died on the sand or were taken prisoner ; and the British and Egyptian loss was only 165.

In that glorious victory Kitchener commanded the cavalry. His task was to head the enemy off some hilly country which he was attempting to reach, until the Egyptian infantry and artillery could bring him to battle and destroy him ; and by skilful and spirited manœuvring, Kitchener helped to lure the dervishes to destruction. He would have relished a greater share of the fighting, but he made no selfish attempt to turn his comparatively minor rôle into a major one. Baring telegraphed his warm appreciation of Kitchener's services to Lord Salisbury, and Kitchener was awarded a C.B.

The Battle of Toski caused great rejoicing in Egypt. The danger of a dervish invasion appeared to be at an end, and as that danger had been frequently cited as the principal reason for the continuance of the British occupation, Sir Evelyn Baring had to think about first principles : ' The argument based on danger from the dervishes', he had already told[2] Lord Salisbury (15 June, 1889), ' . . . is an excellent working argument ; but it does not in reality constitute the real reason why the evacuation policy is wellnigh impossible. The main argument—which it is difficult to use—is the utter incapacity of the ruling classes in this country.'

In those circumstances, Baring was bound to ask himself how long it would continue to be possible to restrain the growing public demand for the re-conquest, or liberation, of the Sudan. The new Egyptian

[1] Hatfield MSS. [2] Salisbury Papers, 53.

Army had proved its quality. Financial rehabilitation and material progress were proceeding apace. He began accordingly, very cautiously as his custom was, to look around for a young and capable commander who could be used eventually, under his personal supervision, and with the strictest regard for economy, to conduct a future campaign.

Grenfell reported[1], in 1890, that Kitchener had proved himself to be 'a very capable, clear-headed officer . . . A good brigadier, very ambitious. His rapid promotion has placed him in a somewhat difficult position. He is not popular, but has of late greatly improved in tact and manner ; and any defects in his character will, in my opinion, disappear as he gets on in the service. He is a fine, gallant soldier, and a great linguist, and very successful in dealing with orientals.'

Kitchener's intense unpopularity in Cairo was by no means wholly due to the widespread jealousy which his rapid promotion had aroused. That jealousy could have been allayed if he had shown greater tact. In the confidential reports which were made on him, tactlessness was listed as his principal failing. He set little value on those 'graces' to which Lord Chesterfield, 'contrary to the custom of profound historians, who always assign deep causes for great events', ascribed 'the better half of the Duke of Marlborough's greatness'. Chesterfield told his son that he had known Marlborough and discovered 'nothing shining in his genius. He had most undoubtedly an excellent plain understanding and sound judgement ; but these qualities would probably have never raised him higher than they found him . . . The graces protected and promoted him. His figure was beautiful ; but his manner was irresistible either by man or woman . . . he could refuse more easily than others could grant. . . .'

Kitchener's figure would probably have compared quite favourably with that of Marlborough, but English society in Cairo was never in remote danger of being bewitched by Kitchener's manner. It was a society which took itself seriously, and which was ruled by the wives of certain senior officers and officials who failed to interest Kitchener because their outlook appeared provincial. On his annual visits to England during the 1890's he relished the society of great ladies, and relaxed in the congenial warmth of a number of great country houses which were at that period seats of political influence as well as temples of luxury. As his reputation increased, such houses competed with

[1] War Office Records.

each other for the privilege of welcoming the handsome, unmarried, lonely and glamorous hero from the East ; and after starting with the Grenfells and Cecils, Kitchener was soon intimate with many patrician families, including those of the Duke of Portland, Lord Londonderry, Lord Dufferin, Lord Waterford, Lord Cowper and Lord Powis.

In those circles, viceregal dreams of future glory floated happily in Kitchener's mind ; and he spoke freely to sympathetic great ladies, who fascinated him, about his hopes and plans. He regarded himself as a man of destiny, with a mission to smash Mahdism, avenge Gordon, and re-conquer the Sudan ; but in Cairo he appeared inarticulate and introspective. He made no attempt to conceal how bored he was by commonplace English houses and parties ; and he showed a strong preference for the society of wealthy and civilized Egyptians, Jews and Turks.

Tall, straight, lean as a lance, Kitchener gazed out imperiously over most men's heads, wearing a harsh mask against the world. He spoke with a soft, and almost self-deprecatory drawl, and he remained aloof and self-contained. He often dined in mess, and occasionally demanded a rubber of bridge afterwards ; but he generally went home immediately after dinner either to work indefatigably into the small hours of the morning or to entertain a few of his oriental friends and acquaintances.

There was, in those circumstances, a general disposition to regard Kitchener as a jumped-up professional in a society of gentlemen and amateurs. " We hated the sight of him ", was a remark frequently heard, after he had achieved greatness, on the lips of second-rate people who had known him casually in Cairo ; and many years passed before his social unpopularity began to evaporate. As late as 24 December, 1897, Baring wrote[1] to Lord Salisbury : ' Kitchener is, as Grenfell says, very unpopular. This is partly due to the fact that he is a severe taskmaster, with a harsh and unsympathetic manner ; and partly to his mania for economy which, although generally laudable, he sometimes pushes too far. To my astonishment I sometimes find our natural rôles reversed.'

British policy in Egypt was wholly conditioned by the need to nurse the Egyptian Treasury back to solvency, and Kitchener's burning ambition drove him to ludicrous lengths in a successful attempt to prove to Baring and Salisbury that he was the most ruthlessly economical

[1] Salisbury Papers, 110.

soldier who had ever lived. He was merciless, therefore, on the subjects of pay, allowances and amenities, as well as in cases of sickness or misfortune ; he took no interest in the welfare of the private soldier and he seldom spoke to one if he could help it.

Kitchener always insisted that his few British officers should be well paid ; but in other respects he never scrupled to pare expenditure to the bone. He declined, for example, to allow his army to be clothed in British cloth, which he held to be absurdly expensive. He sent officers, accordingly, scouring eastern and southern Europe at their own expense in search of serviceable bargains in cheap fabrics for making uniforms and shirts ; and he set up workshops in Cairo which produced articles of equipment, with the aid of low-paid native labour, at about one-half of the price of imported British goods.

During the autumn of 1891, Kitchener spent a few weeks' leave in India, which he visited for the first time. He toured some of the principal attractions, and stayed for a few days at Poona with his younger brother, Walter, who was then a Captain in the West Yorkshire Regiment. On his return to Cairo he was summoned to an important interview with Baring.

Baring asked Kitchener to combine temporarily the post of Inspector-General of the Egyptian Police with his existing appointment as Adjutant-General of the Egyptian Army ; and Kitchener was reluctant to assume so thankless a task. Two British inspectors-general had already tried and failed to reform the police, who came under the Ministry of the Interior, which was rightly regarded as a stronghold of corruption. The system could not be radically reorganized without breaking up an immemorial tradition of local government upon which the Egyptian social fabric was based.

Kitchener's British predecessors had failed because they had tried to move too quickly ; and Kitchener was invited to use his Oriental experience to coax the best possible results out of the existing system, and to effect only such minor reforms as that system was capable of digesting.

Before he consented, Kitchener confided to Baring that he wished to be considered for the post of Sirdar whenever Sir Francis Grenfell should relinquish it. Baring promised that Kitchener's chances would not be lessened if he were to accept the inspectorship-general of police, and on that understanding Kitchener agreed. He made no attempt to effect major reforms, but concentrated on the task of improving the working of the corrupt Oriental system which he found in being.

In consequence of his efforts, serious crime diminished in twelve months by one-half, and the overall number of convictions was more than doubled.

On 21 March, 1892, Cromer telegraphed[1] to Salisbury : ' I understand Sir F. Grenfell has accepted a post in England. He and I both think that Kitchener should succeed. Latter has done his police work admirably. His appointment would be well-received by the Khedive and his ministers, and would, I think, be in every way preferable to the nomination of a new man from England . . .'

Salisbury replied, two days later, that he had pressed Kitchener's appointment on the Duke of Cambridge in as strong language as possible, and that the Duke had said that he would appoint Kitchener ' if possible '. Salisbury minuted (23 March) : ' Sincerely hope no difficulty may occur—the matter is of vital importance.'

Later that day the Duke of Cambridge made up his mind to appoint Kitchener to the post of Sirdar, or Commander-in-Chief of the Egyptian Army, with the rank of Major-General ; and he wrote[2] to Salisbury (23 March) : ' I am personally very much pleased that the choice should fall on Colonel Kitchener, whom I always considered a very good man for the place.' That appointment, which was dated 13 April, 1892, was received with surprise and disgust by the entire Egyptian Army.

The surprise died down quickly, and the disgust turned very slowly to admiration. The army's candidate had been Colonel Josceline Wodehouse, R.A., the popular commander of the field force guarding the Sudanese border. Kitchener's appointment was hotly resented, partly on account of his intense unpopularity and partly because it was known to be due to political considerations and influence.

Salisbury, as well as Sir Evelyn Baring who received a peerage in June, 1892, and who will be described hereafter as Cromer, had picked their man for the eventual liberation of the Sudan. Kitchener had more than succeeded in convincing them that merciless economy held first place among his household gods, and that, alone among soldiers, he could be trusted to fight a war as well as to clothe his army on the cheap. It is true that Kitchener had given no proof as yet that he possessed any gift for exercising strategic control, but he was picked as an indefatigable organizer and loyal subordinate. Cromer rightly held [3] that, at 41, Kitchener was ' young, energetic, ardently

---

[1] Salisbury Papers, 54.   [2] Ibid., 105.
[3] Cromer, *Modern Egypt*, II, p. 87.

and exclusively devoted to his profession and . . . that he left as little as possible to chance '. More important even than that, he ' possessed another quality which is rare among soldiers, and which was of special value in the circumstances then existing. He did not think that extravagance was the handmaid of efficiency.'

Kitchener's rapid rise had provoked such furious jealousy that he displayed an even more extreme degree of reserve towards his brother-officers than heretofore. He gave, for a time, the impression of being more like a machine than a man. He liked and, to some extent, he confided in Reginald Wingate,[1] his director of military intelligence ; but he ruled by fear, and was ruthless with anyone who failed to measure up to the standard of efficiency which he set, or to the demands made upon men's stamina by the Egyptian climate in summer.

Kitchener used personally to interview, with the greatest care, candidates for service in his army at the Junior United Service Club during his annual visit to England on leave. Those who were successful started with a two years' contract in the rank of major, but Kitchener made marriage, or even an engagement to marry, an absolute bar. He told candidates that marriage interfered with work because it involved a divided loyalty ; and he told Cromer there was no reason to pay marriage allowances while suitable single officers were available. He succeeded presently in surrounding himself with an impressive band of extraordinarily youthful colonels who were completely imbued with their chief's methods and ideals.

At the British general election of July, 1892, Salisbury was ousted by Gladstone, who took office for the last time. That Conservative defeat was a blow to Kitchener, in so far as it appeared to show that public opinion at home was less ripe than he had hoped for a forward move in the Sudan. No early advance, in any case, had been contemplated either by Salisbury or Cromer ; but between 1892 and 1896 a number of factors combined to focus British attention upon Khartoum and the upper Nile valley.

The cardinal factor was a gradual realization of the astonishing success which had attended British efforts to restore sound government and a measure of prosperity to Egypt. A second was the danger of leaving a big power vacuum in the upper Nile valley at the height of the colonial scramble for Africa, and at a time when France was known to be casting covetous eyes upon the Sudan. A third was the final

[1] General Sir Reginald Wingate, Bt., G.C.B., G.C.V.O., G.B.E., K.C.M.G., D.S.O. (1861–1953).

81

retirement of Gladstone in March, 1894, and the return to office in June, 1895, of Lord Salisbury with a large Conservative majority.

A fourth factor was the publication, during Queen Victoria's inter-jubilee years, of a number of books, of which the most influential was Alfred Milner's *England in Egypt* (1893). Milner, who had served in Egypt as Financial Secretary, touched the pride of a great imperial people which had been smarting under a sense of failure and frustration since the disastrous mismanagement of the Nile expedition of 1884–5. He declared that Great Britain's missionary task was as yet only half-done ; and as Winston Churchill wrote[1] : ' The book was more than a book. The words rank like a trumpet-call which rallies the soldiers after the parapets are stormed, and summons them to complete the victory.'

The liberation of the Sudan was the logical corollary to the British occupation of Egypt. There were, of course, formidable difficulties, financial and political, in the way of crystallizing an incoherent aspiration into a settled plan of decisive action. But as British opinion moved inexorably in a forward direction, the dream of military glory which haunted Kitchener by night and by day evoked a growing response in British political circles : ' Cheer up about the Sudan ', old Lady Waterford wrote to him (12 August, 1894). ' It *must* happen soon, and Ld. Dufferin is quite convinced of it.' Kitchener was in England then, on leave, and Lady Waterford added: ' I am *so glad* you gave the Foreign Office and War Office your opinion, and it *must* all come right, whatever they may say, and I'm sure your dream is not very far off now. Oh ! I should like to see it, or hear of it. Perhaps I shall ; and anyhow if *you* see it, it is all that signifies.' Kitchener had, in fact, complained to Lady Waterford that he had just received what he called a ' wigging ' for pressing too strongly for immediate action.

Kitchener received such wiggings on a number of occasions ; but he disregarded them, as he worked hard for four years, under a cloak of military secrecy, to cement understandings with native chiefs in southern Egypt and the northern Sudan. He was ably assisted in that work by Wingate ; and he made good use also of the services of his Adjutant-General, Leslie Rundle, as he strove to prepare the Egyptian Army for battle. But Cromer was far from convinced, even by 1896, that that army was ready. He thought that war would necessitate postponement of many useful projects ; and he umpired

[1] *The River War*, p. 150.

itchener with his friend and A.D.C., Frank Maxwell, V.C.

Kitchener Pasha

for two years a friendly dispute between the head of the Public Works Department, Sir William Garstin, and Kitchener. As the Egyptian treasury filled, Garstin begged constantly for funds to spend upon the great Aswan Dam, while Kitchener pleaded, in season and out of season, for war.

Kitchener's detractors were active in seeking to persuade Cromer that the Commander-in-Chief did not possess the confidence of his Egyptian officers. They fastened upon an unhappy incident which occurred in 1894, and which led to a permanent estrangement between Kitchener and the Khedive, to suggest that Kitchener was temperamentally unfitted to exercise high command. All details of that occurrence, which throws light on Kitchener's character, were suppressed.

The twenty-year-old Khedive, Abbas Hilmi II, who had succeeded his father, Tewfiq, on 7 January, 1892, announced in December, 1893, his intention of inspecting units of the Egyptian Army on the Nile between Aswan and Wadi Halfa. That was bound to prove an ordeal for Kitchener, who hated ceremonies, banquets and speeches because they made him feel inadequate and ill at ease. He nevertheless arranged a splendid series of parades, festivities, fireworks and illuminations in the sovereign's honour.

Kitchener was desperately anxious that his army should be suitably praised when the Khedive inspected it for the first time. That army's prowess had not yet been fully tested in war, and the question of morale took precedence over all others. Kitchener's nervousness was increased by a secret report, from a source which had been consistently trustworthy, that the occasion would be used by Abbas Hilmi for a trial of strength. The young sovereign, whom Cromer described to Lord Rosebery as ' this most foolish boy ', had been educated in Europe and was surrounded by flatterers. He had been showing increasing signs of discontent with British advice and control, especially in matters affecting the army.

The Khedive was accompanied by Maher Pasha, his Deputy Minister for War, whose strong anti-British proclivities were not manifested until after his appointment. Maher encouraged his master to bait the Commander-in-Chief, and an unpublished diary kept by Reginald Wingate[1] describes the atmosphere which developed from day to day.

The tour began at 17.00 hours on Saturday, 13 January, 1894, at

[1] In the possession of Sir Ronald Wingate, Bt., C.M.G., C.I.E., O.B.E.

Aswan. The Khedive inspected the 10th Sudanese Battalion, which was ' exceptionally well turned out ', but he found fault with the way in which the men held their rifles, and with the disparity in the heights of the soldiers. He told Kitchener that he objected to being required to give commissions to negroes ; and that he had no intention of bestowing praise ' when, in his opinion, none was due '. That evening, without consulting Kitchener, the Khedive presented a robe of honour to a sheikh whom he had brought with him on his yacht from Luxor. The sheikh, who had been condemned to death six years earlier for espionage and rebellion, had been reprieved on condition that he never subsequently re-entered any frontier district.

On the following morning the Khedive criticized Kitchener for not understanding the finer points of arms drill ; later in the day he told Kitchener that the British senior medical officer in charge of the military hospital was ' quite incompetent for his position and excessively ignorant '. Kitchener retorted that the Khedive could not possibly have had an opportunity of forming a judgement, and that, on the contrary, Surgeon-Major Graham was ' exceptionally capable '. The Khedive did not reply.

Kitchener was entertained on the Khedive's yacht that evening, and afterwards a native dance was staged by Sudanese soldiers and their wives. In the middle of the performance the Khedive accused a negro officer, who was perfectly sober, of being drunk. The negro saluted respectfully and obeyed the Khedive's order to depart. The Khedive then said that he was tired and would go to bed ; and he ordered the dancers to be removed forthwith out of sight and hearing. Wingate noted : ' It would seem the H.H. has taken upon him the role of dissatisfaction with everything directly under English control, and that he has spared no pains to convey his impressions to both English and native officers.' Kitchener and Wingate both considered that the Khedive's attitude was subversive of discipline and morale.

During the days which followed the Khedive grew bolder. He constantly criticized individual British officers and compared them unfavourably with their Egyptian comrades. The climax was reached at Wadi Halfa on 19 January after a march-past of the entire garrison. The Khedive had been extremely critical, and as he rode off parade with Kitchener, he exclaimed :

" To tell you the truth, Kitchener Pasha, I consider that it is disgraceful for Egypt to be served by such an army."

Kitchener had not at that time acquired the poise and balance which would have enabled him to take control of that unpleasant situation. He retorted immediately, although according to Wingate, who was not within earshot, ' in a most respectful tone ' :

"I beg to tender Your Highness my resignation."

The Khedive appeared dumbfounded, and Kitchener repeated :

"I beg to resign Your Highness's service."

There was a pause of some moments, after which the Khedive completely changed his tone. He smiled and said :

"Why do you take it in that way, Kitchener Pasha ? "

"Your Highness, I am not in the least angry, but in resigning I consider I am only doing my duty."

Kitchener was so much shaken that ' he repeated several times that it was his duty to resign ', and that he had no alternative.

The Khedive assured Kitchener that his criticisms had not been directed against the Egyptian Army as a whole ; that he had been greatly impressed by the cavalry ; and that he had no prejudice against the English officers. As no overt reference to the English officers as a body had previously been made, Kitchener concluded that the Khedive had unguardedly disclosed the subject which was uppermost in his mind. He replied that ' the position of English officers in the Egyptian Army was both a difficult and exceptional one . . . that H.H. had most pointedly criticized everything under British direction, and that the British officers' position would be almost untenable if they were publicly treated in this manner '.

"I give you my word of honour as a gentleman," the Khedive said, " that I never intended anything against the English officers as a whole." He added that he was ' very pleased ' with Kitchener, but Kitchener insisted that, after what had happened, he would no longer be able to obtain good officers from England to serve in the Egyptian Army.

"I am quite satisfied with the present English officers," the Khedive remarked, with every appearance of cordiality.

"That may be so. But I assure Your Highness that I shall be unable to get the same class of officer again to serve, under the changed circumstances."

The Khedive begged Kitchener to regard the incident as closed. He said that he felt 'the fullest confidence ' in him, and he reminded him that he had supported his claims against those of Colonel Wodehouse for the office of Sirdar in 1892. He said that he was distressed to find that his remarks ' should be treated in such a serious light '. When he dismounted to go on board his yacht, the Khedive boyishly

seized Kitchener's hand and refused to release it. He begged him
over and over again to forget what had occurred and to withdraw his
resignation. Kitchener remained stiff and aloof, but he could not
free himself until he had indicated that his resignation might be withdrawn.

That evening the Khedive absented himself on the plea of 'indisposi-
tion' from a dinner which Kitchener had arranged for him. 'During
the dinner', Wingate noted, 'there was a general disposition to be
silent (though any unpleasantness was avoided) on the part of the
English officers, which marked, in a very significant manner, how
they had felt the uncalled-for criticisms of H.H. on the afternoon
parade.'

Kitchener regarded the situation as extremely serious and he 'expressed his wish to the English officers that they should do all in their
power to prevent a discussion of H.H.s attitude which might be
derogatory to H.H.'s dignity or show any tendency to disloyalty'.
Before he went to bed he telegraphed to Rundle, in Cairo :

'Give following to Lord Cromer and G.O.C. Message begins.
On the parade this afternoon H.H. made various disparaging remarks to the English commanding officers, and subsequently told
me that it was disgraceful for Egypt to be served by so bad an army.
I thereupon respectfully tendered my resignation. Since H.H.'s
arrival on the frontier it has appeared to me, and others, that he
has consistently spoken disparagingly of almost every English
officer, and therefore his remarks this afternoon were rather a
culmination to a series of similar uncalled for criticisms which,
in this case, I did not feel myself able to pass without some definite
protest for the honour and credit of the Egyptian Army. H.H.
became immediately very cordial and repeatedly begged me to
withdraw my resignation . . . H.H. assured me that he had no
intention of specially abusing English officers, but that he treated
them alike with native officers. Eventually H.H. assured me of
his complete confidence and though I did not absolutely withdraw
my resignation, I gave him to understand I would not persist . . .
I hope Lord Cromer approves of my action.'

On the following day (20 January, 1894) the Khedive criticized
nothing. He assured Kitchener 'that on parade the day before he
had felt a rush of blood to the head, and that when this occurred he

hardly knew what he said or did '. But Kitchener was not a light man ; and he was troubled by the fear lest his resignation in a mood of exasperation, followed by its withdrawal when a calmer mood supervened, would appear irresponsible. He therefore missed a great opportunity, and made the serious mistake of rejecting that olive branch. He bowed coldly and formally to the Khedive and turned away ; and the Khedive, accordingly, became bitterly resentful, because he felt that he had humbled himself before the foreigner in vain.

Wingate recorded Kitchener's view—and his own—that ' the Khedive's attitude of displeasure with what he saw was in no way directed against the native officers, but was done with the deliberate intention of driving the English officers into resignation '. But that view was greatly exaggerated. The Khedive's object was to assert himself in the presence of the English who made him feel inferior, and his appeal to Kitchener not to take his remarks seriously was quite genuine. The interests of the Egyptian Army would have been better served if Kitchener had handled the situation with more humour and lightness of touch. Instead he represented the facts to Cromer in too serious a light ; and Cromer took a graver view of them than he need have done because he had been waiting for some time for a suitable opportunity to teach the young Khedive a lesson. He wired to Kitchener (20 January) : ' Entirely approve your action. If you consider advisable you may inform Khedive I greatly regret learning language which he has used about army as to efficiency of which there is no doubt, and that I have reported circumstantially to London.'

Two days later, at Shellal, Kitchener bade farewell to the Khedive on the last day of his tour. The Khedive's attitude was extremely distant, and Wingate noted that two of his A.D.C.s conducted themselves in a manner which seemed designed to afford him physical protection from the Commander-in-Chief. Kitchener asked for a private interview before the yacht sailed, but wounded pride made the conversation abortive. Kitchener began :

" All the officers at Halfa are extremely sorry at Your Highness's displeasure. This is not only the case with the English but with the native officers as well. I hope Your Highness, for the good of the Army, will give me some assistance in modifying this impression, as I consider it a very serious matter, and my position is a very difficult one."

" I cannot, Kitchener Pasha, do anything to modify what I said at

Halfa. I think I was acting within my rights, and both Riaz Pasha[1] and myself look upon the Army as of the first importance."

" I am afraid, Your Highness, that under these circumstances I shall not be able to restore the state of affairs at Halfa to what it was before."

" I can do nothing to help you."

" Then I think it very probable the English officers will resign, and if they do I will be able to get none to replace them."

" They must do as they like. Of course, if they all resign, it will lead to a political question which I may hear more of in Cairo."

" I will return to Halfa and do all I can to avert any crisis in the Egyptian army."

" Thank you. Good-bye."

In that last interview Kitchener had again exaggerated the gravity of the situation, as well as the difficulty of his personal position. There was no serious risk of a crisis in the Egyptian Army, or of a mass resignation of the English officers. But as the Khedive's yacht departed Kitchener received two telegrams from Lord Cromer. The first asked whether the Egyptian Army would mutiny if it were placed ' under the more direct control of the English military authorities' ; the second announced that the Foreign Secretary, Lord Rosebery, considered the matter to be so ' very serious ', that an ultimatum was about to be presented to the Khedive. Abbas Hilmi, accordingly, was required immediately to write a letter to Kitchener, for publication in the *Official Journal*, expressing complete satisfaction with his native and British army officers and particularly with his British officers. He was required at the same time to dismiss Maher Pasha, and to substitute a nominee of Kitchener's as Deputy Minister for War. He was told that if he failed to comply, the army would be placed under direct British control, and that full details of ' the various instances of insult which have occurred of late will be published, so that the English nation may realize the situation '. It was implied that the explosion of British opinion would be so great that the Khedive would be forced to abdicate.

Kitchener advised Cromer that the proposed change in the control of the Egyptian Army would cause no mutiny if it were ' carefully and secretly' carried out. No action was, however, necessary, because the Khedive surrendered at discretion. His letter to Kitchener, in the form of an order of the day, was published on 26 January ; and on

[1] Prime Minister of Egypt.

6 February Maher Pasha resigned. Kitchener had telegraphed (23 January) to Lord Cromer : 'I am very grateful for support . . . There is no doubt the general impression is that the Khedive came up with the deliberate intention of forcing the English officers out of the Egyptian Army. His refusal to me yesterday to do anything to modify the tension of the situation appears to me to show distinctly that such was his object and that he still hopes to attain it.'

Kitchener was mistaken in his appreciation of the Khedive's motives; and his handling of the situation had been clumsy. The young Khedive was more eager to assert himself against Cromer than against Kitchener. Abbas Hilmi regarded Cromer as a kind of tutor, and the older man's incisive directness was peculiarly distasteful to an Eastern mind. Kitchener himself found Cromer formidable, and occasionally referred to him in private as ' Lord Over-Baring ' ; he might have made a friend for life if he had suppressed his feelings and shown comradeship and tact when the Khedive complained about a sudden rush of blood to the head. As soon as the incident was over he tried to forget it, by describing the Khedive as a ' naughty boy ' and by telling his friends that he was too unimportant to dislike. But Abbas Hilmi never forgave Kitchener, and always hated him. His resentment had an unfortunate effect upon Anglo-Egyptian relations, for it helped to impel him into the camp of Great Britain's enemies after the outbreak of war in 1914.

Kitchener was rewarded with a knighthood (K.C.M.G.). Lord Rosebery wrote to him (8 February, 1894) : ' It would be idle to deny that I have chosen this particular moment for the recommendation in order to make it clear to all whom it may concern that I feel the warmest sympathy with you in the very difficult circumstances in which you have been placed for some time past, and which have recently come to a head.'

Kitchener's self-confidence, which was severely shaken by that incident, did not fully recover until after the Battle of Omdurman, over four years later. Wild rumours circulated, in the absence of any official account, which were not quietened by a leading article, strongly favourable to Kitchener, which appeared in *The Times* on 10 February, 1894. Those rumours were revived in March, 1896, when the British Cabinet at last decided to allow the Egyptian Army to invade the Sudan. The Radical Press then used them to suggest that Kitchener was too headstrong and unreliable to be entrusted with the command.

The defeat at Adowa, on 1 March, 1896, of an Italian army, 30,000 strong, at the hands of the Emperor Menelik of Abyssinia, was the spark which fired the smouldering resolve of the British people to undertake the liberation of the Sudan. That Italian disaster, and the castration of the Italian prisoners, compromised European prestige. There was as much rejoicing in the new Sudanese capital at Omdurman, across the river from Khartoum, as there was in the new Abyssinian capital at Addis Ababa.

The Italian colony of Eritrea was threatened with a Sudanese as well as with an Abyssinian invasion ; and an Italian outpost at Kassala, in the eastern Sudan, was plunged suddenly into a position of deadly peril. The Italians had occupied Kassala in 1893 with British and Egyptian assent. That place had now become a liability, and Italy, supported by her ally, Germany, appealed urgently to Great Britain for help in the shape of a diversionary move in the Sudan.

The British Cabinet's decision was taken on 12 March, 1896, and Salisbury wrote[1] to Cromer (13 March) :

'.The decision to which the Cabinet came yesterday was inspired especially by a desire to help the Italians at Kassala, and to prevent the Dervishes from winning a conspicuous success, which might have far-reaching results. In addition we desired to kill two birds with one stone, and to use the same military effort to plant the foot of Egypt rather further up the Nile . . . But the main object was to relieve Kassala. For this reason publicity was essential. For general reasons . . . I could have wished that our friends, the Italians, had less capacity for being beaten, and would let us wait two or three years till we were quite ready in the valley of the Nile.

'But it would not have been safe either from an African or European point of view to sit quite still while they were being crushed.'

Cromer, who was much startled by that sudden decision, begged Salisbury to retain Kitchener in the command : 'I am very much pleased with Kitchener', he wrote[2] (15 March, 1896). 'He is cool and sensible, knows his subject thoroughly, and is not at all inclined to be rash.' Other names, however, were canvassed in the British Press as the result of a leakage of inaccurate information from the War Office, which caused Kitchener acute anxiety.

[1] Salisbury Papers, 113.　　　　[2] Ibid., 109.

Lord Wolseley, who had succeeded the Duke of Cambridge as Commander-in-Chief of the British Army, did not trust the Egyptian Army. He wanted, therefore, to send out two brigades of English troops to reinforce it, and although the Cabinet refused to agree, the Press assumed until the middle of April that they would be sent. All Kitchener's detractors seized that opportunity to suggest that, in those circumstances, some more senior general should be appointed to the supreme command ; and although the misunderstanding was finally resolved during the third week of April, the Press controversy continued into the first week of May.

Salisbury and Cromer were both determined to retain Kitchener in the command ; but Wolseley argued that a general who took his orders from the War Office would be more amenable to restraint than Kitchener, who would take his orders from the Foreign Office through Lord Cromer. Salisbury, who rejected that argument out of hand, sent Cromer two amusing letters on the subject. He wrote[1] (1 April) :

' I can't help feeling some disquietude at the announcement that the Sirdar has bought 5,000 camels. I know a railway can't move. But the camels may be taken on to Dongola ; and if it should turn out that the Khalifa's strength has been overrated, the camels will operate as a powerful temptation to go on to Berber, or possibly to Khartoum. H.M. Government may officially imprecate, but it is a far cry to the heart of the Sudan, and our powers of restraining the Sirdar will be small. I had much rather see him without those camels . . .'

Cromer assured Salisbury that Kitchener had no more than 2,000 camels, but on 1 May, 1896, the Prime Minister was even more explicit :

' Several of my colleagues ', he wrote, ' are still impressed with the fear that Kitchener meditates an expedition into the wilderness at the head of a string of camels. I do not share their apprehensions —tho' I have as much horror of the camel as they have . . . These apprehensions were not the mere tremors of a civilian. Lord Wolseley was fully persuaded that the Sirdar was bent on a camel raid, and he bases on that fear a recommendation that we should

[1] Ibid., 113.

send out some great English General who would take the Command
. . . The supersession of the Sirdar was not pressed, and I hope
we shall hear no more of it ; but the fear of his going forward
without waiting for the completion of his line of communications
was generally felt.'

On the question of employing Kitchener or some more senior
general from the War Office, Salisbury added : ' I look forward to
our having often to tug hard at the bridle during the next few months,
but I expect to find that the Egyptian horse has the better mouth of
the two.' Cromer replied[1] (8 May) : ' I am very glad you resisted
the idea of supplanting Kitchener. So long as I have him at the
end of a telegraph wire, I feel pretty confident that I can keep him and
the Egyptians generally in hand.'

In that way, Kitchener, as Commander-in-Chief, was placed under
the absolute control of Cromer, who was empowered to approve or
reject every plan which Kitchener suggested, and to grant or withhold any demands which he might make for men, money, or supplies.
The Nile expedition of 1884-5 had been controlled through the War
Office. The River War of 1896-8 was controlled instead through the
Foreign Office ; and the War Office, and the headquarters staff of the
British army of occupation in Egypt, issued no orders and had no
responsibility.

The war in the Sudan was started deliberately by England, after
careful planning and preparation, as a calculated act of policy. It
did not, like most of England's wars, break out of its own accord.
That was in some respects an advantage to Kitchener whose preparations had been completed ; but it was also a source of embarrassment and weakness. He became, within a few weeks, the embodiment of the patriotic ardour of the British nation, which possessed
almost unlimited resources. But he was forbidden to make any
demands whatsoever upon those. Instead he had to conduct his campaign as a cold-blooded business enterprise on behalf of a board which
he served as managing director, and of which Cromer was the cautious
chairman.

Such an extraordinary method of waging war helped to inhibit the
development, in Kitchener, of that capacity for bold and imaginative
enterprise, and for taking swift decisions, which has been the hall-
mark of great captains throughout the ages. There were no im-

[1] Salisbury Papers, 109.

ponderable factors ; and every circumstance was known, analysed, weighed and carried in Kitchener's head. The qualities demanded of the Commander-in-Chief were summarized[1] by Cromer with admirable succinctness :

' When once the British and Egyptian troops were brought face to face with the enemy, there could . . . be little doubt of the result. The speedy and successful issue of the campaign depended, in fact, almost entirely upon the methods adopted for overcoming the very exceptional difficulties connected with the supply and transport of the troops. The main quality required to meet those difficulties was a good head for business . . . Lord Kitchener of Khartoum won his well-deserved peerage because he was an excellent man of business ; he looked very carefully after every important detail, and enforced economy.'

[1] *Modern Egypt*, II, p. 107.

CHAPTER 6

THE SUDAN

1896–1898

T HE popular view of England's mission in Egypt and the Sudan was summarized by the brilliant and much-liked correspondent of the *Daily Mail*, G. W. Steevens, in a book entitled *With Kitchener to Khartoum* (1899), which ran into many editions :

' The vindication of our self-respect was the great treasure we won at Khartoum . . . We have made the Egyptian army, and . . . to put the matter brutally, having this field for recruiting, we have too many enemies in the world to afford to lose it . . . We undertook to leave Egypt ; we have redeemed the promise in an unforeseen way, but we have redeemed it amply . . . without us, there would have been no Egypt today. What we made we shall keep.'

The new order which Great Britain had imposed upon Egypt was being extended to the Sudan, where it was strenuously opposed by the inhabitants. The Khalifa was a brutal tyrant, but he symbolized effectively the nationalist aspirations of the peoples over whom he ruled. They had no desire to be liberated, and they showed themselves willing to die in their tens of thousands for the Mahdist cause. The sole argument which served to reconcile them to the acceptance of foreign rule was the overwhelming superiority of modern weapons ; and Kitchener appreciated that their morale was higher than that of the Egyptian Army.

The British Government at the outset forbade Kitchener to advance south of Dongola. The reason for that restriction was purely financial, and Salisbury warned the Queen (14 June, 1896) that nothing more could be expected for a time : ' Egypt has not got the money. She is prohibited by international law from borrowing ; and there is at present no appearance that either the Cabinet or the House of Commons would be willing to impose the burden on the British Exchequer. At present, therefore, the money could not be obtained. It may be obtained without difficulty as Egypt grows richer.'

A need for merciless economy, therefore, conditioned all Kitchener's actions and thoughts. It caused him to adopt expedients from which, in other circumstances, he might have shrunk. He pared, for example, his medical services to the bone, and resented the outcry which arose when they were found to be inadequate. Furthermore, in the absence of funds with which to pay his Egyptian boatmen, he was compelled to place his trust in forced labour and the lash.

One of Kitchener's first actions at the start of the campaign was to send to India for his brother Walter, whom he put in charge of the camel transport which caused such alarm to the British Cabinet. In a letter to his wife (9 April, 1896), Walter Kitchener described[1] his brother as 'a real autocrat—he does just as he pleases'. Walter said that his brother's house in Cairo was 'simply perfection in the way of taste . . . There seem to be rooms in all directions, and armour, carving, tiles, and draperies from floor to ceiling. The furniture is all most handsome . . . How he could have got all these things together seems extraordinary. The carved screens in the large upstairs reception room are bits of work you would go to a museum to see.'

Kitchener, who was with Rundle at Wadi Halfa when his brother reached Cairo, might have quoted Deuteronomy xxv, 4 : ' Thou shalt not muzzle the ox when he treadeth out the corn.' He was at that moment superintending the construction of a military railway from Wadi Halfa to Akasha, 86 miles to the south, which had been occupied on 20 March and turned into the advanced base of the expedition.

Lord Salisbury took the expedition firmly under his wing and called (16 May, 1896) for direct weekly personal reports from Kitchener to the private secretaries' office in London. Those reports were normally written by the Prime Minister's son, Lord Edward Cecil, who joined Kitchener as A.D.C. ; but Kitchener himself wrote[2] (21 May, 1896) to the Hon. Sir Eric Barrington, Salisbury's private secretary, from the headquarters of the 'Dongola Expeditionary Force' at Wadi Halfa :

' We are all pretty hard at work here, getting supplies pushed forward so as to be ready to move when the Nile allows.

' I have now over 10,000 troops south of this place, and all are fit and well and ready for the dervishes . . . I am making success as safe a thing as it is possible to do in wartime . . .

[1] Letter in the possession of Miss Madge Kitchener.
[2] Salisbury Papers, 99.

' Lord Cromer is a splendid man to work under. He does everything one can possibly want and has been most kind.'

On 6 June, Kitchener was ready to assault the enemy's advanced
concentration at Firket on the east bank of the Nile. He marched his
army out of Akasha in two columns on the afternoon of 6 June, and
surrounded the enemy's camp before dawn on the following morning.
The attack, launched at dawn, was brilliantly successful, and, after
the Mahdists' camp was stormed, over 800 enemy corpses were
counted.

The enemy commander was slain and 1,100 prisoners, half of whom
were wounded, fell into Kitchener's hands, in return for a British and
Egyptian loss of 20 killed and 83 wounded. Kitchener wrote [1]
(8 June) to Cromer:

' I think I can place your mind completely at rest as regards the
conduct of the Egyptian troops. The dervishes made a more stub-
born resistance than I expected. Numbers had to be killed as they
would not surrender, though in a hopeless condition . . . The
dervishes were like rats in a trap, and most that escaped did so by
swimming the river, naked and without arms.'

In forwarding that letter to Salisbury, Cromer wrote:[1]

' The essential part of the plan which Kitchener and I arranged
before he left Cairo was that, if possible, an action should be forced
on at a very early period of the campaign. I wanted to know
whether the Egyptian troops would fight. On this everything
depended. Kitchener managed the whole thing admirably, and
even adhered precisely to the exact date (June 7th) which he
had stated weeks beforehand . . . I cannot speak too highly of
Kitchener's conduct. He has fully justified the confidence which,
as you are aware, I always entertained in his abilities.'

Some hundreds of dervishes made good their escape, and Kitchener's
refusal to order his cavalry to intercept the enemy evoked criticism.
The Egyptian cavalry were ordered to pursue, but not to intercept,
because Kitchener wanted, above all else, in that preliminary encounter, to make certain of a cheap victory. He considered that a

[1] Salisbury Papers, 109.

beaten enemy with a possible escape route open is easier to destroy than a cornered and despairing enemy who sees no possibility of escape and who must, therefore, die or surrender.

That battle, for which a special clasp was struck, was classed by the War Office as a general action ; and two days later Kitchener established his advanced base at Suarda, 30 miles upstream from Firket. He might have pushed on to Dongola immediately by means of a somewhat hazardous rush ; but he preferred to await the arrival of gunboats, as well as the seasonal rise in the level of the Nile and the extension of his desert railway.

In preparation for the campaign, Kitchener, with expert assistance, had designed a new and more powerful type of gunboat which became known as the *Zafir* class. Those vessels, which were being built in England, were the children of Kitchener's invention and therefore his joy and pride. He had arranged that three should be transported in sections to Sukkot, where they would be assembled and launched on the clear waterway which extends from that place to beyond Dongola at high Nile. There was, however, no chance that they could be ready for action before September.

In the meantime Kitchener pushed his railway forward to Sukkot (4 August), where a number of ancient gunboats and armed steamers were assembled. But he was assailed by a series of calamities which British radical opponents of the forward policy likened to those sent by God to punish Pharaoh when he oppressed the chosen people before they left Egypt for Palestine.

The first calamity was an outbreak of cholera in the army. Putrefying corpses, swelling and breaking through the earth above the shallow graves into which they had been shovelled at Firket, led to an outbreak which caused the deaths, between the middle of July and the middle of August, of 20 British and 260 native soldiers and of 640 camp followers.

The second calamity was an unprecedented outbreak of storms and torrential rain in a country where rainfall at the height of summer is virtually unknown. The culminating point was reached on 27 August, four days after the army had resumed its march southwards. On that day one of Kitchener's brigades, which had been ordered to take a short cut through the desert, ran into such a severe thunderstorm and sandstorm that 2,000 out of 3,000 men sank exhausted to the ground.

Nine deaths and eighty serious cases of prostration was the final count of what came to be known as 'the death march' in the Egyptian Army. Kitchener was in no way to blame, but he felt his position acutely, partly because he knew that he possessed a reputation for callous indifference, and partly because he was unpopular with the newspaper correspondents whom he tried to confine to headquarters. The eyes of all England were upon him, and the death march was the least of the troubles which the August storms called down upon his head. Every ravine was turned into a raging torrent ; tents, huts and telegraph lines collapsed in a sea of mud ; and a twelve-mile stretch of the vital military railway was swept away by the floods.

At that critical moment Kitchener dominated the situation. Some delay had become inevitable, but a full-scale check might have had serious consequences. Seeds of doubt about the ethical justness of the war had not been eradicated from the minds of many influential liberals and intellectuals in England ; and those seeds might have sprouted into an ugly mood of defeatism which could have ruled out all possibility of the conquest of the whole of the Sudan if the situation had not been brought quickly under control. Kitchener, therefore, with a troubled spirit, concentrated more than five thousand men immediately upon the task of repairing the damaged railway, and ordered them to work until they dropped.

The men worked night and day, and Kitchener slept only in snatches for an entire week. He appeared on the scene wherever the difficulties were greatest, and inspired all ranks to expend unremittingly their last ounces of strength. He constantly encouraged and sometimes even praised individuals, and he frequently took a hand himself in the work with pick or shovel. For a few days he took around with him an English sergeant named Butler, who had won the heavyweight boxing championship in Cairo. Butler delighted the natives by carrying rocks in his arms, to build up the embankment, of a weight and size which appeared too great for human strength.

Traffic along the railway was resumed after one week, and by that time the brigade which had endured the death march was again ready to take the field. On 5 September, 1896, Kitchener sent two brigades to Dulgo, where five days later he concentrated his main striking force of 15,000 men. He had, in addition, a flotilla of five gunboats, including his newest and latest toy, the *Zafir*, and three armed steamers. He planned to embark on the *Zafir* and to advance up-river on 12 September for the assault on Dongola, which was the expedition's objective.

The flotilla was commanded by the Hon. S. C. G. Colville, R.N., and the army shared Kitchener's confidence in the *Zafir*'s ability to destroy the dervish forts along the Nile. That three-decker stern-paddle-wheel vessel, which was one hundred and forty feet in length and twenty-four feet in beam, drew only two feet of water ; she mounted one twelve-pounder gun, two six-pounders, a howitzer, twelve maxims and a powerful searchlight.

On the afternoon of 11 September Kitchener boarded the *Zafir* in the highest good humour. He ordered Commander Colville to take her into midstream and to show her to the troops, who were lining the banks expectantly and cheering. At that moment fate dealt Kitchener another blow. The *Zafir* had barely slipped her moorings when there was a loud explosion and the engines stopped. Clouds of steam drifted through the air, and Colville, who had been standing with Kitchener on the upper deck, rushed below to see what had happened. He found that she had burst her cylinder.

Kitchener displayed iron self-mastery when Colville reported that a new cylinder would have to be sent up from Wadi Halfa, and that the vessel would be out of action until it arrived. Kitchener's face flushed and his eyes twitched ; but all he said was : " By God, Colville, I don't know which of us it's hardest luck on—you, or me ! Well, get her guns out at once, and put them on board the other steamers." He then immediately left the ship, and the work of dismantling the guns began within a quarter of an hour of the accident.

For twenty-four hours Kitchener was unapproachable. He shut himself in the cabin of another gunboat, nursing his disappointment and calculating the altered odds. Lord Edward Cecil found him at one moment with tears of vexation in his eyes ; but on 12 September the advance started as planned.

The enemy was outnumbered by nearly three to one. The Emir, Wad Bishara, who had escaped from Firket, was courageous and energetic ; but he had only 5,600 regular troops, with seven antiquated cannon, and the odds against him were so overwhelming that the issue was never in doubt.

Because he had chosen to proceed cautiously, and to build up his strength methodically, Kitchener longed for a resounding victory, with a tremendous slaughter of dervishes. But Wad Bishara had no intention of fighting a general action. He had taken up a position on the east bank of the Nile at Kerma, which Kitchener planned to storm at dawn on 19 September, 1896. By a masterly manœuvre, however, Wad Bishara transferred his entire force across the Nile to the west bank during the previous night, and took up an entrenched position a short distance up-stream at Hafir—some 36 miles downstream from Dongola.

Separated in that way by the Nile from his enemy, Kitchener was compelled to depend upon his gunboats and artillery for forcing a passage up-stream. He could not advance on Dongola leaving a strong enemy force under a resolute commander astride of his line of communications, and he was reluctant to split his army by leaving a part of it to mask the dervish entrenchments. His infantry were compelled, therefore, to sit idly on the sand under a blazing sun, and to watch the issue being fought out between their gunboats and artillery and the dervishes across the river.

The Nile narrows at Hafir to about 600 yards, and Colville's gunboats came under heavy and concentrated fire. Lacking the aid of the *Zafir*, they found it impossible, after two and a half hours, to crush the enemy's fire. Kitchener, therefore, moved three batteries of artillery through shallow water to an island opposite the dervish entrenchments, and three battalions of infantry as close as possible to the river's edge. He then ordered the naval craft, under cover of that support, to run the gauntlet of the dervish bombardment and to steam up-river to Dongola.

That manœuvre was successful and the action thereafter died down. The opposing forces watched each other across the river, and the dervishes hurled defiance at the invaders. Wad Bishara, however, had good cause to feel uncomfortable about his line of retreat in view of Kitchener's proved command of the waterway and overwhelming artillery superiority. Accordingly, he stealthily evacuated Hafir during the night and retreated on Dongola, which he reached on the evening of 20 September.

Kitchener took his army across the Nile unopposed, in boats which the dervishes had abandoned. The crossing was completed on the afternoon of 21 September, and the march on Dongola was immediately resumed along the west bank. The dervishes lost 200 killed during that action, and Kitchener lost only two.

Kitchener had achieved his purpose, but he felt that the Battle of Hafir was somewhat inglorious and that it needed to be written up for Lord Salisbury. He therefore asked Lord Edward Cecil to show him the weekly letter which he had written to his father. When he read it, Kitchener was scandalized by its brevity and lack of colour ; and he immediately dictated, as a model, a piece of sentimental and elaborate prose which would have brought a blush to the cheek of a hardened reporter for the halfpenny press.

Summoning all his courage, Cecil told[1] Kitchener that the Prime Minister would be astonished beyond measure at receiving such a report from his son. He begged Kitchener not to insist, and, after some hesitation, Kitchener, who did not know Lord Salisbury well, tore up the model letter which he had dictated. He told Cecil to write what he ' damed well ' chose, and then abruptly turned away ; and Cecil thought that he remained only half convinced.

By noon on 22 September Kitchener was only six miles from Dongola, where he had made his name twelve years before. His gunboats, one of which was commanded by the young David Beatty,[2] sailed up and down the river, carrying supplies and pouring shells into the town. The final advance began at three o'clock on the morning of 23 September, and, as dawn broke, Kitchener's eyes were gladdened by the arrival of the *Zafir*, which had been fitted, by extraordinary exertions, with a new cylinder, and which joined in the bombardment of the town. The gallant enemy commander, Wad Bishara, faced with impossible odds, abandoned Dongola without a fight. He used his cavalry skilfully and successfully to secure the retreat of his entire force in good order southwards.

Profound satisfaction was voiced in Great Britain and throughout the Empire ; and, in striking contrast to Gallipoli, for which no award was ever made, a special medal, with clasps for Firket and for Hafir, was issued to all who had taken part in the expedition. Every British officer (save one) was honourably mentioned in dispatches. Kitchener received a K.C.B., and was promoted (25 September) to be a Major-General in the British Army. He pushed his forward units up-river to Merowe, and ordered them to halt there, pending further instructions.

Kitchener rushed off to Cairo immediately and begged Cromer to authorize a renewed advance. He said that he could undertake to occupy Berber and Abu Hamed during 1897 without British reinforcements ; but he declined to commit himself about Khartoum. He told Cromer that his director of military intelligence, Reginald Wingate, had received alarming news from Abyssinia.

Wingate reported that a strong French mission in Addis Ababa was

[1] Lord Edward Cecil, *Leisure of an Egyptian Official*, p. 191.
[2] Admiral of the Fleet Earl Beatty of the North Sea, P.C., G.C.B., O.M., G.C.V.O., D.S.O. (1871–1936).

urging the Emperor Menelik to consent to the establishment of a French sphere of influence across equatorial Africa, including the upper waters of the Nile, from coast to coast. Wingate also reported that the Khalifa had appealed to the Emperor of Abyssinia for joint military action against the invaders of the Sudan. In those circumstances, Cromer sent Kitchener to London to see the Prime Minister, and to ask the Chancellor of the Exchequer, Sir Michael Hicks-Beach, for a contribution of half a million pounds :

' I had thought ', Cromer wrote[1] (30 October, 1896) to Salisbury, ' to stop two or three years at Dongola ' ; and he added that the question was ' *wholly* one of finance '. He explained that Kitchener had done better and spent less than he had anticipated ; that the enemy were evidently alarmed and shaken ; and that the Egyptian Ministry of Finance agreed with Kitchener that an immediate advance would be less costly than a delayed one. Cromer said that he would now recommend an immediate advance if the British taxpayer could be induced to provide £500,000.

Kitchener, who reached London on 9 November, enlisted all his friends immediately in a lightning campaign against the Chancellor of the Exchequer, whom he finally took by storm during the late afternoon of 16 November. On the previous evening, Kitchener and a number of other soldiers had dined with the Duke of Cambridge, who threw all his influence into the scales ; and on 16 November Kitchener lunched at Windsor with Queen Victoria, whom he found extremely sympathetic. He presented her with some trophies, and she noted that he was ' a striking, energetic-looking man, with a rather firm expression, but very pleasing to talk to '. Kitchener then returned to London by train, interviewed Hicks-Beach, and telegraphed that evening to Lord Cromer immediately before starting on his return journey to Cairo : ' Government have approved of scheme proposed, and authorize expenditure on railway and gunboats. The approximate estimate I submitted to Chancellor of Exchequer was—railway, £240,000 ; construction, £30,000 ; gunboats, £75,000 ; armament, stores, etc., £55,000 ; transport, £100,000. Total, £500,000.'

On 27 November, Salisbury wrote[2] to Cromer :

' No doubt Kitchener has fully informed you of his experiences here. His campaign against the Chancellor of the Exchequer was not the least brilliant and certainly the least expected of all his

[1] Salisbury Papers, 109.　　　　　[2] Ibid., 113.

triumphs. But all his strategy is of a piece. The position was carried by a forced march and a surprise. In fact, I had to give my approval at the end of a moment's notice, when the train by which Kitchener was to go away was already overdue. I need not say I was very glad to do so, and the Cabinet, to whom the whole matter was stated on Wednesday, entirely approved.'

Salisbury added that he had been sorry to learn that Kitchener 'looked with apprehension upon the evacuation of Kassala by the Italians'; and that 'as soon as the French find out what Kitchener is after, we shall have an ebullition'.

Hicks-Beach had the reputation of being an even more close-fisted Chancellor of the Exchequer than Gladstone. He explained, however, to the House of Commons on 5 February, 1897, that Egypt would never be permanently secure while a hostile Power remained in occupation of the upper Nile valley. He added, in regard to the Dongola expedition : " I do not think that any more complete success was ever obtained by any expedition that was ever undertaken. I do not say this as wishing to take any credit whatever to Her Majesty's Government. The credit is due, of course, to Sir Herbert Kitchener."

Hicks-Beach said that Kitchener had been authorized to advance 'in the first place to Abu Hamed, and afterwards possibly beyond [loud cheers]. How far I do not think it right to say . . . I am no believer in the mission of even so powerful a country as this to redress the wrongs of humanity all over the world. But here is a case in which the task is ready to our hand.'

The Dongola expedition had charmed the British nation, and 1897 was the year of Queen Victoria's Diamond Jubilee. That was a great imperial occasion, and, to those who celebrated it, war can seldom have appeared more delightful and rewarding or less dangerous and expensive. Nowhere in the world at that time could vicarious pride and honour be more readily gratified—nowhere could vicarious adventure be better enjoyed, than by following in imagination Major-General Sir Herbert Kitchener, K.C.B., K.C.M.G., in his march across the desert to Khartoum.

So Kitchener returned to Cairo in a mood of exultation as a favourite of the Cabinet and a hero of the British masses. His dream had come true, and his plan of campaign had long been formed. He had already explained to Salisbury and Cromer that his route to Khartoum would not lie through Dongola.

Kitchener planned to throw a military railway across the Nubian Desert from Wadi Halfa to Abu Hamed, at the head of the great bend of the Nile. Abu Hamed was already within reach of his advanced detachments at Merowe, and he hoped, therefore, that it would fall to an assault by river and camel transport before his railway came within reach of enemy raiding parties. He secured the acceptance of that plan in the teeth of strong opposition, and preliminary work on the construction of the Sudan military railway—S.M.R.— was started on 1 January, 1897.

In building his railway, Kitchener relied on a posse of picked sapper subalterns who became known as ' Kitchener's band of boys '. They were all devoted to him and he looked after their interests like a father. Whenever a battle was imminent, he arranged that the boys should be given a chance to win distinction by taking part in it ; and most rose to fame and fortune. No member of the band was quite so useful or so close to Kitchener as Lieutenant Percy Girouard.[1]

Girouard was a young French Canadian who had won the D.S.O. in the Dongola expedition after graduating at the Royal Military College, Kingston, and being trained on the Canadian Pacific Railway. He possessed rare good looks, bubbling high spirits, and that happy transatlantic ability to express himself crisply and tartly without causing offence. Many stories were told about his growing influence over Kitchener. On one occasion, for example, Kitchener became impatient when a heavily-laden train was not being pulled fast enough over a corkscrew section of the desert railway by an engine which was almost a museum piece. Mounting the footplate with Girouard, Kitchener seized the driver by the shoulders. He ordered him to detach half the train and to " Go like hell ! " with the other half. The train rocked like a ship in a storm, but it reached its destination in record time. Kitchener turned to Girouard and exclaimed with his habitual drawl :

" What a dreadful journey we have had, Girouard ! A dreadful journey ! Terrible ! Terrible ! "

There was a pause, while Girouard adjusted his eye-glass before replying with an impudent and lazy smile :

" You'll break the record, and your own ruddy neck one day ! "

Kitchener's face flushed with rage, but he could never be angry for long with Girouard, who was the reigning favourite, privileged and indispensable. He sent Girouard to England in February, 1897, to order material, and saw the subaltern off himself with the words :

[1] Colonel Sir Percy Girouard, K.C.M.G., D.S.O. (1867-1932).

"Don't spend too much, Girouard. We are terribly poor." He was delighted when Girouard succeeded in borrowing from Cecil Rhodes a number of 70- and 80-ton locomotives intended for the Cape and Natal government railways.

Girouard helped Kitchener to prepare estimates and specifications with miserly care, in all respects save one. Cromer urged that a gauge of 3 feet 3⅜ inches should be adopted on grounds of economy; but Kitchener successfully stood out for a gauge of 3 feet 6 inches because he hoped that his railway would ultimately form part of Cecil Rhodes's ambitious scheme of a line from the Cape to Cairo on the South African standard gauge of 3 feet 6 inches.

The Sudan military railway reached the summit of its projected track 103 miles from Wadi Halfa on 23 July, 1897, without once exceeding the limits of curve (6 degrees) and gradient (1 in 120) upon which Girouard had insisted from the outset. Wells, sunk in the desert on Kitchener's initiative, produced water in sufficient abundance to supply all needs of the engines and of the construction gangs. Its discovery was attributed to 'Kitchener's luck', and Kitchener always insisted that any General should be scrapped if he failed to earn a reputation for luck. Railhead was being pushed forward at an average rate of over one and a half miles a day; and it became urgently necessary to occupy the projected terminus of its first stage at Abu Hamed.

Accordingly, on 29 July, 1897, Kitchener dispatched a flying column of 2,700 men and 1,300 camels, with all possible secrecy, up the north bank of the Nile from Merowe. The column was commanded by Major-General Archibald Hunter.[1] It consisted of one infantry brigade, commanded by Lieutenant-Colonel Hector Macdonald[2], D.S.O., Royal Fusiliers (Old Mac), who had risen by bravery and merit from the ranks; one troop of cavalry, one mule-battery of six Krupp twelve-pounders, and four maxim guns.

Hunter covered the 132 miles from Merowe to Abu Hamed in eight days at the hottest season of the year. His presence was not discovered by the enemy until he had advanced some 97 miles, and his assault, delivered at two o'clock on the morning of 7 August, was brilliantly successful. Abu Hamed was stormed by 6.30 a.m.; only 2 British officers and 25 native soldiers were killed; at least 250 enemy corpses were counted.

[1] General Sir Archibald Hunter, G.C.B., G.C.V.O., D.S.O. (1856–1936).
[2] Major-General Sir Hector Macdonald, K.C.B., D.S.O. (1853–1903).

Because he expected a vigorous and speedy enemy reaction from Berber, Kitchener exerted himself to push his entire flotilla of gunboats up-stream to Abu Hamed, followed by hundreds of native boats carrying supplies. Two days before the last gunboat accomplished the difficult passage news was received (27 August) that the enemy had abandoned Berber. That astonishing intelligence was confirmed by reconnaissance on 2 September.

The feeble Mahdist commander in Berber had panicked because he was not reinforced from Metemma as quickly as he had expected by the young and resolute Emir Mahmoud, who commanded at Metemma and who had found it necessary first to suppress a mutiny which his brutal methods had provoked. Kitchener extorted Cromer's consent to the immediate occupation of Berber, which he reached on 10 September after riding, with an escort, across the desert.

Kitchener reopened the road from Suakin to Berber, and sent gunboats to reconnoitre Metemma and to shoot up the town. But in rejecting Kitchener's plea for an early advance to Khartoum, Cromer said that nothing more would probably be attempted for some years.

Cromer and the Foreign Office had entirely altered their attitude to the campaign for financial reasons. Sir Eldon Gorst, the adviser to the Egyptian Ministry of the Interior, and Sir Elwin Palmer, the Director-General of Accounts, had become critical of Kitchener, and openly hostile, because they regarded him as the spearhead of the War Office which was, in their view, attempting to force their hands.

Kitchener had appreciated that the occupation of Berber would force the issue of the campaign. He had always intended to call for the assistance of British regular troops before delivering his final assault upon Khartoum ; and he hoped that the impetus which he had acquired would suffice to carry him forward without pause or interference. That hope was now disappointed, but Kitchener was convinced that the occupation of Berber ruled out the possibility of calling off the campaign. He regarded it as virtually certain that the Khalifa would soon advance in strength to attack the long and exposed Egyptian front.

Lord Wolseley, the Commander-in-Chief at the War Office, agreed with Kitchener ; and he therefore pressed the Government repeatedly to send British regular troops to the Sudan to finish a task which had proved to be too great for the financial and military resources of the Egyptian Government. That pressure, however, dismayed Kitchener quite as much as Cromer's refusal to advance. All senior soldiers were furiously jealous of Kitchener, whom they regarded as the spoilt darling of the Foreign Office which employed him. They were bound to feel delighted if the Foreign Office were to let Kitchener down ; and Kitchener was mortally afraid of the consequences to himself which must follow. He considered that the abandonment of the campaign must lead to a strong and early dervish advance which would require the immediate dispatch by the War Office of a British expeditionary force to retrieve the situation. In that case he would expect to find himself superseded by some more senior British General—as Sir Evelyn Wood had been subordinated to Lord Wolseley in 1884—before he had been allowed sufficient time in which to consolidate his personal grip upon the imagination of the British public.

As a preliminary move the War Office, in July, 1897, appointed Sir Francis Grenfell, whom Kitchener had succeeded as Sirdar, to command the British army of occupation in Egypt. Kitchener had often referred caustically to that army as the army of ' no occupation ', and he was now even more afraid of being robbed of the fruits of his labours than Cromer was afraid of being deflected by War Office pressure from the line of policy which he had chosen, and in which he was supported by Salisbury.

Cromer telegraphed[1] (9 July, 1897) to Salisbury : ' Grenfell's appointment, although personally agreeable to me, is rather a hazardous experiment. It ought, however, to do no harm if it is very clearly understood that there will be no change in the position of the Sirdar. Any increased interference by the War Office in military matters would create divided responsibility, and would also be open to grave political and financial objections.'

Salisbury assured[2] Cromer (11 July) that ' no change whatever ' was intended in Kitchener's position, and that he was vexed with Lansdowne, the Secretary for War, for appointing Grenfell without consultation. Lansdowne minuted[2] : ' No change is intended, but I will see Sir F. Grenfell and tell him to be careful.' Nevertheless, Cromer, unfortunately, took no steps until the end of the year to set Kitchener's mind at rest ; and he made grossly insufficient allowance for Kitchener's feeling of acute personal anxiety and frustration.

Kitchener was partly responsible for the difficulties which followed, because he attempted to conceal his personal fears under cover of a very genuine concern for the public weal. But Cromer had two

[1] Salisbury Papers, 110.   [2] Ibid., 113.

motives for his neglect to reassure Kitchener about his position. In the first place, he disliked the thought of discussing his firm intention of retaining personal control of the campaign with a subordinate whose tongue and outlook had, of late, become notoriously caustic and cynical. In the second place, he considered that Kitchener on tenterhooks would be held more securely under his thumb.

Kitchener warned Cromer that he would need additional funds from the Egyptian Treasury in order to hold securely the territories which he had already conquered. Kitchener said, in particular, that he needed money at once in order to pay for the movement of one part of the idle garrison at Suakin to Berber, and of another part to Kassala, which the Italians were about to evacuate. Cromer categorically refused to allow Kitchener an additional penny for any purpose.

On 14 October, 1897, Kitchener explained his difficulties to Grenfell :

'. . . There are other matters in which my position is not an easy one. Discussions, principally of a financial nature, but which involve military considerations, take place between Lord Cromer and myself. How far these ought to be referred to you, I do not know. If I were in Cairo, things would be clear, but . . . I hope you will never imagine that I desire to work off my own bat and not to loyally serve under you . . .

'I have stated that, in my opinion, handing over Kassala to the dervishes renders our position here insecure, and may result in either the necessity of sending a British expedition very rapidly—for which the authorities would not be prepared—or in our being unable to hold our present positions. I pointed out the strategic importance of Kassala more than eight months ago, and wrote to the War Office on the subject . . . All my original intentions for taking and holding Berber . . . were based on our flank being secured by Kassala being held ; and Lord Cromer and Palmer were both fully aware of this. Of course, the question now is that Palmer will not find the money for the Kassala garrison, which ought to have been raised six months ago . . . though personally I think it could be done.'

Kitchener was at that time conducting an acrimonious telegraphic correspondence about finance with Cromer, as well as with Sir

Elwin Palmer, whom he had always detested ; and in a violent fit of passion, Kitchener, on 18 October, telegraphed[1] his resignation to Cromer, from Berber :

'... I do not think that the gravity of the military situation is fully realized. Holding our long line, which is liable to attack at any point, leaves me with a small force at Berber, a place most difficult to defend, and without support. My suspended scheme to move the Suakin garrison here cannot be postponed much longer. The reconnaissance of Mahmoud's position proves that we have in front of us a force of dervishes of better fighting qualities and far greater numerical strength than we have ever met before. In face of this, the financial authorities appear to be unable to grant what I think necessary for military efficiency. My estimate of the situation may be wrong, but feeling as I do my inability to cope with the difficulties, and the grave responsibility of the position in which I find myself, I beg to tender my resignation to your lordship. I do not take this step without careful consideration . . .'

George Gorringe,[2] who was doing temporary duty as A.D.C., never forgot the terrible look which Kitchener turned upon him when he handed him that message to encode. He had the happy idea of suggesting a duck-shoot, which afforded some relief; but Kitchener was not far removed from a nervous collapse. Cromer telegraphed[3] (22 October) to Salisbury : 'I think I should let you know privately that the difficulties here, which are very great, are materially increased by Sir Herbert Kitchener's frame of mind. A few days ago he formally resigned, but as I have heard no more of this I fancy he will not carry out his intention. He complains of the strain, and, generally, leaves on my mind the impression that, for the moment, his nerve has gone. This is very awkward . . .' Cromer added that he was not yet in a position to decide about Kassala, ' but I must to a certain limited extent place the necessity of securing military safety before finance '.

It was not possible to conquer a vast country on the principle of placing finance before the safety of the Army. But on that day

[1] Salisbury Papers, 110.
[2] Lieutenant-General Sir George Gorringe, K.C.B., K.C.M.G., D.S.O. (1868–1945).
[3] Salisbury Papers, 110.

(22 October) Cromer sent[1] Salisbury a fuller account of his attitude towards the war and his estimate of Kitchener :

'. . . It is abundantly clear that the reconquest of the Sudan is beyond the military and financial resources of the Egyptian Government. In moments of retrospection I tear my hair over the hurried decision of March, 1896. It has upset all my calculations and introduced an entirely new factor into Egyptian politics . . .

'In the second place, my Sirdar is a changed man. From the first moment of my return I was struck by the change in the tone of his telegrams. They were diffuse and altogether wanting in the businesslike ring to which I was formerly accustomed. I have had a voluminous correspondence with him which, if my limited staff can find time, shall be copied and sent home to you. In the meantime I send you privately the telegram in which he expressed a wish to resign. The financial point of issue between him and Palmer was not nearly sufficient to justify such a step, and taking the evidence of the telegram alone, I should have been inclined to think it was merely an attempt to force our financial hand. Several of the high officials here have, from time to time, expressed a wish to resign when they were unable to have their way.

'But at the same time as the telegram was received, Dawkins[2] —who is an intimate friend of Kitchener's—received a letter of which I enclose a copy, written a fortnight ago. It is the production of a sick man who has lost his nerve . . . I daresay this will pass over. Those who know Kitchener best tell me that he is liable to fits of extreme depression from which, however, he rapidly recovers. In the meantime his frame of mind causes me some anxiety, for everything depends on his keeping his head, and judging calmly of the situation . . .

'You will see what Kitchener says in his letter to Dawkins. My own opinion is quite clear that no sufficiently important English interest is involved to justify the loss in life and money which would be involved in the capture of Khartoum.'

The capture of Khartoum was the dream of Kitchener's life, and

[1] Salisbury Papers, 110.

[2] Sir Clinton Dawkins, K.C.B. (1859-1905), at that time Under-Secretary for Finance in Egypt, and, later, a partner in Messrs. J. B. Morgan & Co.

in his letter to Dawkins (dated 6 October from Abu Hamed) he had stated :[1]

> 'I hope there will be no question about finishing off the whole thing at Omdurman next year. The strain on all of us, and on the troops, is very great, and if we do not continue the advance, the dervishes will certainly resume the offensive . . .
> 'You have no idea what continual anxiety, worry, and strain I have through it all. I do not think that I can stand much more, and I feel so completely done up that I can hardly go on and wish I were dead. Before next year's work in the field begins I must get some leave, or I shall break down. I have had none for three years now.'

Sir Thomas Sanderson,[2] Permanent Under-Secretary at the Foreign Office, minuted[3] his opinion that Kitchener, without consulting Cromer, had caused a hint to be dropped to the Italians that he needed their continued presence at Kassala ; that Cromer had rebuked him ; and that Kitchener had exploded. But Salisbury was not convinced. He told[4] Cromer (23 October) that his information about Kitchener was 'very alarming. To what cause is his depression due ? Is he irritated at our not moving faster ? Is he afraid H.M.G. will not support him ? Has Grenfell's appointment anything to do with it ? '

Cromer replied[5] (24 October) that Kitchener had withdrawn his resignation, and that its cause had been 'partly irritation at our failure to give him all the money he wanted ; but still more, I think, in reality, the strain due to the climate, and continuous responsible work . . . His relations with Grenfell are very friendly.'

Cromer was suspicious of Kitchener's good relations with Grenfell, because he was constantly afraid that Salisbury would become entangled, by a soldiers' conspiracy, in another disastrous campaign like the Nile expedition of 1884-5, into which Gladstone had allowed himself to be dragged by Gordon, the War Office, and the popular Press. For that reason Cromer constantly wrote to Salisbury, Hicks-Beach and Lansdowne to urge that no forward move should be undertaken during 1898, and that the soldiers should never, in

[1] Salisbury Papers, 110.
[2] Lord Sanderson of Arnthorpe, G.C.B., K.C.M.G. (1841-1923).
[3] Salisbury Papers, 110.   [4] Ibid., 113.   [5] Ibid., 110.

any circumstances, be let loose until a clear understanding had been reached about the method of defraying the expense.

Salisbury did his best to reassure Cromer. He admitted that Wolseley was constantly urging Lansdowne to press on that winter to Khartoum, but he telegraphed[1] (29 October, 1897) :

'I disagree in this view . . . I only know one argument in its favour—the possibility that, if we wait another year, we may find that the French have anticipated us by setting up a French principality at Fashoda. It is, of course, as difficult to judge what is going on in the upper Nile valley as it is to judge what is going on on the other side of the moon . . . but . . . if we ever get to Fashoda, the diplomatic crisis will be something to remember, and the "what next" will be a very interesting question.'

On 11 November, Kitchener paid a lightning visit to Cromer and Grenfell in Cairo. He looked very cross when he met Cromer, but he laughed and joked with Grenfell, and he tried hard to be amiable. He warned Cromer that Wingate's intelligence reports indicated that the Khalifa was preparing a large-scale assault upon the Egyptian positions at Berber ; and he said that, in such an event, he would have to apply to the War Office for British reinforcements.

Cromer, who automatically received copies of all Wingate's reports, refused to accept the construction which Kitchener placed upon them. He agreed, however, in the circumstances, to provide Kitchener with sufficient funds to move some Egyptian troops from Suakin to Berber and Kassala.

Nothing whatever was said about Kitchener's resignation or about the possibility of his eventual supersession by Grenfell. The atmosphere was not, therefore, appreciably cleared, and Kitchener's mood of frustration and exasperation remained unaltered. It reached such a pitch that, on 16 December, Cromer informed[2] Salisbury that Kitchener's 'main idea now appears to be to get away from Egypt, and obtain some English Military Command in order to qualify for higher positions later. I would rather he did not go just yet, as, whatever his defects, he is, unquestionably, by far the best man I know to command the Egyptian Army for the present. However, no one is indispensable, and if he really wishes to go, I do not want to stand in his way.'

[1] Salisbury Papers, 113. [2] Ibid., 110.

Frustrated ambition caused Kitchener agony at that time. He sometimes spoke to his staff about his dream of founding a new viceroyalty of the Near East to include Egypt and the Sudan ; and he complained that Cromer's attitude towards him had been that of a bullying schoolmaster throughout almost the entire campaign. He felt no gratitude for the concession about Kassala which he had wrung from Cromer at the last moment ; and the resentment which he harboured made him more brusque, dour and uncouth between 1896 and 1898 than at any other period of his life. He displayed a lack of consideration for others which alienated most men's sympathies ; but his manner improved greatly after the Battle of Omdurman had restored his self-confidence and secured his fame and position.

In the meantime, Kitchener often vented his spleen by bullying his staff as some men bully their wives. At other times he might remain morose and silent for hours on end. He was a difficult chief, because he liked to slip away by himself, and would subsequently explode if he happened to want anyone who could not instantly be found. He used to take his meals at any hour, and would occasionally keep his staff waiting until close on midnight and then complain because the dinner was spoiled.

Kitchener was always scrupulously clean and well turned out, and he was intolerant of any laxity in those respects. But his office was invariably a sea of papers which were littered over the floor, and on tables, chairs and window-sills. He always seemed to know where anything was that was needed ; but no one else ever knew, and he became furious if anyone touched his papers in any circumstances.

The stress under which Kitchener worked was immensely increased by his total incapacity to delegate even simple things. He insisted upon acting as his own Chief of Staff, and he left his principal staff officer, Leslie Rundle, to eat his heart out in the rear at Wadi Halfa throughout the campaign. Kitchener's extraordinary grasp of detail enabled him to do almost everything for himself, but he seemed to exhaust himself, without any sound cause, in the process ; and his natural surliness was increased by indigestion, as well as by violent bouts of neuralgia which were probably due to eye-strain.

Kitchener normally rose at least an hour before dawn, and he plumed himself upon needing less sleep than other men. He liked to get through three hours' work before breakfast. He detested routine, and was never tired of expressing his contempt for official channels. He normally exercised his command by issuing verbal orders ; but, when necessary, he would issue a stream of laconic telegrams which he always drafted himself. He kept a stock of forms for that purpose inside his helmet.

Kitchener was most approachable at about 6 p.m., when he would talk for a short time, and drink either a gin and soda or a vermouth and soda. He would work afterwards before dinner, which might be held at any hour ; and he told his staff that he wanted them to talk freely, even if he remained silent, so that merely by listening he could become aware of everything that was being said or thought in the army. He never varied his custom of living in mess with his staff ; he drank nothing at luncheon ; and his usual drink at dinner was mineral water, followed by a single glass of vintage port.

Kitchener's conversation at that period was brutally and startlingly cynical. He affected to believe that no action was ever performed except from motives of naked or concealed self-interest. Some of his staff held that that was a result of many years' experience in the East ; but others, who knew him better, argued that he remained a Christian at heart, and had merely assumed a cloak to hide his innermost feelings. He was generous to his personal servants and he had entire confidence in and, occasionally, a deep and strong affection for those who served him really well. But he had a horror of any approach towards a display of sentiment or emotion ; and he much preferred to be misunderstood than to be suspected of a capacity for warm human feeling.

In those circumstances Kitchener inevitably appeared ungrateful to his English officers, and sometimes positively savage to their Egyptian and Sudanese comrades who were all terrified of him. His standards were exalted, and he would not tolerate any form of failure, weakness or even sickness. Any officer who, after doing his utmost, failed nevertheless to execute an order to Kitchener's satisfaction as a result of some act of God, such as a sudden storm or a mechanical breakdown, for which he had no responsibility, had to reconcile his mind to the fact that his misfortune had set him apart, like a leper. In Kitchener's eyes he had become the victim of a fatal accident, and was finished. That was hard and, in a normal sense, unjust. It was, however, 'Kitchener's way', and the position had to be understood and accepted.

There is, in human nature, a masochistic strain which rewards toughness and ruthless efficiency with affection. Kitchener made no attempt to ingratiate himself with the troops, who marvelled at his strength and revered him almost as a god. He treated them sternly but justly, and there were no complaints ; his treatment of civilians, on the other hand, excited Cromer's concern and disapproval. Owing to the financial stringency, Kitchener was dependent upon forced labour ; and stories of constant floggings and occasional hangings trickled through to Cairo. It must be said, however, that Kitchener employed such methods only from necessity.

Kitchener would allow nothing to deflect him from his goal, and he could not at that period afford the more refined pleasure of benignancy. He might, however, have guarded himself better against an unnecessary charge of callousness if he had paid more attention to problems of military government. Sir Michael Hicks-Beach, for example, had informed the House of Commons (5 February, 1897) that Kitchener was occupied in restoring civilization to the province of Dongola. Cromer was, therefore, entitled to express a measure of disquiet when he found Kitchener acquiescing with apparent indifference in the continued infliction of outmoded punishments for trivial offences, such as the lopping off of hands and feet, because the inhabitants were used to them and the Commander-in-Chief was too busy to interfere.

Whatever Kitchener's defects may have been, his love of fighting was known to all and greatly relished. Without being foolhardy, he made a point of taking the same risks as those who were most exposed to the enemy's fire ; and during advances he usually rode close to the contact squadron of cavalry. His appearance was extremely impressive, and his moustache was justly celebrated not only throughout the Army but throughout the Empire. Its length and bushiness were unique, and it would be easy, but wrong, to dismiss it with a smile. It was the ideal of all moustaches of all drill sergeants throughout all the armies of Europe ; and in that exaggerated form it became a symbol of national virility. It appealed to the martial instinct of the British race at a time when the nation had been demilitarized, materially and spiritually, to an extent which can rarely have been paralleled.

During the third week of December, 1897, a tremendous event occurred. On leaving Cairo a month earlier Kitchener had visited Massawa in order to confer with the governor of the Italian colony of Eritrea about the change-over at Kassala. On his return to Wadi

K.—I

Halfa on 18 December, Kitchener was informed by Wingate that the Khalifa was about to march immediately on Berber at the head of his entire host.

Kitchener at once informed Cromer that the Egyptian Army would not be able to resist that onset unaided, and that the position was serious ; and Cromer alerted Lord Salisbury. On 23 December, accordingly, the British Cabinet decided to give Cromer and Kitchener a free hand in dealing with that emergency, and to send them any British reinforcements for which they might ask.

On that day Salisbury telegraphed[1] to Cromer : 'I imagine it will go smoother with you if you can make it clear to the Sirdar that he will not be superseded by Grenfell—a change which I should very much deplore, as it would alter the whole character of our military action in Egypt.' He confirmed (4 January) a Cabinet decision that Kitchener should be placed in supreme command of all British as well as Egyptian troops operating south of Aswan.

Cromer grumbled[2] characteristically to Salisbury (24 December, 1897, and 8 January, 1898) that, being compelled to act prematurely, he had been placed 'in a most difficult position' ; that Kitchener was 'very unpopular' ; and that all the senior soldiers were filled with jealousy towards him. He added (24 December) :

'The only fault I have to find with him is that it is sometimes difficult to extract the whole truth from him. He is inclined to keep back facts which he does not wish to be known. Moreover, like all soldiers, he generally has some personal interest behind the view which he puts forward in public matters.

'But, after all . . . Kitchener has done his work extremely well. For all our purposes out here he is an admirable appointment.'

On 1 January, 1898, Kitchener sent Cromer a telegram which Cromer himself, subsequently, described[3] as 'historic' : 'General Hunter reports confirming news of a dervish advance. I think that British troops should be sent to Abu Hamed, and that reinforcements should be sent to Egypt . . . The fight for the Sudan would appear likely to take place at Berber.'

So Kitchener's hopes and expectations were realized. Cromer's hand, and Salisbury's, had been forced by the Khalifa—not by

[1] Salisbury Papers, 113. [2] Ibid., 110 and 113.
[3] Modern Egypt, II, p. 97.

Kitchener, nor by the War Office, nor even by public opinion ; and the prevailing mood in Cairo, as well as in London, was one of relief. The period of painful uncertainty, which might have lasted for years, had been restricted to a few weeks; and once the war-hounds were unleashed, the necessary finance was found, without trouble, by the British taxpayer. Seldom, indeed, can a more trifling outlay have reaped a speedier or richer reward.

In Kitchener's mind, where a fierce love of country compensated for the absence of more intimate and familiar human ties, relief was drowned in a surge of exultant thankfulness and pride. The eyes of all England were focused upon his head once more, as he concentrated his reinforced army and advanced to wreak vengeance at last for Gordon's death by the overthrow of the Khalifa and the conquest or liberation of the Sudan.

CHAPTER 7

KITCHENER OF KHARTOUM

1898–1899

B Y the end of January Kitchener had concentrated the Egyptian Army upon Berber in an entrenched camp which he formed at Fort Atbara, at the confluence of the Nile and Atbara rivers. He moved up to Berber a brigade of British infantry, which represented the first instalment of the contribution made by the War Office to the campaign. The British contingent, commanded under Kitchener by Major-General W. F. Gatacre,[1] consisted of an infantry division, a brigade of artillery, and a cavalry regiment (21st Lancers) ; and Lord Salisbury asked Kitchener to permit Lord Randolph Churchill's younger boy, Winston, to be seconded to the 21st Lancers for service with the expedition.

Kitchener, who had risen the hard way, was jealous of youthful patricians when they sought to obtain additional privileges by pulling strings ; and although he owed much to the Prime Minister, he rejected Salisbury's request out of hand. But Winston Churchill, with indomitable enterprise, succeeded in persuading the Adjutant-General, Sir Evelyn Wood, to insist upon the right of the War Office to have the last word upon the question of the composition of the British contingent. Wood, therefore, seconded Churchill to the 21st Lancers for service with the expedition, despite Kitchener's expressed wish and intention.

On his arrival in Egypt, Churchill described[2] Gatacre as a man filled with a restless irritability which often left him ' the exhausted victim of his own vitality '. But Kitchener told[3] Cromer (25 January) that Gatacre suited him, and ' that we shall get on first-rate '. Kitchener was himself so irritable during those opening weeks that he quarrelled with almost everyone except Cromer, and set all his staff on edge. Leslie Rundle threatened to resign unless Kitchener would agree to employ the minimum number of officers whom Rundle as well as Cromer believed to be necessary ; and Kitchener had to give way. He was compelled also to cancel an order which he had issued confining newspaper correspondents to the base areas and lines of communications, after John Walter of The Times had appealed to

[1] Major-General Sir William Gatacre, K.C.B., D.S.O. (1843–1906).
[2] The River War, p. 213.   [3] Salisbury Papers, III.

Lord Salisbury. Kitchener was, however, successful in preventing Sir Francis Grenfell from visiting the British troops at Berber.

Internal feuds, which prevented the Khalifa at the last moment from quitting Omdurman, restrained Mahmoud until 10 February from advancing northwards from Metemma with 18,000 men. Mahmoud, therefore, missed his chance of obstructing Kitchener's concentration, but he advanced northwards towards Fort Atbara along the east bank of the Nile.

Cairo buzzed with rumours that Kitchener was ill; but Cromer wrote[1] (5 February) to Salisbury : ' He seems in good spirits. My only fear is his health. I am told that he is nearly blind of one eye and that the other is shaky . . . This may be an exaggeration, for the other soldiers are so frantically jealous that they would welcome any excuse to get him away. He assures me he is quite well.'

After being shelled by gunboats, Mahmoud quitted the Nile (18 March) at Aliab and marched north-east towards Hudi on the Atbara. Forewarned by spies, Kitchener reached Hudi first ; and Mahmoud, after discovering the approximate strength of Kitchener's combined army, changed direction east, and formed an entrenched camp at Nakheila. There with his back to the River Atbara, he awaited Kitchener's assault behind entrenchments which seemed to grow stronger every day, while Kitchener attempted vainly to lure the dervishes into the open.

Kitchener halted his advance at Ras el Hudi, some thirteen miles from Nakheila, and fell a victim there to an astonishing fit of indecision. He spent days trying to make up his mind whether to attack or not ; on 1 April, 1898, he begged Cromer for advice :

' I am rather perplexed by the situation here. Mahmoud remains stationary, and his army is very badly off for supplies, and deserters keep coming in to us, though not in such large numbers as I expected. He is apparently waiting instructions from the Khalifa before advancing or retiring. It seems to be thought by the deserters that, as retirement would be an acknowledgement of fear, he will eventually advance. Here, we are all well off and healthy, with sufficient transport ; fresh bread every second day and fresh meat every day.

' Yesterday I discussed the situation with Gatacre and Hunter. The former was inclined to attack Mahmoud's present position ; the latter to wait here. We should have the great advantage of

[1] Ibid., 111.

ground if Mahmoud will advance ; but if he retires without our attacking him, the opportunity will have been lost of dealing a blow by which future resistance in the Sudan would probably be considerably affected. I have little doubt of the success of our attack on his present entrenched position, although it would probably entail considerable loss . . . I should be glad to learn your views on the subject.'

Devoid of experience as a commander in the field, Cromer referred Kitchener's telegram to Grenfell in Cairo, as well as to Salisbury, in London, who referred it to the War Office, which was much startled. Grenfell advised patience, since Kitchener appeared to be in doubt ; and Cromer was also advised that Her Majesty's Government would in all circumstances support Kitchener, whether he decided to attack or to play for safety.

That oracular advice was of no practical help, and Cromer tele-graphed (2 April) to Kitchener : ' I am disposed to think that you had better not attack for the present, but wait your opportunity for action and allow events to develop.' Before that reply was received, however, Kitchener informed Cromer (3 April) that Hunter had changed his mind, and that Hunter and Gatacre, as well as himself, now unanimously favoured an attack on 6 April. Kitchener added that he would nevertheless postpone action if Cromer should so wish.

Cromer accordingly reversed his advice of 2 April, and begged Kitchener (3 April) to attack. In thanking Cromer (4 April), Kit-chener said that he proposed to be even more cautious than he had originally planned to be, in order to make absolutely sure of success. He had a superstitious dislike of Fridays, but he ordered the attack to go in at dawn on Good Friday, 8 April, in the hope that Mahmoud would not expect to be assaulted on such a sacred day of the Christian year.

At sunset on 7 April the Anglo-Egyptian army bivouacked in mass of brigade squares about three miles from Mahmoud's entrenchment. The great squares stood to arms at about 1 a.m. and plodded steadily forward by starlight until 3.30, when they were deployed in line of battle. The artillery, hauled to the front before first light, opened fire at 6.15 ; and at 7.40, when the bombardment ceased, the bugles sounded the ' General Advance '. Twelve battalions swept forward with bands playing and pipes skirling ; and shouts of ' Remember Gordon ! ' were heard.

With admirable discipline the dervishes held their fire until their enemies were close enough to be mown down ; but the assault was successful at all points, and after forty minutes of hand-to-hand fighting, Mahmoud's camp was stormed. Kitchener then ordered the ' Cease Fire ' to be sounded, and gave the Sudanese permission to loot. He reserved the pick of the loot for himself, and dispatched subsequently to his house in Cairo a mass of swords, spears, chain-mail and similar curios.

While the Sudanese were thus occupied, the other troops came out of the camp by regiments, and grouped themselves around Kitchener in a manner which the press correspondents described as extraordinarily picturesque. They gave him round upon round of applause and called repeatedly for a speech. Kitchener, who was suffering from a headache, resisted for a time ; and when he yielded, the few words which he spoke were drowned in such a renewed storm of cheering that nothing could be heard at all. He raised his hand gravely in acknowledgement, and rode away at the head of his staff with an impassive face.

In later life, Kitchener always insisted that the Battle of the Atbara, and not the Battle of Omdurman, had marked the turning-point in his career. He won the Atbara at a cost of 583 casualties, of which 120 were British. The Queen, Salisbury and Cromer telegraphed their congratulations, and Kitchener assured the Queen that his wounded were being ' carefully attended '. In fact, however, their sufferings were great as a result of the financial stringency which had again tempted Kitchener to economize on his medical services to an extent which public opinion regarded as inhuman.

On the other hand, Kitchener was widely reported to have been quite human for at least a quarter of an hour when he attended the funeral of the five fallen British officers. He assured Cromer that he had given strict orders that prisoners were to be taken, and that enemy wounded were not to be automatically dispatched, as they had been on some previous occasions. In those circumstances, the fact that few wounded prisoners were taken and that more than 3,000 enemy corpses were counted must be attributed less to inhumanity than to the excitement of battle. Walter Kitchener, in a letter[1] to his wife dated 16 April from Berber, stated that he had seen his brother personally attempting to prevent one group of prisoners from being massacred, and rebuking men for wasting ammunition in that way : ' I saw some of them shot a yard off, as they ran forward with bits

[1] Letter in the possession of Miss Madge Kitchener.

of palm held up in their hands. But Tommy was just as bad as the blacks.'

Several hundred unwounded prisoners fell into Kitchener's hands, including the Emir Mahmoud, who was dragged hatless into Kitchener's presence :

" Are you the man Mahmoud ? " Kitchener asked in Arabic.

" Yes. I am Mahmoud. And I am your equal in rank."

" Why did you come here to burn and kill ? "

" I obeyed my orders, as you obey yours."

Mahmoud was a worthy representative, at that moment, of a people whom Gladstone had once described as ' rightly struggling to be free '. After one or two more unsatisfactory exchanges, Kitchener signified with an impatient gesture that the prisoner should be removed. As he was being dragged away Mahmoud shouted that his comrades would be avenged at Omdurman if Kitchener succeeded in getting there ; and those who witnessed the scene felt pity and respect for the dignified and spirited young savage.

Kitchener, however, was unmoved. Condescending to the primitive psychology of the natives, he took Mahmoud with him when he celebrated his victory by a ceremonial parade followed by a march through Berber on 14 April. Dragging chains which were riveted round his ankles, and wearing a halter round his neck, the defeated enemy commander was made to walk, and sometimes run, behind the cavalry. His hands were bound behind his back, and he was driven forward by Sudanese guards who lashed him with whips when he stumbled, while the crowds pelted and reviled him. Kitchener rode on a white horse in triumph.

On that day (14 April) Wolseley wrote Kitchener a note of congratulations which gave food for thought :

'... In common, I may say, with everyone here, I have followed all your moves with intense interest ; and when asked by the Government what answer should be sent to your telegram—" to fight, or not to fight "—my answer was : " You have a first-rate man in command ; trust him, and let him do as he thinks best ! " That was done, and the result was all that the most critical could desire.

' Were I in your place, however, I would not ask such a question. You must be a better judge than Lord Cromer, or me, or anyone else can be. You have your thumb on the pulse of the army you command ; and you can best know what it is capable of. That is my only criticism, and I give it for what it is worth.'

That criticism was much to the point, and it must, furthermore, be conceded that the minute supervision by Cromer to which Kitchener had become habituated was only a minor contributory cause of the mood of doubt and hesitation by which he was visited before the Atbara. Kitchener's indecision anticipated similar moods which ruined his usefulness in council as well as his credit with his colleagues when, in circumstances of incomparably greater difficulty, he was serving as virtual dictator of British military strategy in 1915.

Thoroughness and drive were Kitchener's outstanding attributes, and he had already developed both to an unique pitch of obsessional intensity. Their effective deployment demanded conditions in which the great majority of impersonal factors could be scrupulously weighed and analysed, and in which human factors could be subdued and personally controlled. Throughout almost the whole of his career, Kitchener contrived to avoid conditions—such as service in the War Office—which jeopardized the satisfaction of that demand. It is remarkable that Kitchener was only called upon three times during his life to face critical situations which called primarily for the exercise of that faculty of swift intuitive decision amid a welter of imponderables which has been the characteristic signature of men of action in all ages. The first occasion was at the Atbara. The second was at Paardeberg, in South Africa, in 1900 when he charged like a bull and was defeated. The third was in 1915 when he tried unsuccessfully to make up his mind about Gallipoli, and other difficult problems of high strategy.

After the Battle of the Atbara, Kitchener sent his army into summer quarters along the Nile between Fort Atbara and Berber. Railhead, on his military railway, reached Fort Atbara on 3 July and remained there until the capture of Khartoum. In the meantime, a second British infantry brigade, a cavalry regiment, a brigade of field artillery, and some minor details, including medical units, arrived in readiness for the seasonal rise in the level of the Nile in August, before when no fresh advance was possible by river.

After making arrangements for bringing those reinforcements to the front, Kitchener took a month's leave in Cairo during June. Cromer told[1] Salisbury (11 June) that Kitchener was serenely confident,

[1] Salisbury Papers, III.

' and is inclined to think that his force will be inconveniently large. He assures me that the real dervish opposition is quite broken.'

Early in July, Kitchener concentrated his powerfully reinforced army on Wad Hamed, only sixty miles north of Omdurman. The hypnotized Khalifa made no attempt to interfere ; and on 24 August the invaders began their inexorable march up the west bank of the Nile in a double line of brigades, with the British brigades closest to the river. The front was covered by the cavalry and horse artillery, and each brigade (except the 4th Egyptian) was followed by a battery of field artillery. Baggage and supply columns brought up the rear. Kitchener took with him, on camels and in river transport craft, two months' supply of ammunition and food ; and in reply to protests that his steamers were grossly overloaded, he enjoyed retorting laconically, ' Plimsoll's dead ! '

A flotilla of ten gunboats and five auxiliary transport steamers (Commander Colin Keppel[1]), as well as a force of 2,500 friendly Arab irregulars (Major the Hon. E. J. Montagu-Stuart-Wortley), guarded the east bank of the Nile ; and Kitchener's right flank was protected by the Egyptian Camel Corps (Major R. J. Tudway).

Kitchener had under command 8,200 British and 17,600 Egyptian and Sudanese regular troops. The British division (Gatacre) was organized in two brigades (A. G. Wauchope, C.B., C.M.G., and the Hon. Neville Lyttelton, C.B.), each consisting of four battalions. There were also the 21st Lancers (Colonel R. M. Martin), a brigade of field artillery, and other details. The Egyptian division (Hunter) consisted of four brigades (Hector Macdonald, D.S.O. ; J. G. Maxwell,[2] D.S.O.; D. F. Lewis ; and J. Collinson). The Egyptian cavalry was commanded by Colonel R. G. Broadwood.

The combined Anglo-Egyptian artillery was commanded by Colonel C. J. Long ; and Kitchener had on land forty-four pieces of field artillery and twenty maxims. He had, on the Nile, an additional thirty-six guns and twenty-four maxims. That superiority was overwhelming, and on 30 August Kitchener dispatched a note from Sayol to the Khalifa, under flag of truce, advising the removal of all women and children from Omdurman. He announced that he proposed to destroy the city forthwith by continuous bombardment,

---

[1] Admiral Sir Colin Keppel, G.C.V.O., K.C.I.E., C.B., D.S.O. (1862-1947).

[2] General the Rt. Hon. Sir John Maxwell, P.C., G.C.B., K.C.M.G., C.V.O., D.S.O. (1850-1929).

124

and to overthrow the dervish throne and government 'in order to save the country from your devilish doings and iniquity'.

Two days later, on 1 September, 1898, the Khalifa's great horde, some 60,000 strong, was sighted by British cavalry before noon, advancing rapidly across the plain of Kerreri, only six and a half miles north of Omdurman. Winston Churchill was ordered by his commanding officer to ride back and inform Kitchener at once.

Kitchener was doubly prejudiced against Churchill, who had reached the front in defiance of his wish, and who had then proceeded to combine his military rôle with that of special correspondent for the *Morning Post*. He had never seen Churchill before, and he listened to his account with impassive courtesy. Churchill found the Commander-in-Chief riding impressively alone, two or three horses' lengths ahead of his headquarters staff, with two standard bearers, carrying the Union Jack and the Egyptian flag, riding immediately behind him : 'The heavy moustaches, the queer rolling look of the eyes, the sunburnt and almost purple cheeks and jowl made a vivid manifestation upon the senses.' [1]

The Anglo-Egyptian army was at that moment preparing to camp for the night in a wide defensive arc around the village of Egeiga, on the Nile. As that operation proceeded, Kitchener rode with his staff to the summit of a rocky viewpoint known as Jebel Surgam, some 300 feet above the Nile, where he beheld Khartoum and Omdurman for the first time, as well as the entire dervish army which was advancing to attack him. Then, as a battle appeared imminent, he retired to inspect the defences of the position which he had selected for his camp.

Gunboats had, in the meantime, already started to bombard Omdurman and the forts protecting it. An improved form of high explosive —lyddite—was used on that day for the first time, and great holes were quickly torn in the gleaming white dome—91 feet high—which covered the Mahdi's tomb, and which was Omdurman's most distinctive architectural feature. Breeches were blown at a number of points in the city's walls, and as masses of masonry crashed continuously to the ground in clouds of dust and smoke, western science sounded the knell of the dervish empire.

No battle took place on 1 September, because the Khalifa unexpectedly halted his impetuous advance. Kitchener appreciated that the Khalifa had been goaded to desperation, and he felt confident of

[1] Winston S. Churchill, *My Early Life*, p. 191.

his power to annihilate any dervish assault by night or day. He, therefore, took a calculated risk as night fell. He allowed the main body of his troops to bivouac comfortably in extended order behind the front line of his wide defensive arc which was strongly held and patrolled. He relied upon putting every man into the front line in case of a night attack, but he conserved the energy of his troops by sparing them the extra labour of closing in at night and opening out again in the morning.

Kitchener was at pains to make the Khalifa believe that the Anglo-Egyptians planned to attack during the night : ' The Egeiga villagers were sent out to obtain information in the direction of the enemy's camp, with the idea that we intended a night attack ; and, this coming to the Khalifa's knowledge, he decided to remain in his position ; consequently we passed an undisturbed night . . .'[1] There was a good moon throughout the night and the searchlights of Kitchener's gunboats swept the rising ground continuously, watching for signs of hostile movement. There was none, and at 3.30 a.m. the Anglo-Egyptian invaders stood to arms. They were deployed in close order and in line, with the rear rank standing and the front rank kneeling ; and orders were carried as usual by A.D.C.s and by orderly officers, known as gallopers.

At dawn, mounted patrols which had been sent out earlier reported that a vast body of dervishes was advancing rapidly upon the camp. The Egyptian cavalry, which had been driven back by the enemy, was then ordered to take up a position with the Camel Corps and the horse artillery on the Kerreri ridge, some two miles north-west of Kitchener's right flank. Kitchener was particularly anxious to protect that flank because he entertained doubts about the quality of Lewis's (3rd) Egyptian brigade, which was posted on the extreme north of the defensive perimeter. The remainder of the perimeter was held from north to south by Macdonald and Maxwell (1st and 2nd Egyptian brigades), and by Wauchope and Lyttelton (1st and 2nd British brigades). Collinson's (4th) Egyptian brigade was in reserve, guarding the transport and supplies.

At 6.40 a.m. on 2 September, 1898—the proudest day of Kitchener's life—the shouts of the advancing dervish army became audible. A few minutes later their banners, appearing over the rising ground, began to form a semicircle round the centre and southern flank of the perimeter. At 6.45 a.m., Kitchener's field artillery opened fire at a

[1] Kitchener's despatch, *London Gazette*, 30 September, 1898.

range of 2,800 yards, as 10,000 dervishes under the white banners of Osman Azrak detached themselves from the main body of the enemy and hurled themselves time after time against Kitchener's left and centre.

That attack collapsed at all points after an hour and forty minutes under a concentrated fire of guns, maxims and rifles. The Anglo-Egyptian superiority in weapons was so great that the fight became almost a massacre, and none of the enemy succeeded in approaching within 300 yards of the perimeter of the camp. Many wounded littered the plain, lying singly for the most part, but sometimes in writhing and wriggling heaps. The survivors withdrew shortly after eight o'clock, leaving over 2,000 dead, including Osman Azrak, behind.

Between eight and nine o'clock a desultory battle raged in the Kerreri foothills between the Egyptian mounted troops and some 20,000 dervishes under the dark green banners of the Khalifa's son, Osman Sheikh-Ed-Din. An initial enemy success was quickly converted into a bloody repulse by means of concentrated fire from land-based artillery, and gunboats ; and soon after nine o'clock the mounted troops returned in high spirits to the camp.

The Khalifa, in the meantime, was lying concealed with the flower of his army, about 20,000 strong, behind the western ridge of Jebel Surgam. If the frontal attack had succeeded, he had planned to advance under his black banners, and to clinch Kitchener's annihilation with his own powerful force and, if necessary, with the aid of another 8,000 men who had been posted below the south-eastern ridge of Jebel Surgam to guard his line of communications with Omdurman. He had, however, appreciated, that if his frontal attack were to fail, Kitchener would at once quit the shelter of his camp and march across the plain to Omdurman. In that event, the Khalifa planned to ambush Kitchener from behind Jebel Surgam. He hoped that the advancing Anglo-Egyptians would be destroyed after being caught between his black banners, appearing suddenly from the west, and the green banners returning from the Kerreri hills in the north.

As soon as it became clear that the attack on the camp had been decisively defeated, Kitchener, as the Khalifa had foreseen, decided to march immediately on Omdurman by the shortest route, and to occupy the city while it was still empty, before nightfall, in order to avoid, if possible, costly street fighting. He had some difficulty in restraining his excited native troops from firing at wounded dervishes in front of their positions. As he rode along Maxwell's front he was heard to exclaim repeatedly, in a tone of agonized reproach :

" Cease fire ! Cease fire ! Cease fire ! Oh, what a dreadful waste of ammunition ! "

At 8.30 a.m. the 21st Lancers were ordered to reconnoitre the route between the southern flank of the camp and the city, and to head off any retreating dervishes from Omdurman. Half an hour later, Kitchener ordered his army to quit the camp in echelon formation of brigades from the left, with the British brigades leading. He knew that the Khalifa was lying somewhere concealed ; but he defied him to renew the attack anywhere and at any time. In that way the second phase of the battle began.

The Lancers, after crossing the eastern slope of Jebel Surgam, encountered a body of dervishes concealed in the bed of a dried-up stream. The regiment, which had never been in action before, was eager to win renown ; and the famous charge which followed, for which three Victoria Crosses were awarded, has been inimitably described[1] by Sir Winston Churchill, who took part in it. It was a magnificent folly, which had no effect upon the battle, and which accounted for a high proportion of the day's small total of British casualties.

In the meantime the invaders were fulfilling the Khalifa's hope that their formation would be spoiled as they advanced. Gatacre, suspecting that the Khalifa was concealed somewhere with a reserve army, was anxious that his two British brigades should occupy as quickly as possible the ridge running east from Jebel Surgam to the Nile. He moved them off, therefore, almost together, instead of observing the regular echelon, with the result that a gap opened between Wauchope and Maxwell.

That situation was complicated as a result of Hunter's eagerness to guard against the danger of a dervish assault from the direction of the Kerreri hills. Hunter shared Kitchener's distrust of Lewis's brigade, and he therefore moved Macdonald from his place immediately behind Maxwell to the post previously held by Lewis on the right of the echelon. Macdonald, strengthened by three batteries of field artillery and eight maxims, moved westwards a short way into the desert in order to give Lewis room to pass.

By 9.30 a.m. the two British brigades, which were both eager to be the first into Omdurman, were ascending the ridge which they coveted.

---

[1] *The River War*, II, pp. 282–7 ; and *My Early Life*, pp. 203–10.

Kitchener had just sent them an order to halt for a few moments while the gaps in the rear were eliminated, when the Khalifa seized his opportunity to strike. He left his position on the western slope of Jebel Surgam and attacked Macdonald, who was then separated by a gap of 800 yards from the rest of the army.

Macdonald accordingly faced west and ceased to conform with the movements of the other Egyptian brigades which were wheeling south as fast as possible. He remained firing at the enemy, and he sent a galloper to ask Hunter for support. Hunter galloped to join Macdonald, and sent an A.D.C. to inform Kitchener—whose view was blocked by Jebel Surgam—of what was happening ; and Kitchener at once began to fling his brigades about the battlefield. He issued orders direct to brigade and even battalion commanders ; and in that way, for about an hour, he threw into vivid and dramatic relief the methods which he had used consistently throughout the campaign. He short-circuited his divisional commanders and ignored his staff ; Walter Kitchener told[1] his brother, Chevallier, that from start to finish, Herbert had run ' the show . . . absolutely off his own bat. His staff were not given the chance of remembering the most ordinary details. As a matter of fact, I think he was afraid to trust any of them, and he was just about right.'

The Anglo-Egyptian superiority in weapons was so overwhelming that the Khalifa's second attack was repulsed with as little difficulty as the first. Kitchener's only problem was to bring the full weight of his fire power to bear to the best advantage in the shortest time. He ordered his three leading brigades to change front in order to face the enemy ; and then, as Macdonald became hotly engaged, he ordered Wauchope to double back across the plain and to go into action in the gap between Macdonald and Lewis.

While Wauchope executed that order, Lyttelton and Maxwell advanced to relieve the pressure on Macdonald by attacking the Khalifa's right flank. Kitchener, who was riding with Lyttelton, watched the dervish attack wither under a storm of well-directed fire. The attack was pressed, like the first, with dauntless courage ; but Wauchope's leading battalion had not yet had time to come into action when the surviving dervishes melted away westwards into the desert, leaving thousands of dead behind, including their commander, Yakub, a brother of the Khalifa.

The second phase of the battle was thus ended, and the third began

[1] Letter dated 16 September, 1898, in the possession of Miss Madge Kitchener.

without an instant's pause. At the moment when the Khalifa's second great attack, under black banners, had collapsed at all points, Macdonald suddenly found himself menaced by the green banners of what appeared to be a new army advancing from the north.

The Khalifa's timing had miscarried. He had tried to co-ordinate the attack by his brother, Yakub, from the west, with an attack by his son, Osman Sheikh-Ed-Din, from the Kerreri hills in the north. Had the two attacks been successfully co-ordinated, Macdonald's difficulties would have been increased ; but the dervishes' discipline was less remarkable than their courage, and Macdonald was at no time in serious danger. He was capable and experienced, and he moved his battalions one after the other, as he could spare them, from a line facing west to a line facing north. That right wheel, executed faultlessly, with parade-ground precision, under a heavy but ill-directed fire, was featured prominently at the Staff College for many years.

Wauchope had been ordered by Kitchener to come into action on Macdonald's left. But without waiting to inform Wauchope, Kitchener subsequently ordered the commanding officer of Wauchope's leading battalion (1st Lincolns) to help prolong Wauchope's right. While Lewis enfiladed the dervish attack on Macdonald's left, the Camel Corps and three batteries of artillery came into line between the 1st Lincolns and Macdonald ; and by 11.15 a.m. the last dervish attack had been repulsed as bloodily and decisively as the former two. The mounted troops killed thousands of the fleeing enemy, and turned his defeat into final and irremediable rout.

At 11.30 a.m. Kitchener handed his binoculars to an A.D.C. and remarked to Lyttelton that the enemy had had ' a thorough dusting '. He ordered his brigades to re-form and to renew their interrupted march on Omdurman. After a midday siesta, which lasted an hour and a half, Kitchener mounted a fresh horse at 2 p.m. and rode at the head of Maxwell's brigade, and at the side of its commander, through the suburbs of Omdurman to the great wall of the Khalifa's enclosure, where he appointed Maxwell to the office of Military Governor. A decrepit emir, riding on a donkey, approached Kitchener and then dismounted. He prostrated himself at Kitchener's feet and offered the keys of the city.

The conqueror accepted the keys, and disclaimed any intention of putting women and children to the sword. He said that males also would be spared, if no attempt at resistance was made, and if all arms

130

were surrendered at once. After that merciful proclamation, the streets and walls which had at first appeared deserted, began to swarm with old men, women and boys in a great state of excitement.

Leaving three battalions and two guns to guard that approach, Kitchener rode with one Sudanese battalion and four guns along the north side of the wall towards the river. His movements were covered by gunboats. Penetrating one of the many breaches made in the walls by his howitzers, Kitchener rode south along the line of forts, which had suffered less damage than he expected, and entered the city by its main gateway, whence he followed a straight road to the Khalifa's house and the Mahdi's tomb. Those were occupied as the remainder of the army poured into the town to link up with the advanced elements which Kitchener had accompanied. Guards were placed over the Khalifa's stores and the principal buildings.

Walter Kitchener noted[1] that his brother ' did all he could to get himself shot, and *would not* stop until well after dark.' He wanted to see everything, including the prison which he was almost the first to enter ; and at one moment Kitchener's career was nearly ended by a stray shell from one of the gunboats which killed the Hon. Hubert Howard, special correspondent of *The Times* and of the *New York Herald*. Some sporadic resistance was encountered, and the troops presently killed several hundred dervishes and civilians, after a fusillade of shots had been fired from a window at a bivouac.

Most of the troops bivouacked inside the walls ; but Lyttelton managed to unite his brigade and to march it in line of quarter columns out of the foul and stinking city into the clean night air of the desert. Long after dark Kitchener arrived with Wingate and Hunter at Lyttelton's bivouac, where he allowed himself to be persuaded to lie down at last and rest. Grenadiers were posted as sentries to guard Kitchener, who remarked, as he dropped off to sleep, that he was filled with a deep sense of thankfulness to the Lord of Hosts who had permitted him to achieve the first of his life's major ambitions at an insignificant cost in British blood. Hunter and Wingate, who slept, later, beside Kitchener, sat up for a time composing telegrams.

The victory had been won at the very low cost of 48 killed (including 3 British officers and 25 British other ranks) and 434 wounded. In return, over 11,000 dervish corpses were counted on the battlefield, and several hundreds more were killed in Omdurman. The total of

[1] Letter (16 September) to Mrs. Walter Kitchener, in the possession of Miss Madge Kitchener.

enemy wounded and prisoners was estimated at around 16,000, and many of the wounded died later from neglect. Kitchener informed Cromer by telegram that he had, in addition, some 30,000 female cooks and concubines on his hands ; and he added that he had no occasion for their services in either capacity, and no means of supplying them with food.

The Khalifa, on leaving the stricken field during the early afternoon, had re-entered Omdurman. He made a vain attempt to collect old men and boys for street fighting, and then went to the Mahdi's tomb, where he prayed silently to Allah for some moments under the shattered dome. On leaving the tomb, he mounted a fresh camel and escaped southwards with a small escort. He left the Nile and rode west, in the direction of Kordofan ; and it must be recorded that, despite the cruel tyranny which he had exercised, all his surviving emirs as well as the routed remnants of his army remained faithful to his person and cause during the fourteen months which elapsed before he was hunted down like a wild animal and killed. Gunboats and mounted troops set off southwards immediately in pursuit, but the Khalifa made good his escape to Kordofan. He joined the garrison at El Obeid, and he remained until the last, the indomitable embodiment of the nationalist aspirations of the peoples over whom he had ruled.

Kitchener was careful to inform Queen Victoria (5 September) that he had personally seen all the British wounded laid in barges before being towed by steamers down to a hospital at Abadai which he had caused to be prepared for them. He told her also about an impressive service which he had held on 4 September in Gordon's memory, outside the ruined palace in Khartoum. Representative detachments of officers and men from every British and Egyptian regiment were ferried across the Nile from Omdurman, and after the singing of Gordon's favourite hymn, ' Abide with Me,' Kitchener was so much overcome that he had to ask Hunter to dismiss the parade. His staff were astonished to see his shoulders shaken with sobs and tears coursing down his cheeks. No one, at first, dared to approach him ; but soon after the singing of the National Anthem he became, for a short time, as gentle as a woman. He walked in Gordon's garden and spoke about his admiration for Gordon's character ; about the long years which he had spent in working to avenge his cruel abandonment and death ; and about the gratitude which he felt towards all those who had helped him to redeem England's honour.

132

Queen Victoria was greatly moved by Kitchener's account of that memorial service for Gordon. She noted proudly in her journal, ' Surely, he is avenged ! ' But the Khalifa had escaped, and Kitchener was not yet satisfied. On 6 September, four days after the battle, he issued orders that the Mahdi's tomb should be razed to the ground, and that the bones of Gordon's great enemy should be cast into the Nile.

Gordon's nephew, Major W. S. Gordon, R.E., was entrusted with the execution of that order ; and the Mahdi's skull, which was unusually large and shapely, was saved from destruction and presented to Kitchener as a trophy. Some members of the ' band of boys ' with whom it amused him occasionally to relax, suggested that he should cause the skull to be mounted in silver or gold, and that he should use it as an inkstand or as a drinking-cup.

Kitchener played with that idea and with the skull for a short time ; and he acquired somehow the idea that Napoleon's intestines had found their way from St. Helena to the museum of the College of Surgeons in London. Accordingly, he announced incautiously to some of his staff that he proposed to send the Mahdi's skull to the College of Surgeons with a request that it should be placed on exhibition alongside the guts of Napoleon.

That story of the Mahdi's skull obtained a wide currency ; and it caused, in February, 1899, a great howl of rage against Kitchener, which was compounded, in approximately equal parts, of frothy but sincere sentiment and of jealousy. Radical and intellectual circles[1] hated Kitchener at that time ; the Army was intensely jealous of him ; and he had gone out of his way to insult the Press. For a few weeks, therefore, while unfriendly questions were being asked in Parliament and elsewhere, Kitchener felt extremely uncomfortable.

On 27 February, 1899, Salisbury telegraphed[2] to Cromer : ' The Queen is shocked by the treatment the Mahdi's body has received, and thinks the head ought to be buried. Putting it in a museum, she thinks, will do great harm.' On 2 March, Cromer replied :[3]

' The dead set against Kitchener was sure to come, sooner or later. Apart from the natural reaction, he has not the faculty of making friends. The soldiers are furiously jealous of him, and many

[1] cf. in this connection, Wilfred Scawen Blunt, My Diaries, I, pp. 386, 390–1, 394–5.
[2] Salisbury Papers, 113.   [3] Ibid., 112.

of the newspaper correspondents, whom he took no pains to conciliate, have long been waiting for an opportunity to attack him. He has his faults. No one is more aware of them than myself. But for all that, he is the most able of the English soldiers I have come across in my time. .

'He was quite right in destroying the Mahdi's tomb, but the details of the destruction were obviously open to objection . . .

'Kitchener is himself responsible for the rather unwise course of sending the skull to the College of Surgeons.'

Kitchener's relations with the Press had been bad from the start of the campaign. He made two exceptions among the newspaper correspondents in favour of *The Times* and *The Daily Mail* (Hubert Howard and G. W. Steevens) ; but that favouritism caused trouble ; and he seldom let slip an opportunity of demonstrating the contempt in which he held the profession as a whole. Only a day or two before the Battle of Omdurman he was informed that a group of correspondents had been waiting outside his tent for some time in the belief that he had a statement to make. He let them wait, until he was ready to emerge, and then, as he strode angrily through their midst he made a statement, which consisted only of the words : " Get out of my way, you drunken swabs ! "

In those circumstances the commotion in the British and American Press about Kitchener and the Mahdi's skull was prolonged maliciously for several weeks. It was combined with charges that Kitchener had left all the dervish wounded to die without succour on the battlefield of Omdurman, and that he had personally ordered a massacre of civilians in Omdurman after the battle. Those attacks worried Kitchener, who wrote (7 March, 1899) to the Queen :

'Lord Kitchener is much distressed that Your Majesty should think that the destruction of the Mahdi's tomb, and the disposal of his bones was improperly carried out. He is very sorry that anything he has done should have caused Your Majesty a moment's uneasiness.

'A few days after the battle, I consulted with some native officers of the Sudanese troops, and spoke on the matter with some influential natives here ; and they told me that, although no educated person believed in the Mahdi being anything but an impostor who had attempted to change the Mohammedan religion, . . . some of the soldiers in our ranks still believed in the Mahdi ; and they recommended the destruction of the tomb, and that the bones should be thrown into the Nile, which would entirely dissipate any such belief.

'Nothing in the matter was done in a hurry, but four days after the battle, before I left for Fashoda, I gave the order for the destruction, thinking it was the safest and wisest course ; and this was carried out in my absence. There was no coffin, and when the bones were found the soldiers seemed all astonished, and exclaimed —" By God ! This was not the Mahdi after all he told us ! " They had previously believed that the Mahdi had been translated bodily to heaven.

'When I returned from Fashoda, the Mahdi's skull, in a box, was brought to me, and I did not know what to do with it. I had thought of sending it to the College of Surgeons where, I believe, such things are kept. It has now been buried in a Moslem cemetery.'

Kitchener added that cerebro-spinal meningitis had recently broken out among his Sudanese troops, and that they might have been tempted to think that they were being punished by God for having fought against the Mahdi's successor, the Khalifa, if the conqueror of the Khalifa had not ordered the tomb to be desecrated : 'I am exceedingly fond of my black troops, but I fully know how hot-headed they are, and how quickly an idea may make them act rashly.'

The Queen was as unwilling as the vast majority of her subjects were to find fault with her handsome and glamorous general on the morrow of his glorious victory which had, in Cromer's words,[1] done ' more than appease those sentiments of honour which had been stung to the quick by the events of 1885 '. The Queen, therefore, told Kitchener (24 March, 1899) that while she agreed that the destruction of the tomb had been ' absolutely necessary ', she felt that ' the destruction of the poor body of a man who, whether he was very bad and cruel, after all was a *man* of a *certain* importance . . . savours in the Queen's opinion, too much of the Middle Ages . . . The graves of our own people have been respected, and those of our foes should, in her opinion, also be. However, she is quite satisfied now, as the skull has been buried.'

Kitchener had the skull buried secretly by night in the Moslem

[1] *Modern Egypt*, II, p. 110.

cemetery at Wadi Halfa. He told Cromer that the structure of the tomb had been rendered dangerous by shell-fire and that it ' might have caused loss of life left as it was '. A White Paper[1] issued late in March, 1899, by the Government in an effort to quieten public opinion, printed a letter (1 February) from Kitchener to Cromer denying categorically a number of specific charges of inhumanity. It also contained, in two letters written by Cromer to Salisbury, personal expressions of Cromer's opinion about the two principal charges which had been brought against Kitchener. The first of Cromer's letters (4 March) stated that : ' To the best of my belief, all that was, under the circumstances, possible, was done for the dervish wounded. But the first duty of the medical officers was, naturally, to look after the British and Egyptian wounded.' The second letter (12 March) expressed Cromer's view that : ' under the very exceptional circumstances of the case, both the destruction of the Mahdi's tomb, and the removal of the body elsewhere, were political necessities '.

The plea of political necessity is always suspect ; but Cromer loyally supported his subordinate, and Kitchener, who had become a hero to schoolboys of all ages, was rewarded with a peerage, the Grand Cross of the Bath, the thanks of both Houses of Parliament, and a Parliamentary money grant of thirty thousand pounds. Apart from that grant, the total cost of Kitchener's campaign amounted to only £2,354,000, towards which the British taxpayer contributed £800,000. No increase was, therefore, necessary in the standard rate of British income-tax which stood at eightpence from 1894 until 1900, and was regarded as excessive.

Kitchener boasted to Cromer that he had conquered a country of approximately one million square miles and two million inhabitants at a cost of two pounds, six shillings and sixpence a square mile, and of only one pound, three shillings and threepence a head. Cromer retorted that he had managed to conduct the general direction of a war of some magnitude without increasing his office staff in Cairo by so much as a single clerk. After the victory both men continued to pay the most scrupulous regard to economy, and one story will serve to illustrate Kitchener's difficulties and mordant wit.

A new Sudanese reserve battalion was formed out of screened prisoners taken at Omdurman ; but money was so short that the men

[1] *Egypt No. 1. (1899). Dispatches from Her Majesty's Agent and Consul-General Respecting the Conduct of the British and Egyptian Troops after the Battle of Omdurman.* March, 1899.

had to be clothed in discarded Egyptian uniforms which were so
ragged as to be indecent in some cases. When Kitchener inspected
the battalion for the first time he congratulated its commanding officer,
Charles Ferguson, Grenadier Guards, with such unwonted amiability
that visions of brevet promotion danced before the youthful colonel's
eyes. He seized his chance to tell Kitchener that his men had been
compelled to pay for their own underclothes, and to beg that an
issue of uniforms should be made ; but Kitchener cut him short at
once :

" The fact is, Ferguson, you extravagant young devil, you feed
your men too well ! Can't you see they're bursting out of their
uniforms ? Good day to you ! " and he rode off at speed.

Kitchener, who took the title of Lord Kitchener of Khartoum and
of Aspall, in Suffolk, which had been his mother's home, was well
satisfied with his rewards. Some of his methods had been crude,
but he was particularly delighted by Salisbury's statement in the House
of Lords (8 June, 1899) that his victory had come out ' with absolute
accuracy, like the answer to a scientific calculation '. There was
some opposition in the Commons to the money grant (5 June) and to
the thanks of Parliament (8 June), although the Leader of the Opposition (Sir Henry Campbell-Bannerman) supported both. John Morley,
who voted against the money grant, described at length the ' extraordinary feelings of shock and disgust ' which Kitchener's brutality
had excited in his sensitive mind ; but Kitchener, who was home
at that time on leave and present with Lord Roberts in the Peers'
Gallery, described Morley's speech as ludicrous and puerile. Kitchener's self-confidence had by that time been restored, and when
the Committee divided, the money grant was voted by 399 against 51.
The thanks of Parliament were voted three days later (8 June),
unanimously in the Lords, and by 321 against 20 in the Commons.

CHAPTER 8

RULER OF THE SUDAN

1898-1900

DURING the first week of August, 1898, Kitchener had received, from the Foreign Office, sealed orders which he was directed to open immediately after the capture of Khartoum. He opened them accordingly on 3 September, and found that he was required to take personal command of an expedition up the White Nile in order to bring to a head the issue created by French action and pretensions in the upper Nile valley.

Kitchener's attention was specifically drawn to a speech made by the Foreign Under-Secretary, Sir Edward Grey, in the House of Commons on 28 March, 1895. Grey had stated that the whole length of the Nile valley was a British sphere of influence, and that ' the advance of a French expedition under secret instructions right from the other side of Africa into a territory over which our claims have been known for so long, would be . . . an unfriendly act, and would be so viewed by England '. Despite that warning, however, a French expedition, led by the gallant and intrepid Major Marchand, had started in June, 1896, from the Atlantic coast of French Equatorial Africa, on its perilous journey through unmapped and unexplored country to Fashoda, which was regarded, hydrographically, as the key-point on the upper Nile.

Speculation about that expedition's progress, which had been rife ever since, was ended on 5 September, 1898, three days after the Battle of Omdurman. On that day Kitchener received unimpeachable proof that Marchand had reached Fashoda. A dervish steamer, from a flotilla which the Khalifa had sent to destroy the mysterious intruders, returned to Omdurman to report failure and to ask for reinforcements. The steamer's captain, who did not know that Kitchener had ousted the Khalifa, made his report to the conqueror instead.

On 10 September, therefore, Kitchener left for Fashoda, with Wingate, in a flotilla of five gunboats which carried a detachment of 100 Cameron Highlanders, two Sudanese battalions, a battery of Egyptian artillery and a quantity of maxim guns. Marchand, who had reached Fashoda on 10 July, was short of ammunition and other necessities. He had only seven French officers and 120 Senegalese soldiers, and was wholly at Kitchener's mercy.

The British and French Governments each professed to believe that the other was bluffing ; and the situation was so tense that any false move by Kitchener, or by Marchand, could easily have started a conflagration which the statesmen would have been powerless to control. Kitchener, whose only positive instructions were to meet Marchand and to say or do nothing which could imply a British recognition of the right of any power ' to occupy any part of the Nile Valley ', was fully aware that the issue of peace or war rested at that moment in his hands.

After shooting up a dervish camp on 15 December, Kitchener anchored three days later only 12 miles north of Fashoda. He immediately wrote to Marchand, whom he addressed as ' the chief of the European mission at Fashoda ', to announce that he had overthrown the Khalifa and liberated the Sudan ; and that he had brought a substantial force of British and Egyptian troops to Fashoda.

Marchand's reply, received late that evening, congratulated Kitchener upon his victory. It took leave to inform him that a treaty, signed on 3 September with a local potentate, had placed a considerable extent of territory in the upper Nile valley under French protection, ' subject to ratification by my government '.

On the following morning (19 September), Kitchener steamed to Fashoda, where he saw the French flag flying over the old government buildings. Kitchener had already decided to insist only upon the hoisting of the Egyptian colours, as a symbolic assertion of claims which Egypt had never renounced to sovereignty over the whole of the Sudan. He appreciated that if, as at Khartoum, the British flag had been hoisted as well, the wound to French pride would have been even more galling. He therefore ordered all his British vessels to fly the Egyptian colours ; and he met Marchand wearing the uniform of an Egyptian general, with a tarboosh on his head.

Marchand came aboard Kitchener's gunboat on 19 September and was entertained to lunch. By a happy chance Kitchener and he took an instant liking to each other, and the atmosphere was tense but cordial when they sat down at a small table aft of the cabin to discuss the situation over coffee and liqueurs, when lunch was ended.

Kitchener wrote[1] (21 September) to Cromer : ' I proceeded at once to inform M. Marchand that I was authorized to state that the

[1] *Parliamentary Papers, Egypt*, No. 3 (1898), pp. 3-4.

presence of the French at Fashoda and in the Valley of the Nile was regarded as a direct violation of the rights of Egypt and Great Britain ; and that, in accordance with my instructions, I must protest in the strongest possible terms against their occupation of Fashoda, and their hoisting of the French flag in the dominions of His Highness, the Khedive.'

Marchand stated in reply that, as a soldier, he had to obey orders, and that those orders were precise. Kitchener stated that his orders were equally precise, and that, unlike Marchand, he had at his disposal the necessary force to execute them. He said that he would hate to use force, but that he intended to occupy the whole of the Sudan ; and he offered to place sufficient river transport and supplies at Marchand's disposal to convey his entire party in luxury to Cairo.

Marchand said that if Kitchener were to use force, he and his companions would all die at their posts ; and that war between France and Great Britain would be the inevitable consequence. He said that he could not quit Fashoda without orders from Paris, and he added that he thought that such orders would probably be sent in due course, if Kitchener would exercise patience.

Kitchener then asked : " Do I understand that you are authorized by the French Government to resist Egypt in putting up its flag and re-asserting its authority in its former possessions, such as the Mudirieh of Fashoda ? "

Marchand, after a brief hesitation, admitted that he was in no condition to stop Kitchener from hoisting the Egyptian flag, if that was his intention. Kitchener at once stated that he proposed to hoist the Egyptian colours with all ceremony and without an instant's delay, and that the French colours would be left undisturbed until the interested governments had sorted the matter out by diplomatic means.

A site had already been selected which commanded the river as well as the only road into the interior ; and at 1 p.m. on 19 September the Egyptian flag was duly hoisted to the accompaniment of a salute of twenty-one guns. In his report (21 September) to Cromer, Kitchener expressed ' the highest admiration ' for Marchand's toughness and courage, but he added, ' our general impression was one of astonishment that an attempt should have been made to carry out a project of such magnitude and danger by the despatch of so small and ill-equipped a force which, as their commander remarked to me, was neither in a position to resist a second dervish attack, nor to retire.

Indeed, had our destruction of the Khalifa's power at Omdurman been delayed a fortnight, in all probability he and his companions would have been massacred.'

Kitchener left his artillery, together with one Sudanese battalion, at Fashoda ; and he established a post higher up the river. He sent Marchand a present of wine and other comforts, accompanied by a formal written protest against ' any occupation by France of the countries in the Valley of the Nile '. He obtained easily, from the minor potentate with whom Marchand had concluded a treaty, a written categorical denial that any treaty existed ; and he warned Marchand that ' all transport of munitions of war on the Nile is absolutely prohibited '. Salisbury told[1] Cromer (25 September) that Kitchener's actions, as well as the language which he had used, were endorsed and commended by the Cabinet.

At Cairo, where he received a hero's welcome on 6 October, Kitchener expressed the view that France would presently give way. But the Fashoda crisis was at its height when he landed at Dover on 27 October, 1898. The Press of both countries was using wild and irresponsible language, while statesmen worked hard for a settlement ; and in that mood of excitement and hysteria the British public took Kitchener to its heart. Women in particular were fascinated because he was unmarried and mysterious, and because he seemed so lonely and so stern. Writing from Khartoum (4 December) to his wife, Walter Kitchener said[2] that his brother was ' not in the least swollen-headed ' ; but that he was occasionally liable to ' behave abominably ' through ' shyness '.

Kitchener landed at Dover in a grey lounge suit and was not, in consequence, recognized immediately by the crowd. He was greeted on behalf of the Government by the Under-Secretary for War, George Wyndham, M.P., and on behalf of the Army by Sir William Butler, while a band played, ' See, the conquering hero comes ! ' A civic luncheon followed, at which Kitchener said that the Battle of Omdurman had at last opened the whole of the Nile valley ' to the civilizing influences of commercial enterprise '.

After the luncheon, Kitchener was drawn by special train to London, where Charing Cross station had been beflagged. The official reception committee on the platform included the Princes Francis and Adolphus of Teck ; Prince Christian of Schleswig-Holstein ;

[1] Salisbury Papers, 113.
[2] Letter in the possession of Miss Madge Kitchener.

Lords Roberts[1] and Wolseley ; and Sir Evelyn Wood. Outside the station the police had difficulty in controlling the enthusiasm of the crowds which cheered Kitchener as he drove to 17, Belgrave Square to stay with Pandeli Ralli. *The Times* commented (28 October) : ' No incident of recent times, not even the arrival of Lord Beaconsfield and Lord Salisbury after the Berlin Conference, has elicited such a remarkable demonstration of popular feeling.'

After staying at Hatfield with the Prime Minister, who confirmed that he would be Governor-General of the Sudan as well as Commander-in-Chief of the Egyptian Army, Kitchener went up to Balmoral to stay with the Queen. She found him ' very agreeable and full of conversation ' ; but Arthur Balfour, who was a fellow-guest both at Hatfield and Balmoral, was more critical. He told Lady Elcho (2 November) that after helping Kitchener with some speeches that he had to make, he found it hard to make up his mind about the nation's idol : ' He possesses, without doubt, boundless courage and resolution. How far he could adapt himself to wholly different and perhaps larger problems than those with which he has been dealing, I do not feel confident. He seems to have a profound contempt for every soldier except himself, which, though not an amiable trait, does not make me think less of his brains.'

After a visit to the Gaiety Theatre on 3 November, when the whole house rose and gave him a standing ovation, Kitchener drove at 12.30 p.m. on 4 November to Guildhall. There, in the presence of 3,000 spectators, the conqueror of the Sudan was presented with the Freedom of the City of London, together with a costly but tasteless and barbaric sword of honour. The hilt, made of 18-carat gold, was embellished with crudely-carved figures of Justice, Britannia and the British Lion. Kitchener's monogram, K. K., was picked out in diamonds and rubies upon both sides. The blade was of steel, damascened with gold ; and the scabbard was encircled with massive gold bands on which Kitchener's arms as well as the arms of the City of London and the names of all Kitchener's victories were emblazoned. The City Chamberlain spoke at some length, and when he had finished, Lord Edward Cecil, who was one of Kitchener's three A.D.C.s, unbuckled the hero's ivory-hilted sword and substituted the coruscating gift of the wealthiest city in the world.

That afternoon, the French Ambassador called upon Lord Salisbury

[1] Field-Marshal Earl Roberts of Kandahar, V.C., K.G., K.P., P.C., G.C.B., O.M., G.C.S.I., G.C.I.E. (1832–1914).

to announce that Major Marchand had been ordered to quit Fashoda. The French had chosen their ground too imprudently, and without first making sure of Russian and other support. Good sense, therefore, prevailed, and a convention signed a few weeks later (21 March, 1899) helped to pave the way for the *entente cordiale*. The watershed between the Nile and Congo rivers was declared to be the boundary between French and British spheres of influence ; and every effort was made to ease the humiliation of that French retreat. Marchand ceased forthwith to be described as a representative of France ; he became instead a bold explorer and a standard-bearer of European civilization. In return, the name Fashoda was expunged from the map, so that Frenchmen should never have occasion to recall it. The name Kodok was substituted ; and it has remained unchanged ever since.

That evening, in the company of the leaders of the nation's life in every field, Kitchener was entertained by the Lord Mayor at a State banquet in the Mansion House. The Duke of Cambridge was present, and Lord Rosebery made a felicitous speech. But the speech of the evening was made by the Prime Minister, who proposed Kitchener's health. Lord Salisbury praised Kitchener as the most economical of all the great captains of history ; and he said that he had an important announcement to make. The Fashoda crisis was ended. The French Government had decided to withdraw. After a prolonged outburst of cheering and laughter the Prime Minister generously attributed ' that gratifying and, to some extent, unexpected news ' to ' the chivalrous character and diplomatic talents ' which Kitchener had displayed in a situation of extreme delicacy and responsibility.

In reply, Kitchener made no reference whatever to that dramatic announcement. He was too inexperienced a speaker to risk any departure from the notes which Balfour had helped him to prepare. But he concluded amid thunderous applause : " We have freed the vast territories of the Sudan from the most cruel tyranny the world has ever known [cheers]. We have hoisted the British and Egyptian flags at Khartoum [loud cheers]. Never, I hope, will they be hauled down again [loud and prolonged cheers, which lasted for several minutes]."

The Queen wrote to congratulate Kitchener upon that speech which he had told her he dreaded having to make ; and the five weeks which followed were devoted to feastings and celebrations.

At Chatham, Woolwich and Aldershot (8, 17 and 18 November) the soldiers made amends for their former jealousy of Kitchener, who was, however, even more impressed by the academic honours which were accorded him at Cambridge and at Edinburgh. He much regretted having to postpone his visit to Oxford owing to pressure upon his time.

At Cambridge, on 24 November, Kitchener received an honorary degree as well as the freedom of the town. He visited the Union Society and addressed a few words to the undergraduates who rose in a body to sing, " For he's a jolly good fellow ! " Undergraduate imperialism was uninhibited at that period, and bonfires blazed all night in Kitchener's honour on Market Hill and in most of the college quadrangles. A very few unpopular members of the University who chose that moment to speak perversely against the slaughter of dervishes were flung fully clothed into the icy river, while fireworks cascaded in the sky.

Kitchener went on to Sandringham to stay with the Prince of Wales ; and from Sandringham he went north (28 November) to stay with Lord Rosebery and to receive an honorary degree from Edinburgh University as well as the freedom of the Scottish capital. He chose that moment to launch an appeal (29 November) for a fund of one hundred thousand pounds to found a college in Gordon's memory at Khartoum. He said : " We shall have to give justice to the people. We shall have to organize a police force. There is a great civilizing power in the policeman [laughter and cheers] . . . I should wish to see the English race step in and give what the government cannot provide—namely, education to the children of these poor people."

Salisbury had written[1] (21 November) to explain to Kitchener that no money was available from the public purse for education because the interests of European bondholders were paramount, and were protected by treaties. He advised Kitchener, therefore, to appeal to rich men who had made money in Egypt, and he added :

' The reconciliation of the races which inhabit the Nile Valley to a Government that, in its principles and in its methods must be essentially Western . . . will tax the resources of the present generation of Englishmen, and of those who come after for many years . . .
' The only method by which that reconciliation can be attained is

[1] Salisbury Papers, 113.

'DREAMING TRUE'

PUNCH, December 10, 1898

to give to the races whom you have conquered access to the literature and knowledge of Europe.

' Your scheme, therefore, for establishing a machinery by which European knowledge can be brought to the inhabitants of the Valley of the Nile, is not only in itself wholly admirable ; but it represents the only policy by which the civilizing mission of this country can effectively be accomplished.'

Kitchener accordingly appealed to private charity in a letter (30 November) to *The Times*, which stated that ' those who have conquered are called upon to civilize. In fact, the work interrupted since the death of Gordon must be resumed.' He obtained large sums from many rich men, including Lord Rothschild, Lord Revelstoke, Lord Hillingdon, Sir Ernest Cassel and Hugh Colin Smith ; and over £111,000 had been subscribed before the end of the year. A characteristic passion for ponderable detail caused Kitchener to request the Fund's trustees to estimate the monetary value of his name, in comparison with that of other names, when used in different kinds of charitable appeals.

In summoning the Sudanese to support Kitchener's educational experiment, Rudyard Kipling wrote (8 December, 1898) :

" Go, and carry your shoes in your hand, and bow your head on your breast ;
For he who did not slay you in sport—he will not teach you in jest."

It has, however, to be recorded that Kitchener found it impossible in practice to take any genuine interest either in the Gordon College or in education. He wanted to do his duty, but he was concerned about governing and not about educating the Sudanese. He needed a supply of reliable native clerks ; and a small primary school, and a small training centre for teachers, which were both opened in 1900, answered his limited and immediate purpose well enough. They developed within two generations into an independent university ; but Kitchener never rose to the height of the generous argument which Lord Salisbury had used ; and as early as 19 May, 1899, Cromer reported[1] regretfully to Salisbury that Kitchener had become ' especially bored with his own creation—the Gordon College—at which I am not at all surprised '.

[1] Salisbury Papers, 112.

Kitchener left England on 7 December, 1898, after a final visit to Windsor, where he thanked the Queen for sponsoring his appeal. She gave him a gold cigarette-case with a ruby clasp, as he hurried off to Cardiff in order to receive the freedom of that city. With characteristic directness he let it be known that, in future, if cities should continue to express a wish to enrol him as an honorary freeman, he would have little use for fancy caskets or jewelled swords. He said that he needed plate, furniture and pictures, which he was too poor to buy, for a house with a park surrounding it which he hoped ultimately to acquire as an appropriate background to the dignities which his sword had won.

Before he left England, Kitchener complained strongly to Lord Salisbury about the terms upon which Cromer proposed that he should govern the Sudan. Cromer had asked that Kitchener should be forbidden to pass any law, or to spend any sums of one hundred pounds or more, without previous authority ; but Kitchener declined to accept the government on those terms. Salisbury told[1] Cromer (9 December, 1898) that Kitchener insisted 'that the Governor-General of the Sudan is to govern, and is to spend the money he has'. Kitchener had been exasperated by Cromer's control in the past, because it had been exercised through subordinates ; and Salisbury directed Cromer to give Kitchener his head in future, subject to a right on Cromer's part to alter or reverse any of Kitchener's actions. Salisbury warned Cromer that 'too great a centralization' was 'exposed to that mania for paper-piling which is the endemic pest of British departments . . . and . . . involves endless temptations to pedantry and circumlocution when an ordinary official is exposed to them'.

After staying a few days in Cairo with Cromer, who gave him avuncular advice, Kitchener returned (28 December) to Khartoum in a mood of prickly impatience and overweening self-confidence. He had made up his mind either to quit or to be supreme in the Sudan ; and the rigorous autocracy which he exercised provoked unrest throughout the country which he governed and mutiny in the army which he commanded.

The exalted mood which visited Kitchener after the Battle of Omdurman was well illustrated in a chance remark which Wingate recorded in his diary[2] as early as 26 September, 1898. Lady Cromer was then dying of cancer, and Cromer was reported to have said that

[1] Ibid., 113.
[2] In the possession of Sir Ronald Wingate, Bt., C.M.G., C.I.E.

he would lose all interest in Egypt if she were to die : " In that case," Kitchener coolly observed, " Cromer will quit, and I shall probably be appointed in his place."

Lady Cromer died on 16 October, 1898. Cromer, in reply to Kitchener's letter of sympathy, said that he meant to continue his work for Egypt and the Sudan. He added that he intended always to be ' a true friend' to Kitchener ; and he tried in his own way to make that promise good. He visited Khartoum on 4 January to lay the foundation-stone of the Gordon Memorial College ; and he told an assembly of Sudanese notables that they must look for justice neither to Cairo nor to London, but to Kitchener alone.

On 19 January, 1899, the British and Egyptian Governments signed an agreement which established an Anglo-Egyptian condominium over the Sudan. That hybrid arrangement, which lasted for over half a century, gave Great Britain a virtual trusteeship, based upon a right of conquest, which proved extraordinarily successful although without precedent in international law. On that day, Cromer, with all proper apologies, sent Kitchener a private letter of advice. He begged him to guard a sense of proportion ; to cease being jealous and secretive ; and to encourage his subordinates ' to speak up and tell you when they do not agree with you. They are all far too much inclined to be frightened of you.'

Kitchener was no longer willing either to consult Cromer or to keep him fully informed ; and his rough-and-ready methods caused increasing consternation in Cairo. As early as 21 November, while he was still being dined and wined in England, he had privately ordered work to be begun on rebuilding Khartoum, starting with the palace ; and he directed Wingate (26 January) to ' loot like blazes. I want any quantity of marble stairs, marble pavings, iron railings, looking-glasses and fittings ; doors, windows, furniture of all sorts.'

By the first week of February, 1899, five thousand men were being employed on the task of rebuilding Khartoum ; and the palace and government offices were beginning to arise out of the surrounding rubble. New roads and streets were laid out on a military plan, and Kitchener ordered seven thousand trees to be planted to give shade to the people. To Anglo-Egyptian officials, conditioned to frugality, such lavishness was astonishing ; but Cromer wrote kindly (9 February) to Kitchener : ' Don't be alarmed about your finance ... When you can lay the whole matter before me, I will do my best to help. Gorst is most reasonable and conciliatory. *Treat him tenderly*.'

148

Kitchener was not in the habit of treating people tenderly ; and he loathed Sir Eldon Gorst, who had recently succeeded Palmer as financial adviser. He was determined to allow nothing to stand in his way, and he declined categorically to account in detail for the inadequate annual subvention of £E.350,000 which had been allotted to the Sudan. He never consulted Cromer ; and he kept repeating to his staff : " Don't dare to quote regulations to me ! They are made for the guidance of fools." He constantly diverted funds on his personal initiative and without telling anyone, from one specified purpose to another ; and he forbade Government auditors from Cairo to visit Khartoum.

The buildings which sprang up in Kitchener's capital bore little relation to previous official sketches. There were no contractors, detailed plans, specifications or estimates. It became well known throughout the Sudan that no close inquiry would be permitted into means, so long as Kitchener's ends were attained with the maximum speed and the minimum expense or publicity ; and, in those circumstances, Cromer's letters to Salisbury sounded an increasingly critical note.

' Kitchener's methods ', Cromer wrote[1] (14 January, 1899), ' are perhaps a little more masterful and peremptory than is usual in dealing with civil affairs . . . I went through all his fiscal measures with him. His ideas are reasonable enough. . . . I have got Kitchener to relax his leave rules in favour of the English officers. It is an important point as everything depends on them, and they are all so terrified of their Chief that they do not dare to state their own grievance.'

The first governors and inspectors of Sudanese provinces were all British officers attached to the Egyptian Army. But Kitchener took immediate steps to recruit, from the public schools and universities, young Englishmen of outstanding character, excellent health and good all-round abilities to form the nucleus of what became a model civil service. He told[2] them not to trust in laws, regulations or proclamations, which could effect little : ' It is to the individual action of British officers, working independently, but with a common purpose, on the individual natives whose confidence they have gained, that we must look for the moral and industrial regeneration of the Sudan.' Kitchener added : ' All insubordination must be promptly and severely repressed. At the same time, a paternal spirit of correction

[1] Salisbury Papers, 112.
[2] *Parliamentary Papers, Egypt*, No. 1 (1900), pp. 55-7.

for offences should be your aim in your relations with the people, and clemency should be shown in dealing with first offences, especially when such may be the result of ignorance, or are openly acknowledged. In the latter case they should be more than half-pardoned in order to induce truthfulness.'

Kitchener ordered his governors of provinces to respect the Mahommedan religion, while repressing unorthodox fanaticism; and to discountenance slavery, without interfering with existing conditions ' as long as service is willingly rendered by servants to masters'.

On 10 February, 1899, Cromer told[1] Lord Salisbury: 'My Sirdar's very drastic methods of dealing with civil affairs are a never-failing source of amusement to me. The other day I told him that land speculators were sending money to the Greeks in the Sudan in order to make purchases, and that some little care was necessary, as these men at present had no legal means for acquiring a valid title. He replied that he abounded in my view, and would I like him to expel every Greek from the country who bought or sold anything without his consent.

'... I endeavour to impress on him that if he tries to manage not only the public affairs but also the private business of all his new subjects—after the Napoleon and Frederick the Great system—he will find he has far more to do than he can get through. That is rather his weakness.'

Kitchener resented criticism, and Cromer wrote a week later (18 February): 'I am rather concerned about my Sirdar. He writes that "the work is somewhat beyond him"—which I feel is the truth. He does not understand civil government, and, moreover, he is such a terrible hand at quarrelling with everyone, except myself. However, the present system must have a fair trial.'

Kitchener's momentary depression was caused by the outcry which had arisen about the Mahdi's skull; but Cromer continued to complain. Trouble broke out in the army, and on 21 March Cromer telegraphed[1] to Salisbury: 'I have ascertained the principal cause of disaffection in the army. Money was provided in the estimates for continuing the payment of extra allowances to all ranks serving in the Sudan. Sirdar, without reference to any authority at Cairo, abolished those allowances, in order to apply money to other objects! I consider this step most injudicious, especially as the pay of junior English officers has recently, and very wisely, been increased.'

[1] Salisbury Papers, 112.

Cromer added that he had rebuked Kitchener for taking a measure of such importance ' without my consent ' ; and that he had ' expressed to the Sirdar my strong opinion that the order should be at once cancelled '. But Kitchener refused to cancel the order, on the ground that such an unprecedented display of weakness would be bad for discipline. He consented to make a few concessions, but the major contrast between the increase of pay which had been granted to junior English officers, and the cut which Kitchener had imposed in the field allowances paid to their Egyptian comrades serving at their side in the same army, created a fierce undercurrent of discontent.

A month later (22 April, 1899) Cromer had further occasion to complain about Kitchener : ' There is ', he told[1] Lord Salisbury, ' a state bordering on famine at Omdurman, and further south, due to the Sirdar not allowing sufficient scope to private trade. He is, I fear, terribly bureaucratic, and does not see with sufficient clearness the difference between governing a country and commanding a regiment.' Cromer asked Kitchener to come to Cairo for a talk, and Kitchener came, grudgingly, during the second week of May. He flatly refused to alter his trade policy, on the ground that the southern Sudan was still a theatre of military operations.

Kitchener was preparing an expedition into the southern Sudan in order to hunt down and kill the Khalifa, who was still at large. Kitchener proposed to lead that expedition himself, in September, after he had enjoyed a spell of summer leave in England ; and he told Cromer that famine conditions suited his policy well, because they would assist the hunt by depriving the Khalifa of local support. Cromer begged Kitchener to remember that he was a civilized Christian ruler who had to deal with human beings, and not with blocks of wood ; and he told[1] Salisbury (19 May) that Kitchener had, thereupon, exploded. Kitchener had exclaimed that he had ' had about enough of the Sudan ' ; that he needed rest ; and that he would presently seek employment in India. Cromer admitted to Salisbury that Kitchener would be difficult to replace.

Without altering his trade policy, which caused great suffering and hardship, Kitchener took two months' leave in England during June and July. He stayed with the Duke of Connaught, who had already visited him in Khartoum, as well as with Lord Salisbury, the Duke of Portland and Lady Cowper. He crossed to Ireland to discuss with Lord Roberts, who was serving as Commander-in-Chief at the

[1] Ibid.

Curragh, the possibility of being employed in South Africa in the probable event of an outbreak of war with the Boer republics, and in the possible event of Roberts being entrusted with the chief command. He also called at the India Office to inquire about the possibility (which he had discussed some time previously with Curzon) of being appointed to the post of military member of the Viceroy of India's council. Both conversations were satisfactory.

Kitchener saw much of the Prime Minister's son and daughter-in-law, Lord and Lady Cranborne ; and he cultivated close personal relations with the Duke of York (King George V), who dined with him several times. The Duke and Kitchener were often seen taking their early morning ride together in Rotten Row ; and H.R.H. accompanied Kitchener to Oxford on 21 June, when an honorary degree was conferred upon Kitchener.

Kitchener was less successful in impressing Lord Esher, the subtle and extremely influential secretary of the Office of Works. He called on Esher on 26 July to request help in furnishing his palace at Khartoum, and Esher noted[1] : ' Kitchener is not attractive. None of the men who served with him were attracted to him. I should doubt anyone loving him. It is the coarseness of his fibre, which appears in his face to a marked degree. The eyes are good—but the mouth and jaw and skin are those of a rough private . . . '

In such matters, Esher wrote as a connoisseur, and he added that Cromer shared ' the personal coolness towards Kitchener which appears to be felt by everyone who comes in contact with him '. But Kitchener did not ask to be loved ; he wooed nothing except opportunity ; and he was perfectly content so long as his strength was feared and admired.

Soon after his return to Khartoum, Kitchener led an expedition, 9,000 strong, into Kordofan, in an attempt to hunt down the Khalifa. A previous expedition, led by Walter Kitchener in January, had failed ; and Kitchener himself was unsuccessful during September and October. He enjoyed the hunt, however, and he went to Cairo at the beginning of November to discuss finance with Lord Cromer in a refreshed and exhilarated mood. He wrote[2] (6 November) to Lady Cranborne : ' Lord Cromer . . . gives me no trouble at all. Such a blessing, when one has one's hands full.'

A few days later, the Khalifa's movements were betrayed to

[1] *Journals and Letters*, I, p. 238.
[2] Hatfield MSS.

Kitchener by spies. Reginald Wingate was despatched from Khartoum on 19 November, and he ran his quarry to earth five days later some 200 miles south of Khartoum. The dervishes attacked with their usual reckless courage, and were mown down like running partridges by concentrated rifle and machine-gun fire. When all was over, the Khalifa and his principal emirs were found dead together in a cluster upon the field with their faces turned towards Mecca. They died somewhat after the manner of the chosen band of Thebes, and Kitchener, who often neglected to date his letters, wrote[1] to Lady Cranborne : ' Well, at last we have settled matters out here, and the Khalifa is done for. Wingate's column had the luck to come on them much as I expected, and the Khalifa and his principal emirs died game, though his men made rather a poor fight of it.'

In that way Mahdism was finally destroyed in the Sudan, six weeks after the outbreak of the Boer War in South Africa, and one month before Kitchener himself sailed for South Africa to wage war upon what was at that time popularly known as Krugerism. Barely a month after Kitchener had left, the discontent which his harsh rule had provoked flared into open mutiny at Omdurman.

On 28 January, 1900, the 14th Sudanese battalion arrested all its British officers, broke into the guard-room, and seized 300 rounds of ammunition per man. It then put the British officers' quarters into a state of defence and defied all authority. Reginald Wingate, who had just succeeded Kitchener as Governor-General of the Sudan and as Commander-in-Chief, handled that most serious situation with great prudence and success. He refused the offer of a British division to suppress the mutiny ; and he induced the men to return to their duty by the promise of an amnesty. The seven native officer ringleaders, whom Kitchener would certainly have hanged, were merely cashiered, and paraded in front of the army while their badges and insignia of rank were ceremoniously torn from their uniforms which they had dishonoured.

The mutinous battalion was mostly composed of ignorant former prisoners who had fought on the Khalifa's side at Omdurman. Their Egyptian officers, provoked by the cut which Kitchener had imposed upon their field allowances, had told their men that the Egyptian Army was about to be ordered to South Africa to be slaughtered by the formidable Boers. Cromer informed[2] Salisbury (9 February 1900) that the outbreak had been caused by the loss of prestige

[1] Hatfield MSS.   [2] Salisbury Papers, 112.

occasioned by the British defeats in the Transvaal ; by the attitude of the Khedive, and of the native Press ; and by 'the very harsh rule of the late Sirdar'. He said that he had never been able to make Kitchener understand the gravity of the discontent which he had provoked among his Egyptian officers by his unsympathetic handling of their grievances on the subject of pensions and allowances : 'His sole idea was to rule by inspiring fear, and the fear he inspired was such that it is conceivable that the present trouble would not have occurred had he remained in the Sudan.'

Later (27 April and 12 June, 1900), Cromer reported[1] that the mutineers had not intended to kill their British officers, 'except perhaps Kitchener', but to use them as hostages. He had, he said, found serious defects in 'the civil schooling' which officers and officials had received under Kitchener : 'When Kitchener left, he said something to me about coming back here. I did not encourage the idea, and, from what I now learn, I am persuaded that his return is quite out of the question. He would not be able to hold the Sudan without a large British Force.'

Kitchener, in the meantime, was in South Africa, fighting Dutch racialism which had become incarnate in the person of Paul Kruger, President and virtual dictator of the Transvaal. The clash between Krugerism and British imperialism had blazed into war on 11 October, 1899.

The Boer republics of the Transvaal and the Orange Free State had come into existence as a result of the Great Trek in 1836. Many thousands of Boers had then migrated into the interior from the Cape of Good Hope which Great Britain had acquired in 1815. The trekking Boers had hoped in that way to preserve their backward-looking, patriarchal form of society from British interference and control ; but the remote Transvaal could barely maintain its existence against the hostile and warlike native races which surrounded it. Disraeli, accordingly, annexed the Transvaal (1877), and dispatched an army to crush the Zulus (1879), who were its most dangerous local enemies.

Gladstone in 1881 restored the independence of the Transvaal ; but he waited to do so until the Boers had risen in revolt and inflicted a humiliating defeat upon the British at the Battle of Majuba Hill. He thereby embittered British opinion in South Africa and deluded the Boers into believing that they could do with the British as they

[1] Salisbury Papers, 112.

pleased. That delusion was a contributory cause of the war of 1899–1902.

Gold had been mined in the Transvaal for many years, but the discovery in 1886 of the banket reef of the Witwatersrand changed the character of the republic in the most dramatic manner. An isolated community of some 20,000 farming families spread over a country of about the size of France was swamped by foreign-born immigrants— mostly British—who considerably outnumbered the Boers by 1896. Many thousands of adventurers flocked to Johannesburg and to the diamond metropolis of Kimberley ; and the annual revenue of the Transvaal rose from £200,000 in 1886 to over four millions in 1899.

The conflict between the old and the new ways of life appeared to be almost irreconcilable. The woman-hating multi-millionaire, Cecil Rhodes, who focused the aspirations of the capitalists, dreamed of securing world dominion for the Anglo-Saxon race and the English-speaking peoples. He used his immense wealth and power to forward his plan of effecting a sub-continental federation of the two ruling white races, and he enjoyed the support of a majority of the Dutch in Cape Colony, as well as that of the leading Dutch in the Orange Free State.

Those plans and dreams were anathema to Paul Kruger, who fought stubbornly and truculently to preserve the narrow Old Testament way of life to which the Boer farmers of the Transvaal were wedded. He denied civil rights to the foreigners, known as outlanders, who flocked to his country, while making a shrewd use of the wealth with which they enriched it. He embarked on a great programme of railway development, and proceeded to arm his people on the most modern lines. He conceived the ambition of transforming the Transvaal into a South African Prussia ; and he dreamed of annexing and imposing Dutch racialism upon the Cape Colony and Natal, and of forming a Republican United States of South Africa. He passed repressive laws against public meetings and the Press. In those cir- cumstances, the leading capitalist outlanders, after failing to come to terms with Kruger, conspired to overthrow Kruger's Government by revolution in order to free themselves from the many difficulties which that government threw constantly in their way.

Joseph Chamberlain, the British Colonial Secretary, knew that a rebellion was planned. He regarded it as inevitable ; but he did not know that Cecil Rhodes, the Prime Minister of Cape Colony, had promised to assist it from outside by dispatching the administrator of Rhodesia, Dr. Jameson,[1] across the border at the head of 500 troopers armed with field pieces and maxim guns. Jameson lost patience when the capitalist conspirators inside the Transvaal failed to formulate their plans for rebellion on time. He marched, therefore, prematurely against the urgent advice of Rhodes, on 29 December, 1895, and was surrounded in the outskirts of Johannesburg on 2 January, 1896. He surrendered on condition that the lives of the invaders should be spared.

The scandal reverberated around the world. Rhodes, who was implicated beyond hope of whitewash, resigned his office as Prime Minister of the Cape, and forfeited overnight the goodwill of the Dutch in Cape Colony and the Orange Free State. Summoned to London to face a Parliamentary Committee of Inquiry, he confessed to all his friends that he had been a naughty boy. But the telegram of congratulations which the young German Emperor sent to Kruger, and the violence of the abuse which was heaped on the British name throughout the world, helped to unite the British people and Empire in a convulsive transport of patriotic ardour and excitement. Elsewhere, except in Italy, Hungary, Greece, and what *The Times* called ' the best elements of American society ', Great Britain appeared to have few friends left in the world.

The reprehensible Jameson raid might have been justified on grounds of expediency if it had met with instant and resounding success. Its catastrophic failure united all the South African Dutch against the British. The Orange Free State concluded an intimate offensive and defensive alliance with the Transvaal ; and Kruger proceeded to enlist foreign aid on an entirely new scale ; to arm his people to the teeth with the most modern weapons ; and to prepare openly for a war of conquest and independence.

All attempts to achieve a settlement broke down. Some 22,000 British subjects in the Transvaal, who were being taxed without representation and subjected to other humiliations, petitioned the Queen for redress. Sir Alfred Milner,[2] who was sent to South Africa as British High Commissioner, met the Presidents of the two Boer republics in Bloemfontein without result. He declared that the cause of strife lay not in British policy but in Krugerism ; and on 9 October, 1899, Kruger's patience was exhausted. He issued an ultimatum demanding the withdrawal of all British troops from the

[1] Rt. Hon. Sir Leander Jameson, Bt., P.C., C.B. (1853–1917).
[2] Viscount Milner, K.G., G.C.B., G.C.M.G. (1854–1925).

frontiers ; the evacuation from South Africa of all troops landed since
1 June, 1899 ; and the immediate recall of all reinforcements on the
high seas. Hostilities began on 11 October, when that ultimatum
expired.

The British had planned a victorious advance through the Orange
Free State to Pretoria ; but a series of disasters quickly made them the
laughing-stock of a jealous and bitterly hostile world. In the east,
Sir George White, commanding in Natal, was besieged in Ladysmith.
In the west, Baden-Powell was besieged in Mafeking ; while Cecil
Rhodes, with many senior executives of the great De Beers combine,
was surrounded in his diamond metropolis of Kimberley. Crossing
the Orange River at two points, Boer commandos invaded Cape
Colony in an attempt to raise that country against the British.

In one black week of December the Boers inflicted three serious
defeats on their arrogantly self-confident but ill-prepared and bewildered adversaries. On 9 December, Lord Methuen, advancing
with 8,000 men to the relief of Kimberley, was defeated at Magersfontein on the Modder River. On the following day, Sir William
Gatacre, who had been sent with 4,000 men to clear the Boers out
of Cape Colony, was defeated at Stormberg. Five days later (15
December), Sir Redvers Buller, who had landed at Durban a month
earlier to assume supreme command, attacked the Boer positions at
Colenso, on the Tugela River, with 20,000 men, in an attempt to
raise the siege of Ladysmith. He was bloodily repulsed, and so
shaken that he advised the War Office to abandon Ladysmith to its
fate, and warned Sir George White, in Ladysmith, to burn his cyphers
in preparation for surrender.

Sir George White indignantly repudiated all idea of surrender ;
and the Cabinet lost all confidence in the bloated and incompetent
Buller. Lord Roberts told Lansdowne, the Secretary for War, that
the war would be lost unless a radical change were made immediately
in the Supreme Command ; and he offered to go out to South Africa
in order to take Buller's place. But Salisbury (aged 69) objected that
Roberts (aged 67), whose only son had been mortally wounded at
Colenso, was too old.

On 17 December, Salisbury was persuaded to agree to Buller's
supersession by Roberts, on condition that Kitchener, who was aged
49, should accompany Roberts as Chief of Staff. On 18 December,
accordingly, the announcement that Roberts of Kandahar and Kitchener of Khartoum were proceeding immediately to South Africa to

restore a deteriorating situation was received at home and throughout the Empire with extraordinary enthusiasm. Cromer telegraphed[1] (21 and 22 December) to Salisbury that Kitchener was ' evidently rather nervous lest Roberts's age and the loss of his son may not have affected him ' ; and that Kitchener, therefore, wished to be given ' local rank senior to the other generals, of whom I gathered he had a somewhat poor opinion ... He seemed to attach so much importance to the point that I thought I had better let you know.'

Jealousy of Kitchener was still far too strong to permit of such local rank being accorded ; but Roberts agreed that Kitchener should serve, in effect, as his second-in-command. The British Army at that period was more like a social institution than a fighting machine ; and in the absence of any scientific system of staff organization, Kitchener's appointment as Chief of Staff implied no specific duties and called for no specialized training. Kitchener was employed, accordingly, less to work out plans and convey orders, than as the right-hand man of his ageing chief. There was in fact no system at all, and those conditions accorded admirably with Kitchener's temperament. He was liable to be dispatched at any moment to take charge of some operation, or of some important piece of work ; everything remained fluid and informal ; and so long as he did not fall out with Roberts, he could do more or less as he pleased.

Between 1899 and 1902 the British imperial forces in South Africa reached a grand total of 449,000 men. Of those, 256,000 were regulars and 193,000 were volunteers ; and a large proportion were employed on line of communication, transport, remount, supply, and other non-combatant duties. They opposed an enemy who disposed of a maximum force of 60,000 to 65,000 men.

The Boers, on the other hand, were all mounted, and it was reckoned that one mounted man on the veldt was worth three or four soldiers on foot. The Boers were, moreover, two little nations in arms, and they deployed almost the whole of their strength in the field. They had learnt commando tactics in dealing with wild beasts and natives, who had always menaced their security.

Roberts and Kitchener differed as much in character as they did in appearance. Roberts was short and genial, and filled with a genuine kindliness which won the hearts of all ranks. His interest in the welfare of the common soldier had earned him the nickname Bobs, and the love of the Army as a whole. Kitchener was tall and

[1] Salisbury Papers, 112.

intensely reserved ; and filled with a ruthlessness which took no account of personal feelings. He never made the smallest attempt to cultivate the arts of popularity ; but he and Roberts worked together happily and without strain.

After handing over the Sudan and the Egyptian Army to Sir Reginald Wingate, Kitchener left Khartoum on 18 December. He boarded the cruiser *Isis* at Alexandria three days later and reached Gibraltar on 26 December. At Gibralter Kitchener joined Roberts on the *Dunottar Castle* which sailed on 27 December for Cape Town, where he disembarked on 10 January, 1900. On the voyage out he evolved with Roberts an entirely new plan of campaign.

CHAPTER 9

KRUGERISM

1900–1901

Roberts and Kitchener planned an advance up the western flank of the enemy republics, along the railway which ran from Cape Town through De Aar junction to Kimberley, Mafeking and Bulawayo. That new plan was based solely upon Cape Town, instead of upon Cape Town, Port Elizabeth and East London; and it threw the whole burden of maintaining the army upon the longest and most exposed railway in South Africa. But the plan possessed the great merit of flexibility; it threatened both the enemy's capitals, as well as his line of communications; and it left the invaders free to strike east at any point at any time.

Disregarding all protests on landing, Kitchener tore in pieces immediately the organization of the army's transport. He pooled the transport on an army service corps basis, and abolished the existing regimental system; and that unwise change created chaos. The Egyptian army had operated in conditions which made it natural for all its transport to be parked normally in one place. But in South Africa, where a large army was dispersed over a wide area, Kitchener's centralized system proved to be unworkable. Many officers drafted into the army service corps establishment were incompetent misfits who deserved to be sent home, so that regiments soon found it imperative to disregard Kitchener's order and to appropriate army wagons to their own use. Kitchener was rebuked by the War Office for changing regulations without authority; and he grumbled (30 January, 1900) to Pandeli Ralli about the obstructive tactics of ' old red-tape heads of departments' who quoted regulations to him ' generally dated about 1870 and intended for Aldershot manœuvres', and who ' seemed quite hurt when I do not agree to follow their printed rot'.

Lack of trained staff officers was a great handicap to Kitchener. The British Army was still the preserve of gentlemen who disliked having to take their profession seriously, and Kitchener wrote[1] ruefully (29 April, 1900) to Lady Cranborne, who quickly became his principal confidante :

' It is quite impossible to calculate on anything in this army. I

[1] Hatfield MSS.

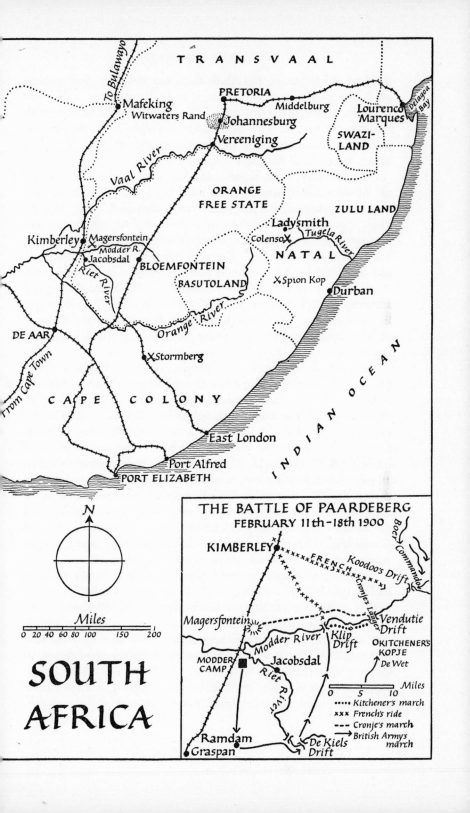

TRANSVAAL

To Bulawayo

Mafeking

Witwaters Rand

PRETORIA

Middelburg

Johannesburg

Vereeniging

Lourenco Marques

Delagoa Bay

SWAZI-LAND

Vaal River

ORANGE
FREE STATE

ZULU LAND

Ladysmith

Colenso ✕

Tugela River

Kimberley

Magersfontein ✕

Modder R.

Jacobsdal

Riet River

BLOEMFONTEIN

NATAL

BASUTOLAND

✕ Spion Kop

Durban

Orange River

DE AAR

From Cape Town

✕ Stormberg

CAPE   COLONY

INDIAN   OCEAN

East London

Port Alfred

PORT ELIZABETH

N

Miles
0 20 40 60 80 100   150   200

SOUTH
AFRICA

THE BATTLE OF PAARDEBERG
FEBRUARY 11th -18th 1900

KIMBERLEY

FRENCH

Koodoo's Drift

Boer Commando

Cronje's Laager

Magersfontein

Modder River

Klip Drift

Vendutie Drift

OKITCHENER'S KOPJE

De Wet

MODDER CAMP

Jacobsdal

Riet River

Ramdam

Graspan

De Kiels Drift

Miles
0   5   10

····· Kitchener's march
✕✕✕ French's ride
--- Cronje's march
→ British Army's march

must say, I like having the whole thing cut and dried, and worked out ; but people here do not seem to look upon war sufficiently seriously. It is considered too much like a game of polo, with intervals for afternoon tea . . . I try all I can, day and night, to get the machine to work. But a thorough reorganization will have to take place before we can call ourselves a fighting nation.'

On 8 February, 1900, Roberts and Kitchener reached the front on the Modder River, where 37,000 men, 113 guns, 12,000 horses and 22,000 transport animals had been secretly assembled. They speeded their preparations in the light of a war situation which was still deteriorating. In Natal, two more attempts to relieve Ladysmith had been repulsed by Louis Botha at Spion Kop and Vaal Kranz ; and in Kimberley Cecil Rhodes was reported to be at odds with R. G. Kekewich, the military commander. Kitchener telegraphed authority to Kekewich to place Rhodes, if necessary, under arrest. In those circumstances the offensive was launched on the night of 10/11 February—ten days before the provisional date which had been envisaged.

The tactical plan was very simple. The 1st Division (Lord Methuen) was ordered to contain General Cronje's army at Magersfontein, while the 7th Division (Charles Tucker) seized Jacobsdal to the south-east. The main punch was to be delivered by the Cavalry Division (John French), by the 6th and 9th Divisions (Thomas Kelly-Kenny and Henry Colvile), and by one brigade of mounted infantry (O. C. Hannay). Those formations were ordered to march 17 miles south to Ramdam, in order to deceive Cronje, and then to change direction east to De Kiel's Drift, where they were to ford the Riet River and to change direction north. They were ordered to ford the Modder River at Klip Drift and then to march north-west on Kimberley. The objects were to destroy Cronje's army, relieve Kimberley, and afterwards strike east at Bloemfontein.

Kitchener, who accompanied Kelly-Kenny, rode always with the leading infantry, and the operation went according to plan. French's cavalry rode in triumph into Kimberley on the afternoon of 15 February, while the infantry plodded wearily a great distance behind. The only jarring note was struck by Christian De Wet, who had been despatched by Cronje with a commando, over a thousand strong, to discover what the British were doing. De Wet fell upon the British supply column as it was crossing De Kiel's Drift ; and the British army was placed, in consequence, upon short rations for a month.

162

Hemmed in upon all sides, Cronje started to withdraw eastwards on Bloemfontein along the north bank of the Modder at dusk on 15 February; and the British reconnaissance was so inefficient that he nearly succeeded in slipping unobserved through the gap between French's rear and Kelly-Kenny's van. The dust made by his wagons was, however, observed at dawn on 16 February by patrols which Kitchener had sent out, and, scenting blood, Kitchener at once switched Kelly-Kenny and Hannay from the march on Kimberley to the pursuit of Cronje. He sent gallopers to order French to ride without an instant's delay from Kimberley to Koodoo's Drift, on the Modder, in an effort to intercept Cronje.

Throughout 16 February, which was about the hottest day of that South African summer, Kitchener strove to maintain contact with Cronje's rear. He spent much of his time riding ahead with Hannay's mounted infantry. His order did not reach French until 10 p.m. that day, when the cavalry was exhausted after riding around the country north of Kimberley. Less than 1,500 men with twelve pieces of artillery were fit to start at 4 a.m. on 17 February on the 30-mile ride to Koodoo's Drift.

French covered the distance in six and a half hours, and he arrived at 10.30 a.m., at the moment when he was needed. Fifteen years later, when, as Commander-in-Chief of the B.E.F., his personal relationship with Kitchener, who was then Secretary for War, was on the point of collapsing completely, French frequently referred with tears in his eyes to that early morning ride. Cronje had planned to cross the river at Vendutie Drift, 4½ miles west of the place predicted by Kitchener; and, from the high ground overlooking the river, the Boers were observed by French as they approached the ford. Cronje's leading wagons were preparing to enter the water when his oxen were stampeded by shells from French's guns.

Cronje knew that if he crossed the ford he would almost certainly meet De Wet, as well as reinforcements which were being rushed up from Bloemfontein. Nevertheless, he would not purchase safety at the cost of sacrificing his wagons which were the property, and often a large part of the working capital, of the 5,000 burghers who accompanied him. He did not know how exhausted the British cavalry were, and he was hampered by the presence in his convoy of many women and children. He bared his teeth, therefore, like an old wolf at bay, and proceeded to dig himself into a naturally strong defensive position.

Cronje's laager, on the north bank of the Modder at Vendutie near Paardeberg, was encircled by commanding heights, sloping down gently to the river which provided water for man and beast. At that spot the shallow stream was about 50 yards wide, and it wound through steep banks which rose to an average height of 30 feet. The banks, and the ground for a short distance adjoining them, were covered with mimosa, thorn and other scrub, which gave excellent cover on an otherwise bare and shelterless plain. Innumerable ravines, which ran into the river on both sides, made admirable trenches for defence. Throughout the remainder of 17 February, and throughout the night, the Boers improved those trenches and dug fresh ones, where necessary. They worked feverishly to elaborate a system of defence which gave an all-round field of fire over the surrounding veldt. They built dug-outs in the steep river-banks which provided complete protection for women and children. Between those overhanging banks they enjoyed a protected passage from one end of the laager to the other.

Roberts, who was prostrated by a feverish chill at Jacobsdal on 17 February, ordered Kitchener to take command. But apart from Kitchener he notified only Kelly-Kenny to whom he wrote (17 February) : 'I hope to join you to-morrow. Meanwhile, please consider Lord Kitchener is with you for the purpose of communicating to you my orders, so that there may be no delay—such as reference to and fro would entail.' Kelly-Kenny replied pompously at 4 p.m. that day : 'With regard to my position and Lord Kitchener's, your description of it I perfectly understand. This is not a time to enter into personal matters. Till this phase of the operation is completed, I will submit to even humiliation rather than raise any matter connected with my command.'

Kitchener, as a Major-General, was junior in rank to Kelly-Kenny, Colvile and French, who had all been given the local rank of Lieutenant-General ; and at that period men did not hesitate to stand resolutely upon their personal rights in a way which modern bureaucratic society has made unsuitable and even impossible. Kelly-Kenny was, in consequence, profoundly mortified ; but no one disputed, although many failed to understand, the right to command which Kitchener assumed.

The Battle of Paardeberg fought on 18 February, 1900, was the most controversial episode in Kitchener's career. He spent the night of 17/18 February with the mounted infantry west of the laager near

Paardeberg Drift on the south bank of the Modder ; and he rode forward before dawn to inspect the Boer positions from some high ground. The great majority of the Boers were entrenched upon the north bank ; but a small body had been detached to hold the approaches to the south bank.

Kitchener had to decide whether to besiege Cronje and then to shell and starve him into surrender, or whether, at the cost of heavy casualties, to attempt to storm the laager without preparation or delay. Remembering his doubts before the Atbara, less than two years before, Kitchener did not hesitate. He announced to the few officers who accompanied him on his dawn reconnaissance : " Gentlemen ! It is now six-thirty. By ten-thirty we shall be in possession of that laager ; and I shall then load up French and push him on to Bloemfontein with the cavalry ! "

Such tactics would have served at the Atbara, and it was partly Kitchener's fault that at Paardeberg they proved unavailing. The decision to attack was sound, but it was taken too precipitately, without allowing time for adequate reconnaissance or consultation. Kitchener's intentions were never made clear to his subordinate commanders, and his handling of the battle would have been open to serious criticism even if it had been won instead of lost.

Kitchener's tactical plan possessed the merit of simplicity. He ordered Kelly-Kenny to launch a frontal attack from the south, and to engage the enemy's attention while simultaneous attacks were launched upon the laager at 10 a.m. by Colvile from the east, along the north and south banks, and by Hannay's mounted infantry from the west along the north bank. Kitchener tried to order French also to attack with his cavalry from the north ; but French explained by heliograph soon after dawn that his men were too much exhausted. Kitchener accepted that explanation, and French undertook to prevent the enemy from escaping northwards, and to deal with any Boer commandos which might attempt to intervene from the north.

That plan could certainly have been improved if time had been allowed for reconnaissance. It was not well adapted to the nature of the ground. Kitchener did not, for example, appreciate that a strong attack delivered eastwards along the north bank offered much the greatest prospect of success ; he did not appreciate the extreme difficulty of the frontal attack from the south ; and he discovered too late that the Boers relied mainly not, as he had at first supposed, upon their inner stronghold, but upon a system of outlying trenches and ravines which were barely visible through the scrub which covered them.

Kitchener was fighting white men for the first time in his life, and he badly underrated their strength and morale. He failed to make Kelly-Kenny and Colvile understand clearly the parts which he intended them to play ; and, mainly for that reason, the quality of their co-operation was half-hearted throughout the day. Kitchener had, in fact, assumed the responsibility of command without the usual means of exercising it. He lacked machinery for co-ordinating the movements of his dispersed forces.

Kitchener had no headquarters from which to direct the battle, and virtually no staff to assist him. He tried to compensate for that lack by galloping like a whirlwind from point to point throughout the day, and by issuing verbal orders, as at Omdurman, to subordinate commanders, most of whom did not even know that he was in command. He had acquired in the Sudan a withering contempt for established channels and routine ; and at Paardeberg he created confusion by hustling troops into battle wherever and whenever he found them, without regard to orders which they might previously have received, and often without informing, because he lacked the means, the formations to which they belonged. In that way he succeeded in hurling into action practically all the troops who were in the field ; but the result was chaotic.

Long before dawn Kitchener ordered Hannay to take his mounted infantry along the south bank of the river and to cross to the north bank by a ford east of the Boer laager. Hannay was ordered to work his way westwards along the north bank and to prepare to rush the laager as soon as Colvile's attack from the east was fully developed. Soon after the first phase of the battle began, Kitchener telegraphed to inform Roberts at 8 a.m. that the enemy was completely surrounded, and that ' I think it must be a case of complete surrender ! '

The battlefield presented the extraordinary spectacle of the Boer laager, like a bull's-eye, encircled by a British army which was ringed, in its turn, by a number of Boer commandos of unknown strength. By intervening at about 10 a.m. one of those commandos administered a major check. Kitchener was absorbed in the task of co-ordinating the assaults from east and west, when Hannay's mounted infantry were suddenly attacked in the rear by enemy reinforcements which had been rushed up from Bloemfontein.

From his central position south of the laager Kitchener had no view of Hannay on the north bank. He had, however, a clear view of Kelly-Kenny's 18th Brigade (T. E. Stephenson), which he had ordered to support Hannay along the south bank ; and he was dismayed to see that it had suddenly faced east instead of west.

Kitchener sent an A.D.C. to ask Stephenson for an explanation. The A.D.C. reported that Stephenson appeared to have no firm grasp of Kitchener's intentions. Kitchener at once galloped furiously to see Stephenson and to order him to ignore the threat to Hannay's rear. He then galloped to see Hannay, after sending the senior of his two staff officers to order French to deal with the Boers in Hannay's rear.

Kitchener's plan had been temporarily upset, but he expected that the situation would soon be brought under control, although another enemy commando was threatening French's rear. The most disquieting feature was the skilful and determined opposition which Cronje was offering to Colvile's advance from the east and to Kelly-Kenny's attack from the south. Both assaults were held and pinned down ; and Horace Smith-Dorrien, commanding Colvile's 19th Brigade, complained[1] that he was left throughout the day 'in a complete fog, and knew nothing of the situation either of our own troops, or of the Boers, beyond what I could see, or infer, myself'.

That confusion was typical of the way in which the battle was fought ; but it must be said that Smith-Dorrien's attitude was supine. If he had shown greater initiative he might have linked up with advanced units of Colvile's 3rd (Highland) Brigade (Hector Macdonald), which had secured a precarious foothold on the north bank.

Time was passing ; and at 1.30 Kitchener, who had ridden to see Colvile, ordered that every available man should be sent to reinforce Smith-Dorrien on the north bank. At the same time he ordered that Smith-Dorrien's attack should be pressed home, regardless of casualties, in association with Hannay's expected attack from the east. Colvile dispatched his last reserves, under Lieutenant-Colonel W. A. Aldworth, who had been guarding the baggage ; but he omitted to order Aldworth to notify his arrival on the north bank to Smith-Dorrien. Furthermore, by some gross muddle which has never been satisfactorily elucidated, Kitchener's second order never reached Smith-Dorrien.

East of the laager, Hannay and Stephenson attacked in obedience

[1] General Sir Horace Smith-Dorrien, *Memories of Forty-Eight Years Service*, p. 152.

to Kitchener's order ; but that attack was quickly brought to a stand-still by the fierce resistance of the Boers. Kitchener thereupon issued two orders to Kelly-Kenny. He ordered that Stephenson's brigade should cross to the north bank of the Modder and launch a renewed attack on the laager in support of Hannay ; and he ordered that the 13th Brigade (C. E. Knox) should undertake a new frontal attack from the south.

Kelly-Kenny passed on the first order, but he protested strongly against the second. He said that Knox was seriously wounded and that the troops were exhausted. Kitchener did not insist ; but he rode to see Stephenson again in order to superintend his crossing of the river. While he was with Stephenson he received a note from Hannay, dispatched at 1.30 p.m., which stated that the mounted infantry could make no further progress.

Kitchener immediately dispatched a strongly-worded order to Hannay :

' Time has come for a final effort. All troops have been warned that laager must be rushed at all costs. Try and carry Stephenson's brigade on with you. But if they cannot go, mounted infantry should do it. Gallop up, if necessary, and fire into laager.'

Kitchener had not, in fact, found it possible to warn all troops, or even many troops, that the laager would have to be rushed at all costs at once. Hannay received Kitchener's note at 3 p.m., and as he had reported that further progress was impossible, he construed the order to gallop up and fire into the laager as a reflection upon his personal courage. Ignoring, therefore, the injunction to co-operate with Stephenson, Hannay collected three officers and about fifty men who were within hail, and ordered them to follow him in a charge upon the laager. He galloped forward, immediately, over open ground, and fell, riddled with bullets.

Unmoved by that futile gesture, Kitchener urged Stephenson to hasten and press home his attack. That attack from the east coincided with a spirited attack led by Aldworth from the west, without the knowledge of Smith-Dorrien. Both attacks were beaten off by the Boers by about 5.30 p.m., and Aldworth was killed.

While Kitchener and Kelly-Kenny were absorbed in following the development of that last attempt at a concerted assault from east and west, a fresh diversion inaugurated the final phase of the battle. De Wet galloped up from the south with five hundred men and launched an attack against Kelly-Kenny's rear. He seized a prominent feature, known as Kitchener's Kopje, and put to flight a newly-raised body of Cape volunteers, known as Kitchener's Horse, which had been ordered to hold it. From that eminence De Wet started to shell the British artillery which was continuously shelling the laager.

Swearing violently, Kitchener was compelled to turn his attention to De Wet ; but at that late hour it proved impossible to dislodge De Wet from Kitchener's Kopje. That failure brought the battle to a close ; it died down into a few convulsive attempts to draw closer to the laager in obedience to orders which Kitchener had constantly issued earlier and which had been, in many cases, delayed. The troops were exhausted by lack of food and sleep, as well as by the exertions of the previous night and day ; and at 7.40 p.m. Roberts received a telegram from Kitchener :

' We did not succeed in getting into the enemy's convoy, though we drove the Boers back a considerable distance along the river bed. The troops are maintaining their positions, and I hope to-morrow we shall be able to do something more definite. Late this afternoon the Boers developed an attack on our right which is still going on, but is kept under control by our artillery. Our casualties have, I fear, been severe.'

Kitchener, who had never lost a battle before, ordered all troops to dig themselves in at the furthest points which they had reached, in preparation for a renewed attack next morning. But in the confusion caused by De Wet's dramatic intervention that order failed to reach most of the advanced units. The troops were completely worn out, and it was imperative that they should be rested and fed. Smith-Dorrien's brigade, for example, had only arrived on the scene an hour before they were hurled into battle. The Boers chivalrously allowed some of their opponents, who were desperate from want of water, to fill their bottles from the river towards dusk. After dusk most of the troops were quietly withdrawn from the most exposed positions by their colonels or brigadiers.

Boer losses amounted to about 300 ; but all their oxen and most of their horses were killed or irretrievably scattered, so that Cronje's mobility was destroyed. British losses totalled 1,262, including 24 officers and 279 men killed. By pre-1914 standards that price would have been considered high, even if Cronje had been overwhelmed ; but Kitchener was as contemptuous of suggestions that he had been reckless of human life as he was of criticism of his decision to attack.

When all was over, he wrote[1] (4 March, 1900) to Lady Cranborne :
' The army requires really months of hard work to get it fit for the
work it has to do. I never thought it was quite as bad as I have found
it.' He wrote[1] again (16 March) :
   ' I have been having rather a bad time lately . . . I hope the authorities
will keep their hair on ; and if they want a victim to sacrifice, I am
always at their disposal. War means risks, and you cannot play the
game and always win ; and the sooner those in authority realize this,
the better.'

On 19 February, the day after the battle, Roberts was well enough
to join Kitchener and to resume control of operations. The 7th
Division (Tucker) was brought up from Jacobsdal ; and Roberts,
after inspecting the ground, conferred with all his senior commanders.
Kitchener strongly urged that the attack should be resumed forthwith ;
but Roberts decided that the laager could not be stormed without a
' further loss of life which did not appear . . . to be warranted by the
military exigencies of the situation '.[2] He therefore ordered that
Cronje should be besieged, and that he should be shelled and starved
into surrender.

The controversy aroused by that decision was as great as that
aroused by Kitchener's precipitate attack, and by his handling of the
battle. Roberts' decision was severely criticized in the histories of the
war published by the German General Staff, and by The Times (L. S.
Amery) ; but it was endorsed by the British official history. It was
justified by results, for Cronje surrendered on 27 February, only nine
days after the battle, and one day after the relief of Ladysmith.
Roberts then swept forward in overwhelming strength from Paardeberg, and rode in triumph into Bloemfontein on 13 March, 1900.

Roberts never reproached Kitchener for his decision to attack, or
for his tactical handling of the battle ; and Kitchener never permitted
even the mildest criticism of Roberts to pass his lips. Lord Esher
noted[3] (13 January, 1901) that Roberts had ' no words to express
his high commendation ' of Kitchener. Roberts explained that
' Kitchener's self-possession, his eagerness to undertake all the hardest
and most difficult work, his scorn of notoriety, and his loyalty, were
beyond all praise. He was the only officer who shrank from no
responsibility, and no task, however arduous.'

[1] Hatfield MSS.
[2] Robert's despatch No. 3 (28 February, 1900) from Paardeberg Camp.
[3] Journals and Letters, I, p. 273.

Kitchener was not present at the surrender of Cronje or at the entry into the capital of the Orange Free State. On the former occasion he was helping his old favourite, Percy Girouard, on a task of railway construction ; and on the second he was away suppressing a minor revolt in Cape Colony. He rejoined Roberts on 25 March in Bloemfontein, where a difficult supply problem and an outbreak of enteric fever imposed a delay of six weeks.

It seemed for a moment that all resistance might collapse ; but the enforced delay gave Marcus Steyn, the President of the Orange Free State, and General Louis Botha a chance to reorganize their forces for partisan warfare on a sub-continental scale. They welcomed volunteers from Europe and sent a deputation to appeal to the conscience of the Great Powers. In the meantime they braced themselves to fight to the last man and the last round.

Christian de Wet opened British eyes to the nature of the new style of warfare by bringing off two brilliant lightning strokes on 31 March and 4 April. The second cost Sir William Gatacre his command. That gallant soldier was judged to be incompetent, and was awarded a ' bowler hat ' ; and Gatacre complained publicly that Kitchener had treated him with uncomradely and cold-blooded ruthlessness.

At the beginning of May, Roberts was ready to march northwards into the Transvaal with 70,000 men and 178 guns. He advanced in overwhelming strength and on such a wide front that the Boers were outflanked on both wings. Mafeking was relieved on 13 May, and on 31 May the British entered Johannesburg. On 5 June, 1900, Roberts and Kitchener rode in triumph into Pretoria.

During the advance, Kitchener found time to write[1] (13 May) to two of Lord Desborough's boys :

' My dear Julian and Billy,

' Many thanks for your letters which caught me on the march here, and I read them while our guns were pounding away at the Boers who were sitting up on some hills and trying to prevent our advance. However, they soon cleared out and ran before we could round them up . . .

' Sooner or later we are bound to catch them, but they give a lot of trouble. The Boers are not like the Sudanese who stood up to a

[1] Letter in the possession of Viscountess Gage.

fair fight. They are always running away on their little ponies. We make the prisoners we take march on foot, which they do not like at all.

'There are a good many foreigners among the Boers, but they are easily shot, as they do not slink about like the Boers themselves. We killed a German colonel yesterday.

'Now I must get back to work, so goodbye.

'Mind you work hard.'

The Boers, unlike the Sudanese at Omdurman, had no intention of being mown down in a 'fair fight'; and on 7 June, Kitchener wrote[1] to Lady Cranborne: 'It is rather nice putting Pretoria on the address above, but it is not going to be my address for long, as I have to be off to-day to look after our line of communications which has been cut by those annoying Free State Boers at Vredefort. I hope I shall soon be able to put things right again.... I think the Boers have had nearly enough of it, and in another fortnight or three weeks we may have peace.... I have always to be the one to go, but I am quite glad to be useful, and it was very nice when the Chief thanked me when we got here.'

The Queen wrote constantly to Kitchener. She told him (8 June, 1900) that the relief of Mafeking and the conquest of Johannesburg and Pretoria had been 'hailed with wild delight and thankfulness'. After her death (22 January, 1901) Princess Beatrice wrote (8 February) that 'the day before my dear mother died, when hardly conscious of her surroundings, she suddenly asked, "What news is there from Lord Kitchener? What has been happening in South Africa these last days?" Her whole mind was wrapped up in her soldiers, fighting for her.'

Before the end of September, 1900, Paul Kruger was a fugitive in Europe, and both Boer republics were overrun and cut off from communication with the outer world. The Boer forces were scattered into fragments, and their British prisoners were freed. Almost everyone supposed in consequence that the conquered territories would quickly be pacified; and in July, 1900, the British Government decided that Roberts should return to England as Commander-in-Chief at the Horse Guards, in succession to Wolseley; and that Kitchener should succeed Roberts as Commander-in-Chief in South Africa. After a series of delays Roberts laid down his South African

[1] Hatfield MSS.

command at midnight on 28/29 November, and Kitchener was left to deal with a baffling problem of guerrilla warfare.

The Boers hoped that guerrilla warfare would exasperate and ultimately exhaust their opponents' patience until such time as one or more of the Great Powers might be moved to mediate or to intervene. Marcus Steyn, of the Orange Free State, remained at large as an armed outlaw to encourage his people's will to resist ; while Botha, H. J. De La Rey, Jan Christian Smuts, and the intrepid and ubiquitous Christian De Wet amazed the world and made the British look ridiculous by winning an almost unbroken series of minor successes. As late as 7 March, 1902, a year and three-quarters after the fall of Pretoria, a column of 1,300 men under Lord Methuen was destroyed by De La Rey at Tweebosch, in the western Transvaal, after a fight in which the British mounted troops fled in uncontrollable panic. Methuen, who was wounded, surrendered to De La Rey with 600 men and 6 pieces of artillery.

Lord Salisbury's attempt, in October, 1900, to capitalize the emotions of military victory, afforded encouragement to the Boers. Salisbury appealed to the country, in a general election, and at that ' khaki ' election the pro-Boer attitude of a majority of the Opposition was uninhibited. The Conservatives increased their majority by a bare three seats, and the Boers continued to hope that British public opinion would presently change in their favour. A noisy Welsh radical, David Lloyd George, made his name at that period by the vehemence of his expressions of sympathy with the enemy.

The unexpected prolongation of hostilities was a bitter disappointment to Kitchener, who had set his heart upon becoming Commander-in-Chief in India. He had reached an understanding with Curzon, the young and vigorous Viceroy, who was ambitious to secure the services of such a famous soldier as Commander-in-Chief ; and the question became urgent after the death of Sir William Lockhart on 18 March, 1900.

The Commander-in-Chief in India held his appointment for five years, and Lockhart's term would have expired in November, 1903. When Lockhart died, the British Cabinet promoted Sir William Palmer to the post of acting Commander-in-Chief, and left the question of Kitchener's appointment to be decided after the situation in South Africa had become more clear.

Kitchener's friends, including Curzon, continued to press his claims ; and when, after the khaki election of October, 1900, St. John

Brodrick[1] succeeded Lord Lansdowne as Secretary for War, Kitchener telegraphed[2] (3 November) to Brodrick : ' Best congratulations. Am anxious to get to India. Can you help ? ' Brodrick replied (9 November) that he would try ; but he added : ' There is a very strong feeling, not only in the Cabinet, but outside it, that your presence at the War Office, as soon as you can be spared from South Africa, would give much confidence.'

Kitchener was well aware of the Government's strong desire that he should serve in the War Office and play a leading part in setting the British military machine in order upon German lines. The gross defects of that machine had been fully exposed by the Boer War ; but Kitchener was convinced that in the absence of conscription, which he conceived to be absolutely impossible, Brodrick's plan was futile. He considered that even if Brodrick were to succeed in persuading the country to accept a permanent standing army of six corps, that army would be far too small to play any useful part in a great European war against the conscript armies of the continent. Kitchener knew that he lacked entirely the arts of insinuation and address which would be needed in full measure if the British people were to be transformed into a military nation ; and he declined to ruin his fame and reputation by taking part in a politico-military controversy for which he was temperamentally unsuited. For that reason he told his friends that he meant to avoid service in the War Office at any cost. He wrote[3] (5 November, 1900) to Lady Cranborne : ' I could do no good there, and would sooner sweep a crossing. What I should like is India, or the Sudan again. The Government took me out of the latter for a not very pleasant situation in this war ; and I think they ought either to give me my old place again, or India. Otherwise I do not see my way out of it, except to leave the service and try for other employment.'

Nothing but a supreme call of duty could ever have availed to draw Kitchener to the War Office in any capacity. He knew his strength and limitations too well. He could lead and command ; but he was incapable of teamwork because he was wholly deficient in the civilian arts of discussion and persuasion. His adult life had been passed upon the frontiers of the Empire which he had helped to expand; and he had stolen the hearts of his fellow-countrymen because he helped them to fulfil vicariously the nostalgic dreams of their adolescence.

---

[1] Earl of Midleton, K.P., P.C. (1856-1942). [2] Midleton Papers.
[3] Hatfield MSS.

He inspired them with a confidence which the strenuous attempts of three administrations to effect a root-and-branch reform of the Army failed to impart between 1902 and 1914 ; but he was realistic enough to know that distance lent enchantment to the kind of influence which he exercised. He was not popular in the Army, and he dreaded having to start afresh in London, without the support of a wife or any family connections, in a position which would have deprived his background of the quality of romance, while reducing to ordinary human proportions the long mysterious shadow which he cast.

Brodrick did all that he could to overcome Kitchener's objections. He promised him direct access to the Cabinet, through the Secretary of State, and begged him to permit his great driving power to be harnessed for a brief period to the task of military reorganization. He repeatedly told him that the climate of opinion which made possible a root-and-branch reform might never return ; and Roberts seconded those appeals. Queen Victoria herself expressed a wish, shortly before she died, that Kitchener would consent. Brodrick reminded Kitchener (15 December, 1900) that he had no experience of India, and no knowledge of Hindustani : " Are you sure ", he asked, " that Indian command is as good an avenue to other high military positions as the War Office ? "

Kitchener remained adamant. He told[1] Brodrick (13 December, 1900) that if he was not fit for India, he was fit for nothing ; and that his lack of Indian experience ought to be regarded by the Cabinet as a positive advantage, because he would be able to take a detached view and ' to look at military matters from a larger view than India alone . . . I wish I were at home to explain to you verbally about my going to the W.O. I feel sure that I am not the man for the place ; that I should be of little use ; and that I should be a certain failure. That is my personal conviction.'

Kitchener's popular reputation, which he was firmly resolved not to jeopardize, was already beginning to cause embarrassment. He wrote[1] moodily (8 March, 1901) to Lady Cranborne : ' I hear Palmer, the acting C.-in-C., is to get India, so I shall have to look out for civil work, which I rather prefer. The army is quite terrible, and I am afraid, incurable.' But two days later Kitchener received welcome news. The Cabinet was so strongly impressed by the strength of the representations which Kitchener and his friends had made, that its attitude weakened ; and Brodrick telegraphed (9 March) : ' I have

[1] Midleton Papers.

175

arranged with India Office that Palmer's appointment should be confirmed for one year only from now. I earnestly trust, on conclusion of war, you will give us your assistance here until India is vacant. Above arrangement is made in your interest.'

Brodrick and Kitchener both thought at that time that the war would be over within a few months ; but in a laconic note of thanks, Kitchener pointedly refrained from saying anything to indicate a willingness to serve in the War Office. Curzon wrote (31 March, 1901) to assure Kitchener that he was eagerly awaiting his arrival in India after the victorious conclusion of his campaign, and to warn him that he would have to deal with a 'masterful Viceroy', strongly prejudiced against 'over-centralization', who was sternly resolved to suppress 'the mild jobbery in which all the great military panjandrums indulge'. Curzon took leave to remind Kitchener that 'in the last resort, the Viceroy can stop anything'.

Curzon enclosed a letter, dated 31 August, 1900, which he said that he had held up when it had become clear that Kitchener was likely to be detained in South Africa for some time. In that letter Curzon warned Kitchener not to interfere with the frontier problem, which he described as 'the principal military interest of India'. Curzon explained that he understood that problem better than anyone else, and that 'I take its management exclusively into my own charge.'

After informing Kitchener that he intended to be supreme in military as well as in civil affairs, Curzon added that there were nevertheless many reforms which he hoped to effect with Kitchener's help : 'I see absurd and uncontrolled expenditure. I observe a lack of method and system. I detect slackness and jobbery. And in some respects I lament a want of fibre and tone. Upon all these matters I shall have many opportunities of speaking to you, and of suggesting abundant openings for your industry and force.' He warned Kitchener that the appointment of a Commander-in-Chief who had no Indian experience and who did not belong to the Indian Army was certain to provoke jealousy, and he told him : 'I know well, from our conversations before I left England, how greatly set your heart has been upon Indian service ; and I can only say that, as the results show, I have not myself been backward in assisting you to realize your ambition.'

Those two letters sounded a patronizing note which cannot have been agreeable to Kitchener ; but with his mind at rest on the subject of his future employment, he was the better able to concentrate exclusively and cheerfully upon his three main methods of destroying

176

the Boers' will to resist. Between December, 1900, and May, 1902, he carved up much of the South African sub-continent into a series of fenced areas by means of blockhouses. He dispatched columns of British troops in a series of great drives or man-hunts. And he scorched the countryside by burning farms, by carrying off sheep, cattle and supplies ; and by herding enemy women and children into concentration camps.

Kitchener's blockhouses impaired the Boers' mobility by dividing the country into districts. Every blockhouse was garrisoned and oined to its neighbours by barbed wire ; and the intervals between them were gradually reduced from an average of one and a half miles to an average of under half a mile. They were built on the assumption that protection against small arms' fire alone was necessary, since the Boers had almost no artillery left ; and the system, which was only moderately successful, finally consisted of some 8,000 blockhouses extending for some 3,700 miles.

Kitchener often dispatched as many as sixty columns of troops at one time on man-hunts through the fenced areas into which he had divided the country. The strain of looking after them all was severe, and he employed sporting metaphors throughout the campaign. He wrote every week to Roberts and Brodrick about his ' bag ' and he told[1] Roberts (23 August, 1901) : ' I look more to the numbers I kill or capture than anything else.' He reminded[2] Brodrick on that day that ' the real criterion of the war is my weekly bag ' ; and as he grew more impatient, he complained[2] to Brodrick : ' It is no longer real war out here, but police operations of considerable magnitude to catch various bands of men who resist, and do all they can to avoid arrest. Like wild animals they have to be got into enclosures before they can be captured.'

The drives were often bitter disappointments to Kitchener. Despite all his efforts, the principal Boer leaders invariably escaped ; the captures very rarely exceeded 200 men ; and a series of humiliating minor disasters occurred. Kitchener had about 200,000 men, of whom 130,000 were fully effective, to chase about 60,000 guerrillas —Boers, Cape and Natal rebels, and foreign volunteers—of whom not more than 20,000 were ever in the field at one time. In that struggle the mounted infantryman was supreme, and Kitchener's first demand from Brodrick was for 30,000 additional mounted infantrymen.

[1] Roberts Papers.   [2] Midleton Papers.

The war did not cost an excessive number of lives. On the British side, apart from 16,000 who died from enteric fever and other diseases, less than 6,000 were killed in action. On the Boer side, less than 14,000 died in action, and a remarkable degree of chivalry was shown. White lives were precious in the Boers' eyes, because they feared a revolt on the part of the Africans who were silent witnesses of the white man's quarrel in which they were not permitted by either side to participate. The British were well aware that, after surrendering, they would merely be disarmed and deprived of their boots and trousers before being set immediately at liberty. They showed, in consequence, a tendency to put up their hands when hard-pressed in a way which would have been inconceivable in the two world wars which followed. Much of Kitchener's correspondence was concerned with the need to tighten up court-martial procedure in such cases.

In those circumstances the war, in one of its aspects, took on the appearance of a tournament which inspired Baden-Powell, the defender of Mafeking, to bequeath the game of scouting to children. But, although Kitchener strove constantly to suppress extravagance of all kinds, the war cost the British taxpayer 222 million pounds.

Brodrick complained confidentially to Kitchener (11 May, 1901) that Roberts 'had no idea of money'; and Kitchener knew that his proved capacity for combining cheese-paring economy with efficiency was a most important element in the confidence which he inspired : 'I am selling, and eating as much captured stock as I can', he told Brodrick (15 March, 1901) ; and his letters contain numerous references to his concern for the interests of the British taxpayer. Even so, the standard rate of income-tax rose from eightpence in 1900–1 to one shilling and threepence in 1902–3. It was reduced to elevenpence in the following year.

'As long as De Wet is out', Kitchener told[1] Brodrick (28 December, 1900), 'I can see no end to the war. If we could only catch him, I believe all the others are heartily sick of it.' But at the end of the war, Kitchener described De Wet as merely 'a cute and active small farmer', and reserved all his admiration for the Boer Commander-in-Chief, Louis Botha. He wrote to Botha (16 April, 1901) to explain his reasons for establishing a system of concentration camps which quickly aroused a storm of criticism in Great Britain and throughout the world. He told Botha that he had been driven to adopt that repugnant expedient 'by the irregular manner in which

[1] Midleton Papers.

you have conducted and are conducting hostilities, by forcing unwilling and peaceful inhabitants to join your commandos '.

That was not, however, Kitchener's principal reason. The concentration camps had been started as a means of protecting, from the
vengeance of their fellow-countrymen, prominent Boers who were
willing to co-operate voluntarily with their conquerors. But after
the widespread and systematic adoption of the policy of burning farms,
it became necessary to make provision for housing, feeding and
clothing large numbers of destitute old men, women and children,
who would all have perished miserably if Kitchener had not ordered
that they should be dispatched to concentration camps.

Because the need was unforeseen, no adequate preparations were
made, and many camps became scandalously overcrowded. Owing
to the army's needs, and a policy of strict economy, rations were
scarce ; and journeys to the camps which sprang up along the railways
had sometimes to be made in open trucks which took several days
to reach their destination. Most Boers had no experience of living
at close quarters in large numbers ; and even friendly or impartial
observers described their habits as filthy. Many camps, in consequence,
became so insanitary that epidemics broke out, which caused the death
of some 20,000 of the 117,000 inmates of Kitchener's 46 camps between
1 January, 1900, and 28 February, 1902.

Those bad facts were widely reported, and every effort was made
by the authorities, as well as by charitable organizations, to improve
conditions. In the end those efforts were successful ; and the arrangements made by Lord Milner, the High Commissioner, for meeting
children's educational needs were excellent. Many Boer children,
for whom no schools had been available in the remote districts from
which they had been lifted, attended school for the first time in
the camps ; and young adults were also encouraged to attend. The
British took full advantage of the opportunity to influence the minds
of the younger generation of Boers.

Conditions inside the camps varied greatly at different times.
They depended upon the capacity of the commandant, as well as
upon such factors as the proximity of wood, water and a supply base,
and the effectiveness of an informed local public opinion. There
were a number of cases of inexcusable overcrowding and mismanagement, and the pro-Boer and pacifist sentiments of a section of the
British Press and Liberal Opposition crystallized around those scandals.
Sir Henry Campbell-Bannerman described Kitchener's methods as

'methods of barbarism', and the Boers derived encouragement from his words. Lloyd George compared Kitchener's methods with those of Herod, who had also 'tried to crush a little race by killing its young sons and daughters'.

Many of the camps were visited early in 1901 by Emily Hobhouse ; and almost all were visited later that year by a ladies' commission, presided over by Millicent Fawcett, which was sent out by the War Office and provided with a special train. Kitchener grumbled[1] to Roberts (19 July, 1901) about that visit : 'I hope it will calm the agitators in England. I doubt there being much for them to do as the camps are very well run.'

Kitchener had no time to spare for investigating conditions, and he never inspected a camp himself. He suggested that responsibility for running the camps should be transferred from the War Office to the Colonial Office, and the Colonial Secretary, Joseph Chamberlain, accepted formal responsibility as early as 1 March, 1901. Joseph Chamberlain professed himself to be shocked by the conditions which were disclosed, but Kitchener was impenitent. He conceived an especial prejudice against Miss Hobhouse, whom he always described to his staff as 'that bloody woman' ; and he had her arrested when she arrived at Cape Town in October, 1901, on a second visit, without his consent.

Miss Hobhouse was deported after making a scene and struggling violently with her guards. On her behalf, Lord Bryce, Sir William Harcourt, and some others took counsel's opinion about bringing an action against Kitchener. Kitchener, who was grimly amused, defied them to do their worst ; but counsel's opinion was unfavourable and no proceedings were started.

Kitchener was not squeamish, and he grumbled constantly about 'the woman question'. He told[1] Roberts (4 December, 1900) that the Boer women were 'keeping up the war, and are far more bitter than the men'. He tried to separate the reconcilables from the irreconcilables, and formed elaborate plans for deporting the latter permanently overseas. But the British Cabinet refused to consent.

Brodrick frequently warned Kitchener that concentration camps were causing great difficulty in the House of Commons : 'War is war', he told him (12 April, 1901) '. . . We must do the best we can . . . Tell me everything that will help the defence.' He said

[1] Roberts Papers.

(26 April) that almost all Liberals and quite a few Conservatives were 'hot on the humanitarian tack'.

That problem fidgeted Kitchener, and the Cabinet was reluctant to press him too hard : 'We are doing all we can for the inmates,' he informed[1] Brodrick (26 July, 1901), 'but it is impossible to fight against the criminal neglect of the mothers . . . I am considering whether some of the worst cases might not be tried for manslaughter.' He told[2] Lady Cranborne (2 August, 1901) that the inmates of his camps were 'far better done in every way than they are in their own homes, or than the British refugees whom no one seems to care for. The doctors' reports of the filth and dirt these Boer ladies from the wilds revel in, are not very pleasant reading.'

Kitchener regarded the Press and Parliamentary agitation against concentration camps as a species of defeatist propaganda. He appeared callous because his mind was wholly concentrated upon winning the war in the shortest possible time and with the minimum of expense ; but there was no deliberate cruelty. The sufferings of the inmates were caused invariably by administrative incompetence, and by lack of foresight ; and there was no justification for the preposterous German claim, made forty years later, that Kitchener's concentration camps had served as models for those established by Hitler. Many men would have been more concerned to remedy conditions than Kitchener was ; but the scandal of the South African camps was a manifestation of a species of imaginative weakness which characterizes the English. It is an aspect of their character which is frequently a source of strength, but which can be productive of misfortune.

[1] Midleton Papers.   [2] Hatfield MSS.

CHAPTER 10

CONQUEST OF SOUTH AFRICA

1901–1903

A T his headquarters in Pretoria, Kitchener delegated as little as possible and acted as his own chief of staff. He accepted, in November, 1901, the offer of Ian (Johnny) Hamilton's[1] services in that nominal capacity, but he never used Hamilton to formulate plans or to transmit his orders. He welcomed him instead as a hero-worshipping friend, whose sensitiveness, refinement and charm satisfied a craving in his nature ; and he employed him, during the last few months of the war, in a variety of convenient ways.

Kitchener took no leave and enjoyed almost no recreation. His working day began punctually at 6 a.m. and usually ended late at night. His carelessness with papers was a perpetual source of worry to his staff, but the laconic orders and telegrams which he issued were models of lucidity. For the sake of his health he rode for an hour— sometimes less—most afternoons at four o'clock, and he played an occasional game of billiards after dinner.

Kitchener gave an impression of very great strength because he was so natural and unpretentious. He had no vanities and he never showed impatience about anything important ; but he could be childishly petulant about trivial matters. He did not seem to care, or to take into his calculations, what other people might say or think about him. He received a stream of callers every day, each concerned with his particular job—transport, discipline, press censorship, supply, and so forth—and he gave each his undivided attention ; but few, even of those who saw him most frequently, felt that they had really come to know him. He did not, in the final analysis, appear to possess a judicial mind, because he was so much absorbed by the task immediately in hand that he lost the habit, and to some extent, even the power of looking ahead. Once he had decided upon a course of action he took little account of considerations of precedent, prudence or even of logic.

One man who came to know Kitchener extremely well was Frank Maxwell, who had won the V.C. in action against De Wet in March, 1900, and who had previously served in India as A.D.C. to his uncle, Sir William Lockhart. Kitchener appointed Maxwell to be his

[1] General Sir Ian Hamilton, G.C.B., G.C.M.G., D.S.O. (1853–1947).

A.D.C. in December, 1900 ; and Maxwell's widow wrote[1] many years later that ' an extraordinary kinship of feeling and sympathy which never waned ' arose between Kitchener and her husband. Maxwell started to give Kitchener lessons in Hindustani ; but Kitchener lost interest as soon as he secured the promise of the Indian command. To the amazement of his staff, Kitchener remained totally and unashamedly ignorant of Hindustani throughout the seven years which he spent later in India as Commander-in-Chief.

Kitchener addressed Maxwell invariably as ' Brat ', and allowed him many liberties ; and Maxwell, who was killed in action as a brigadier-general in France in 1917, hero-worshipped his chief. He admitted,[2] however, to his father that Kitchener could be rough and rude : ' He is awfully shy, and, until he knows anyone, his manners, except to ladies, are not engaging. He really feels nice things, but to put tongue to them, except in very intimate society, he would rather die.'

Early in 1901 Boer commandos raided Natal and Cape Colony. The Dutch inhabitants of those colonies failed to rise in strength, and that failure induced Botha to approach Kitchener about a meeting to discuss possible terms of peace. The meeting took place on 28 February at Middelburg, and on that day Kitchener informed[3] Roberts that Botha had been ' quite reasonable about the conduct of the war '. He had merely ' asked that greater care might be taken in bringing in the women . . . He made no complaint about burning farms.'

Kitchener had already reported[4] to Brodrick (21 January, 1901) that the Boers appeared to be ' absurdly afraid of certain Jews, who no doubt wield great influence in this country '. He now found Botha extremely sensitive on that subject, and suspicious of the motives of the High Commissioner, Lord Milner, whom Botha called the tool of alien financial vultures. Botha asked for representative government immediately after the conclusion of peace, and for a promise that non-whites would not be enfranchised. He asked also for a complete amnesty for all acts of war committed in good faith by Boers, as well as by Cape and Natal rebels.

Kitchener was more anxious than Milner or the British Cabinet were to make concessions. He was instructed to state that Crown Colony government would be instituted on the conclusion of peace, and that a

[1] Mrs. Maxwell, *Frank Maxwell, V.C.*, p. 7.
[2] Ibid., p. 89 (letter dated 13 September, 1901).
[3] Roberts Papers.   [4] Midleton Papers.

representative element would be added later. He was authorized to promise that after representative government had been established 'in both the new colonies', the African franchise would be 'so limited as to secure the just predominance of the white race'. He was forbidden to make any promises about the disfranchisement of persons of mixed blood.

Negotiations broke down over the question of an amnesty for Cape and Natal rebels. Milner was supported by the British Cabinet and by the law officers of the Crown as well as by British public opinion, in insisting that British subjects who had aided the enemy must be punished as traitors. Botha, on the other hand, insisted that Boers who, although technically British subjects, had chivalrously borne arms in support of their blood-brothers in the two republics, did not deserve to suffer the fate of traitors. Kitchener agreed warmly with Botha. He was longing to finish the war and to take up his appointment in India; and after the negotiations had been broken off he wrote[1] bitterly to Brodrick (22 March, 1901):

'I did all in my power to urge Milner to change his views, which seem to me very narrow on the subject . . . Milner's views may be strictly just, but to my mind they are vindictive, and I do not know of a case in history where, under similar circumstances, an amnesty has not been granted.

'We are now carrying on the war to be able to put 2 or 300 Dutchmen in prison at the end of it. It seems to me absurd, and I wonder the Chancellor of the Exchequer did not have a fit.'

Kitchener considered that a generous peace would best suit the interests of all concerned. He was not, however, prepared to allow the best course to become the enemy of the good. When he was forbidden to concede terms which he considered expedient and reasonable, he at once started to recommend the employment of draconian methods.

Kitchener's intense concentration upon the task immediately in hand caused him to execute that sudden change of front. He had found Botha quite congenial; but he denounced[1] him (26 April, 1901) to Brodrick as 'an excellent actor' with 'the mind of an unscrupulous pettifogging attorney'. He demanded authority to shoot all Cape and Natal rebels out of hand, and to confiscate the property of all Boers who failed to surrender within a time-limit to be fixed by proclamation.

[1] Midleton Papers.

The Cabinet was as strongly opposed to that drastic proposal as it had been to Kitchener's previous plea for a general amnesty. Brodrick explained (21 June) that it would be ' awkward ' to shoot rebels out of hand : ' If we had begun by it, it would have been well enough.' He reminded Kitchener of the undesirability of outraging the conscience of Europe, and of the risk of exasperating the government of Cape Colony, where a majority of the population was cowed but disaffected. He suggested that confiscation would not ' weigh much with a man whose farm is burnt, stock scattered, and furniture destroyed '.

Kitchener was contemptuous of the legal scruples by which he considered that the Cabinet was consistently swayed. He complained[1] (9 August, 1901) to Roberts that he could not even induce the Cape government to declare martial law : ' The Boers will not believe in banishment, as they feel sure that a change of government would bring them all back again. Confiscation is the one thing that will touch them : I quite understand that confiscation is repugnant to British lawyers ; but in this war we have had to do much that is repugnant to us all.'

Despite the Cabinet's negative attitude, Kitchener urged[2] Brodrick in a fulminating letter dated 21 June, 1901, to make a clean sweep of the Boer population of South Africa. He said that it had become hopeless to expect Boer and Briton to settle down peaceably together after the war, which was likely to drag on for a long time : ' I feel that it will be many generations before they forget or forgive this war, and that they will bide their time and, when we are least prepared for it, try the issue again.'

It was a mistake, Kitchener suggested, to regard the Boers as a civilized race which could ever be an asset to the British Empire : they ' are uncivilized Africander savages with a thin white veneer . . . The Boer woman in the refugee camps who slaps her great protruding belly at you, and shouts, " When all our men are gone, these little khakis will fight you," is a type of the savage produced by generations of wild lonely life . . . The leaders and townspeople are sufficiently educated and civilized. I only refer to the bulk of the population.'

In those circumstances, Kitchener begged the Cabinet to be realistic, and to authorize the forcible and permanent banishment of all Boers who had at any time borne arms against the British, together with their families and dependants :

[1] Roberts Papers.   [2] Midleton Papers.

'We have now got more than half the Boer population either as prisoners of war, or in our refugee camps. I would advise that they should not be allowed to return. I think we should start a scheme for settling them elsewhere, and S.A. will then be safe, and there will be room for the British to colonize.'

Kitchener asked that the bulk of the Boer population of South Africa should be transported to the Dutch East Indies, Fiji and Madagascar. He argued that the Dutch would certainly welcome their blood brothers to the East Indies, and that the French could probably be persuaded to accept Boer settlers in Madagascar. It would be necessary to assimilate completely those Boers who had from the start co-operated with the British, and to confiscate without compensation the property of all the rest.

Kitchener suggested that the only realistic alternative policy would be to divide and rule. It might, with difficulty, be possible to bring about a more or less permanent state of civil war between the Boers who had co-operated with their conquerors from the start, and those who had 'unjustifiably carried on the war to the ruin of their country'. If that policy were accepted by the Cabinet, the British objective would be obtained if the Boers could be induced to hate each other more than they hated the British ; but Kitchener stated that he was by no means convinced that a sufficient degree of hatred could be permanently and artificially sustained.

The British Cabinet's reaction to that carefully elaborated plan greatly disappointed Kitchener : 'Hitherto', Brodrick wrote (20 July, 1901), 'the effects of severity have not been all that we could have wished.' He pointed out that 'farm-burning' appeared merely to have toughened the enemy's spirit, and he suggested that if Kitchener's more drastic proposals failed likewise to break that spirit, 'Europe would be needlessly scandalized'.

Brodrick suggested that Kitchener should execute some Cape rebels, and Kitchener acted with alacrity on that advice. But he was not naturally bloodthirsty, and he would have been equally happy to be magnanimous if that had suited his purpose. He frequently commuted death sentences early in 1902, when the war was nearing its end ; but he remained wedded, in the meantime, to measures of rigorous severity.

Kitchener succeeded in extracting from the Cabinet authority to issue, on 7 August, a proclamation demanding unconditional surrender by 15 September. The Boers' prospects were declared to be hopeless ;

186

officers and officials who failed to surrender by the date named were threatened with permanent banishment ; and all Boers who remained in the field were notified that their families and dependants would be sent to concentration camps, and that the expense of their maintenance would be recovered by means of an immediate levy upon their property.

That proclamation had no effect, and Kitchener stated openly that it was far too mild, and that action, and not threats, was required.   He succeeded in obtaining a declaration of martial law in Cape Colony at the beginning of October ; and he announced, at the beginning of November, that he proposed forthwith to start transporting overseas irreconcilable women from the concentration camps. He had, however, exceeded his instructions, and he was compelled to cancel that announcement.

Kitchener grumbled to Roberts that he could see no end to the war. He complained[1] (29 November) that the Boers were ' not governed by common sense ', and (20 December) that the operations on which he was engaged were ' like hunting Greek or Italian bandits '.   Roberts wrote to Kitchener (15 November) offering to come out again to South Africa and to resume the command in order to set Kitchener free to take up his appointment as Commander-in-Chief in India.   But Kitchener replied (13 December) that he wished to see the war through, however long it might last.

Kitchener's relentless pressure gradually wore the enemy down ; and the Stock Exchange in Johannesburg was reopened in December, 1901. Kitchener failed, however, to capture any of the principal guerrilla leaders, and he told[1] Roberts (16 February, 1902) : ' What are left of the Boers are really fine fellows.'   Efforts which were being made on both sides at that time to arrange conditions for a conference were not interrupted when Kitchener, on 7 March, 1902, suffered his greatest shock of the campaign.

Lord Methuen, surprised at Tweebosch by De La Rey, was wounded and taken prisoner, and his column, after putting up a poor fight, was scattered and destroyed. Kitchener, who had been under great strain for many months, collapsed when he heard the news, and remained in bed without food for thirty-six hours. He told Frank Maxwell that his nerves had ' gone all to pieces ' ; but the A.D.C. managed to coax him into a better humour. He ordered a gargantuan meal to which the Commander-in-Chief, under protest,

[1] Roberts Papers.

did full justice. After that, Kitchener immediately regained his poise.

On 30 March, Kitchener told[1] Brodrick that although he was not sanguine about the prospects of reaching a satisfactory accommodation, he believed that the time had come to offer generous terms, if the Boers would admit that they were beaten. He was intent only upon his objective, and was as happy to obtain it by magnanimity, when magnanimity appeared expedient, as he would have been, if necessary, to use brutal methods.

On 10 April, 1902, Schalk Burger, acting President of the South African Republic (Transvaal), and Marcus Steyn, President of the Orange Free State, who had been given safe-conducts to confer with their friends and with each other, asked Kitchener for a meeting to discuss terms of peace. The conference began two days later in Kitchener's office in Pretoria. Burger was gloomy and silent, and Kitchener described[1] Steyn to Brodrick (13 April) as 'the man who rules the whole'.

Kitchener added that Steyn was a sick man and bitterly hostile, but, like Burger, a gentleman. He found that all the Boers were 'very polite', although, in general, 'The Free Staters are a very low-classed lot compared with the Transvaalers.' Kitchener said that the Boers appeared to be :

'rather frightened of me. I gave it to them pretty straight on their treatment of natives . . . They are much afraid of a native rising, and I have told them they are entirely responsible if such an event occurs . . . They retaliated somewhat feebly by saying our troops incite natives against them. I said we only incited natives by example. They [the natives] are an imitative people ; and when they see us chasing Boers over hills, they want to take revenge for the bad treatment of the natives by the Boers. They did not much like this, and Botha was a good deal impressed.'

Kitchener relished his rôle of preaching humanity to the Boers ; and he made the most of that opportunity to parade before the Cabinet as a man of feeling. He repeated several times that he had 'given it to their generals pretty hot' on the native question. He strongly opposed the popular clamour for unconditional surrender, and he handled the British Cabinet, as well as the Boer leaders, and his

[1] Midleton Papers.

principal colleague, Lord Milner, with remarkable dexterity. He told[1] Brodrick (27 April) that he had advised the Boers not to haggle, but to lay down their arms and trust to British generosity ; he deferred as much as possible to Milner ; and he suggested to Botha, behind Milner's back, that the Liberals would be in power within two years in Great Britain and that they would almost certainly grant self-government at once.

Kitchener adapted his tactics to his estimate of the characters of individual Boer leaders whom he constantly saw privately in order to consult, browbeat or cajole. He worked especially hard on J. C. Smuts and on J. M. B. Hertzog, an Orange Free State judge who had been active as a commando leader. He refused to declare an armistice while negotiations were in progress because he wanted the enemy to continue to feel his power. But he agreed to what he called a ' go slow ', and he issued numerous safe-conducts while the Boer leaders polled their followers, and while a representative conference of Boers met at Vereeniging on 15 May, 1902, to consider the peace terms which Kitchener had drafted with the aid of Lord Milner and of Sir Richard Solomon, the Attorney-General of Cape Colony.

Those peace terms conformed to a general directive which the Cabinet had issued. The Boers were required to lay down their arms and to acknowledge King Edward VII as their sovereign. In return, the British undertook that all prisoners who took an oath of loyalty to King Edward would be restored to their homes and possessions as quickly as possible, and that an amnesty would be granted for all acts of war committed in good faith. From that amnesty British subjects who had aided the Boers were excluded.

The British undertook to substitute civil for military government ' at the earliest possible date ' ; and to introduce, as soon as circumstances should permit, ' representative institutions leading up to self-government '. The British also undertook that the Dutch language should be given equality with English in the schools and law courts ; that no tax should be levied on landed property to defray the cost of the war ; and that three million pounds should be contributed by the British taxpayer towards the cost of restoring and re-stocking farms which Kitchener had burnt.

Kitchener suggested that the Transvaal and Orange River colonies should be compelled to raise a loan of 200 million pounds in order to relieve the British taxpayer of the entire cost of the war. He asked

[1] Ibid.

that the loan should be guaranteed by the British Treasury and secured on the Rand goldfields ; but Sir Michael Hicks-Beach, the Chancellor of the Exchequer, rejected that proposal. He considered that the new colonies would be unable to pay interest and sinking fund on such a huge loan, and that those charges would have to be met, in consequence, by the shareholders in the gold-mining companies. Kitchener argued, unsuccessfully, that the mines were probably worth three thousand million pounds, and that it would not be unjust to mulct the shareholders for a large part of the cost of the war.

Botha and Smuts, of the Transvaal, spoke strongly for acceptance of the British terms, while Steyn and De Wet of the Orange Free State held out longest for rejection. The vote was finally taken at Vereeniging by the Boer representatives at 3.30 p.m. on 31 May, 1902, after a fortnight of agonized discussion. The majority in favour of acceptance was 48 (54 against 6), and the Boer commissioners appointed to sign the treaty were rushed immediately to Pretoria by special train.

The terms were signed at 10.30 p.m. that night (31 May) in the dining-room of Kitchener's headquarters : by Kitchener and Milner on behalf of the United Kingdom ; by S. W. Burger, F. W. Reitz, Louis Botha, J. H. De La Rey, L. J. Meyer, and J. C. Smuts acting as the Government of the South African Republic (Transvaal Colony) ; and by C. R. De Wet, W. J. C. Brebner, J. M. B. Hertzog, and C. A. Oliver, acting as the Government of the Orange Free State (Orange River Colony). Handshakes were exchanged, and the atmosphere quickly became cordial. " We are good friends now," Kitchener exclaimed, three days later, as he linked his arm in Botha's and patted the head of Botha's young son to whom he had taken a fancy.

On 17 June at a victory banquet given in Johannesburg by the gold-mining interests and by the Stock Exchange to Kitchener and other senior commanders, Kitchener told his fellow-guests : " You have tasted the salt of life, and its savour will never leave you. You can never forget the sweet, pure, healthy life on the veldt—the morning ride, gallop, scrap, and capture." He commended to his audience the example set by their former enemies whom he described as a courageous, disciplined, tenacious and warlike race : " Judged as a whole, I maintain that they are a virile race, and an asset of considerable importance to the British Empire, for whose honour and glory I hope before long that they may be fighting side by side with us."

On 23 June, immediately before he sailed for England, Kitchener received a rapturous welcome in Cape Town. He declared, at a civic luncheon in the Castle: "Boer and Briton alike have had the horrors of war brought home to them. They have had a good fight and have shaken hands over it ; and now they are working as one man to set right the damage."

Kitchener left Cape Town with a great quantity of loot. His luggage included some life-size statues of Kruger and other famous Boers, which had been removed by his orders from public squares in Bloemfontein and Pretoria. He planned to re-erect them in his park whenever he acquired a home of his own ; and in the meantime he stored them at the Chatham headquarters of the Corps of Royal Engineers. They were restored secretly to South Africa in 1909 after Kitchener had received strong private representations from the Colonial Office.

Honours were showered upon Kitchener even before he landed at Southampton on 12 July, 1902. He had been awarded a G.C.M.G. in November, 1901 ; and on 5 June, 1902, he was informed that he was to be created a Viscount, appointed to the Order of Merit as one of its twelve original members, and promoted to the rank of General. He was voted the thanks of Parliament together with a Parliamentary money grant of fifty thousand pounds. His friends thought that he should have had an earldom, like Roberts, with a grant of one hundred thousand pounds ; but Kitchener was careful to tell[1] the Commander-in-Chief (8 June) that he liked his promotion to the rank of General best, ' as it completes the series of my ranks from Captain on, having all been obtained by brevet for active service.'

Kitchener took the title of Viscount Kitchener of Khartoum, and of Vaal in the Colony of the Transvaal, and of Aspall in the County of Suffolk ; and he asked that, as he was unmarried, a special remainder should be settled upon his brothers and their sons. That request was granted at once, and Kitchener's military secretary, Major William Birdwood,[2] who conducted the correspondence on Kitchener's behalf, asked Kitchener for the names of his nephews. Birdwood was astonished when his chief, who normally carried a mass of detail of all kinds in his head, said that he had no recollection.

The necessary information was soon obtained, but the name of Kitchener's younger brother, Arthur, who died unmarried in 1907, was inadvertently omitted from the remainder. Birdwood apologized

---

[1] Roberts Papers.
[2] Field-Marshal Lord Birdwood, G.C.B., G.C.S.I., G.C.M.G., G.C.V.O., C.I.E., D.S.O. (1865-1951).

to his chief for that oversight, and said that he would have the matter adjusted.

"Don't bother," Kitchener replied.

"Don't you care for that brother, sir?"

"Oh, I dare say he's as good as any of them. But he's not a soldier, Birdie. Leave it alone."

Birdwood, accordingly, said no more; but he always felt that Kitchener's attitude had been cavalier.

On landing (12 July) at Southampton, Kitchener accepted the freedom of the town. His train was stopped at Basingstoke for ten minutes in order to allow the freedom of that place also to be presented in a brief ceremony on the platform. At Paddington Station Kitchener was greeted, amongst many others, by the Prince of Wales, the Dukes of Cambridge and Connaught, Prince Arthur of Connaught and Lord Roberts of Kandahar; and the hero was observed to fidget impatiently while the Mayor of Paddington read an address of welcome. When the reception on the platform was ended, Kitchener drove with the Prince of Wales in a triumphal procession to St. James's Palace through decorated streets lined with troops, including colonial and Indian detachments. Stands, gay with flags and bunting, had been erected for spectators, and high prices were paid for good seats.

At St. James's Palace the Prince of Wales entertained Kitchener and a glittering company to luncheon. The Prince was deputizing for the King, whose coronation had had to be postponed because he was recovering from an operation for appendicitis. After the luncheon, however, the Duke of Connaught took Kitchener to Buckingham Palace to see the King, who invested the hero with the Order of Merit and the G.C.M.G.

Kitchener stayed as usual with Pandeli Ralli at 17, Belgrave Square; and a round of banquets and receptions followed. At a South African banquet (31 July) at Guildhall, when a sword of honour from the Corporation of Cape Town was presented, Kitchener declared:

"Gold, coal, and iron are very good assets [cheers], and when you add to them the development of agriculture and the introduction, by assisted immigration, of fresh blood into the country [loud cheers]—I think you may assure yourselves that you have nothing less than the making of a new America in the southern hemisphere [cheers]. The question of who will supply the energy,

EASTWARD HO!

Britannia (to India). "We can ill spare him; but you see we give you of our best!"

PUNCH, July 16, 1902

193

the brains, and the money . . . is one more for you than for me. But when . . . patriotism is joined to self-interest [loud laughter and applause], I am not afraid that you will fail to sow the seed and reap the harvest for which I hope that we have prepared the soil" [loud and prolonged applause].

The first matter which occupied Kitchener in London was the date of his assumption of the Indian command. He discussed it with the Commander-in-Chief, Lord Roberts, and with the Secretary for India, Lord George Hamilton, who informed the Viceroy, Lord Curzon (15 July), that Kitchener would reach Bombay on 28 November.

Curzon replied (16 July) that he urgently needed Kitchener's presence by the middle of October ; but Kitchener insisted rightly that he was entitled to a much longer leave. His view was upheld, and he used the interval to pay court to the wealthy daughter of a great Tory political house. That suit was unsuccessful ; but Kitchener's heart was not involved. He rejected Pandeli Ralli's suggestion of a Greek heiress as a consolation prize ; and on the voyage to India he tore up a mass of private correspondence before casting it into the Red Sea.

On 16 August Kitchener accompanied Joseph Chamberlain and Roberts to Southampton where he greeted Louis Botha, Christian De Wet and Jacobus De La Rey, who had come to England in an effort to secure some concessions, including a larger grant than three million pounds for rebuilding farms. They were unsuccessful, but the three generals received a warm popular welcome in tribute to the gallant fight which they had made.

The King had invited the Boers to attend a naval review that afternoon ; but the generals explained privately to Kitchener that they wished to go to London instead, in order to procure suitable clothes. Two days later, accordingly, attired in frock coats and silk hats, they were received by the King at Cowes. Botha assured the King in Kitchener's presence that he intended to be a loyal subject and that he would do his best to carry his people with him ; and all three generals were escorted round the Fleet by Kitchener. They told Kitchener that they were surprised and touched by the warmth of their welcome, and by the many courtesies which had been paid to them.

Towns and cities competed for the honour of making Kitchener an

First meeting between Kitchener and Boer envoys at Middelburg
Sitting, l. to r. : Christian De Wet, Louis Botha, Kitchener, Col. Ian Hamilton

Kitchener at 22nd General Hospital, Pretoria, 14 June, 1900

'Fallen Leader'. President Kruger

'Laughing Cavalier'. Kitchener at Southampton on return from South Africa

honorary freeman ; and the hero again surprised some of his friends by announcing that he was urgently in need of gold plate. He said that he wanted it in order to impress the Princes of India when he took up his appointment as Commander-in-Chief. On 6 August, accordingly, when he went again to Guildhall with Roberts in order to receive the thanks of the City of London, the address to Roberts was contained in a jewelled casket, while the address to Kitchener was accompanied by two very heavy, large and ugly gold vases crudely copied from Renaissance models.

During the late summer and early autumn Kitchener paid a series of visits to the country houses of his friends. He stayed at Balmoral with the King and at Whittingehame with A. J. Balfour, who had, on 11 July, succeeded his uncle, Lord Salisbury, as Prime Minister. Besides visiting Hatfield, Knowsley, Powis, Welbeck, Wrest and Ashridge, Kitchener paid two visits to Lord Londonderry. He stayed with him at Wynyard towards the end of August, and again at Castle Stewart in Northern Ireland at the beginning of October.

On 14 October, Kitchener gave evidence[1] in London before the Royal Commission on the South African War. He laid especial stress upon the need for efficient training in staff duties, and for fostering the growth of a new professional spirit in the Army. He called for the elimination of weaklings, and expressed the view that ' hunting and polo are the best and quickest means of developing the qualities and muscles required in the field '. He advised that ' captains and subalterns should be *real* commanders, and battalion and brigade commanders should confine themselves to supervision '.

Kitchener condemned the inefficiency of the Intelligence Branch of the War Office, and called for more information about ' the manufacturing capabilities and resources of different countries '. He also declared : " I am of opinion that all infantry and artillery should carry with them sufficient tools to enable them to construct hasty entrenchments ; for as the accuracy of weapons increases, so in equal degree will the value of such entrenchments."

Kitchener's advice was held to be extremely valuable, and regret was publicly expressed that it had been found impossible to persuade him to serve in the War Office. R. B. Haldane, for example, who presently reorganized the Army, said at Dundee (2 October, 1902) that he despaired of the future unless somebody like Kitchener was let loose in the War Office and given a completely free hand.

[1] *Minutes of Evidence, Royal Commission on the War in South Africa*, I, pp. 7–13.

Kitchener himself had no regrets on that subject when he left Victoria Station on 17 October on his way to India. He travelled under an assumed name in conditions of strict secrecy, and he was seen off only by Pandeli Ralli and William Birdwood. He reached Cairo on 27 October, and, after inspecting the Aswan Dam, he revisited Khartoum, where he opened the Gordon Memorial College on 8 November. He then returned to Port Said and embarked for Bombay, where he landed on 28 November.

Kitchener arrived in India with a fixed obsession that a Russian invasion was being prepared. That conviction was reinforced by letters which he frequently received from members of the Rothschild family as well as from the British Ambassador in St. Petersburg, Sir Cecil Spring-Rice, about Russian activities in central Asia. Kitchener landed, accordingly, with an urgent sense of mission, and with the firm resolve to take drastic and immediate steps to prepare the Indian Army to meet the Russian threat.

The early disasters of the South African War had exposed the inefficiency which had overtaken the British Army as a result of the long Victorian peace. Kitchener and his friends believed that the state of the Indian Army was even more deplorable ; and the ruling class in England as well as in India understood clearly that Kitchener would allow nothing and no one to stand in his way.

The Viceroy of India was as eager as Kitchener was to see necessary reforms effected. Lord Curzon, who was nine years younger than Kitchener, and ambitious that his viceroyalty should be the most memorable in British imperial annals, was in urgent need of an efficient instrument for effecting military reforms. The Viceroy's personal relations with the Army had been unhappy, partly on account of the ineffectiveness of Kitchener's immediate predecessor, Sir Power Palmer, but mainly on account of Curzon's own rashness and arrogant temper. Shortly before Kitchener's arrival Curzon had imposed collective punishments, for reasons which the Army considered inadequate, upon two regiments, one of which, the 9th Lancers, was a crack regiment of the British Army with many friends in high places. In that way a potentially dangerous feud had been opened between the Viceroy and the Army.

Kitchener's foundations had been laid deep in public opinion, and he did not intend to be any man's tool. He intended to do his duty in the autocratic way which had answered in the Sudan and South Africa ; and he worked in the closest association with friends and

supporters at home. Many of those friends distrusted the forward
policy which the vigorous Viceroy was pursuing in Afghanistan and
Tibet ; and that policy was, in fact, disavowed by the Conservative
Government before it fell at the general election of December, 1905.

Curzon was as quarrelsome and impatient of control as Kitchener.
He quarrelled not only with Kitchener and with the Army, but with
Brodrick, who had been his intimate friend, and with Sir Mackworth
Young, the Governor of the Punjab. He was obstinate and touchy
and frequently wrong-headed. His partition of Bengal nearly caused
a Hindu revolt, and his attempt to stop the growth of a seditious
intellectual proletariat by checking the flow of Indian candidates for
university degrees caused great ill feeling.

Kitchener, in those circumstances, inspired rather more confidence
in patrician circles at home than Curzon did. He was, like Curzon, a
Conservative, and before he left England he took the precaution of
making Lady Cranborne[1] his confidante and unofficial contact with
the inner circle of the Conservative political and social establishment.
Lady Cranborne's husband, who was first cousin to the Prime Minister,
A. J. Balfour, succeeded as Lord Salisbury in August, 1903. He became Lord Privy Seal in September, 1903, and President of the Board
of Trade in March, 1905. Kitchener had enjoyed a long friendship with
the Cecil family, and its influence was considerable. Its members
acted always from a sense of disinterested duty and from motives of
the highest patriotism. They were prominent in a ruling class which
felt that it possessed a direct personal responsibility for the safety of
the Empire which was the pride of the British race and which had
been entrusted by providence to its hands.

To Lady Salisbury, therefore, Kitchener confided week by week his
most intimate hopes, troubles and plans. He did so in the certain
knowledge that his confidence would be secure when he vented his
spleen, and that his friends would be kept informed about whatever
it behoved them to know. Elaborate arrangements were made by
Kitchener's military secretary, Hubert Hamilton, to ensure the secrecy
of that correspondence. Top secret documents and plans were delivered
personally by Hamilton's lawyer into Lady Salisbury's hands, ' under
the guise ', as Hamilton wrote[1] to her (5 August, 1903), ' of legal
documents '.

As soon as Kitchener reached India, Curzon started to fence for

[1] Lady Cicely Alice Gore (1867-1955), 2nd dau. of 5th Earl of Arran ; m.
(1887) Viscount Cranborne (4th Marquess of Salisbury).

position. Lady Curzon wrote with feminine subtlety (9 December, 1902) : ' Do please take the army and all the military straight into your heart ! It will be a wonderful load off George . . . I suppose you know that the prayer of the soldiers has been that the two giants would fall out, and it will be a great grief for them to see you work in harmony, and to know the intense satisfaction it is to George to know that you are here at last . . . *Please don't answer this.*'

Curzon wrote (15 December) in a different but equally characteristic vein : ' How are you going to sign,' he began, ' while you are in India ? ' The Viceroy explained that he always signed ' Curzon', and not ' Curzon of Kedleston ', ' for the additional labour, with the thousands of signatures I have to write, would be prodigious. I hope, therefore, unless you have strong views to the contrary, that you will sign " Kitchener ", and will instruct the Department to that effect'.

Curzon had no desire to hear the name ' Kitchener of Khartoum ' resounding more euphoniously throughout India than the truncated ' Curzon' which he had felt constrained to adopt ; and Kitchener, who was quite indifferent about such matters, complied with Curzon's request. At the same time, however, he announced that both the organization and administration of the Army in India were in need of immediate and fundamental reform.

' The idea that pervades everyone in India,' Kitchener told[1] Lady Salisbury (30 December, 1902), ' is that the army is intended to hold India against the Indians . . . I think this is a wrong policy.' He explained that it was folly to continue to think in terms of the Mutiny of 1856–7. The Army's main task was no longer to support the civil power in remote districts, but to guard the frontiers against external attack.

In letters to Brodrick before he left South Africa, Kitchener had strongly recommended that the British Army should be organized primarily and unequivocally upon a corps and divisional basis, in standard units of approximately equal size and strength. He had stressed the importance of the personal factor in war, and of ensuring that general officers should have the duty of leading in war the men whom they had trained in peace. Those principles accorded with the best contemporary continental practice, and Kitchener was resolved to apply them in India without delay. He found his army, as he told[1] Lady Salisbury (16 July, 1903), scattered ' all higgledy-piggledy over the country, without any system or reason whatever '. The

[1] Hatfield MSS.

men were not even collected for training at big centres like Aldershot, but were distributed about the sub-continent, usually in units of one battalion, in accordance with obsolete notions about internal security or in consequence of the Government's stingy reluctance to build barracks. No one knew with certainty how those units would be brigaded in an emergency or which general officers would command them.

The quality of the troops varied to an extraordinary extent. Prolonged peace and an enervating climate had sapped the martial virtues of the southern regiments, as much as experience of warfare and unsettled conditions had fostered those qualities among the virile races of north India. Most southern regiments were held in such contempt that British officers with means and influence invariably contrived to avoid service with them. Some northern regiments, on the other hand, like the Guides, enjoyed much the same reputation as the Guards.

Kitchener's plans for reforming those conditions were not original ; but he forced them into effect without delay. He reduced his garrisons to the minimum compatible with safety, and thereby saved enough material to form nine field divisions instead of four.

Kitchener divided those nine divisions, each of which consisted of ten thousand bayonets, into two groups. A northern group of five divisions was deployed to guard the frontier along a line from Peshawar to Lucknow ; while a southern group of four divisions was disposed southwards, with one forward division at Quetta, facing Afghanistan. In that way the divisional system was effectively applied in India for the first time ; and that reorganization was an immense improvement. Divisional generals and brigade commanders were told what their precise rôles were and would be in any emergency ; and they were ordered to assume a greater degree of responsibility than heretofore. Lieutenant-generals commanding each group of divisions were ordered to leave all detail and paper work to their subordinates, and to devote the whole of their energy to training.

In order to bring his divisions up to a uniform standard of efficiency, Kitchener disbanded fourteen southern regiments, and replaced them by regiments recruited from the best fighting stocks of the north. Disregarding all protests and opposition, he ordered a drastic re-numbering and re-naming, on a consistent pattern, of the regiments of the Indian Army. During that process Kitchener was careful to preserve a few names which had earned real distinction in past wars. Flushed with success, Kitchener tried to ensure that all regiments should be given equal spells of service on the frontiers. That proved impossible, because men who had been born close to the frontier were found to be much better fitted in practice to deal with raiding tribesmen and local conditions. Nevertheless, Kitchener quickly made the sub-continent vibrate with the force of his strong personality ; and he coolly ignored from the outset Curzon's reiterated hints that questions of frontier policy and defence were the Viceroy's preserve. Kitchener embarked immediately upon a series of arduous frontier tours, during which he seldom spent two nights at one place, but often arrived unexpectedly at isolated posts. In that way his magnetic influence soon became widely spread among the tribes.

As he travelled with a small escort, riding hill ponies or mules, Kitchener wove in imagination a network of strategic railways aimed at Russian communications and at the heart of Afghanistan. He did his best for years, without success, to lull the suspicions of Habibullah, the ruler of Afghanistan, who was Great Britain's ally. Those plans of railway construction were highly congenial to Kitchener ; they were the subject of prolonged discussion in council ; but they dissolved into air when the Liberals came to power in Great Britain because John Morley, who became Secretary for India, rejected them out of hand.

Despite all that activity, Kitchener found that he had much time to spare. That was due partly to his contempt for existing departmental methods which caused him to neglect paper work, and partly to the fact that wide aspects of military organization, including the whole of the supply, transport and ordnance services, were outside his province. His methods were described[1] by his military secretary, Hubert Hamilton, in a letter to Lady Salisbury (9 August, 1903) : ' It is wonderful how he gets through his work—3 or 4 hours a day does it all, and only 5 days a week ; yet I think he does more than an ordinary man in a similar position working 8 or 10 hours for 6 days. He discards all detail on the one hand and, on the other, makes his staff work very hard, and very willingly, at all the bigger questions he takes up. He chucks ideas and projects at us anyhow and in no time, and then goes off.'

Most of Kitchener's letters to Lady Salisbury between 1903 and 1905 were concerned with a single exceedingly controversial problem which bedevilled the relations between the Viceroy and the Commander-

[1] Hatfield MSS.

in-Chief from the day on which Kitchener landed at Bombay. Kitchener found that he was not allowed to control his army autocratically, as he had done in Egypt and South Africa. He had, on the contrary, to share many facets of his command with, and to leave others entirely in the hands of a junior officer, Major-General Sir Edmund Elles, who was the military member of the Viceroy's Council. As an efficient and ambitious staff officer, Elles had a good reputation; but Kitchener was determined to be supreme. He quickly resolved, therefore, to annihilate Elles as well as the military department which Elles controlled.

The military department was responsible for all non-combatant army services. It enjoyed a watching brief over expenditure, and its head served as the channel of communication between the Viceroy and the Commander-in-Chief. Because he was expected to advise the civilian Viceroy upon broad aspects of military policy, the military member of council was entitled to criticize freely the plans and projects of the Commander-in-Chief; and Elles made full use of that privilege. He attended all meetings of the Viceroy's Council, while Kitchener, who ranked second to the Viceroy in official precedence and the Indian social hierarchy, was expected to attend only when matters with which he was closely and immediately concerned were being discussed.

That system of dual control was anathema to Kitchener. It had grown up in response to conditions of active warfare and inadequate communications which had ceased for a long time to exist; and it caused endless duplication of correspondence and delay. It had worked smoothly when Roberts was Commander-in-Chief, because the Viceroy, the Commander-in-Chief, and the military member had been in close and friendly agreement. But that had ceased to be the case before Kitchener arrived in India. Curzon's temperament and honest desire for reform had made him so eager to look closely into military detail, that he had taken the ambitious military member under his wing. Kitchener's ineffective predecessor, Sir Power Palmer, had allowed Elles to trespass still further upon the Commander-in-Chief's province, so that great friction and intense jealousy had arisen between the two staffs. In those circumstances the military member, who was always a general officer, began to look more like the Commander-in-Chief's rival than like a loyal and junior colleague.

At his first meeting with Curzon in India on 1 December, 1902, Kitchener disingenuously asked whether he would have found it easier to accomplish his mission if he had come to India as military member of council instead of as Commander-in-Chief. Curzon begged him to be patient and to study the system of dual control ; and in a letter (2 December) to the Secretary for India, Lord George Hamilton, Curzon praised Kitchener's ' honesty, directness, frankness, and combination of energy with power '.

As Kitchener studied the system his mood became dark. He told Curzon on Christmas Day that he regarded it as preposterous, but that he would give it a trial. Curzon told Hamilton (13 January, 1903) : ' He seems to think that the government of India is to be conducted by concordat between him and me. Accordingly he comes and pours out to me all sorts of schemes to which he asks my consent. It is all so frank and honest and good-tempered that one cannot meet these advances with a rebuff . . .'

On 25 January, 1903, Kitchener opened his mind[1] to Lady Salisbury :

' Curzon is all that one could wish, and as kind as possible, but the system by which a member of council is made responsible for the administration of the army, independent of the C.-in-C, while the latter has only executive functions, is extraordinary . . . I asked Curzon why he liked to keep up such a farce, and his answer was, " If the C.-in-C. had anything to do with the machinery, he would become too powerful." . . . As to power, I do not want more power outside the Army, but I do want power to do good in the Army . . . I am sorry to say that under the present system I find initiative for good in the administration of the Army so checked that it ceases to be workable . . . I suppose one ought to be able to work it, but there it is . . . We have to deal with the human nature of a collective body of men which is quite a different thing to the human nature of an individual. To make an Army efficient, you must be able to feel the pulse of the whole army collectively, and instinctively to know how things will affect it as a whole. Common sense does not seem to be the best guide to understanding collective human nature.'

Kitchener constantly explained that no army could be efficient unless its commander was allowed complete control ; but he honestly attempted for some weeks to keep his promise to Curzon that he would give the existing system a trial. He considered that his hand

[1] Hatfield MSS.

was forced at the beginning of February, 1903, when an order of which he strongly disapproved was drafted in his name, but without previous consultation, by Elles : 'Luckily,' Kitchener told[1] Lady Salisbury (12 February), 'I was just in time, and as I intimated to Curzon that I should be inclined to resign if it were issued, it naturally got hung up ; and now they are asking my opinion on it.'

The 'opinion' which Kitchener wrote called for the resignation of Elles and the abolition of the military department ; and that display of bull-headed intransigeance caused a temperamental clash to develop between the spoilt, scholarly, patrician Viceroy—the cultivated flower of Eton and Balliol—and the blunt, forceful sapper Commander-in-Chief, whose schooling had been neglected, and who owed the whole of his success to obsessional thoroughness and drive. Kitchener sent copies of his opinion secretly to Lady Salisbury, Lord Roberts and Ian Hamilton ; and Curzon's letters to the Secretary of State became filled with complaints about Kitchener. Curzon constantly referred to Kitchener's neglect of files and hatred of routine ; and he compared him (7 May) with 'a caged lion, dashing its bruised and lacerated head against the bars'. He said that 'having hitherto been in a position of undisputed command and in circumstances, such as those of active warfare, where his voice was supreme, and where military dominated political considerations, he expects to find the same conditions revived here'.

A week later (16 May) Curzon wrote : 'He stands aloof and alone, a molten mass of devouring energy and burning ambition, without anybody to control or guide it in the right direction.' He added that he was doing his best 'to govern this remarkable phenomenon' ; but it was harder to govern Kitchener than to govern India.

[1] Ibid.

CHAPTER 11

THE QUARREL WITH CURZON

1903–1905

KITCHENER in India indulged a taste for magnificence which he had previously controlled. He told[1] Lady Salisbury as early as Christmas Day, 1902, that he had dressed all his servants 'in white liveries with red bibs and belts, and a good deal of gold embroidery'; and he began to cultivate orchids and to beautify his grounds. At the same time he ordered expensive and extensive alterations to be set in train at once to his two principal residences, Snowdon at Simla, and Treasury Gate outside Calcutta; and he made that work his main recreation throughout his stay in India.

At Snowdon, which had been a gloomy villa, Kitchener built a great hall panelled in walnut, which unfortunately he varnished, and a new dining-room, drawing-room and library. He worked out every detail of that reconstruction himself, and had a tremendous row with the Finance Department before he succeeded in compelling it to pay for the entire cost of the work. The ceiling in his library was an exact copy of the one at Hatfield, while the ceiling in his florid drawing-room was his own design. He experienced a grim satisfaction from standing over his A.D.C.s, usually Victor Brooke and Frank Maxwell, V.C., as they pounded up masses of files belonging to the military department. Kitchener, who described those files as 'bumph', turned them into papiermâché in order to provide, economically, for the construction of his ceilings.

At Treasury Gate, which had formerly looked like a dingy barracks, Kitchener's virtuosity was displayed on an even more impressive scale. He transformed a number of small, undistinguished rooms into princely halls in which he loved to entertain on a large scale. Little that was original was left of either house in the end, except the servants' quarters, which were totally neglected and left for the attention of Kitchener's successors.

William Birdwood, who was then Kitchener's assistant military secretary, used, in his old age, to describe one aspect of Kitchener's life at Calcutta. Kitchener had never been taught to drive as a young man and, as a whip, he terrified the inhabitants of what was then the imperial capital. He owned a magnificent pair of black horses which

[1] Hatfield MSS.

he loved to drive in a mail phaeton ; he was quite fearless ; and he left the reins loose on the horses' backs while his left hand held not only the reins but often a long cigar and a spare glove as well. He was frequently seen driving furiously on the wrong side of the road, shouting at intervals to other carriages—" Get to Hell, damn you, out of my way ! " Birdwood used to recall that he had often seen the sentry who stood on the bridge leading out of Fort William flee for his life as Kitchener, with rolling eyes and a set expression, appeared to be bent on running him down.

A Miss Ella Christie, who visited Simla in June, 1907, in a letter (23 June) to her sister left an account[1] of one of Kitchener's normal dinner parties at that time : 'We were forty at six tables—the centre one all gold plate, and, on one sideboard, five gorgeous gold vases. He must have a regiment of *cordons bleus* in the kitchen, for I never saw such a repast . . . We began with iced soup, just stiff enough to spoon comfortably, with little dots of truffle ; next fillets of fish with mushrooms and prawns ; then *filets de bœuf à la banquetine*.' A *mousse de canetons*, followed by quails, constituted the fourth and fifth courses. The sixth was ' a dream of a fruit compôte, with cream ices '. There was no savoury, but biscuits and butter were handed round as a seventh course ; and the eighth consisted of a sumptuous dessert : ' Such peaches, apricots, mangoes, and prunes, just softened with a dash of brandy ! ' After dinner, Victor Brooke led individual guests one by one up to Kitchener, who dismissed Miss Christie by rising from his chair after three minutes' conversation about the weather.

The massive gold plate which Kitchener loved to use became celebrated. Lady Curzon successfully made her peace in May, 1903, with a gift of two gold mustard-pots after an unhappy incident at a ball at Viceregal Lodge in Simla. By a strange oversight no place was left for the Commander-in-Chief in the small supper room to which, by tradition, the viceregal party withdrew. Kitchener, with rare discourtesy but characteristic impetuosity, immediately ordered his carriage and drove off without saying good-bye, half a minute before Lady Curzon, after discovering that the Commander-in-Chief was missing, rushed in horror into the hall to find him and apologize. That story travelled quickly round official India.

In that month of May, 1903, Curzon's discovery that Kitchener had been intriguing behind his back precipitated a major crisis. Lord George Hamilton told Curzon that Kitchener was trying to convince

[1] *Alicella, A Memoir of Alice Stewart and Ella Christie*, p. 163.

Roberts, the Commander-in-Chief at the War Office, that the system of dual control was unworkable. Roberts strongly supported that system, on the basis of his experience in India ; and Kitchener's efforts to convince him were unsuccessful. But Curzon, on 12 May, sent Kitchener a courteously worded rebuke :

'In his letter which came by yesterday's mail, the S. of S. mentioned that he had heard from members of the Imperial Defence Committee of "schemes of wide reform and of great alteration" being put forward by you—as he assumed in private letters to the W.O. or C.-in-C. ; and he asked me to warn you that—" although communications between the two C.-in-C.s are always recognized, any changes of an important character must be referred through the Indian Government and the India Office here. Otherwise we shall have a double set of communications which will be a source of great embarrassment and personal friction " . . .'

Kitchener admitted (13 May) his offence, and explained that he felt the need of Roberts' experienced advice. He added that he was 'quite ready for the future to stand alone' ; but he made no attempt to keep that promise, and he made light of that rebuke both to Lady Salisbury and to Roberts. He merely begged[1] Lady Salisbury (13 May) to be 'very careful that everything I write is considered *quite private*', and added : 'I have just had a wigging from the S. of S. for writing home too much . . . You, Ld. R., and Ian Hamilton are the only people I have written to ; as you know, I am not a great letter-writer. I enclose a copy of the wigging, and of my reply. It seems rather petty . . .'

In a similar letter (28 May) to Roberts, Kitchener said[2] that he found the matter 'very amusing, as I never was a great letter-writer'. Curzon, of course, knew nothing about the correspondence with Lady Salisbury ; but he angered Kitchener by attempting to veto all private correspondence with Roberts. He maintained those efforts after the post of Commander-in-Chief of the British Army had been abolished, when Roberts retired and became an ordinary member of the Committee of Imperial Defence.

One of the first tasks of that Committee was to obtain enough factual information to enable it to form a judgement upon the dispute between Curzon and Kitchener upon the subject of the dual control of the

[1] Hatfield MSS.   [2] Roberts Papers.

Indian Army; and the British Government's embarrassment was well illustrated in an undated letter which Lady Salisbury sent Kitchener to see early in 1904. It had been written to her by her husband and was marked 'Very Private':

'A. J. B. (Balfour) is very much concerned about the situation in India. He is much hampered because the information K. sends is secret, and he therefore can't use it. He is doing his best to act through Roberts in order that the Govt. of India may be approached, officially or semi-officially, and an opportunity afforded for that Govt. to give, officially or semi-officially, this information which K. has given secretly to you. A. J. B. earnestly hopes that K. will do his best to make the effort successful.'

Curzon believed that a plot against his Government was being hatched by Kitchener in association with certain members of the British Cabinet; and Kitchener was convinced that his Indian mission was being deliberately frustrated by an unholy alliance between an obstinate and suspicious Viceroy and a jealous and ambitious Military Member of Council. Kitchener hoped to neutralize Roberts, who made no secret of his support of Curzon; and as Curzon continued to complain about the correspondence between the two soldiers, Kitchener eventually sent a member of his staff to see Roberts secretly in London. As a result, Roberts wrote (3 March, 1905) to Kitchener: 'I have written to Curzon, telling him that I wrote to you at the desire of the Prime Minister, who still wishes me to communicate with you on all matters connected with the defence of India.'

In the meantime, Kitchener concentrated all his principal efforts upon Balfour, through Lady Salisbury. He wrote[1] to Lady Salisbury (21 May, 1903), 'notwithstanding the censure for writing too much,' and enclosed his first plan for 'the defence of that portion of the frontier I have seen'. He begged her to 'draw lines on the map', to 'imagine yourself the general defending the position', and to appreciate how 'gloriously secure' such a general must feel. Hubert Hamilton offered her the aid of his brother, an 'absolutely discreet' officer, who had passed high out of the Staff College, in studying the plan.

In a covering letter (21 May) Kitchener told[1] Lady Salisbury that he had promised Curzon to let the problem of dual control alone for

[1] Hatfield MSS.

twelve months, and to concentrate upon other matters : ' I shall then resign on a very similar proposition, so if Curzon gets a year's extension, as everyone here seems to think probable, you may see me in London again about this time next year . . . I am sure you will be careful that *nothing* comes from me, and that my name is never used.'

That strong hint that the Government might have to choose between retaining Kitchener's services as Commander-in-Chief in India and extending Curzon's term of office as Viceroy, was significant ; but two days later the situation was temporarily relieved by an explosion followed by a brief reconciliation. A routine order drafted by Kitchener was sent to the Military Department for issue in the usual way. Sir Edmund Elles duly issued it ; but he detected, immediately afterwards, a small grammatical error which might, he suggested, have caused confusion. He therefore cancelled the order and reissued it in a very slightly amended form, without further reference to the Commander-in-Chief.

Curzon told Kitchener that the matter was so trivial as to be ludicrous. That was true, but it was the latest in a series of pinpricks, and Kitchener was sensitive to anything which served to remind him of his educational deficiencies. Kitchener accordingly informed Curzon by letter (25 May, 1903) that he would resign forthwith unless the Viceroy were to instruct Elles immediately that no order of any kind was in future to be issued to the Army upon any pretext without reference to the Commander-in-Chief.

Curzon surrendered to that ultimatum, because, as he ruefully admitted (28 May) to the Secretary of State, if Kitchener were to resign, 'public opinion in England (though certainly not in India) would side with him'. That was always Kitchener's strongest weapon ; and on that day he reached an understanding with Curzon. Curzon promised that he would no longer regard Kitchener's frontier tours with suspicion or disfavour ; and Kitchener renewed his promise to let the problem of dual control alone for one year. On that understanding they shook hands.

Thereafter the atmosphere improved marvellously for some weeks, and both men made a determined effort to work in harmony. Kitchener wrote[1] (1 July, 1903) to Lady Salisbury : ' The Curzons, both of them, have been *very* kind and nice to me. When you write to them you might say how much I appreciate it all. He is really a

[1] Hatfield MSS.

first-rate Viceroy and we work together much better now—quite cordially in fact.'

That halcyon period was ended early in August, when Curzon announced that his term of office as Viceroy was being extended, and that he hoped to have a law passed permitting him to return to England for a brief period of leave. Kitchener grumbled[1] (6 August) to Lady Salisbury :

' Curzon has announced that, though he feels how important it is for him to go, still he is staying on for an indefinite period, rather like the lover who, while protesting, yet relents—always going, never goes.

' I hope if a law is passed to let him leave the country, Mr. Balfour will not forget to let the C.-in-C. have a chance of seeing people at home . . . The fact is no C.-in-C. worth his salt could go on with the military department organized as it is now . . . C.-in-C.s can be provided, I have no doubt, for the pay, who will shut their eyes and let things go on ; but I cannot ; and as the Viceroy likes the present system, there is no doubt I ought to clear out.

' Why not put Cromer into the Govt. at home, and give me his billet ? That is what I should really like.'

Cromer was still ruling Egypt and the Sudan from Cairo.

Kitchener enclosed with that letter a copy of his completed plan for the defence of India against a Russian invasion. He said that he would let Lady Salisbury know if he should decide to send an ' expurgated ' copy to Roberts, in case she would care to discuss the plan with him. Expurgated copies were, in fact, sent to Curzon as well as to Roberts, because, despite Kitchener's promise to let the question of dual control lie dormant for a year, the full document was prefaced by a scorching indictment of that system, which Kitchener described as the greatest obstacle to military victory in the event of an Anglo-Russian war. In the meantime an officer was sent home to explain the plan privately to Lady Salisbury, and to the Prime Minister, if that could be arranged.

Kitchener's personal plans were interrupted by a serious accident on Sunday, 15 November, 1903. He was riding alone for exercise at Simla, between his town house, Snowdon, and his country house, Wildflower Hall, when his horse shied and his foot caught an

[1] Ibid.

obstruction. He was heavily thrown, and both bones in the left leg were broken a short distance above the ankle. They were badly set by army surgeons after he had been carried two miles to Snowdon by rickshaw, and he was in consequence slightly lamed for the rest of his life. He was an execrable patient and was plunged in gloom for some weeks. He told[1] Lady Salisbury (30 December, 1903) that, unless he could be active bodily, he found all mental activity impossible : ' I do not know why it is, but the brain refuses to do anything.'

The Curzons were solicitous and kind, and sympathy poured in from all quarters. Frank Maxwell, in a letter[2] to his mother (16 December, 1903), gave an amusing account of Kitchener in bed :

' He got a stitch, or something, from always lying in one position, which made him very unsociable. He couldn't read, nor play bridge, and lay and moped all day. He never allows anyone to do anything for him . . . I found him at about 5 p.m. looking grievously sorry for himself and without a kick in him. Following is the dialogue . . . which ensued :

' " Bridge to-night, Sir ? "

' " Oh dear, no."

' " That's a pity. Aren't you feeling quite up to the mark ? " '
Kitchener replied with a groan.

' " Here's to-day's paper. Would you like to read it ? "

' " I can't possibly."

' " All right. I'll read you out some of it, shall I ? "

' " No. Don't bother." '

[The Brat, as Kitchener always called him, proceeded nevertheless to read the paper out loud to Kitchener, who groaned and sighed at intervals.]

' " Paper's finished. What book are you reading, Sir ? "

' " I don't know."

' " No ? But I do. You were reading Gough's *Life*. How far have you got in it ? "

' " I don't know."

' " All right then. As you haven't finished it, I'll read the last chapter out loud." '

At that point the Commander-in-Chief fetched a deep sigh, and

[1] Hatfield MSS.   [2] Mrs. Maxwell, *Frank Maxwell, V.C.*, pp.107–8.

Lord Curzon of Kedleston, 1898
General Charles Gordon

Kitchener at Simla

Seated (second from right) next to C.-in-C. Gwalior. (Second from left) Col. Hubert Hamilton.

indicated feebly to the A.D.C. the point which he had reached in the book. 'We soon got started,' Maxwell continued : ' Moans, frequent at first, gave place to short exclamations on anything that interested him in the book ; and he never suggested a stop till more than two hours afterwards, when I had to go and change for dinner.'

Kitchener appeared in Council on 5 February, 1904, for the first time after his accident. He hobbled on two sticks, and clashed with Elles about his anti-invasion plan. He said that he had an army without any means of feeding, mounting, moving or supplying it ; and he complained that he had to rely for those services upon a totally distinct and separate Department which he knew to be incompetent and ignorant of the true requirements of war.

A few days later (15 February) Kitchener left Calcutta on a tour of inspection. He started to compose a fresh paper, calling for the abolition of dual control, which he intended to send to Curzon as soon as the year's time limit, to which he had agreed, should expire in May, 1904. In that paper he exposed in detail the inefficiencies and delays of which the Military Department had been guilty, and the waste of public money which it had caused.

As Kitchener recovered from his broken leg the military controversy overshadowed all else. Hubert Hamilton told[1] Lady Salisbury (24 March, 1904) that although Curzon was always working, ' Ld. K. works less than ever. There's nothing left for him to do. The Military Department is gorged to repletion, and can't possibly digest a fraction of what he gives them.' Kitchener, in fact, found it impossible any longer even to attempt to make the best of a system which required the military member to digest and criticize every plan which the Commander-in-Chief prepared and every suggestion which he made before they could be given effect. Kitchener had based his case on the argument that the system was unworkable, and if he had succeeded in making it work that argument would have fallen to the ground. He therefore sulked like Achilles, and was constantly described by his staff, as well as by his friends, as a Hercules chained to the Himalayas. He dismayed the British Government, which was already torn by internal discussions about tariff reform, by announcing unequivocally that he would resign if he were overruled.

Curzon, whose term of office as Viceroy had been extended in August, 1903, left India on 30 April, 1904, to enjoy a period of leave in England. While in England, the Viceroy was, of course, invited

[1] Hatfield MSS.

to state his views on the military controversy ; and St. John Brodrick, who succeeded Lord George Hamilton as Secretary for India in September, 1903, wrote to Kitchener (29 April, 1904) : ' We have got to the point where it is absolutely essential that you and the home Government should understand each other.' He invited Kitchener to state his views with the utmost frankness, and added that he was laying protocol aside, on the principle that ' while the cat's away, the mice will play '.

In the course of their correspondence Kitchener told[1] Brodrick (21 September) that his anti-invasion plan was held up indefinitely in the Military Department, which he dubbed ' the baboo department '. He said that ' the dual control of the Army out here is fatal to efficiency or economy. If the Military Dept., instead of giving themselves up to tinkering in all military affairs such as discipline, promotion, military training, etc., were to devote themselves to military finance and, working with the C.-in-C., attempt to introduce economies in the Army, I fully believe they could save between one and two million pounds a year.'

That argument failed, in some respects, to convince Brodrick, who replied (13 October) : ' The difficulty lies in the fact that officials of almost every degree, including Lord Roberts, who are conversant with the past working, adhere to what I call the dual control. They are fortified by what most people regard as the failure of successive attempts to improvise a better system.'

Roberts, who continued to the last to support Curzon strongly, remained on friendly terms with Kitchener, who told Lady Salisbury that ' the little man ' was too old to be taught how much conditions in India had changed. Roberts told Kitchener frankly (28 December, 1904) ; ' My reasons for not concurring in the abolition of the military member are that I do not think any one could carry on both duties in a thoroughly satisfactory manner. Even you, with your remarkable power of work, would, I think, find it extremely difficult ; and I know no one likely to take your place who could possibly hope to succeed.'

Kitchener was strong and uncompromising. He replied[2] (9 November, 1904) to Brodrick :

' I had rather hoped you would send out a Commission to inquire into the whole subject on the spot . . .

[1] Midleton Papers.   [2] Hatfield MSS.

' If we go to war under the present system, I can see nothing but disaster ahead . . .

' My judgement in the matter may be wrong ; but, if it is, all I ask is that you will spare me and let me go. My health will not stand the strain much longer.'

The blind trust of the British masses in Kitchener was an asset of value to the Government. War between Russia and Japan had broken out in February 1904, and the skies were stormy. The weak and divided British Cabinet was tottering towards its fall, and in those circumstances its members were strongly averse from quarrelling with the famous soldier who had been sent to India to effect necessary reforms, and whose positive character inspired the British public, which hardly knew him, with that confidence which Ministers failed to give. Balfour himself informed Kitchener by letter as early as December, 1903, that 'at least as at present advised' he leaned to the view that 'the existing division of attributes between the Commander-in-Chief and the Military Member of Council is quite indefensible'.

Curzon was much hampered while on leave in England by his own ill-health as well as by the serious illness of Lady Curzon. But he attended, by invitation, meetings of the Committee of Imperial Defence ; and he was dismayed to discover how much detailed information it possessed, and how much support Kitchener appeared to enjoy. He concluded rightly that Kitchener had been intriguing behind his back.

Balfour made a strenuous effort to win Curzon round to the view that some drastic change was needed in the Indian military system. He informed[1] Curzon (3 November, 1904) that he and Brodrick had become convinced that Kitchener's resignation would have a disastrous effect upon public opinion, and that they had both reached the conclusion that the system of dual control would have to be altered. Balfour begged Curzon, accordingly, to consider the matter again with a view to finding some method of reaching an accommodation with Kitchener.

Curzon returned to India on 13 December, 1904, after promising reluctantly to re-examine the problem of dual control. He undertook to report officially and as quickly as possible to Brodrick, the views of Kitchener and of Elles, together with his own recommendations. In

[1] Mrs. Dugdale, *Life of Arthur James Balfour*, I, pp. 406-8.

the meantime, Kitchener had had a tremendous row with the Governor of Madras, Lord Ampthill, who became Acting Viceroy during Curzon's absence on leave.

Sir Edmund Elles had objected to an unimportant movement order which Kitchener had issued, on the ground that it trespassed upon the province of the military member. Kitchener warned Ampthill that his patience was exhausted, and when Ampthill, prompted by Elles, asked Kitchener to withdraw the order, Kitchener cabled his resignation to Brodrick on 26 September, 1904.

Ampthill saw Kitchener immediately and surrendered unconditionally. The disputed order was allowed to stand ; Kitchener's resignation was withdrawn ; and the affair was successfully hushed up. That act of calculated impetuosity advanced Kitchener's cause, because it helped to convince Brodrick that the Commander-in-Chief was indispensable. Kitchener, who had told[1] Lady Salisbury (29 September) : 'I continually repeat to myself, "patience, patience", when pin-pricks are sent to me by the Military Department,' wrote[1] to her (29 September) : 'I found there was a limit to my endurance. I knew I was right by the feeling of intense relief when it was over. I felt quite a young man again, instead of a worried, preoccupied old cripple.' In a covering letter, Hamilton was careful to explain[1] to Lady Salisbury that Kitchener was often considered 'impatient and impetuous, and so, in a way, he is—but never when patience and moderation are the elements of success'.

On 22 December, 1904, Kitchener informed[1] Lady Salisbury that he was 'in the throws' [sic] of writing his final denunciation[2] of the system of dual control. His personal hatred of Elles had become by that time almost pathological, and he had, in consequence, difficulty in restraining his language. He argued that the existing system was 'faulty, inefficient, and incapable of the expansion necessary for a great war . . . No one dislikes changes more than I do ; but, if necessary, I do not fear it. I would certainly not continue a rotten system because I was afraid to stretch out my hand and take a sound one.'

Kitchener said that dual control caused 'enormous delay,' 'endless discussion' and 'duplication of work'. It precluded the possibility of formulating or executing 'any consistent military policy'. The English counterpart of that system had nearly caused complete

[1] Hatfield MSS.

[2] *Parliamentary Papers, East India (Army Administration)*, 1905 (Cd. 2572).

disaster during the South African War, and that war had proved that 'the services on which the Army depends for its subsistence, equipment, armament, and movement' must be controlled exclusively by the Commander-in-Chief: 'It is impossible for a commander to administer them in war unless they have been trained and administered under him in peace.'

After quoting many examples of gross extravagance and inefficiency, Kitchener pointed out that if ever he happened to find himself in accord with Elles, one of them became automatically a useless and expensive luxury ; and that, when they differed, an *impasse* resulted which left decisions on all military questions to be decided by civilian members of council who had no responsibility for the execution of those decisions. An efficient system of military administration required, besides much else, 'that control and responsibility shall never be separated, but shall always rest in the same hands'.

Kitchener told[1] Lady Salisbury (5 January, 1905) that he had warned Curzon that he would resign unless his views were upheld by the Cabinet, and that Curzon had accepted that 'as the natural consequence'. He sent a copy of his paper to Lady Salisbury and asked[1] her (16 February) to 'thank A. J. B. for his very kind message. It was a great relief to me to feel that he approved of the course I have taken.' Kitchener referred to a series of encouraging secret telegrams which he had recently received from a former member of his staff, Major R. J. Marker, who had left India after being jilted by Lady Curzon's sister. Marker had been appointed private secretary to H. O. Arnold-Forster, the new Secretary for War. Kitchener, who inspired fervent loyalty from those who had been close to him, described that appointment as 'very lucky . . . as through him anything can be safely transmitted to me. I pay for all telegrams, so they are private and absolutely safe.' Kitchener forgot, at that moment, that Curzon had power, under security legislation, to require the Telegraph Department to produce for his inspection copies of all private or secret telegrams.

On 23 February, 1905, Kitchener told[1] Lady Salisbury that he had warned Curzon that if he had reason to think that the delay was being unduly prolonged, he would resign forthwith on that account alone, before any decision was reached in London : 'I hate always threatening to resign, but what is one to do ?' All useful work was at a standstill, but Kitchener secretly canvassed all officers in India, except Elles,

[1] Hatfield MSS.

of the rank of Major-General and above. He obtained warm assurances of support from everyone, except Horace Smith-Dorrien,
commanding the 4th Division, whose reply was brilliantly tactful and
equivocal. Curzon, who termed that canvass an act of disloyalty,
sent Kitchener a strongly-worded rebuke.

Kitchener's proposal to annihilate Elles and the Military Department
was taken in Council on 10 March, 1905. Kitchener's paper lay on
the table, with Elles's reply, and Curzon's observations on both. The
Viceroy's Council at that period was exclusively British, and the
Indians, like the Africans during the Boer War, had no voice and took
no part in the white man's quarrel.

Kitchener, who had been given copies of Curzon's and Elles's papers
to study a few days before the fateful meeting, described Curzon's
defence to Lady Salisbury as a most able document. It stressed the
immense amount of good which Kitchener had managed to accomplish under the existing system, and it continued : ' Administrative
systems are not constructed to test exceptional men, but to be worked
by average men . . . I believe that the combined duties which Lord
Kitchener desires to vest in the head of the Army are beyond the
capacity of any one man, of whatever energy, or powers.' Curzon
pointed out that Kitchener's proposal would have the effect of depriving the Viceroy of an adequate military adviser when the Commander-
in-Chief took the field on the outbreak of a great war ; and he ended
by accusing Kitchener of an ambition to subvert the civil supremacy
in India and to substitute a military dictatorship.

At the Council on 10 March, Elles defended himself point by point
against the charges which Kitchener had brought. But Kitchener, to
everyone's surprise, said nothing at all ; and some members construed
his silence as tantamount to a display of contemptuous arrogance.
That silence, however, although premeditated, was due to a different
cause. Kitchener knew his limitations : he could lead or command,
but he had no gift of eloquence or argument. He had stated his views
on paper, and on that paper he took his stand. He knew that he would
be outvoted, and in fact, when the vote was taken, he found himself
in a minority of one.

After that vote, Curzon drew up a dispatch which he sent to Brodrick on 23 March. He emphasized that Kitchener's proposal would
have the effect of establishing a ' military despotism ' which would
' dethrone the Government of India from their constitutional control
of the Indian Army ' ; and he denied that the duplication of military

advisers caused waste or inefficiency. Kitchener added a brief minute in which he dissented entirely from the Viceroy's views, and the dispute was then referred to Brodrick for the decision of the British Cabinet.

In reporting[1] the scene at the Council to Lady Salisbury (14 March), Kitchener outlined facetiously, but with a serious underlying intent, the reply which, he suggested, Brodrick should make to Curzon's dispatch. He suggested that Elles should disappear with a G.C.I.E., and that the Commander-in-Chief should take over all his duties. He said that Curzon's face could be saved, and his mind eased, if the Commander-in-Chief were given a deputy. That deputy should be a general officer whose principal duty would be to keep out of harm's way on the outbreak of war, and to hold and stroke Curzon's hand. Kitchener added that the post could be abolished when Curzon relinquished the viceroyalty ; and he begged Lady Salisbury to communicate the substance of that proposal to Brodrick.

Kitchener mentioned that Curzon had sent for him in order to complain that ' it was very mean of me to let it to be known at home that I would resign if the dual control were continued, as it would coerce the government my way, and they were thus unable to judge the case on its merits '. When Kitchener replied that he had done ' the straight thing ' Curzon ' shifted the base of his attack and said if I resigned, all the papers would have to be published and my reputation would in consequence suffer severely as my paper was a very bad one and would do me a lot of harm. I replied that I did not agree . . .' Kitchener told Curzon that soldiers who fought and died for their country were entitled to ' a fair chance for their lives. I said I thought it was not far from murder to continue the present system . . .'

Only a few months earlier, in October, 1904, war between the British and Russian Empires had seemed very close after the Russian Baltic Fleet, on its way to the war in the Far East, had fired, off the Dogger Bank, on a British trawling fleet from Hull which it mistook for torpedo-boats. The Russo-Japanese War was still in progress, and it was almost inconceivable that Kitchener could be permitted to resign his command at a time when public opinion was still greatly disturbed, and when large-scale military changes were in progress and only half-completed in England as well as in India. In influential quarters a bare majority held that Kitchener was probably right,

[1] Hatfield MSS.

while a much larger majority was convinced that, even if he were wrong, to allow him to throw up his task would involve choosing the greater evil.

Curzon had, like Kitchener, dispatched emissaries secretly to London, so that both points of view were well known ; and the dispute became for some months the principal topic of conversation in the social and political worlds. The Cabinet had a difficult and distasteful task in making up its mind, and its decision was conveyed at last to Curzon in a despatch from Brodrick dated 31 May, 1905.

That decision was presented as a compromise which gave Kitchener about two-thirds of what he had demanded. The Military Department was retained, as a result of strong representations by Roberts, and by three ex-Viceroys, including Lord Lansdowne, the Foreign Secretary ; but it was stripped of most of its power to interfere with the Commander-in-Chief. The military member, who was in future to be known as the Military Supply Member, and to wear plain clothes in order to emphasize his civilian character, was to be disassociated from all strictly military work ; he was to retain control only of supply and transport. He was empowered to advise the Viceroy on the financial and political aspect of any matter which came before the Council for discussion.

The Viceroy and the Commander-in-Chief were instructed for the future to communicate direct, instead of through the Military Supply Member ; and the Commander-in-Chief was empowered to communicate with the Viceroy as he pleased. He was to be provided with a secretariat for that purpose. A second confidential dispatch informed Curzon that the resignation of Sir Edmund Elles before 1 October was considered imperative ; and that pecuniary compensation would be offered.

The hasty and somewhat harsh manner in which that dispatch was drafted by Brodrick wounded Curzon's pride. The India Office had hoped that it would be drafted instead by Sir Arthur Godley (Lord Kilbracken), the Permanent Under-Secretary, who was a much better master of English. In a confidential letter (1 June, 1905) Roberts explained to Kitchener that although the Military Supply Member was to be ' disassociated from all strictly military work ', he and Lansdowne had insisted that the Viceroy's Council should not be deprived of the assistance of ' a colleague to whom they could look for advice on all the delicate and difficult questions which often

218

arise in regard to the Native Army'. Kitchener told Roberts (22 June) that he was 'a good deal surprised' by that letter, but that he hoped that it would be possible 'to work out something practical'.

Kitchener was relieved to find that Curzon regarded that decision as a resounding defeat. Lord Lansdowne informed the House of Lords (1 August, 1905) that in the dispute between Kitchener and Curzon on the subject of the military member, 'we decided against Lord Kitchener'; but Curzon was at no pains to conceal from his friends the intense mortification which he felt. He told them that the creation of a new Military Supply Member, whom he described as 'disembowelled', represented a half-hearted attempt to save his face.

Lady Salisbury assured Hubert Hamilton (1 June) that, 'in fact, even if not technically', Kitchener had obtained all that he required, and that their friends were in consequence well satisfied: 'They all say, "K. is so sensible ; he will see he has got what he wanted, and will go ahead in comfort."' But Kitchener, after he had digested Brodrick's dispatch, told[1] Lady Salisbury (22 June) that the decision was less favourable than he had expected. He inferred that the Cabinet strongly wished to avert Curzon's resignation ; and at an important interview with Curzon on 25 June, he regulated his conduct in the light of that inference.

At that interview, Curzon opened the conversation by threatening to resign at once unless Kitchener would recommend Brodrick to accept certain modifications of the new arrangements. As Curzon enumerated his points, Kitchener saw that they were matters of trivial detail ; and he had no difficulty in agreeing. The discussion then grew warm and, finally, heated on the subject of the Military Supply Member. Curzon said that he would resign within the hour unless Kitchener would promise to ask Brodrick to consent that the Military Supply Member should revert to his former title of Military Member, and that he should always be a soldier. He then flopped into a sofa and appeared to burst into tears. His shoulders were shaken by sobs, and Kitchener gave way : 'I hope,' Kitchener wrote (26 June) to Sir Edward Stedman, the Military Secretary at the India Office, 'Mr. Brodrick will approve of my attitude in this matter. I have done everything possible (perhaps too much) to conciliate the Viceroy and prevent a crisis. I have had a pistol held to my head which I really

[1] Hatfield MSS.

believe was loaded, as he is very much upset at the terms of the dispatch and his loss of prestige.'

Kitchener was much troubled about that incident. He preserved an undated copy of a letter which he sent to Lord Stanley (Derby), Financial Secretary to the War Office : ' The only tip I had was yours, to let him down easy . . . Even before I got downstairs I felt I had made a mistake, but has no one ever said more than he intended ? . . . Had he gone, on the dispatch, he would have had much sympathy, both here and at home, and might have done a good deal of harm. No retort about his conduct in Tibet and Afghanistan would have been possible, as these had been condoned, and it would have widened the discussion to a considerable extent. He would have appeared as a martyr to the cause of constitutional government.'

To Lady Salisbury, Kitchener wrote[1] (6 July) :

' I wonder whether I have done what Mr. Balfour would have wished in keeping Curzon from resigning ? . . . I can well understand that there are several matters in connection with Afghanistan which would have made a change of Viceroy advantageous ; but looking at the whole position of affairs, I could not help coming to the conclusion that Curzon's resignation at this juncture would do the Government harm . . .

' I made one slip of the tongue in these negotiations, which I much regretted afterwards, as I was afraid it might be misunderstood by my friends at home. After an hour and a half storming at Curzon about the title of Military Dept., which he insisted on and I strongly objected to, he suddenly gave way and collapsed. I was so surprised that I said in that case I would associate myself with him in obtaining his puerile requests . . . I could not go back on what I had said without upsetting everything again . . . and I therefore left it alone, trusting my friends would not dream for a moment that I had been disloyal to them in any way. . . I could have bitten my tongue out for making such a stupid remark. I suppose I was rather excited by the discussion. I was prancing up and down his room, talking to him very straight on the subject. I told him if he insisted on the title, everyone would know what he meant by it, and that he did not intend to loyally carry out the decision of the Govt. ; and when he collapsed I rather lost my head. *Mea culpa !*

[1] Hatfield MSS.

I hope, however, I am forgiven. Please let me know if I am. It has been a trying time . . .'

Kitchener's tactical mistake encouraged Curzon to delude himself with the belief that he had won significant concessions ; and Kitchener found it difficult to disillusion the sick Viceroy. He told[1] Lady Salisbury (16 July) that he had just seen Curzon : ' He was not very pleasant ; nor more was I, as I had to speak to him pretty straight about his absurd view of the modifications he has obtained. I told him they were all safeguards against a military autocracy which I had entirely repudiated the notion of imposing.'

Two days later (18 July), Curzon deliberately put to the test the view which he had formed about the significance of the modifications which Kitchener had agreed to recommend. In a speech to the Legislative Assembly, Curzon took leave to observe that the Government of India had received ' with regret' the British Government's instructions to introduce a new form of military administration, ' contrary to the advice which they had all but unanimously tendered to His Majesty's government' ; and that they were ' somewhat surprised at the manner in which it was thought necessary to convey those orders '. Curzon paused at that point, and then announced that he had succeeded in obtaining a number of important modifications. ' We have converted the position of the Military Supply Member into one of greater utility and efficiency. We have very considerably strengthened the guarantees for civil supervision and control.'

The astonished India Office cabled a request that the full text of that speech should immediately be cabled home ; and Kitchener, who was very sensitive to the charge that he was seeking to subvert the civil supremacy, wrote[1] (20 July) to Lady Salisbury : ' Curzon has, I think, given himself away by his very improper speech. I wonder what action the Government will take—he is evidently at their mercy.' Curzon, in the meantime, goaded to desperation, claimed the right to nominate, as of old, the new Military Member of Council in succession to Sir Edmund Elles.

Brodrick refused to admit that right, or to accept Curzon's interpretation of the so-called modifications. He refused also to appoint Curzon's nominee, Major-General Sir Edmund Barrow, in Elles's place, because he knew that Kitchener would object. He insisted at the same time that the term ' Supply', which Kitchener had agreed to

[1] Ibid.

drop, should be restored to the title of Elles's successor ; and Kitchener reported[1] (10 August) to Lady Salisbury a painful interview which he had had with Curzon five days earlier :

> ' He said he would resign, and I said he must do what he thought right, and so I left him.   Next day I got a letter from Eddy Stanley telling me what misrepresentations the Viceroy has been making in secret telegrams about my views.   I *was* angry.   I always thought his misrepresentations were about the so-called modifications, and it never occurred to me that he could have told such unwarrantable lies about my views of the whole scheme . . .   I do not now believe a word he says, and I hope neither you nor any of my friends will do so in the future ; and to think that, out of pity for the man when he was down, I could be fool enough to make such a gross mistake —it makes me wild.
>
> ' I am so glad it is understood at home that I have not been disloyal to my friends.   If I only had not made that one mistake I should feel quite happy.'

Pity was not a weakness for which Kitchener had just cause to reproach himself.   He had failed to appreciate that a man of Curzon's temperament found it much easier to deceive himself than to deceive others.   Curzon resigned when Brodrick reiterated his refusal to appoint Barrow in place of Elles, and the announcements of his resignation and of the appointment of Lord Minto as Viceroy were both made on 21 August, 1905.

After first showing that he was prepared to compromise on the question of principle, and then, characteristically, resigning on a personal issue, Curzon severed his friendship with Brodrick.   At the same time the quarrel with Kitchener was made bitterly personal as a result of Curzon's misrepresentation of Kitchener's views about the rôle of the new Military Supply Member.   After reading a minute which set forth Kitchener's proposals for implementing the new scheme, Curzon told Brodrick that the new member would be left with less than two hours' work a day, and that the post would be a sinecure.   But Kitchener, who was determined to work the new system loyally, repudiated that suggestion.

An angry correspondence followed between the Viceroy and the Commander-in-Chief, in the course of which Curzon alleged that

[1] Hatfield MSS.

Kitchener had seen and agreed with a minute signed by the head of the Ordnance, showing the number of ordnance officers who would, in future, come directly under the Commander-in-Chief. On 26 August, Kitchener denied in writing, for the second time, that he had ever seen that minute.

To Kitchener's intense surprise, Curzon refused to accept that denial. He wrote (28 August) that he had made inquiries and found that the sheet containing the figures ' *was* included in the file sent to you, and was marked with a green slip, to which your attention was especially drawn . . .'

That letter virtually accused Kitchener of lying, and Kitchener wrote[1] (30 August) to Lady Salisbury :

' Curzon has rather surpassed himself, I think, by writing me the last letter of the enclosed correspondence. In old days I suppose I should have called him out on it and shot him like a dog for his grossly insulting letter. All I can do now is to have nothing more to do with him. . . . Everyone knows I never saw the paper in question—not through any carelessness of mine, but because it was hid away in a big file which was referred to me on a different question (which I answered), without any reference to this paper having been placed at the bottom of the file. I am going away on tour, to be clear of the whole thing. It all seems to me so low and disgusting.'

Kitchener asked that Balfour should be informed about the gross insult to which he had been subjected.

Kitchener, who was never at home among files, had been let down on that occasion by his staff. His nerves, as well as Curzon's, were badly frayed, and although his letter to Lady Salisbury was too violent, he had just cause to be angry. Curzon retired for ten years into private life, nursing his grievance, while Kitchener, after his triumph, presently forgot and forgave. But Kitchener insisted that his angry correspondence with Curzon should be published in the Press, in association with a White Paper containing the telegrams which had passed between Curzon and Brodrick. *The Times* commented (28 August) that such a ' lamentable spectacle ought to have been impossible ', and it censured Kitchener as well as Curzon for ' an offence against the public interest '.

[1] Ibid.

In response to a pathetic letter of appeal from Lady Curzon, who was mortally ill, Kitchener agreed, with great reluctance, to shake hands with Curzon at a farewell ceremony on the lawn of Viceregal House at Simla before the Curzons left India for England. Kitchener was still furious at that time, and he told[1] Lady Salisbury (26 October) that he had consented, ' only to stop people talking, although it was not very pleasant to shake hands with a man who has called you a liar. However, I consoled myself by the consideration that it was the Viceroy to whom I was saying goodbye, not Curzon.'

After Curzon had departed, Kitchener told[1] Lady Salisbury (2 November) that he was troubled by the suspicion that Curzon had used his security powers ' to see my private telegrams, all of which I personally paid for and thought safe . . . My position was that I had told the Viceroy, if no change in army administration was allowed, that I wished to resign my command. Under these circumstances I think it was only natural that I should keep my friends informed of how things went on, and of my views ; and I looked upon these telegrams exactly the same as private letters.'

Kitchener said that he had reason to believe that Curzon was thinking of publishing those telegrams : ' This would be very unpleasant and should be stoppped . . . The only person I know of who would be likely to influence him would be the King, and if Curzon is desperate it might be as well to invoke his aid ; as if I have to justify my action in public it will do no possible good, but will, I fear, only tend to lower our public life at home and abroad.' Kitchener was referring to the telegrams which he had exchanged with R. J. Marker, private secretary to the Secretary for War ; but, except for their caustic wording, and for the proof which they afforded of the distrust which Curzon had evoked in influential political circles at home, there was little in any of them to which serious exception could have been taken ; and they never were published.

Kitchener and Curzon were both inspired by a profound sense of duty. They were strong, proud, confident, self-willed men of outstanding character and illustrious reputation which had been richly earned ; and their quarrel involved not only a clash of temperaments, but a difference of opinion about the best method of advancing the interests of a mighty empire to whose service both their lives were dedicated. A last word, therefore, must be said, about the merits of the military controversy out of which their personal quarrel sprang.

[1] Hatfield MSS.

In March, 1907, Kitchener obtained from the Viceroy's Council a unanimous vote in favour of the new system of military administration. He told[1] Lady Salisbury (24 April, 1907) that a dispatch had been sent home : ' signed by the whole Council, stating that the new system was a complete success and an immense improvement upon the old ; that none of the anticipations against it had been realized ; and that the Viceroy and Govt. of India had as much, if not more, power over the Army than before ; that there was no autocracy, etc., etc.   I think I must have the three dispatches bound up—Curzon's original, signed by all the Council, except myself ; then the dispatch establishing the new system ; and this last one, signed by everyone. Poor Curzon ! How angry he would be ! '

That resounding triumph did nothing to increase the respect felt by Kitchener for his civilian colleagues who had unanimously reversed an opinion which they had expressed with an equal degree of unanimity only two years before, ' and yet ', Kitchener added disingenuously, ' they were—more or less—clever and unbiased people '.   He assured[1] Lady Salisbury (19 July, 1906) that his work was ' less than it used to be ', and (20 June, 1907) that the new system had ' more than justified my wildest hopes '.

In pursuance of his policy of strict economy, John Morley, the new Liberal Secretary for India, asked Minto in July, 1907, whether it was worth while to retain the new Military Supply Department. Kitchener advised Minto to make no change, because the system was working well, and because his personal relations with the new Military Supply Member, Major-General Scott, were so happy.   But Morley saw no reason to continue to pay a salary to any official, however popular or efficient, whose employment could be regarded as otiose, and the post of Military Supply Member was accordingly abolished on 1 April, 1909. Kitchener, thereafter, assumed personal control of the Department, while retaining its separate identity.

Sir Horace Smith-Dorrien, an excellent soldier and a warm admirer of Kitchener, held[2] that his chief went too far. He maintained that, after Curzon's overthrow, ' the personal inspection of troops by the C.-in-C. diminished, and his magnetic influence grew small by degrees, and dangerously less ' ; and Roberts sent Kitchener a friendly warning (17 June, 1909) that his method of command was becoming too

[1] Ibid.
[2] General Sir Horace Smith-Dorrien, *Memories of Forty-eight Years Service*, p. 329.

impersonal : ' It is for this reason that I have been unable to agree altogether with the changes that have been made in the military administration of the Indian Army. Few men can get through the amount of work that you can, and no soldier that I know has your power of organization ; and my fear is that future C.-in-Cs. will not have time to attend to the Council work, and look after the Army at the same time.'

War must always remain the ultimate test of any military system ; and it has to be admitted that the report of the Royal Commission on the ill-starred expedition to Mesopotamia, which was conducted during 1916 by the Indian Army, stated unequivocally (July, 1917) that ' the combination of the duties of Commander-in-Chief in India and Military Member of Council cannot adequately be performed by any one man in time of war '.

It may be suggested, nevertheless, that that report, which deliberately echoed past controversy, was too kind to the commanders of the expedition to Mesopotamia, and too hard upon the new system which Kitchener had instituted. The weight of responsibility resting upon the shoulders of any one man, however exalted, is never a true measure of the amount of work which he is called upon personally to perform. It is an elementary principle of administration that the latter must always be a question of organization, and of the delegation of power. Were it otherwise it would be impossible for any man, however exceptional, to attempt to guide the destinies of a great nation or organization, such as the United States or the Roman Catholic Church.

The system of military administration which Kitchener destroyed in India was obsolete and on the point of breaking down. It is true that while he remained in India after its reconstruction, his organization of the work was open to serious criticism. He refused to delegate responsibility, and he centralized all power in himself to an excessive and wholly unnecessary degree. That was always his weakness, and some of his less competent successors were confused and misled by the example which they inherited.

Nevertheless, on an impartial survey and despite the report of the Royal Commission on the campaign in Mesopotamia which was completed hastily in circumstances of peculiar difficulty, Kitchener's system must be accounted greatly superior to the one which it displaced. It was better adapted to needs and conditions which, together with the highly personal machine which Kitchener devised to meet them, have passed, like a dissolving view, into history.

CHAPTER 12

APOTHEOSIS

1906–1910

THE overthrow of Curzon enhanced Kitchener's reputation with the British public. The fierceness of the contest touched a chord in the popular mood which had exulted in the carnage at Omdurman and which was becoming increasingly attuned to violence. The smooth surface of contemporary political and social life was growing seismic ; and within a few years the action of the House of Lords in rejecting a Liberal Budget, the militant suffragette campaign and the drift towards civil war in Ireland afforded preliminary intimations of the existence of deep-seated internal stresses which were soon to precipitate the gigantic earthquake of 1914 and the convulsive break-up of the former pattern of European civilization.

Strenuous efforts were being made in those circumstances to set in order the British military machine ; and more than a year after a War Office Reconstruction Committee, under the chairmanship of Lord Esher, had issued its report, Esher wrote [1] (26 July, 1905) on his own initiative, but with the tacit approval of A. J. Balfour, to sound Kitchener about the possibility of his acceptance of the new post of Chief of the General Staff. Esher skilfully employed such arguments as might have been expected to attract Kitchener :

'. . . The position, if you would accept it, would have to be enhanced in importance, and this could best be done by marking your advent—

' (a) by an increase in the emoluments of the post,

' (b) by giving you a Field-Marshal's baton.

' Nothing could mark more clearly the intention that you should have as free a hand as is consistent with our parliamentary institutions to mould the Army into shape . . .

' Perhaps you do not altogether perceive, at a distance from home, the immense power which, under the existing system, a Chief of the General Staff potentially exercises.

' No Commander-in-Chief under the old limitations enjoyed such authority.

[1] Esher, *Journals and Letters*, II, pp. 94–6.

' The statutory powers of the Secretary of State rendered all real power in a Commander-in-Chief nugatory ; whereas under the present system a strong and determined Chief of the General Staff could *administer* the Army practically unchallenged . . .'

Esher begged Kitchener to forgo his ' moral and material ease ', and to come home in order to ' wield an authority which has never been exercised in this country to the same degree since the death of the Duke of Wellington '. But Kitchener was unimpressed. He had told [1] Lady Salisbury (28 October, 1903) that Esher was ' an outsider, who knows little or nothing about the Army ', and (11 November, 1903) that there was not one man on Esher's War Office Reconstruction Committee who had 'the faintest idea of what the machine is wanted to turn out. You can make a beautiful machine to make carpets—but it won't chop meat.'

Kitchener had warned Lady Salisbury (28 October) that politicians were, by nature, incapable of reforming any army ; and that Esher's Committee would have been useless, even if it had been composed entirely of soldiers. He had explained that soldiers, unlike sailors, had little in common : ' You see, Navy men are all more or less alike. They go through almost exactly the same experiences during their service, and come from commanding a fleet to the Admiralty Board. In the Army, you rarely get two soldiers who think alike on even the fundamental military questions, as, during their service, they have all had totally different experiences in the totally different services that exist.'

As for the politicians, Kitchener wrote [1] (4 August, 1904) : ' Poor Army ! It is the happy or unhappy playground of politicians who have to leave their mark ; and *what* a mark they leave ! . . . I do not think the country would stand conscription, but, if it did, who would dream of paying the men 1/- a day, as Arnold-Forster calmly supposes—1d. a day would be more like it.'

Kitchener would have liked to see the principal administrative duties of the Secretary of State for War transferred to the province of a plenipotentiary Commander-in-Chief. He knew that such an arrangement was impossible in England ; and he, therefore, kept away from the War Office and from all attempts to reform the Army at home. He condemned [1] Esher's report to Lady Salisbury (2 March, 1904) on the ground that it effected ' an absolute divorce between administrative

[1] Hatfield MSS.

228

and executive functions in the Army . . . In peacetime the feeling in the Army of distrust of W.O. administration will be accentuated ; and in wartime the Army in the field will have absolutely no confidence in a civil administration assisted by some officers who may be entirely out of touch with the Army, and know practically nothing of the necessities of a campaign. It is only through the loyal administration of the Army by executive officers that true economy combined with efficiency can be obtained.'

Kitchener had done his best to reform the military machine in India on the centralized autocratic system in which he placed his entire trust ; and he wrote [1] to Roberts (22 March, 1906) : ' I have had a very unpleasant time in all this, but it is a lesson I shall not forget. No more attempts at Army reform for me—either here, or in England. I do not think, if one tries to do one's best for the Army, one deserves to be made to live a dog's life . . . but I suppose this is the English way.'

It was the democratic way, and Kitchener's abilities were oriented otherwise. Suggestions were already being made in responsible quarters at home—by Lord Rosebery, amongst others, with whom Kitchener seldom corresponded—that Kitchener's appointment as Secretary for War would reassure the country. Kitchener scoffed at that idea, and he was equally scornful of Esher's suggestion that he should return to England in order to serve as Chief of the General Staff at the War Office. He wrote [2] to Esher (14 August, 1905) :

' Patriotic convictions, my dear Lord Esher, have led many men to commit great follies, and will, I presume, continue to do so in the future.

' You must pardon this opening . . . but what I want to impress upon you is that it would take a great deal to convince me now that it was my patriotic duty to accept the post of C. of G.S. Why ? Because I should fail ! I think I know what I can do, as well as my limitations. I can, I believe, impress, to a certain extent, my personality on men working under me ; I am vain enough to think I can lead them ; but I have no silver tongue to persuade . . .'

With that letter, Kitchener enclosed *A Note on the Military Policy of India*. It was a secret and most statesmanlike document, dated 19

[1] Roberts Papers.　　　　[2] Esher, *Journals and Letters*, II, p. 98.

July, 1905 ; and it greatly impressed the Cabinet in general, and
Balfour in particular. Kitchener argued that no consistent policy
had hitherto been followed ; that policy had been apt to change, in
whole or in part, with every change of Secretary of State, or Viceroy,
and that it ought in future to be controlled by the Committee of
Imperial Defence instead of by the Government of India.

Balfour remained eager to tempt Kitchener home ; but at the
general election of December, 1905, the Conservatives suffered an
overwhelming defeat at the hands of the Liberals, under Sir Henry
Campbell-Bannerman. That event almost coincided with the arrival
of the new Viceroy, and Kitchener found that he had to deal with
Minto in place of Curzon, and with John Morley, who succeeded
Brodrick as Secretary of State for India.

Kitchener was in no doubt about what he wanted to do. He told
Birdwood and other intimates that he would like his term as Commander-in-Chief to be extended for a sufficient time, after it expired
in November, 1907, to give him a chance of being selected, after a
year's holiday, to succeed Minto in 1910 as Viceroy of India. He
said that if the Viceroyalty were denied to him, as a soldier, or as a
Tory, or for any other reason, he would like to rule Egypt as Cromer's
successor.

Cromer, when he retired in 1907, strongly advised the Liberal
Government not to send Kitchener to Egypt. Sir Eldon Gorst was,
accordingly, appointed and Kitchener, thereafter, set his heart on
becoming Ambassador at Constantinople, in default of either India or
Egypt. He told Birdwood that he would quit the Army and retire
into private life in preference to entering the War Office in any capacity,
because he believed that the War Office would prove to be the grave
of his great reputation.

The Embassy at Constantinople would have been quite a good
appointment for Kitchener. He understood the Turks, and he told [1]
his friend and solicitor, Arthur Renshaw (27 May, 1909) that, if he
were appointed as Ambassador, he was certain that he could ' manage
to retrieve our position in the East '. It is just possible that, if Kitchener
had been in Constantinople instead of in Cairo in 1913–14, the weight
of the Turkish Empire would have been thrown into the first World
War upon the British instead of upon the German side ; and it may
be regretted that he was not offered that appointment in 1910–11,
when he found himself temporarily unemployed. The Foreign

[1] Letter in the possession of Lady Winifred Renshaw.

Secretary, Sir Edward Grey, vetoed that suggestion on the ground that Kitchener's appointment would have excited jealousy among professional diplomats.

After the change of government in England, a fierce battle continued to rage between Kitchener's and Curzon's partisans. Curzon tried hard to stir up prejudice against Kitchener, and pressure was exerted on Morley to reverse Brodrick's decision on the subject of dual control. Kitchener informed Minto and Morley that he would resign within the hour if such action were taken.

Kitchener sent his adjutant-general, Sir Beauchamp Duff, to London to represent his interests, and to attend meetings of the Committee of Imperial Defence. He told [1] Lady Salisbury (28 February, 1907) that ' Duff has done a lot of good at home with Mr. Morley ' ; but he rejected her advice that he should write often and fully to Morley himself. He explained [1] to her (17 October, 1907) : ' Curzon's agents do all they can to poison the S. of S.'s mind with most unwarrantable and baseless reports. I wonder he listens to them. I know he would like me to write more often and fuller, and, possibly, it might do good. But, between ourselves, it is much more important for me to keep well with the Viceroy than with the S. of S.'

Kitchener constantly assured Lady Salisbury, and other friends, that ' the Viceroy and I get on first-rate ' ; and Minto told Morley (1 February, 1906) that he had been much puzzled by reports that Kitchener was ' overbearing, self-seeking, and difficult to deal with. One can only speak of people as one finds them, and all I can say is that I find him very broadminded, very ready to see both sides of a question, and perfectly easy to deal with ; whilst his minutes on the questions we have had to consider since I have been here, have been much the ablest and most moderate I have had before me . . .'

Minto, a somewhat indolent Whig patrician in his sixty-first year, had been a successful Governor-General of Canada. He was a little startled soon after his arrival in India to hear Kitchener remark ingenuously after dinner, as he stubbed out a cigar in a gold ash-tray and fed biscuits to his poodle, that he thought that he should have been awarded the Nobel Peace Prize. Kitchener explained that he had brought peace to the Sudan, and subsequently to South Africa.

A visiting maharajah rashly remarked : ' Nobel wanted the reconciliation of peoples through contact and negotiation, not by conquest ! ' and Kitchener's blue eyes blazed, although their focus, as always,

[1] Hatfield MSS.

remained uncertain : ' Nobel ', he exclaimed, ' was a dreamer. He was no realist, but a weaver of fantasies. How could such a man understand what our Empire means for the future of the whole of mankind ! '

As a former professional soldier, Minto found that he understood and quite liked Kitchener. Morley and Kitchener, on the other hand, were antipathetic. Nicknamed ' Priscilla ' by Campbell-Bannerman, and not too popular with his colleagues because he seemed too much imbued with a sense of his importance, Morley was a polished intel-lectual who once [1] told Esher that he found Kitchener ' a most un-interesting type'. At other times he was, in fact, fascinated by Kitchener ; but Kitchener's opinion of Morley never varied. He described [2] Morley to Arthur Renshaw (13 April, 1909) as ' pig-headed and dangerous ' ; to his staff as ' sand-paperish ' ; and to Lady Salisbury [3] (25 April, 1909) as a man who ' positively hates military efficiency'. After three years' experience of Liberal Ministers, Kitchener told [3] Lady Salisbury (6 April, 1909) that he ached to see them ' kicked out—the harm they do is great'. He explained that ' with this Government, military or naval efficiency are looked on with disgust, and, whenever they can, they act accordingly, notwith-standing fine words to the contrary '. Nevertheless he did his utmost to work loyally and without friction with Morley.

At the end of February, 1906, Morley confirmed Brodrick's arrange-ments about the system of military administration : ' All's well that ends well ', Kitchener told [3] Lady Salisbury (1 March, 1906). ' I *am* thankful, as it has been a most trying time. I owe a great deal to Ld. Minto as, without his support, I believe they would have enjoyed upsetting St. J.'s scheme . . . Minto . . . was of course a bit nervous about me at first, but confidence came. It . . . has quite taken away any desire to have anything further to do with Army reforms.'

Kitchener quickly discovered that he had only won the first round. The Liberals were pledged to economy, and Morley was a ruthless anti-militarist in the Gladstonian tradition. He took the view, with which Kitchener strongly disagreed, that as the Russian menace had been reduced, a number of Kitchener's military projects could safely be scrapped. All plans for strategic railways fell, accordingly, under

---

[1] Esher, *Journals and Letters*, II, p. 175.
[2] Letter in the possession of Lady Winifred Renshaw.
[3] Hatfield MSS.

the axe ; and work on new military buildings, including a number of much-needed barracks, was arbitrarily suspended.

A passion for cheese-paring economy constituted the sole bond of sympathy between Kitchener and Morley ; but Kitchener was particularly irritated when he was denied the means to build a new cavalry cantonment near Quetta and to convert his garrison artillery into heavy batteries. He would have preferred to economize by postponing, temporarily, a number of rises in the pay, allowances and pensions of junior officers and other ranks—British as well as Indian—upon which Morley insisted in order to offset a fall in the value of the rupee. Kitchener successfully resisted Morley's attempt to reduce his establishment of 71,000 British troops, exclusive of officers ; and he was supported consistently by Minto, who handled him extremely well when he grumbled and growled that his mission was being frustrated by ignorant politicians, and that he might at any moment have to consider resignation.

Kitchener managed, nevertheless, to complete his reorganization scheme, and to effect a number of useful but unspectacular reforms. He improved training, equipment and armaments; and he established in September, 1906, a Staff College at Quetta which worked in association with its British counterpart at Camberley. He raised his Army's morale by providing it with better rations ; by encouraging sport ; and by establishing regimental institutes and clubs. He caused factories to be built in order to make his Army self-supporting in war ; and he warmly encouraged the establishment of grass and dairy farms throughout India.

Kitchener strongly disapproved of the action of R. B. Haldane, the Liberal Secretary for War, in creating a Territorial Army in England. His professional jealousy was aroused, and he wrote [1] (7 June, 1906) to Lady Salisbury : ' What a heterogeneous committee he has got together ! I suppose the militia and volunteers will demand greater expenditure, and probably get it. Then, whatever is given, plus all the economies in the Budget, will have to come out of the regular Army, which we shall be told we can do without. That sort of thing is all very well until the bullets begin to fly. Then surprise, grief, and rage will result. If the people are sensible, they won't allow this sort of thing, after all the experience we have been through recently.'

Throughout the latter part of his stay in India, Kitchener was troubled by the growth of sedition. He told [1] Lady Salisbury (6 June,

[1] Hatfield MSS.

233

1907) that it was 'pretty strong underneath the surface. The principal agitators are the more or less educated lawyer class. They . . . are doing all they can to get at the loyalty of the Army. They preach another mutiny, to drive us out of the country. It will require careful handling . . .'

Kitchener laughed at Minto's suggestion that the situation might be improved if an Indian were appointed to membership of the Viceroy's Council; and he strongly opposed that idea. He pressed for the rigorous prohibition of all obnoxious public meetings and seditious publications, as well as for the infliction of the death penalty upon anyone who attempted to tamper with the loyalty of his soldiers, which was never, at any period, in serious doubt.

Minto, guided by Morley, failed to act as swiftly or as vigorously as Kitchener would have wished; but he pleased the Commander-in-Chief by asking him (1 November, 1907) to thank his sepoys 'for the contempt with which they have received the disgraceful overtures which I know have been made to them'.

Kitchener never concealed his view that India would become untenable whenever the different sections of the population ceased to hate each other more than they feared their British overlords. He told Minto frequently that it was 'unrealistic' to worry about outrages committed in Bengal. He explained that he drew no soldiers from that unwarlike country where, if necessary, he could easily scotch sedition by the employment of ruthless methods. He said that he was much more concerned about outrages committed by Punjabis because 'they are the fighting classes from which we draw our Army'; and because, in an emergency, they would be more difficult to cow.

On 15 March, 1907, after consulting Minto, Morley offered Kitchener a two years' extension of his command, which was due to expire in November. In accepting that offer (7 April), Kitchener complained about his health; and he suffered, in fact, throughout that year from brief but recurrent bouts of malaria. Birdwood found him on one such occasion in bed at Simla with all his clothes on, including his boots, cap, and even his spectacles, and with every window closed. He had difficulty in persuading his chief to undress and to go properly to bed. When he had succeeded, Kitchener exclaimed in a hoarse whisper : " Send at once for my brother, Walter. He will wish to be here at the last." Birdwood coaxed him into a more cheerful mood and took him away presently for a few days' rest.

Kitchener was not really ill, but friends noticed that, in his fifty-seventh year, a kind of nervous irritability appeared to have gripped him. Accordingly, after consulting Minto, Kitchener wrote (24 September) to ask Morley for permission to leave India early in 1908, in order to take a holiday in the form of a long sea voyage to Singapore, China and Japan. He was debarred by law from revisiting Europe during his tenure of command ; and while he awaited Morley's answer he displayed an extraordinary degree of high-strung nervous excitement and impatience.

Kitchener's depression was only partly caused by fever and by Morley's reluctance and hesitation to take swift and strong action against sedition. Kitchener told [1] Lady Salisbury (29 August, 1907) that he felt himself ' a prisoner in India ' and that he longed ' to be out of it all ', because Morley was being so ' nasty ', and showing him ' no consideration '. But there was also at that moment a more personal cause of Kitchener's discontent.

What Kitchener sometimes described as his ' happy family of boys ', who understood and looked after him so well, had broken up. Frank Maxwell, V.C. (the ' Brat '), who had been the reigning favourite for six years, had left to attend the Staff College in England, where he had become engaged to be married ; and Victor Brooke, elder brother of the future Lord Alanbrooke, had become military secretary to the Viceroy. To replace Maxwell, who had previously promised to return, Kitchener, after taking a great amount of trouble, appointed Captain O. A. G. FitzGerald, 18th Bengal Lancers, to be his A.D.C. But at the end of July, 1907, FitzGerald went home to England on leave ; and while he was away Kitchener was intensely lonely for some weeks. After his return, FitzGerald established himself so securely in the affections of his chief that Kitchener never looked elsewhere, and their intimate association was happy and fortunate. FitzGerald, like Kitchener, was a bachelor and a natural celibate ; he devoted the whole of the rest of his life exclusively to Kitchener ; and, except for a brief period early in 1910, he never quitted Kitchener's side until they met death together on the fatal voyage to Russia in June, 1916.

Morley's reply to Kitchener's application for leave of absence was dated 7 November, 1907 ; and Birdwood used to recall that its cleverness caused Kitchener intense annoyance :

'. . . It is only, I think, three or four months since I received,
[1] Hatfield MSS.

as the foundation of the case for sundry measures of repressive legislation, a strong memorandum of yours depicting the dangers of disaffection in the Indian Army . . . In the state of things so emphatically pressed on my close attention, you won't think it unnatural that I should feel uneasy at the idea of your being off the scene, even for a week.

' Then there is another difficulty. You represent military things upon the Executive Council of the Governor-General. What is to become of them in your absence ? You will not, I think, refer me to the head of the Military Supply Department. Even if you did, I cherish the hope that the Department may vanish into limbo almost before you start . . .'

Morley added that ' Indian military business in all its aspects ' was likely to be ' an object of much interest and importance for some months to come. Are we to hang it all up ? ' He said that he would ' get into a scrape ' for having extended Kitchener's period of command if the Commander-in-Chief's health had become so precarious that a sea voyage was really necessary.

Kitchener appreciated that he had met his match, and he withdrew his application for leave ; the prompt award of a G.C.I.E. may have been intended as a kind of consolation. Nevertheless, for the first time in his life, Kitchener reacted by relapsing into idleness, and that startling and wholly unexpected development was noted [1] with dismay by Minto as well as by Morley.

Kitchener informed his friends that his Indian mission had been faithfully discharged ; that no one appeared to want him any more ; and that the Liberal Government had extended his term in India only because it did not know what future use to make of his popular reputation : ' We jog along ', he told [2] Lady Salisbury (13 August, 1908), ' and hope things are better. But are they ? I really do not know. Anyway, my office and staff work happily, and though the India Office are not, perhaps, all one could wish, they have not worried me much lately. I have been amusing myself in my spare time by redecorating the drawing-room.' He added : ' Have you heard a rumour that I was to be offered the embassy at Berlin ? . . . Constantinople would be more my line if anything of that sort were contemplated.'

Shooting tigers, exhibiting his orchids, arranging his porcelain,

[1] Cf. Esher, *Journals and Letters*, II, pp. 406, 437.   [2] Hatfield MSS.

caring for his poodle, raising the ceilings of his suites of reception rooms and playing with his investments helped to solace Kitchener's leisure during his last two years in India.   He was concerned about his future, but he had the means to retire temporarily, if necessary, into private life.   He had instructed [1] his solicitor, as early as 7 February, 1906, to look out for ' a nice old house ' with a good property in England, for which he said that he might be prepared to pay, as an investment, up to fifty thousand pounds.

Nevertheless, in comparison with his friends, Kitchener was a poor man.   His ambition, furthermore, was unsatisfied.   He asked Minto privately to help him to obtain Egypt, before Gorst's appointment, and India thereafter ; while his friends at home continued to press his claim to succeed Minto in India.

Kitchener was not snobbish, but he had made few contemporary friends in early life.   Nearly all his friendships dated from the period of his manhood, and among the patrician ruling class he had a host of eager and devoted friends to whom he was invariably charming.   In adapting his means to his aims and ambitions in that way, Kitchener was true to his nature which impelled him to concentrate exclusively upon the task in hand.   But he made no attempt to court the affection of his Army, or of ordinary people, because neither his temperament nor the social climate of his age made him dependent upon their affection for success.

In those circumstances, Kitchener's celebrated coldness and reserve were sometimes construed, outside the patrician world and his small circle of intimates, as rudeness and selfish opportunism ; and his great popularity with the British masses, who hero-worshipped his shadow, was not reflected among the rank and file of the Army which he commanded.   He neglected those small courtesies and gracious acts which help to make life agreeable, whether prompted by the heart or by the head ; and unlike Roberts and Sir Power Palmer, his immediate predecessors, he seldom troubled to thank those who were responsible for his comfort when he made tours of inspection in his special train.

Because he was entirely devoid of vanity, Kitchener cared little for ceremony ; and he often gave scant notice of his arrival when he was on tour.   But during his visits he radiated no warmth, and he occasionally behaved more like an uncouth old-time accountant, intent only upon satisfying himself that value was being obtained for

[1] Letter in the possession of Lady Winifred Renshaw.

money, than like a Commander-in-Chief who values the love of his men. He professed interest only in official and technical matters. A typical comment by one commanding officer, whose prowess as a cricketer was blazed throughout the sub-continent, was that the chief had spoken of cricket as though it were a medicine to be taken twice weekly by the troops in summer. Kitchener had refused to hear details about battalion successes and scores.

The obsessional aspect of Kitchener's temperament was much in evidence in India. He seemed unable to rest, and to wish always to control the material world around him. Garrulous in congenial company, he belied his taciturn reputation ; but he seldom sat and talked quietly as most men do. He loved to recall and discuss his past exploits and to polish, as he did so, some dervish spear or similar trophy with a strange intensity, as if he could not bear to relax.

When his table was laid for guests, Kitchener invariably inspected it himself. He arranged the flowers with his own hand, and took immense pains to ensure that no glass or vase, and no knife, fork or spoon was a fraction of an inch out of position. He was proud of the trouble which he took, and he often called attention to it ; and he liked to attend personally to all the needs of his pet poodle. On one occasion, when they were about to leave Simla for a ten days' tour, FitzGerald remarked that there was only one tennis court at Wildflower Hall. Unknown to FitzGerald, Kitchener immediately issued orders that a sizeable hillock should be removed and that tennis courts should be laid out where it had stood. That work was completed within a week by engineers working night and day, and Kitchener was re-warded on his return by gasps of unfeigned astonishment from his A.D.C. In small things as in great, Kitchener loved to alter and improve ; but he was apt to lose interest quickly after his changes had been effected.

Kitchener discharged well, under protest, the larger social duties of his position. He had a reputation for meanness which was not wholly undeserved ; but he had been poor in his youth, and the hospitality which he dispensed in later life was invariably upon a most lavish scale. His balls and suppers were celebrated throughout India and, although he spoke only to his more distinguished guests, he always made a point of appearing happy and in splendid form. On lesser social occasions, however, except when he was displaying his porcelain, when he was glad to meet even humble strangers upon a human level of equality, Kitchener lost his geniality and became once more the

grim and unsympathetic taskmaster. Those who knew him super-
ficially had no conception of the powerful emotional undercurrents
which he had schooled himself to repress, and which found an outlet
in his passion for art and flowers.

In all his financial dealings, Kitchener was scrupulously honest ;
but he did not hesitate to use his position and prestige to beg for any
choice article which he wanted to add to his collections, either as a
knockdown bargain or as a goodwill offering and outright gift.
Dealers learned to close their shops, fellow-collectors to be suddenly
indisposed, whenever it was known that the Commander-in-Chief
was engaged upon an artistic prowl, as he frequently was, especially
during his last two years in India.

As Kitchener's period of command drew towards its close, the Liberal
Government became concerned about his future employment. He
was nearly sixty, and a little too closely identified with the Conservatives ; but his popular reputation was great and he had no intention
of retiring if he could help it. During the summer of 1909, accordingly, the Government seized an opportunity to make use of Kitchener
in order to extricate itself from an embarrassment in which it had been
involved by its Secretary for War, R. B. Haldane.

Haldane had established, two years earlier, a Mediterranean Command, based on Malta, for what he believed to be reasons of high
strategy ; and, at the Government's request, the King had persuaded
his brother, the Duke of Connaught, to invest the new post with the
prestige of his name by accepting it. The Duke, who had been very
reluctant to accept, informed the Government privately within a year
that he intended to resign because the command, in his opinion,
served no useful purpose.

The Government was committed to the view that the post was of
the first importance ; and the King had so informed his brother. The
King told H. H. Asquith, the new Liberal Prime Minister, that he was
furious with his brother, who would have to consider his military
career to be at an end. After the failure of all attempts to induce the
Duke of Connaught to change his mind, the Government decided
that Kitchener would have to be cajoled into consenting to succeed
the Duke.

The first overture to Kitchener was made by Haldane with extreme
tact on 7 July, 1909 :

' I am writing merely tentatively and informally with the purpose
of ascertaining what you might hereafter be prepared to consider,

rather than with the desire to make a definite proposition. I may, however, add that not only are the Prime Minister and my principal colleagues in the Cabinet cognisant of what I am doing, but that I have gone over the substance of it with Mr. Balfour, who is anxious to lay the foundations of continuity in military policy.'

Haldane explained that the Government wished to give 'the new Mediterranean command, including as it does the British forces in Egypt', an enhanced importance ; that the Duke of Connaught was about to resign ; and that it was hoped that Kitchener might be persuaded to combine 'the post of Commander-in-Chief in the Mediterranean with a seat on the Committee of Imperial Defence, and the Presidency of the Selection Board when you are in London'. He notified Kitchener, who had been awarded a G.C.S.I. on 25 June, together with a diamond pendant valued at 16,000 rupees, that he would be promoted to the rank of Field-Marshal in November, whether he agreed to go to Malta or not. Haldane promised, in addition, that Kitchener would be paid five thousand pounds a year in addition to his full pay and allowances as a Field-Marshal ; and that two Maltese palaces, one 'with a beautiful garden', would be placed at his disposal.

On 22 July, Morley informed Kitchener by telegram that the Duke of Connaught had resigned and that the Government begged him to come to its help by taking over the command from H.R.H. But Kitchener informed Morley (25 July) that he was 'looking forward to a period of unemployment' ; and he replied formally to Haldane on the same day : 'I regret that after 35 years' continuous service I could not accept the Mediterranean Command'. He explained that he needed a long holiday, and that a tour of Japan, Australia and New Zealand, to which the Government had already agreed, and upon which he intended to embark as soon as his successor reached India, 'will, I think, afford me valuable experience which will then be at your disposal'.

Morley and Haldane had anticipated that refusal, and had concerted their plans to meet and overcome it. Esher had seen the King on behalf of the Government and of the Committee of Imperial Defence, and had asked him to exert pressure upon Kitchener. The King, prompted by Kitchener's friends, had hitherto been pressing Kitchener's claims to succeed Minto ; but he was preoccupied by the controversies about Irish home rule and the House of Lords' veto ; his health was failing ; and he was averse from having to admit, even to himself,

240

that he had pressed a command which was of less than first-rate importance upon his recalcitrant brother. He yielded the more readily, therefore, to his Government's request.

Accordingly, on 26 July, 1909, Kitchener was dismayed to receive a personal appeal from his Sovereign :

'I take a personal interest in this matter, and attach great importance to your acceptance—Edward, Rex Imperator.'

That telegram was accompanied by another, from Haldane, asking Kitchener to ' make it convenient to take over a little sooner ' than would have been necessary if the Duke of Connaught had not behaved so badly in resigning in so unexpected and precipitate a manner.

On the evening of 26 July, Kitchener telegraphed to the King : ' Your Majesty's wishes are always commands to me. My reply to Mr. Haldane was sent off yesterday declining the Command for certain reasons. I leave the matter entirely in Your Majesty's hands, and will loyally carry out whatever Your Majesty may decide.'

The King replied that he would confer with Haldane ; and he subsequently telegraphed (1 August) a third time to Kitchener : ' On consideration I am anxious that you should accept the Mediterranean Command, at all events for a short period, for the purpose of initiating its development under new conditions. Your acceptance of the Command would in no way prejudice your being considered for any higher appointment, hereafter becoming vacant, which may be more agreeable to you.'

Esher noted [1] on 28 July that he had pressed the King to take Kitchener at his word, and that he assumed that Kitchener would probably read between the lines of the King's telegram ' that this may lead to the Viceroyalty '. That was, in fact, the conclusion which Minto, as well as Kitchener drew ; and Kitchener had reason to know that, despite potential Cabinet opposition, the King and the Prime Minister both supported his claims. He replied (2 August) to the King : ' I am very grateful to Your Majesty for the consideration you have given to my case, and I am telegraphing to Mr. Haldane in the sense of Your Majesty's wishes.'

Kitchener failed to induce the Government to appoint Sir Beauchamp Duff to be his successor ; but in other respects everything possible was done to placate and accommodate Kitchener. He was made a

[1] *Journals and Letters*, II, p. 397.

Field-Marshal on the day (10 September, 1909) on which he relinquished his Indian command to Sir O'Moore Creagh, the Military Secretary at the India Office; and he was authorized to travel with his friend, FitzGerald, at the public expense to Japan, Australia and New Zealand. He had been invited to represent Great Britain at the annual manœuvres of the Imperial Japanese Army, and subsequently to advise the Australian and New Zealand governments about defence policy. A British cruiser was placed at his personal disposal in the Antipodes; and he was paid a special personal allowance of ten pounds a day while on land and three pounds a day while at sea.

On 28 August, Kitchener informed Haldane that he could not undertake to return from Australia during the spring, 'as the climate of March and April will not suit me in England'. He said that he proposed to take a few months' leave before taking up his new command, and Haldane reluctantly agreed (31 August). Kitchener calculated that those additional months would bring him very close to the time when Minto would be ready to quit India; and he hoped that, by then, some fresh means of filling the Mediterranean Command would have been devised by the Government. He placed his principal trust in King Edward, but Esher noted [1] (14 and 25 January, 1910) that although the King was 'violently in favour' of sending Kitchener back to India as Viceroy, and although Morley was eager 'to get rid of Minto before June, as he has broken down in health . . . he will not send K. out, as he has become hopelessly idle'.

No public announcement was made about Kitchener's acceptance of the Mediterranean Command, although *The Times* reported it, unofficially, on 7 August. The matter, therefore, remained veiled in uncertainty, and Kitchener's resentment would have been much greater if he had not formed a high expectation of by-passing Malta and of succeeding to India. He merely told [2] his solicitor (12 August) that it would be impossible to live suitably in Malta upon the inadequate salary which the Government had proposed; and he told Lady Salisbury [3] (5 August) that he had 'no wish to replace the Duke in a billet which he found the fifth wheel in a coach'. He added: 'If the Govt. play the King, we poor soldiers are done, and can only obey—at least such are my principles . . . I do not see that I could have done anything else.'

[1] *Journals and Letters*, II, pp. 437, 442.
[2] Letter in the possession of Lady Winifred Renshaw.
[3] Hatfield MSS.

On the day he left India, Kitchener thought it prudent to explain to Morley why he had rejected the Secretary of State's overtures to enter into a regular personal correspondence. At the same time he took that opportunity to hint, with consummate skill and delicacy, that his views about some subjects might be expected to differ, as Viceroy, from those which he had formerly held as Commander-in-Chief.

'I felt', Kitchener wrote (10 September, 1909), 'that . . . any regular correspondence between the Secretary of State and myself might, however unintentionally, trench on questions which afterwards assumed increased importance, and that my privately expressed opinions might not be in accordance with those held by the Viceroy when he subsequently came to deal with the subject, and therefore be embarrassing to him. To make my letters of much interest to you under these circumstances seemed to me almost impossible, and it appeared to me safer not to attempt it.'

On 20 August, Kitchener attended a farewell banquet in Simla at which Minto proposed his health. Kitchener read his reply, which was dull and much too long ; and it was subsequently discovered that one entire paragraph as well as a few felicitous phrases had been lifted almost verbatim from a similar speech which Curzon had delivered at Bombay on 16 November, 1905. Much amusement was caused and a newspaper correspondence followed, during which Kitchener kept silent. He had always dreaded the ordeal of speech-making, and at his request Sir Beauchamp Duff had drafted the speech for him.

After handing over his command to Creagh at Poona on 10 September, Kitchener reached Peking on 12 October. He was received with high honours by the Chinese Regent, who presented him with four pieces of peach-bloom porcelain. Kitchener assured FitzGerald that they were worth thousands of pounds, and he was mortified when London dealers informed him, later, that they were modern copies and almost worthless. He told [1] Arthur Renshaw (5 and 21 October) that he had spent over seven hundred pounds in Shanghai and nearly a thousand pounds in Peking upon art purchases.

Shortly afterwards, accompanied by the Japanese War Minister, Kitchener toured the battlefields of the Russo-Japanese War. He visited Mukden, Port Arthur and Seoul before reaching Tokyo on 2 November. He was met at the station by the Prime Minister as well as by the Commander-in-Chief, and he drove in an imperial carriage through streets lined with troops to a palace which had been

[1] Letter in the possession of Lady Winifred Renshaw.

placed at his disposal. Children carpeted his route with flowers and he received extraordinary honours as the embodiment of virtues which the Japanese were being taught to revere. He told [2] Lady Salisbury (20 November) that he had never enjoyed himself more, and 'I only wish the spirit of our people . . . was more like that of the Japanese.'

From 5 to 11 November, Kitchener accompanied the Emperor of Japan upon a visit to his army's manœuvres. Kitchener was critical of the Japanese cavalry, but he gave high praise to the infantry and to Japanese staff work. He received presents and high decorations from the Emperor before he left Japan on a lightning holiday tour of the Dutch East Indies.

On 21 December, Kitchener joined H.M.S. *Encounter* at Port Darwin in northern Australia ; and he ordered *Encounter* to proceed at once to Thursday Island, where he spent Christmas before starting his official tour of Australia on 1 January, 1910. He visited Brisbane, Sydney, Melbourne, Adelaide, Fremantle, Perth, Albany and Hobart before returning to Melbourne, where he pieced together his Report [1] on Australian Defence which was dated 12 February and published six days later.

After explaining that he had visited military camps in every State, Kitchener criticized Australian forces as 'inadequate in numbers, training, organization, and munitions of war' ; he detected 'a distinct tendency to go too fast, and to neglect essential preliminaries of training for more advanced studies which the troops engaged were not capable of carrying out properly'. He called for the provision of a fully trained 'citizen force' of 80,000 men, which 'should be kept outside politics' ; for the establishment of a Military College on the lines of West Point in the U.S.A. ; for the formation of a Staff Corps 'which should be entirely drawn from the Military College' ; for the construction of strategic railways ; and for the division of the sub-continent into ten military areas. Alfred Deakin, the Australian Prime Minister, declared (14 February) that, having appealed to Caesar, his Government would 'defer to Caesar's judgement'.

On 12 February Kitchener wrote [2] to Lady Salisbury from Government House, Melbourne :

'I have just finished here . . . It has been rather hard work,

---

[1] *Commonwealth of Australia Parliamentary Papers, General Session*, 1910, II, pp. 83–104.   [2] Hatfield MSS.

not so much from the military point of view, but on account of the innumerable receptions by mayors, and those sort of people . . . I *am* glad it is all over, though I fear New Zealand will be quite as bad.

'I am very sad at losing my last connection with my happy Simla family . . . FitzGerald has been recalled to India and left me entirely on my own a fortnight ago. I must say I feel rather lonely without a companion after being so many years surrounded by my boys who always looked after me so well and were such friends.'

After complicated negotiations, Kitchener recovered FitzGerald two months later ; and in the meantime he sailed (13 February, 1910) for The Bluff, South Island, New Zealand, where he was met on 17 February by the Prime Minister, Sir Joseph Ward. He went by train to Dunedin, and was publicly embraced on the platform by his sister, Mrs. Parker, who lived at Kurow, Otago. To Kitchener's disgust, Mrs. Parker informed [1] reporters that women bored her brother, and that he possessed ' a most fascinating ' squint.

At Dunedin, before he started on a processional tour of the town, the Mayor shouldered Sir Joseph Ward out of Kitchener's carriage after punching the Prime Minister's jaw. He then sat himself next to Kitchener in Sir Joseph's seat. It was noticed that Kitchener did not blink an eyelid while the scuffle was taking place ; and he seemed to grow increasingly democratic as the tour continued. To the amusement of his staff he often went out of his way to exchange reminiscences with veterans who had served with him in South Africa and elsewhere.

After visiting Wellington, Lyttelton, Napier and Auckland, Kitchener wrote (2 March) to Sir Joseph Ward : ' I do not think that it is necessary to write you a special memorandum on the defence of New Zealand, as from what I have seen during my inspection, the necessity for improved training is just as equally marked in this country as in Australia . . .' He called for the adoption of ' homogeneous ' systems in order that New Zealand and Australia might be able ' efficiently to support one another in the event of national danger '.

Kitchener left Wellington on 16 March for Tahiti, whence he sailed for San Francisco, which he reached on 8 April. The *San Francisco Chronicle* reported (9 April) that ' His Lordship declined all offers

---

[1] *Otago Daily Times* (17 February, 1910).

of interview by the newspaper correspondents'. After visiting the Yosemite Valley, Kitchener left, via Chicago, for New York where he arrived on 15 April. He visited the Military Academy at West Point on 16 April, and the *New York Herald* reported (17 April) that 'in deference to his known dislike for demonstration, there was no escort or booming of salutes'.

After being entertained (18 April) by the Pilgrims, Kitchener suddenly cut short his stay in the United States. He had arranged to tour the Civil War battlefields, but he decided to return immediately to London in order to secure, if possible, his appointment as Viceroy of India in succession to Minto. He had been warned in letters from friends that his prospects were becoming less favourable than they had hoped ; and a letter dated 1 February from Minto caused him particular anxiety : 'I have no idea at all', Minto wrote, 'as to my successor. All sorts of strange people are mentioned ; and I wish for your own sake you were at home to watch the run of events.'

Refusing all information to reporters about his reasons for leaving so suddenly, Kitchener embarked on the *Oceanic* on 20 April. He told the *New York Herald* that he had been fascinated by the beauty of American women, and some newspapers suggested that the bachelor Field-Marshal was fleeing for his life from the women of New York. Kitchener landed at Plymouth on 26 April, 1910, and went immediately to London to stay, as usual, with Ralli in Belgrave Square.

Many newspapers headlined Kitchener's return, and urged the Government to employ him quickly in some new and important capacity ; and Kitchener did not waste a single hour. His first action was to arrange an audience with the King for the morning of 28 April, in order to receive his Field-Marshal's baton ; and his first call, on the morning of 27 April, was made at the India Office, where he saw Lord Morley. Morley wrote [1] (29 April) to Minto :

'I was a good deal astonished, for I had expected a silent, stiff, moody hero. Behold he was the most cheerful of men, and he hammered away loud and strong, with free gestures and high tones. He used the warmest language . . . about yourself . . . We got on very well—he and I—for nothing was said about his going back to India as Governor-General.'

Kitchener felt that Morley had played with him, as a cat plays with a mouse ; and he much regretted that Asquith had taken advantage

[1] Morley, *Recollections*, II, p. 331.

of the parliamentary recess to accompany Reginald McKenna on the
Admiralty yacht, *Enchantress*, on a visit of inspection to Gibraltar.
Nevertheless, on the afternoon of 27 April, Kitchener tried the atmosphere at the Colonial Office by calling on the Colonial Secretary, Lord
Crewe. That interview was even more unsatisfactory, and Kitchener
told Birdwood that he had been disgusted by his reception.

Kitchener expected that the Minister would have been interested
in his recent impressions of Australia and New Zealand, and he
hoped in that way to be able to form an indirect view about the
Cabinet's general attitude towards him. Crewe had, however,
appeared nervous and preoccupied, and had merely exclaimed : " Ah,
Field-Marshal ! Back, so soon ? Well, did you have a good time of
it ? " Shortly afterwards, pleading that he had to preside at a meeting,
he had bowed Kitchener out.

Morley had an audience with the King immediately before Kitchener
on the morning of 28 April. He said that Asquith was in favour of
recommending Kitchener's appointment as Viceroy of India in
succession to Minto ; but that the Prime Minister had left the decision
about that recommendation in the hands of the Secretary of State for
India. Morley then advised the King to appoint Sir Charles Hardinge,[1]
the Permanent Under-Secretary at the Foreign Office, who was one
of the King's intimates.

The King, who was feeling unwell, urged Kitchener's claims with
all the vigour of which he was still capable. He said that Hardinge
was a diplomat, and that a man should ' stick to his last '. He asked
Morley to explain his objection to Kitchener.

Morley said that if Hardinge was a diplomat, Kitchener was a soldier ;
and that it would be wrong to send the most famous active soldier of
the day to rule India immediately after the India Councils Act, 1909,
had come into effect. That Act had liberalized the Government of
India by introducing an important elective element into the Indian
legislative councils ; and Kitchener's appointment would destroy
much of the goodwill created by that reform, because it would cause
educated Indians to conclude that a new era of paternalism and repression was about to begin.

When the King pooh-poohed those arguments, Morley said that
he might feel impelled to resign ; but, in deference to the King's
friendly insistence, he promised to turn the matter over in his mind

[1] Lord Hardinge of Penshurst, K.G., P.C., G.C.B., G.C.S.I., G.C.M.G.,
G.C.I.E., G.C.V.O., I.S.O. (1858–1944).

for one month. He then withdrew, and Kitchener was ushered into the Royal presence. According to Birdwood, the conversation began :

" Ah, Kitchener ! I'm sorry you're going to such a rotten billet as the Mediterranean."

" Thank you, Sir. I only accepted it at Your Majesty's command."

" It's a damned rotten billet."

" It is. Have I Your Majesty's permission to refuse it now ? "

" Certainly. I wouldn't go, if I were you."

The King was then overtaken by a fit of coughing. When he recovered, he told Kitchener about his unsatisfactory conversation with Morley, and promised to do his best to overcome Morley's scruples. Kitchener thanked the King very warmly indeed, and said that he would in no circumstances now consent to take up the Mediterranean Command. He was so pleased and impetuous that he inadvertently gave offence by leaving behind the Field-Marshal's baton which the King gave him before he left.

Morley, like Kitchener, had not wasted a single hour. He saw Haldane immediately after leaving Buckingham Palace ; and Haldane announced officially in the House of Commons that afternoon that Kitchener would shortly be going to Malta to take up the Mediterranean Command. That evening, Kitchener dined alone with Haldane at his house in Queen Anne's Gate, and he told Birdwood that the atmosphere had been sulphurous.

Kitchener reproached Haldane for his action in having induced the King to exert pressure upon him during the previous July ; as well as for the statement which he had seen fit to make that afternoon in the House of Commons. Haldane retorted that the King had acted as a constitutional sovereign on the advice of his Ministers ; and that it had been necessary to quieten rumour by making a public announcement as soon as possible after Kitchener's unexpectedly early return. He pointed out that *The Times* had published the news of Kitchener's acceptance of the Mediterranean Command as early as 7 August, 1909.

Kitchener felt that he had been the victim of sharp practice ; but he kept his poise and temper, and said that, as the King had changed his mind, he would never now consent to take up the Mediterranean Command. He added that he would prefer to remain permanently unemployed ; but Haldane insisted that he had in his possession Kitchener's letter of acceptance dated 3 August, 1909.

A WASTE OF GOOD MATERIAL

Britannia (to Lord Kitchener). "Welcome back! I wish a better post could have been found for you—but our politicians are a little afraid of strong men."

PUNCH, April 27, 1910

249

Kitchener said that the Mediterranean Command was quite useless, and that it could be a menace to the best strategic interests of the Empire. He said that he would make that viewpoint clear when he took his seat on the Committee of Imperial Defence. Haldane retorted that he disagreed with Kitchener's view about the utility of the Mediterranean Command, and that the offer of a seat on the Committee of Imperial Defence had been made conditionally upon Kitchener's acceptance of the Mediterranean Command.

Kitchener said that Haldane was well aware that his whole heart was set upon succeeding Minto as Viceroy; and he vehemently expressed his firm hope and expectation of being offered that glittering prize. Haldane said that while he personally hoped that Morley would reach a favourable decision, the Government would expect Kitchener to take Malta if he failed to obtain India.

Thereafter the conversation took a more cheerful turn and the two elderly bachelors reached an accord. Haldane promised, before Kitchener left, that he would try to influence Morley in Kitchener's favour, and that nothing more would be said for one month about the Mediterranean Command.

Exactly one week later, on 6 May, 1910, King Edward VII died; and Kitchener felt that his luck had failed at last. It is just possible, but unlikely, that if the King had lived, some means of overcoming Morley's genuine scruples might have been found. Morley asked Kitchener to see him at the India Office during the week of the King's funeral, and was offended, on that occasion, by the language which Kitchener used. He explained to him fully then, as well as at a small dinner-party which he gave on 14 May when Haldane and Esher were also present, the nature of the difficulty which he felt. Morley noted,[1] in his feline way, that he had found that dinner ' curiously interesting '; and Esher noted[2] that Kitchener had held himself under perfect control. Esher thought that Kitchener had made a better impression upon Morley, and that his chances had, in consequence, improved.

On 1 June, however, Morley informed[3] Minto that he had made up his mind, and that he had warned Asquith to expect his resignation if the Cabinet were to insist upon sending Kitchener to India as Viceroy. Asquith, who strongly pressed Kitchener's claims, was unwilling to permit Morley to resign on that issue; and the Cabinet, with some

---

[1] Morley, *Recollections*, II, p. 331.   [2] *Journals and Letters*, III, p. 4.
[3] *Recollections*, II, p. 333.

reluctance and hesitation, upheld Morley. In those circumstances Sir Charles Hardinge was appointed to succeed Minto.

On 9 June, 1910, Morley wrote to Kitchener :

' At last, after some delay, for which I am not responsible, a decision has been reached about the Indian Viceroyalty . . . We are not going to invite you to go back in a new capacity . . . The sole difficulty arises from misgivings as to the impressions which would be likely to arise in India from a military appointment . . .

' Let me add that I do not think that I ever had a more disagreeable task in my life than the writing of this letter . . . and let me hint to you that the Indian post by no means exhausts the demands of the hour for a man of supreme capacity and many proved successes.'

That letter conveyed the most bitter disappointment of Kitchener's life. He wrote, on that day, laconically to Haldane, in order to confirm his refusal to take up the Mediterranean Command ; and Haldane so informed the House of Commons, without comment, on 13 June. Nothing was said about the Committee of Imperial Defence, and Kitchener informed his friends that he had been dismissed from that body after having accepted a seat upon it. He then withdrew from London and went on a motor tour of southern Ireland, where he revisited the scenes of his childhood.

CHAPTER 13

RULER OF EGYPT

1910–1914

SINCE he had failed to obtain India, Kitchener wanted Egypt, or at least the embassy at Constantinople. Both were in the gift of the Foreign Office, of which the new Viceroy, Lord Hardinge, had been the permanent head ; and Kitchener wrote [1] (26 June, 1910) to Lady Salisbury from an hotel at Glengariff, Co. Cork : ' I wrote to congratulate Hardinge before I left, and got a nice reply. Do you think you could see him, and find out if there is any chance in Egypt ? He ought to play up, as he has quite bowled me out, and might be useful.'

Kitchener wrote several times to Lady Salisbury from the same address : ' I see Gorst is on his way to England ', he wrote [1] (5 July), ' so I suppose something will be settled soon about Constantinople and Egypt. I should much prefer the latter, but if the authorities will not kick Gorst upstairs into a position which would be more suitable for him, then I should prefer Constantinople to anything Haldane may devise to use my name for, without really letting me do anything . . . I cannot go cap in hand to these people.' He wrote [1] again, pathetically, three days later : ' If you hear anything hopeful, will you send me a wire ? One word—" Hope "—will do.'

In the meantime questions were being asked, in Parliament and elsewhere, about the Government's plans for employing Kitchener. Evasive Government statements provoked indignant articles in the Press, most of which called attention to Kitchener's absence from the Committee of Imperial Defence. The Government had more serious problems on hand at that time, but the problem posed by Kitchener's position and reputation was a minor irritant.

Kitchener would have been more than human if he had repressed his delight when Wingate informed him that Gorst's health was causing serious anxiety. Kitchener told [1] Lady Salisbury (7 August) that Gorst might not be able to return to Egypt, ' so it might come off, after all '. Gorst, in fact, was mortally stricken, but he returned for a short time to Cairo, while Kitchener visited Balmoral before going on to stay at Welbeck, Powis, Hatfield, and other great Tory houses and attending Army manœuvres and a naval review. He was

[1] Hatfield MSS.

extremely prickly when Asquith wrote (29 September) to offer him an unpaid seat on the Committee of Imperial Defence.

'Before again accepting a seat', Kitchener replied (1 October), '. . . . I should, if possible, like to know the reason of my removal not long ago.' He explained that he disagreed with Haldane about the utility of the Mediterranean Command, as well as about 'other questions of defence and Army policy', and he concluded haughtily : 'I have arranged to shoot in the Sudan this winter, and, in these circumstances, perhaps you might prefer to leave the matter until my return.'

After posting that letter, Kitchener wondered if he had sounded too defiant a note : 'No answer !' he complained [1] (6 October) to Lady Salisbury. '. . . He is probably consulting Haldane and preparing a lawyer's reply. I have not told anyone, so please keep this quite secret.' Kitchener had, from the first, been contemptuous of the Territorial Army which Haldane had created ; and he regarded as absurdly optimistic and inadequate the extremely tentative plan which the Defence Committee had formed for joint military action with France upon the outbreak of war with Germany. Nevertheless, as a professional soldier, Kitchener had no wish to quarrel openly with the Government at a time when politics were more embittered than at any period within living memory owing to the Parliament Bill, and to the implications which it held for the next phase of the struggle for Irish Home Rule.

Kitchener's sympathies and social connections were known to be predominantly Tory ; and his letter had annoyed Asquith, who waited a fortnight before replying (14 October) :

'I think that you are under some misconception when you speak of your " removal " from the Defence Committee. As you are aware, appointments to that Committee are made by the Prime Minister alone ; but when, in July, 1909, the question arose of your being asked to undertake the Mediterranean Command, I authorized Mr. Haldane, as part and parcel of the same offer, to request you to become a member of the Committee. In August, 1909, you accepted Mr. Haldane's proposal ; but subsequently, for reasons which seemed to you sufficient and which I do not presume to discuss, you withdrew that acceptance. What was, from the first, a composite proposal therefore fell to the ground.

[1] Ibid.

'I am now suggesting that you should give your services to the Defence Committee without regard to any other appointment. The offer is quite unconditional, and I would not regard your acceptance of it as implying on your part any abandonment or modification of the opinion you hold either in regard to the Mediterranean Command, or to the more general questions of defence and Army policy.'

Kitchener had hoped to use public discontent at his absence from the Defence Committee as a lever to force the Government to employ him ; but he dispatched (15 October) a curt note of acceptance, and hastened his preparations to take a long winter holiday and shooting-trip through Egypt, the Sudan, Uganda and British East Africa. He announced that he had not spent a winter in England since 1874, and that he had no intention of spoiling his health by remaining at home. He would not wait either to take his seat on the Defence Committee or to complete personally negotiations into which he had entered for the purchase of the Broome Park estate, near Canterbury, from the ruined Oxenden family. Instead he left England on 5 November, 1910, accompanied by FitzGerald as well as by Major A. McMurdo, who had been his first A.D.C. in Egypt during the 1880's.

Travelling by way of Rome, Venice and Vienna, Kitchener reached Constantinople on 27 November. Writing [1] from Cairo to Lady Salisbury on 8 December, Kitchener deplored the state of affairs which he had found in the Turkish capital : 'We are out of it altogether, as the present Ambassador does nothing, and the German is allowed to do as he likes . . . I was rather afraid my presence might attract attention and [be] thought to mean something, though I refused to see any of the young Turks ; so after 3 days I thought it wiser to go on to Alexandria.'

Kitchener had long been convinced that, as Ambassador at Constantinople, he could, if given a free hand, retrieve the British position. For success, however, he would have needed to be provided with funds in order to outbid the Germans in purchasing the support of Turkish leaders ; and Grey would have been much too high-minded to make sufficient funds available. Grey was, moreover, strongly opposed, on trades-union grounds, to the idea of appointing ambassadors from outside the Diplomatic Service. Kitchener, therefore, contented himself by characteristically securing a private understanding

[1] Hatfield MSS.

in Constantinople that Turkish approval would be forthcoming in the event of his being offered Gorst's post in Cairo. That approval, known technically as an 'exequatur', was necessary because Egypt at that time was still technically a part of the Turkish Empire.

In Cairo, where Kitchener was joined by his nephew, Toby, the future Lord Broome, Kitchener lunched with the Khedive, Abbas Hilmi II, who eyed him askance. He stayed with Gorst, who was looking desperately ill, and he left on 19 December for Khartoum. On the Nile steamer, Kitchener's nephew introduced him to a woman tourist at her insistent request. She was nervous, and remarked stupidly, " Isn't it a nice, sunny day ? " Kitchener replied politely, " It generally is sunny here," and he never acknowledged her existence again. He explained to his nephew that he had consented to the introduction under duress, but that, the experiment having failed, inane chit-chat with wealthy widows formed no part of the agreement.

Kitchener, who had a great reception in Khartoum, was delighted to observe the progress which the city had made since he had delivered it from the curse of Mahdism. He made many visits of inspection and was particularly interested in irrigation projects. He visited Suakin, before borrowing a steamer from Wingate to convey his party up the White Nile to Entebbe. He took with him a case of books which consisted entirely of bound volumes of *Country Life* and of novels by Stanley Weyman ; and strict security precautions had to be taken. Sir Edward Grey warned Gorst, who alerted the Governors of Uganda and British East Africa (Kenya), that Indian as well as Egyptian nationalists had hatched a plot for Kitchener's assassination. Kitchener, who said that he felt flattered, was not inconvenienced in any way. He shot elephant, lion, hippopotamus, buffalo, a rare and magnificent white rhinoceros, and at least six different species of antelope.

From Egypt, Kitchener had cabled to invite Major E. H. M. Leggett (late R.E.), who had served on his staff in South Africa, to join his party. Leggett met Kitchener, FitzGerald and McMurdo on the Sudanese–Uganda border, and acted thereafter as their host. He had been resident in Kenya for some years, having been lent by the War Office to the Colonial Office in 1906 for duty in charge of the development work of the British East African Corporation.

With Leggett's help, Kitchener and his friends made exhaustive inquiries about the prospects of land development in Uganda and Kenya. As a result, they decided to obtain the largest possible free grant of Crown lands in Kenya, and to develop them in partnership.

They agreed that Leggett should be the working partner, and that all financial questions should be adjusted subsequently between the partners.

The Governor of Kenya was Kitchener's old favourite, Sir Percy Girouard ; and Kitchener, on Leggett's advice, asked Girouard for the largest possible free grant of land in the district of Muhoroni, which had formerly belonged to the Nandi tribe. That tribe had, in 1906, been dispossessed by the British Government of all land lying between the main railway and the Nandi escarpment.

The land thus made available for development and exploitation by white capitalists had been the favourite grazing area of the Nandi tribe. But it was also a first-class agricultural district ; and in response to Kitchener's application Girouard explained, with regret, that, under the Crown Land's Ordinance, which may have reminded Kitchener of the Encumbered Estates Act of his Irish boyhood, he had power to allot only 2,000 acres each to Kitchener, FitzGerald and McMurdo. He said that Leggett had already received elsewhere the full amount to which he was entitled.

The law required that Kitchener, FitzGerald and McMurdo should all reside in Kenya, and either manage their properties themselves or employ a separate European manager upon each of their three separate estates. But that did not satisfy Kitchener, who brushed the regulations aside and reached a private agreement with Girouard while he was staying as his guest at Government House, Nairobi.

Girouard agreed to allot 5,000 instead of 2,000 acres to Kitchener because, as he explained, the circumstances of the applicant were such as to give grounds for expecting especially active development. He allotted 2,000 acres each to FitzGerald and McMurdo, and agreed to treat the whole area of 9,000 acres as a single property, which was known as the Songhor Estates. Girouard waived, furthermore, the requirement that Kitchener, FitzGerald and McMurdo should reside in Kenya ; and he arranged that Leggett, as one of the partners, should represent the ownership, and be treated, for legal purposes only, as the resident European owner of the entire property.

Kitchener, FitzGerald and McMurdo promptly rounded off that somewhat irregular transaction by executing powers of attorney in favour of Leggett ; and Kitchener told Girouard that, as soon as he retired, he would spend all his winters on his property in Kenya, and all his summers at Broome Park. The four partners subsequently agreed that Kitchener should provide 50 per cent of the working capital needed for development ; that FitzGerald and McMurdo should each provide 20 per cent ; and that Leggett should find the remaining 10 per cent.

When McMurdo died in April, 1914, the three surviving partners bought out his share from his executors. But none of the partners ever provided nearly enough money for development, and stagnation would have resulted if the British East Africa Corporation, out of goodwill towards Kitchener who had friends upon its board, had not continuously made loans to defray the expense not only of development but of maintenance.

After the deaths of Kitchener and FitzGerald in 1916 the British East Africa Corporation refused to continue to finance the Songhor Estates. It demanded the repayment of an outstanding debt of about five thousand pounds, and it informed Kitchener's executors that a further sum of about eight hundred pounds was owed to the Government in payment for the formal grant of the leases. Several thousand pounds of additional working capital were also at that time urgently required, which the partners, immediately before Kitchener's and FitzGerald's deaths, had decided to raise by floating a private company, and by taking, as a fourth partner, a rich man to whom half their joint interest would have been transferred in the form of shares.

Kitchener sailed from Mombasa on 7 March, 1911, in response to a request from King George V that he should command the troops at the Coronation. He reached Naples on 22 March, and stayed for a few days in Venice with Lady Layard, at whose house he met the Kaiser. He landed at Dover on 2 April and, four days later, he bought Broome Park, near Canterbury, with about 500 acres of land, for fourteen thousand pounds. He acquired 50 additional acres later for an additional thousand pounds ; but he failed to secure all the heirlooms of the Oxenden family which he coveted.

Kitchener was enchanted by his purchase. The house, built in 1635–8, is the best surviving example of a new style of architecture which became fashionable during the 1630's, when bricklayers raised the prestige of their craft for the first time to a level with that of the masons. Broome was built with unprecedented virtuosity by a bricklayer-contractor who used brick instead of stone even for the ornamental parts, including a well-proportioned scheme of pilaster strips leading up to gables of extreme complexity, with curved broken pediments.

The formalities of sale could not be completed for some months, because flaws were discovered in the title. But the lawyers straightened matters, and almost the whole of Kitchener's leisure for the last five years of his life was devoted to the tasks of beautifying the grounds ; of reconstructing the interior of the house which he gutted completely ; and of filling it with the treasures which he had managed to accumulate by purchase, gift and loot. None of those tasks was completed when Kitchener was drowned in 1916. The remainder of Kitchener's leisure was devoted to an attempt to run his East African property verbally, as well as by private, informal correspondence with his partners. He bequeathed his lion's share of the Songhor Estates to FitzGerald, if FitzGerald should survive him, and to members of his own family if FitzGerald should die first ; and the lawyers' difficult task was complicated by uncertainty as to whether Kitchener or FitzGerald had died first when the *Hampshire* sank. The last surviving partner, Leggett, reported at the beginning of 1917 that only 200 out of the total area of 9,000 acres were actually cultivated and planted.

England, when Kitchener came home in April, 1911, was gripped by the aftermath of the great crisis caused by the action of the House of Lords in rejecting the Liberal Budget of 1909. Two subsequent elections had left the Liberals in power, and it was not known whether or not several hundred peers would have to be created in order to secure the passage of a Parliament Bill drastically curtailing the powers of the Upper House. In those circumstances, party feeling ran so high that normal social relations between Conservative and Liberal patricians were, for the most part, temporarily suspended ; but it was vital for Kitchener at that moment to maintain close social contact with Liberal Ministers.

Kitchener accordingly had himself introduced as a viscount into the House of Lords on 26 April, 1911, by two Liberal peers—Morley and Milner ; and he lunched and dined frequently at 10 Downing Street with Mrs. Asquith, who lionized him. He took advantage of confidential chats with the King, while preparations went forward for the Coronation ; and he bowed stiffly to Curzon at a formal luncheon party which Haldane gave for the Kaiser on 28 May. He consented to meet Curzon again at a dinner-party given by Lady Salisbury, and that encounter was unkindly described as a momentary concurrence of two icebergs.

The progress of Gorst's illness, and the intentions of the Government if Gorst should die, continued to preoccupy Kitchener, who was by no means sanguine about his prospects. He wrote [1] (26 April) to his solicitor and friend, Arthur Renshaw :

' I rather expect I may be asked to become chairman of the East Africa Corporation. I believe that it is all right, and of course, with property in East Africa, it will be useful to become chairman of the Co., . . . I am also trying to get on to the Board of the South Eastern and Chatham Line . . . I must try and make something in the City if I can get no Govt. employment, as Broome will eat money. *You* might put me on the Texas Board, or on something of the sort.'

To his delight, Kitchener joined the board of the London, Chatham and Dover Railway ; and he took steps at once to improve the service to Canterbury in order to avoid waste of time in travelling to Broome. He began also at that time to take a great interest in Boy Scouts, and he became president of the North London Association. Parties of scouts camped constantly in his park at Broome, and Kitchener enjoyed the boys' presence, and appeared to take a genuine interest in their training.

Early in May, Kitchener became aware that Gorst was dying of cancer, and that Cromer had written to suggest to Grey that Gorst had only one possible and suitable successor. Kitchener became, in consequence, extremely restless until 17 June, when he received a letter from Grey asking him to call at the Foreign Office in order to discuss ' a matter which, though important, is not urgent '. Kitchener saw Grey, accordingly, at three o'clock on the afternoon of Monday, 19 June.

Grey said that a strong man was needed to replace Gorst ; and he asked Kitchener whether, without putting the clock back, he would be able to channel the energies of the Egyptians into constructive work, and away from a nationalist agitation which almost amounted to rebellion. Kitchener expressed his complete confidence that he would be able to pacify Egypt, and to guide the country along progressive lines towards a prosperous and happy future ; and on 20 June Grey wrote to him :

' The King approves very cordially of your going to Egypt, and the arrangement is one that has evidently given him much pleasure ; . . . I should like the formal announcement and appointment to be dependent, to some extent, upon the news of Gorst's

[1] Letter in the possession of Lady Winifred Renshaw.

health ; but as the question is now practically settled, there is no reason why your friends should not know.'

Gorst did not formally resign until a few days before his death, which occurred on 10 July at his Wiltshire home. The Khedive, Abbas Hilmi, who had loved him, came over especially to see him immediately before the end. Six days later, on 16 July, Grey informed the House of Commons that Kitchener had been appointed as British Agent, Consul-General, and Minister Plenipotentiary in succession to Gorst in Cairo ; and that no change ' from civil and administrative reform to military policy' was contemplated.

In the meantime, when King George V was crowned in Westminster Abbey on 22 June, 1911, Kitchener commanded over 50,000 troops who lined the streets of the capital. The unprecedented rigour of the precautions which he took to control the crowds of liberty-loving sightseers excited some good-humoured comments ; and he was rewarded by being made a Knight of St. Patrick, in recognition of the boyhood which he had spent in southern Ireland as a member of an alien, Protestant ruling caste.

Before he left England for Egypt on 16 September, Kitchener had already started the work of gutting the interior of Broome as drastically as he had previously gutted the interiors of his official residences in India. He raised the height of floors and ceilings, shifted walls, and altered and concealed drainpipes. He tried to do the entire work out of income, and refused, in consequence, to employ more than a dozen men at a time. He told [1] Lady Salisbury (27 August) that Broome was ' a mass of girders inside the house ' ; and he told [2] Renshaw (11 December) that he hoped, in January, ' with good dividends and a quarter's pay ', to be in a position to meet most of his bills. In addition to his pay and allowances as a Field-Marshal, he received a special personal annual salary of £7,600.

After spending a few days at Balmoral, Kitchener was seen off from Liverpool Street Station on 16 September by a troop of North London boy scouts. His party included FitzGerald, a French chef, and two black spaniels to which he had become greatly attached ; and he arrived at Cairo on 29 September. To everyone's surprise, but at Sir Edward Grey's suggestion, Kitchener was wearing a grey frock-coat and a black silk hat, which he was seldom seen to wear in Egypt again. He

[1] Hatfield MSS.
[2] Letter in the possession of Lady Winifred Renshaw.

was received with full military honours, and, despite the efforts of the nationalists, his reception was impressive. As he drove to the British Agency with an escort of 21st Lancers he had constantly to acknowledge the handclaps of Egyptians who had assembled in unprecedented numbers along his route.

On the day he reached Cairo, Kitchener's problem was complicated by an outbreak of war between Italy and Turkey. Italy had barely a shadow of an excuse for declaring war, but an Italian army, which was despatched to conquer Libya, experienced initial reverses which damaged European prestige. Egypt was commanded by Kitchener to observe strict neutrality, although the sympathies of her people, as Moslems, were ardently pro-Turk. In those circumstances, Kitchener's prompt gesture in contributing one hundred pounds to the Turkish Red Crescent as a personal gift was extremely well received by Egyptian opinion.

The immense prestige which Kitchener enjoyed in an Oriental country where personalities counted for more than policies, enabled him to control the situation with a degree of virtuosity to which Gorst could never have hoped to attain. Gorst had been an ambitious, competent and conscientious official, but he had lacked personality and the gift of leadership. His principal task had been to liberalize the autocracy which Cromer had exercised.

The British were pledged to evacuate Egypt at some time in the future; and Gorst, accordingly, encouraged Egyptians to assume a greater share of responsibility by relaxing controls and by restricting his interference to matters which directly affected British interests. He already possessed the confidence and he thereby won the affection of the Khedive, Abbas Hilmi II; but their intimate friendship harmed both men. Gorst, who had calculated that he would be able to use the Khedive against the nationalists, was accused by the British of having plunged Egypt into anarchy by pandering to its factions, which he was powerless to control; and the Khedive, who had calculated that he would be able eventually to wring unlimited concessions from a weak and sentimental British Agent, was accused by Egyptian nationalists of having sold himself to his country's invaders.

When controls are relaxed after a long period of autocratic rule a strong hand is needed to tide over the transition. Gorst, unlike Cromer and Kitchener, who were both known in Egypt as 'The Lord', was a weak man; and a dangerous situation developed. Cromer complained to Kitchener (30 July, 1913) that the inevitable and desirable 'relaxation in the personal system which was a necessity in my day' had been 'too brusque and radical' under Gorst : 'Instead of a gradual change, the entire system was wholly and also very suddenly upset, with the result that the edifice which I had taken 25 years to construct was very nearly toppled over. The reaction which was certain to occur then ensued. You were appointed, and we have now gone back to a system of personal government, probably in a more accentuated form than was the case in my day. For the time, everybody seems very well content, but do not imagine for one moment that this state of things will last . . .'

In congratulating Kitchener upon his appointment, Haldane and other Liberal Ministers had told him that ' a strong man was needed in Egypt'. Kitchener's task was to use his strength and prestige to restore a deteriorating situation, while continuing a policy of cautious liberalization ; but he construed his mission in his own way. He concentrated upon the first part of his task, which he discharged extremely successfully ; but he neglected the second, and threw dust impartially into the eyes of Egyptian nationalists and British Liberal Ministers.

Kitchener's most characteristic political action was to tear up the constitution of Egypt and to promulgate a new one which made a number of trifling and widely publicized concessions to Egyptian nationalist sentiment as well as to British liberal idealism. In so doing, however, he had no long-term end in view, and no intention whatever of preparing the way for representative government. Kitchener regarded that side of his work as purely tactical, and he took a detached and cynical view of his so-called constitutional experiment.

Kitchener, on the other hand, concentrated the whole of his attention with his habitual thoroughness and drive upon the great work which he undertook for Egyptian agriculture, upon which the country's economy depended. In that field he had both a long term strategic and an immediate tactical purpose. He derived almost unlimited satisfaction from the thought that he was placing countless succeeding generations in his debt in a land which he loved second only to his own ; and he tried to discourage windy debate and unprofitable political agitation by directing the people's minds to matters of greater practical interest and significance. He was helped by a sudden upsurge in the economic prosperity of Egypt, which occurred in 1911 after four years of leanness and austerity.

The spirit in which Kitchener approached his task was sounded in a few sentences of the first of the three annual reports which he sent to Sir Edward Grey :

> 'I am glad', he wrote [1] (6 April, 1912) 'to be able to report that . . . the consideration of practical reforms for the good of the country has apparently become more interesting to the majority of the people than discussions of abstruse political questions which are unlikely to lead to any useful result . . . Whatever the value of a party system may be in Western political life, it is evident that its application to an intensely democratic community, the essential basis of whose social life is the brotherhood of man, combined with respect for learning and the experience of age, is an unnatural proceeding, fraught with inevitable division and weakness.
>
> 'The development and elevation of the character of a people depends mainly on the growth of self-control and the power to dominate natural impulses, as well as on the practice of unobtrusive self reliance and perseverance, combined with reasoned determination. None of these elements of advance are assisted in any way by party strife. Calm and well considered interest in political affairs is good for both the governed and those who rule ; but fictitious interest, generally based on misrepresentation, and maintained by party funds and party tactics, does nothing to elevate or develop the intelligent character of an Oriental race . . .
>
> 'The future development of the vast mass of the inhabitants of Egypt depends upon improved conditions of agriculture . . .'

While he was on leave in England in 1912 Kitchener consulted Cromer about the undertaking which he had given to Grey to continue Gorst's policy of replacing personal rule by some gradual advance towards a more liberal system. Cromer put his views on paper (25 July, 1912) :

> 'As regards any real representation of the Egyptian people which could ultimately, in some degree, take the place of personal Government, probably the wisest thing for the moment is to leave the whole question alone . . . National representation in Egypt, in the sense in which that term is generally used, is a sheer absurdity . . . The Egyptians are not a nation . . . They are a fortuitous agglomeration of a number of miscellaneous and hybrid elements. My idea

[1] *Parliamentary Papers, Egypt*, No. 1 (1912) (Cd. 6149).

always was that gradually, by a steady course of statesmanlike procedure . . . all those various elements could . . . be fused together.'

In those circumstances Kitchener sought to devise an acceptable constitutional framework under cover of which he could rule Egypt in the manner dictated by the conditions which he found, as well as by his temperament. He considered that the existing constitution had broken down in practice because it had failed to settle satisfactorily the problem of the Suez Canal; and the new constitution which he promulgated on 21 July, 1913, was based upon principles of expediency.

Egypt in 1911 possessed a small and select Legislative Council, and a more democratic General Assembly. Their function was purely consultative, except that the consent of the Assembly was required to measures involving the imposition of fresh general taxation, and that foreign policy and the Civil List were excluded from the debates of both bodies. Nevertheless, under Gorst both bodies had grown increasingly obstreperous, and in 1909–10 a major crisis had occurred.

The Suez Canal Company asked that its concession, which was due to expire in 1968, should be extended for another forty years, until 2008, in return for a payment to the Egyptian Government of a sum of four million pounds and an annual share of the profits. That offer was accepted by Butros Pasha, the Coptic Christian Prime Minister of Egypt, and by his Ministers, in face of a shrill and angry nationalist outcry.

Butros then suggested that his hand would be strengthened if the deal could be endorsed by the General Assembly. Gorst weakly and foolishly agreed, and the event proved that both men had over-estimated that body's prudence and sense of responsibility. When the ministerial decision was submitted to a vote, only one member of the General Assembly dared to support it; and after expressing his deep mortification, Butros Pasha was assassinated by a nationalist on 10 February, 1910.

That crime, and the defiant vote of the Egyptian General Assembly, appeared to represent a major setback to the policy which Gorst had pursued; and Kitchener told [1] Grey (28 March, 1914) that they had proved ' how dangerous it was to leave the really important interests of the country in the hands of inexperienced persons, swayed by out-

[1] *Parliamentary Papers, Egypt,* No. 1 (1914) (Cd. 7358).

side interests, and moved by political wirepullers . . . No Government would be insane enough to consider that, because an Advisory Council had proved itself unable to carry out its functions in a reasonable and satisfactory manner, it should therefore be given a larger measure of power and control.'

Kitchener, accordingly, promulgated a revised organic electoral law, which was designed to secure a preponderating representation of landlords in what was, euphemistically, termed the Legislature. He then abolished the Legislative Council as well as the General Assembly, and created a new Legislative Assembly of seventeen nominated and sixty-six elected members. He conferred upon the new body all the powers which the former two had possessed, with what he termed ' certain important extensions '. Those extensions empowered the new chamber :

(1) to initiate legislation which the Governor could veto, for reasons stated ;
(2) to delay legislation for a brief period ;
(3) to require the Government to state its reasons for insisting upon legislation of which the Assembly disapproved.

Machinery was established at the same time for enabling the Government, if it so wished, to consult the electors directly, by means of a referendum, about any proposition to which the Legislative Assembly was opposed.

Those minimal concessions, with their necessary safeguards, were paraded by Kitchener with all ceremony in a Liberal uniform before the eyes of the British Cabinet. Kitchener told [1] Grey (28 March, 1914) that the reform might prove to have been ' an important step along the path of true progress ', or that it might ' destroy itself ', and ' convince all reasonable men that this country for the present is not fitted for those representative institutions which are now on their trial '. He reminded Grey that it had taken the British ' almost a thousand years to bring representative institutions to their present state ', and that ' those who have been accustomed to accept almost blindly the decisions of their rulers, are ill-equipped all at once to become their advisers '. Nevertheless, he expressed his confidence in the future.

So long as his strong hands and the glamour of his name and imposing personality continued to hold Egypt under his spell, Kitchener's

[1] Ibid.

confidence appeared to be justified. But the hurricane of the first World War blew his constitutional experiment sky-high. His reform of the Egyptian economy, on the other hand, earned Kitchener a place among the greatest of those who have exercised personal rule in the Nile valley during the past five thousand years.

As an agricultural country devoid of industry, Egypt depended wholly upon the export of cotton. The keystone of Kitchener's economic policy was, therefore, the advancement of that interest and the protection of the peasants, upon whose labour everything depended. In pursuance of that aim he passed two laws of far-reaching importance in 1912. The first, known as the 'five feddan' law, protected the small cultivator of five feddans (5·19 acres) of land, or under, from expropriation of his land or equipment for debt. The second established a new system of local courts of justice, known as cantonal courts, to serve the peasants' needs. Unpaid magistrates were appointed to dispense, throughout the countryside, justice based upon local custom, which the peasants relished and understood. They were delighted to be relieved of the need to make long, expensive journeys to distant towns in order to have disputes settled or cases tried by the ordinary native courts, where the procedure baffled them, and the expense often beggared them when it was not wholly beyond their reach.

Financiers and economists objected strongly to the five feddan law; and lawyers objected equally strongly to the legal reform. Cromer wrote (30 July, 1913) to Kitchener : ' You must bear in mind that whether the five feddan law was right or, as I think, wrong, there can be no doubt that the measure, and also the ease with which it was promulgated, has given a very great shock to confidence amongst all the monied classes. Of this I feel quite certain, but I doubt whether you realize the extent of the shock which has been given.'

Kitchener was glad to ride roughshod over the selfish interests of alien usurers and native lawyers as he fought to transform the submerged mass of the peasantry into a secure and conservative tenant class. He was prejudiced against lawyers, and strongly prejudiced against the many small cosmopolitan financiers who had seeped into Egypt in the British wake. He told [1] Grey (22 March, 1913) that those vultures, protected by the privileges which they enjoyed under the ' capitulations' as Europeans, were ' scattered throughout the country in the villages and financed by various banks'. They preyed upon the Egyptian peasant, who ' has had from time immemorial

[1] *Parliamentary Papers, Egypt,* No. 1 (1913) (Cd. 6682).

an ingrained habit of spending more money than he can afford on ceremonies, such as marriage, etc.', by lending money on mortgage ' at exorbitant rates of interest—30 to 40 per cent, and even higher, being not unusual charges '.

In an effort to encourage thrift among the peasants, Kitchener extended the savings bank system to remote country districts, and decreed, under severe sanctions, that no loans should be advanced to peasants by moneylenders at a higher annual rate than 3 per cent. He switched completely into reverse his predecessor's policy of non-interference in matters which did not directly concern Great Britain ; and he was as much concerned about small matters as about big. He instituted a scheme for draining and clearing village ponds ; he established centres where the peasants could have their cotton weighed and stored ; and he enrolled a corps of midwives for service in Egyptian villages. But the work for which he will always be best remembered was a gigantic scheme of land drainage and reclamation.

That costly scheme was strenuously opposed, on behalf of Egypt's foreign bondholders, by Sir Paul Harvey, the Financial Adviser to the Egyptian Government. Kitchener, who had an old score to settle with the Finance Department, requested Harvey to resign forthwith from the Egyptian service. He would brook no opposition, and he appointed the Financial Under-Secretary, Lord Edward Cecil, who had once been his A.D.C., to succeed Harvey. Kitchener knew that Cecil would obey him without question, and the event proved that Kitchener had been right in insisting that the Egyptian Treasury was strong enough to stand the strain. But Harvey had been well liked ; his case was not unique ; and his virtual dismissal for the crime of having offered unpalatable advice was resented by a bureaucracy which Kitchener regarded as too presumptuous and too large.

Kitchener frequently went on semi-royal progresses in his special train in order to visit the provinces and inspect the progress of his land drainage work. He would sit on a dais with local notables under an immense marquee, and listen patiently to addresses of welcome and to poems extolling his virtues which were recited in classical Arabic by advanced pupils in schools. Over the dais would hang a huge coloured portrait of his familiar features, with the virile moustache duly emphasized ; and over the portrait would appear the legend : ' Welcome to Lord Kitchener—the Friend of the Peasant '. Those tours were extraordinarily popular, and few who accompanied him were ever able to erase from their memories the expression of deep contentment which was printed upon Kitchener's face as he gazed hour by hour from his railway coach upon the green, illimitable wealth of the Nile Delta.

In addition to those beneficial and imaginative reforms, Kitchener forced his Government to spend capital upon roads, bridges and light railways ; upon hospitals and imposing public buildings ; and upon preserving Arab monuments and Egyptian antiquities. At the same time he constantly and vigorously prosecuted the great work of heightening the Aswan Dam in order to increase its storage capacity as a precaution against drought.

Kitchener was so strong that he never minded beating a retreat when a question in dispute concerned means and not ends. A good example of that trait occurred when he impetuously summoned a meeting of the twenty largest landowners in Egypt. He informed them that he had brushed from his path everyone who had dared to oppose his agricultural policy, which had placed them all in his debt ; and he invited them, in return, to use their great influence with the Legislative Assembly, whose consent would be necessary to a new form of taxation which he wished to introduce. He explained that he hoped to institute death duties in order to provide money for agricultural and technical education.

Everyone present admired Kitchener, and some genuinely liked him. One or two might have been willing to consider sacrificing their comfort, and even risking their lives, if he had proposed some arduous and exciting service to them. But on the subject of death duties their silence was so oppressive and profound that Kitchener's broad shoulders shook with laughter ; and he dismissed the matter promptly and for ever from his mind.

By switching into reverse Gorst's policy of non-interference, Kitchener exposed himself to a great quantity of work. Most of his day was spent in receiving callers and deputations. He would never receive women on account of a morbid fear of scenes, but he plumed himself upon being accessible to all men without regard to rank or class ; and that policy was extremely popular with almost everyone except the Khedive. The Egyptians understood the advantages of being ruled by a benevolent autocrat ; and they rejoiced to find that their privilege of direct access to supreme authority, which had been suspended under Gorst, had been restored.

Gorst had considered it necessary, from the highest motives, as he saw them, to turn a deaf ear to the cries of the oppressed. But

Kitchener, who constantly exerted himself on behalf of the oppressed, saw no reason to inhibit his joy and pride in ruling Egypt effectually. He liked and understood the Egyptians, and they warmed to his strength and to the simplicity of his manner. His worst fault was a petulance which occasionally betrayed him into actions which he subsequently regretted. An example occurred in 1913, after a number of unpleasant incidents at the elegant and agreeable Gezira Sporting Club.

Kitchener often deplored the way in which, in Egypt as in India, the increasing swarms of British officials and European tourists had caused a social cleavage to develop between Europeans and Egyptians. Kitchener blamed the British club habit and sports system ; but, at the Gezira Club, well-born Egyptians of wealth and position had always been welcome as members. Most were well liked, but a few, who were close to the Khedive, caused trouble by talking politics, and by openly criticizing the British. Kitchener, accordingly, threatened action if further complaints were received that the club's harmony was being disturbed, and he ruthlessly executed that threat when fresh incidents were reported. He had himself installed as president of the club ; and he insisted that all Egyptian members should be asked to resign, or be expelled forthwith if they refused. He made no exceptions, and the place become exclusively British. Great ill-feeling was thereby caused, and many British members resigned, or threatened to resign, in protest. But Kitchener was unmoved. He exhorted the club's committee to ignore all threats ; to treat letters of resignation as irrevocable ; and to show no weakness. Another club was established later in which Egyptians and British could meet on equal terms.

In general, nevertheless, Kitchener ignored national and racial differences. He was courteous, urbane and sometimes delightfully humorous. On one occasion, for example, General Sir Rudolph Slatin Pasha, ' Old Rowdy ', the charming Austrian adventurer whom everybody loved, and for whom the post of Inspector-General of the Sudan had been specially invented, invited himself to lunch with Kitchener in order to talk about his pension. He opened the subject by observing :

" Well, Lord Kitchener, I'm afraid I've not made a great financial success of my life."

" No one who knew you, my dear Slatin, ever thought you would."

" Here was I, for twelve years a prisoner of the Mahdi—naked, in

269

chains, captured on active service. Yet not one piastre of pay throughout that period !"

"Well, Slatin ! You can't say your expenses over that period
amounted to much."

Kitchener thereupon turned the conversation to the prospects of
aviation, and the cotton crop.

Another story, about Kitchener and the Khedive, was widely
repeated throughout Europe. Kitchener had found it necessary to
rebuke Abbas Hilmi for some small act of defiance ; and the Khedive
had excused himself upon the ground that, as the vassal of the Sultan
of Turkey, which, in legal theory, he remained, he was bound to try
to please his suzerain. Kitchener had rapped out immediately :
" My own position here is anomalous enough. We really can't have
two incomprehensibles !"

At the Residency, outside Cairo, and at his summer quarters at
Ramleh, outside Alexandria, Kitchener worked hard all day, and
insisted upon congenial company in the evenings. He loved to speak
of his youthful work in Palestine, and of his two great heroes—General
Gordon, who had been the inspiration of his life, and Lord Salisbury,
who had constantly supported him, after launching him upon his career.
Most of all, he loved to talk about Broome, and the alterations which
he was making there ; and even in Cairo he could not resist the urge
to set similar works in train. One of his first actions upon arriving
at the Residency was to order the construction of an immense new
ballroom. He turned the old ballroom into a new state reception
room, and his hideous drawing-room into a gallery for the reception
of his collections of porcelain and Byzantine ikons. At the same time
he changed all his servants' liveries from chocolate and yellow, which
Gorst had favoured, into scarlet and gold.

Despite a growing love of talk, Kitchener's staff found that their
chief remained incapable of dictating minutes or dispatches. He
wrote everything out laboriously in his extraordinarily bold, large
and legible handwriting ; and he sometimes expressed amused
annoyance when words refused to accept the logical discipline which
he tried to impose upon them. He had, for example, a habit of referring to a ' choate ' system, meaning an orderly one. When he was
told that no such word existed, he exclaimed : " Inchoate—half-baked :
choate—apple-pie." He tried, similarly, to force the word ' détente '
into his dispatches in the sense of disagreement : " Entente—you
agree : détente—you don't !"

When confronted by a crisis, Kitchener had two habits which his staff found slightly disconcerting. He might propound a number of outrageous solutions—" String 'em up ! " " Mow 'em down ! " " Martial law ! "—partly to clear his mind, and partly to see how they were countered ; or he might invite opinions ; tear all answers to pieces with mordant flashes of wit ; and immediately adopt, as if it had been his own, the most sensible solution which had been suggested. All his personal staff agreed, however, that he was the most delightful chief whom it had ever been their privilege to serve.

The voyage up the Nile to Khartoum had become, since the turn of the century, a fashionable winter attraction to European Royalties and other distinguished people. Kitchener loved to entertain them at the start and on the completion of their tours ; and he welcomed a constant stream of visitors from England, including all his closest friends. Every summer he left Egypt in order to enjoy three months' leave in England, when he stayed with his friends, went up to Balmoral, shot grouse, stalked deer and inspected the long work of reconstruction at Broome. At Broome he stayed in the agent's house, and always took a guest or two with him. They noticed that, motoring from London, he was normally silent except when he pointed out from time to time, with emphatic gestures, places where he thought that the road should be widened or a corner eliminated. He worked hard in his garden, and he made his guests work also ; and he used often to say that he was astonished to observe how few people understood the immense amount of trouble which it was necessary to take in order to accomplish successfully even the smallest task—such as the siting of a flower-bed or the arrangement of choice porcelain in a cabinet.

After returning to Cairo in November, 1913, for the last time from his annual summer leave in England, Kitchener effected two more reforms of great significance. He established a Ministry of Agriculture, which proved an immense boon ; and he established a new Ministry to take control of the Waqfs, or Moslem religious charities, which had been administered previously by the Khedive. That second reform provoked controversy.

It had long been known that the palace favourites of Abbas Hilmi were continuously misappropriating the vast funds which pious Moslems had bequeathed in the past for religious, educational and social purposes. But, as Christians and foreigners, Cromer and Gorst had considered it to be impossible to interfere. Kitchener had no such inhibitions. He transferred the control of those endowments to a responsible Minister, assisted by an under-secretary and a council of five, who were all Moslems ; and he secured the Khedive's consent by threatening, if it were withheld, to publish details of a large number of irregularities of which the Sovereign had been guilty.

Kitchener had deliberately set himself the task of humiliating the Khedive in order, if possible, to predispose him towards an act of abdication. He followed up his success by delivering in rapid succession two further blows. He bluntly informed Abbas Hilmi that he would not in future be permitted to confer titles or decorations except upon the recommendation of his Ministers, countersigned by Kitchener ; and he abrogated the right which the Sovereign had hitherto possessed to preside at meetings of the Council of Ministers. Kitchener said that Abbas Hilmi would in future attend only upon special occasions, by invitation, and with the consent of the British Agent.

Kitchener's relations with the Khedive could hardly have been worse. Abbas Hilmi had never forgotten the frontier incident of 1894, when he had first been humiliated by Kitchener ; and Kitchener made insufficient allowance for the bitter sense of frustration from which the Sovereign suffered. Abbas Hilmi was self-indulgent, as well as mildly vicious and corrupt ; and he did a number of foolish things. But in those respects he was not unique among Oriental potentates. He was excellent company and very intelligent, and he possessed many attractive and amiable qualities. He felt that he had been defrauded of his birthright, and for that reason he sought such consolations as were open to him.

Kitchener's letters to Lady Salisbury between 1911 and 1914 were filled with complaints about ' this wicked little Khedive '. He told [1] her, for example (May, 1914), that he often felt that he was playing a part in a comic opera, rather than conducting ' serious government '. By the summer of 1913 he had made up his mind that serious government implied government by himself and the disappearance of Abbas Hilmi ; and he consulted Cromer about the best method of deposing the Egyptian Sovereign.

Cromer, who was a good deal startled, wrote to Kitchener (30 July, 1913) :

' I gathered from what you said yesterday that you are now on

[1] Hatfield MSS.

the point of coming to a serious collision with the Khedive. This was perfectly certain to happen. Further, you are, I think, rather inclined to go so far as to say that he ought to be deposed, and his son put in his place. That is a very serious matter. That the Khedive has behaved very badly . . . is sufficiently obvious, but . . . I do not think the Khedive's conduct . . . is sufficient to afford justification in the public mind for such an extreme measure as deposition . . . It would not be at all difficult to create a state of things in which, in spite of his personal character and unpopularity, he would attract public sympathy, and afford a centre around which Nationalist proclivities might cluster.'

It was almost as though the question of dual control, which had been settled in India, had been revived in Egypt in a wholly different form. But in Kitchener's mind, the deposition of Abbas Hilmi represented only a preliminary step on a great new imperial by-pass road. He wanted to abolish the nominal suzerainty of Turkey over Egypt, and to substitute an advisory council for the board which still nominally controlled Egyptian finance ; he wanted to annex Egypt and to create a new viceroyalty of Egypt and the Sudan ; and he wanted, above all, to abolish the régime of the foreign capitulations which were the principal bar to the progress of Egypt as a self-governing entity because they gave European residents far-reaching privileges and immunities in the fields of legal status and taxation.

The question of annexing Egypt had often been considered by the British Foreign Office, but Kitchener underestimated the effects which his proposed reforms would have had upon Moslem sentiment throughout the world, as well as upon Liberal sentiment in Great Britain, and upon British relations with Turkey and other interested Great Powers. Cromer warned Kitchener (30 July, 1913) that the problem of the capitulations was 'almost unbelievably complicated', and that there was no reason to suppose that annexations would 'once and for all solve the capitulations question'. Cromer added that foreign Powers would never voluntarily consent to abandon their treaty rights, and that even the substitution of an advisory council for the *Caisse de la Dette* would be strongly resisted, at home as well as abroad, on the ground that 'it would place the whole of the legislative power mainly in the hands of yourself'.

In spite of that advice, Kitchener told [1] Sir Edward Grey in his last

[1] *Parliamentary Papers, Egypt*, No. 1 (1914) (Cd. 7358).

annual report (28 March, 1914) that the nettle of the capitulations would need to be firmly grasped : ' Otherwise I cannot foresee the possibility of effecting any radical improvements in a situation the faults of which are inherent in the existing system of the " Capitulations " : The fundamental modification of this system has been urged in the reports emanating from this Agency for many years past, and it may be hoped that a settlement of the question will not now be much longer delayed.'

Before he left Egypt in 1914 for his summer leave in England, Kitchener set up a committee of his own to study the problem of the capitulations. He intended to try to force the British Government to consider seriously, as a start, the possibility of annexing Egypt after the issue of an ultimatum to Abbas Hilmi. Abbas Hilmi, who left Egypt on his annual European tour at the same time as Kitchener, announced his intention of including London in his itinerary ; but Kitchener took prompt action to prevent that visit. He saw the King on 29 June, 1914, and the Khedive was officially informed in Paris, that if he came to England the King would decline to see him. The Khedive's tour ended, accordingly, in Constantinople, in the camp of England's enemies, whom Abbas Hilmi found more congenial than Kitchener and his detested soldiers and officials.

Neither Kitchener nor the Khedive ever visited Egypt again ; and after the outbreak, on 5 November, 1914, of war between the British and Turkish Empires, a British protectorate was proclaimed over Egypt. Abbas Hilmi retorted by issuing a violently anti-British proclamation, after which he was formally deposed and his son ignored. His uncle, Hussein, a man of high character and charm, was installed by the British with the title of Sultan upon the Egyptian throne ; and the suzerainty of the British Crown replaced that of the Sultan of Turkey.

Only one open attempt was made to assassinate Kitchener in Egypt : a nationalist broke through the crowd and pointed a gun at him in the yard outside Cairo Station in April, 1913. While FitzGerald covered his chief with his body, Kitchener advanced imperturbably and asked the man what he wanted ; and the criminal fanatic was so astonished and intimidated that he threw his gun away, sank to his knees, and raised his hands in mute supplication before he was sabred. Other plots were hatched, but all were frustrated, and Kitchener proudly informed [1] Lady Salisbury (3 October, 1913) that at a meeting

[1] Hatfield MSS.

Port Said, 1911

Standing, l. to r. : Khedive Abbas Hilmi II, King George V, Kitchener

Broome Park

of Egyptian nationalists in Geneva 'their headman said that they could do nothing with the people of Egypt so long as I was there'.

After an attempt had been made by an Indian nationalist to assassinate Hardinge in Delhi, reports appeared in the British Press that Kitchener would be asked to exchange Egypt for India. Hardinge, who was seriously wounded, was said to be an unpopular viceroy; but Kitchener's private hope was that he would be invited to succeed Hardinge in India during the autumn of 1915, after he had enjoyed the happiness of presiding over the creation of a new viceroyalty of Egypt and the Sudan, on the analogy of the existing viceroyalties of India and Ireland.

That hope was not destined to be realized; but on 17 June, 1914, Kitchener was delighted to hear that an earldom was to be conferred upon him in recognition of his services to the Empire. He started for home the next day, and told his friends that he intended to take the title of Earl of Broome. They told him, however, that the name 'Kitchener' was an imperial asset, and he allowed them to persuade him to retain it; he took the subsidiary titles of Viscount Broome and Baron Denton.

Kitchener reached Dover on 23 June, five days before the assassination, by Serbian nationalists, of the heir to the throne of Austria-Hungary. One month later the throne of human reason itself was temporarily overwhelmed by the mightiest tornado which had ever risen to the surface of men's minds from some remote atavistic depths to sear and blast humanity.

CHAPTER *14*

SECRETARY FOR WAR

1914

DURING the last few weeks of the glittering London season of 1914, Kitchener again camped in Pandeli Ralli's house at 17 Belgrave Square, which he made his social head-quarters. He lunched and dined out constantly, and Sir Osbert Sitwell has recorded [1] the impression made upon him by Kitchener at that time, at a ball given by the Household Cavalry at Knightsbridge Barracks. Kitchener had chosen a conspicuous seat enfilading the full length of two vistas of rooms :

'. . . One saw only him, for his partner sank into insignificance, since, whatever his faults or his merits, his genius was sufficient to concentrate attention upon him to the exclusion of all others in his neighbourhood, as if he were accompanied by an invisible limelight with an orange slide ; for the colour of his face was tawny beyond sunburn, and pertained to the planet Mars. With an altogether exceptional squareness and solidity, he sat there as if he were a god, slightly gone to seed perhaps, but waiting confidently for his earthly dominion to disclose itself . . . A large square frame, with square shoulders, square head, square face, a square line of hair at the top of a square forehead, he rested there . . . with a slightly unfocused glance which seemed almost in its fixity to possess a power of divination. As well as being the realization of an ideal of Kipling's . . . he plainly belonged to some different order of creation from those around him . . . he could claim kin-ship to the old race of gigantic German Generals, spawned by Wotan in the Prussian plains, and born with spiked helmets ready on their heads. Though his pose offered the same suggestion of immense strength and even of latent fury . . . every trait of his appearance, his blue eyes and the cut of his features, unusual as it was, proclaimed him to be English : not an English leader of patrician type, such as Wellington, but one from the class that had, since the Reform Bill, monopolized power. And you could, in the mind's eye, see his image set up as that of an English god, by natives in different parts of the Empire which he had helped to

[1] *Great Morning* (Macmillan), pp. 262-4.

create and support, precisely as the Roman Emperors had formerly been worshipped. Within a few months' time, when from every hoarding vast posters showed Lord Kitchener pointing into perspectives in space, so steadily perceived, if focused with uncertainty, and, below, the caption " He wants YOU ! ", I often thought of that square figure glowering under the wreaths and festoons of smilax, from among the ferns, and palms and flowers . . . '

At week-ends Kitchener usually went to Broome, and as the Old World slithered into the abyss he prepared to return to his post in Egypt. He went to Broome on Friday, 31 July, after lunching with the King, and saying that he would like to succeed Hardinge as Viceroy of India. He wrote farewell letters to Lady Salisbury and other friends. On Monday, 3 August, he motored to Dover and boarded the 12.55 Channel steamer for Calais. The Foreign Office had reserved a compartment for him on the 2.50 p.m. train from Calais to Paris and sleepers on the 9 p.m. train from Paris to Marseilles ; and the First Lord of the Admiralty, Winston Churchill, had ordered a cruiser to convey him from Marseilles to Alexandria.

The boat train from Victoria was late at Dover, and Kitchener sent FitzGerald and Edward Cecil to urge the captain to start without waiting for the train. While the captain hesitated, a telephone message was received from the Prime Minister, H. H. Asquith, requesting Kitchener to return immediately to London. At Belgrave Square Kitchener found a note from Asquith :

' I was very sorry to interrupt your journey today . . . But with matters in their present critical position I was anxious that you should not get beyond the reach of personal consultation and assistance.'

In reply (4 August), Kitchener asked ' if there is any objection now to my making arrangements to leave for Egypt on the P. & O. next Friday ' ; but Asquith's secretary telephoned to say that there was strong objection, and that, if war were declared, the Prime Minister would wish to see Kitchener for a few minutes alone, immediately before an extraordinary council of war which he would be expected to attend on 5 August at 4 p.m. at 10 Downing Street. Kitchener spent that unwelcome interval in discussing Egyptian affairs at the Foreign Office, and in instructing his solicitor about his will.

Kitchener had gone as close as he ever went towards running away, because he was desperately anxious to avoid a summons to join the Government as Secretary for War. That office had been combined by Asquith with that of Prime Minister since the end of March, 1914, when J. E. B. Seely (Lord Mottistone) had resigned after mishandling the so-called mutiny at the Curragh. On that occasion a section of the entrenched caste of senior army officers felt that it had secured a moral victory in a contest with the Irish policy of the Liberal Government ; and the incident had repercussions after the outbreak of war when a struggle developed between statesmen and soldiers for the control of war strategy.

On 5 August, *The Times*, which was controlled by Northcliffe, urged Asquith in the strongest terms to surrender the War Office to Kitchener at once. Asquith had already made up his mind to embark upon what he privately termed that ' hazardous experiment ', and he noted [1] in his diary that Kitchener, ' to do him justice ', had been extremely reluctant to consent to serve. The Press was informed on the evening of 5 August that Kitchener, aged 64, had entered the Cabinet as Secretary for War, as a soldier and without politics ; and that his post in Cairo would again be open to him at the war's end. He was the first serving soldier to sit in any Cabinet since George Monck, Duke of Albemarle, in 1660 ; and he was paid a special allowance of eleven hundred and forty pounds a year in addition to his pay as a Field-Marshal and his annual salary of five thousand pounds as a Secretary of State.

The ecstatic outburst of popular approval which greeted Kitchener's appointment evoked little echo in the War Office or the highest army circles. That was due less to jealousy than to a fear that Kitchener might be used by the Government as an instrument of political interference with prearranged military plans. All the leading statesmen and Service chiefs cherished the strange illusion that a long war would impose an intolerable strain upon the interlocked economies of the belligerents. They were, therefore, convinced that the issue would be decided, one way or the other, within a few months by a series of bloody battles fought by professional armies in the course of a brief war of movement. In those circumstances, the ruling Liberal politicians, diffident of their ability to control the military caste in war, welcomed the mythical demi-god into their midst. They counted upon using the mass enthusiasm which Kitchener's name commanded, to inspire confidence, and to strengthen the Government's foundation in public opinion.

The British plan for meeting the emergency had been devised

---

[1] *Memories and Reflections*, II, p. 24.

before the war by Haldane and the Committee of Imperial Defence. The basic assumptions were that the war would be short, and that the tremendous disparity between the miniature British Army and the vast conscript hosts of the continental Powers would be balanced effectually by the traditional British weapon of overwhelming sea-power. Kitchener, who disagreed profoundly with both those assumptions, was in cordial agreement with the German Kaiser in regarding the British Army of 1914 with contempt.

Kitchener despised the regular Army because it was much too small for the part which it was certain to have to play. It consisted of about 120,000 men organized in six superbly trained and equipped infantry divisions, with one cavalry division. Another 60,000 regular troops, stationed overseas, were available to be brought home as soon as replacements had been provided by India and the colonies.

Kitchener despised the Territorial Army of fourteen divisions, which Haldane had formed out of the old Volunteers and Imperial Yeomanry, on account of its amateur spirit which he regarded as incurable. Enlisted only for home defence, and designed for unlimited expansion, its embodiment on the outbreak of war was intended to free the regular Army for service on the Continent. Kitchener held that the Territorials were a characteristically untrained and unprofessional product of the years which the locusts had eaten, and of the mind of a philosophical Lord Chancellor, and he persistently declined to place his trust in such a force.

Kitchener had usually contrived to avoid attending meetings of the Defence Committee even on the rare occasions when his presence in London made such attendance possible. But he knew, in outline, about the secret conversations between members of the British and French General Staffs which had been held since 1906, unknown to most members of the British Cabinet, with the object of ensuring the presence of the B.E.F. (British Expeditionary Force) at the earliest moment on the left of the French line in the event of war with Germany. He had regarded with contempt the purpose of those staff conversations ; and he had informed the Defence Committee during the summer of 1911 that he expected that the Germans would walk through the French ' like partridges '. He told [1] Lord Esher at that time that it was ' puerile ' to suppose that the presence or absence of the ridiculously small British Army at any particular time or place could affect the outcome of a Franco-German war ; and that such

[1] Esher, *Journals and Letters*, III, p. 58.

a war could only be won with the aid of ' the last million ' men whom Great Britain could raise, train, equip and hurl into the fight.

As a realist, Kitchener understood that any government which had ventured to propose a substantial increase of military expenditure before the war would have been flung out of power by an indignant electorate. For that reason he had never publicly attacked Haldane ; and he had held entirely aloof from the campaign which Roberts had conducted for years on behalf of conscription in time of peace. Kitchener felt that the British people had enjoyed the kind of government which they deserved ; he despised their unmilitary qualities and the improvidence which they had shown ; and with those thoughts present in his mind he stalked into the Cabinet room at 10, Downing Street, on 5 August at 4. p.m. to attend the council of war at which he met eleven other general officers, including Lord Roberts and Field-Marshal Sir John French, Commander-in-Chief of the B.E.F. Asquith presided, and Lord Haldane, Sir Edward Grey and Winston Churchill (First Lord of the Admiralty) were also present.

Before it adjourned until the following day the council of war recommended that the bulk of the B.E.F. should be dispatched immediately across the Channel and concentrated at the place which would harmonize best with French strategic dispositions. Kitchener urged that it should be concentrated around Amiens ; but almost all his military colleagues pressed for a concentration around Maubeuge, some 70 miles further forward. Kitchener said that it would be wrong to expose the B.E.F. unnecessarily to the hazards of an enforced initial retreat ; and he explained that the Germans, in his opinion, would not have dragged Great Britain into the war by violating Belgian neutrality unless they had decided to stake everything upon a knock-out blow aimed at the heart of France, east as well as west of the River Meuse.

Kitchener's military colleagues pointed out that the B.E.F. had been committed before the war to a suitable alignment with the French ; and they stressed the importance of harmonizing at the outset the military strategy of Great Britain and France. They expressed the view of the French General Staff that the Germans, faced with a war upon two fronts, and with the menace of ' the Russian steam-roller ', did not possess the strength to mount an assault upon the massive scale which Kitchener anticipated. They considered that the Germans would advance either through the Ardennes or through the industrial heart of Belgium, west of the Meuse ; and they explained that, in either case, the French wanted the B.E.F. as far forward as possible, in order that it should be in a position to give the maximum protection to their left, while their right delivered a blow in regard to which no information had been vouchsafed during the secret pre-war staff conversations.

On the morning of 6 August the Cabinet, in deference to Kitchener, decided provisionally that the B.E.F. should be concentrated around Amiens. Kitchener did not attend that meeting because he had not yet kissed hands or been sworn of the Privy Council. He had, of course, no wish to hold back the B.E.F.'s contribution of 100,000 men, but General Joffre, the French Commander-in-Chief, who was opposing 1,500,000 Germans with 1,300,000 Frenchmen, sent officers to London to press strongly for a more forward British concentration.

The French had decided to stake everything upon an initial stroke of reckless audacity in the south. They launched, in the greatest possible strength, an offensive into the lost province of Lorraine with the object of breaking into the heart of Germany. That assault was disastrously repulsed before the end of August, after exacting from the French Army and nation the enormous forfeit of 300,000 casualties. It might have cost the Allies the war, if the Germans had not also committed gross and extraordinary blunders.

Kitchener had appeared too late upon the scene to interfere with the pre-war gentleman's agreement reached between the British and French General Staffs, in which he had taken little interest and about which he had no detailed knowledge. On the afternoon of 12 August, while the B.E.F. were crossing the Channel, he conferred at the War Office with Sir John French and several French officers of high rank. The French insisted that their strategy could not be harmonized with that of the British unless the B.E.F. was concentrated at least as far forward as Maubeuge ; and after a discussion lasting three hours, during which he repeatedly expressed his deep misgiving, Kitchener said that he felt unable any longer to oppose the unanimous advice of the General Staffs of both armies. He then took Sir John French to see Asquith, who said, naturally, that he would accept Kitchener's advice. The Cabinet's provisional decision of 6 August was, accordingly, set aside ; and within a fortnight the B.E.F. was in precipitate retreat from Mons.

Wearing a frock-coat and silk hat, Kitchener entered the War Office on the stroke of ten on the morning of 6 August, 1914. Normally, he always arrived at nine, wearing the blue undress uniform of a Field-Marshal, and stayed until about 8 p.m. without troubling to go out for lunch. He ate little, and was content with a few sandwiches in his office, but it was noticed, as the months passed, that he put on a good deal of weight. His Director of Military Operations, Sir Charles Callwell, recorded [1] that although, at the start, Kitchener was working ' in an atmosphere of latent hostility ', he quickly ' made things hum '. Callwell added that, to his astonishment, he saw, within a few days, elderly War Office messengers, ' dignity personified . . . tearing along the passages with coat-tails flying as though mad donkeys were at their heels, when Lord K. wanted somebody in his sanctum '.

Kitchener led deliberately a dedicated life from which he assumed that with God's help he would emerge victorious in three or four years' time as the saviour of his foolish but chastened and beloved country, with a dukedom like Marlborough and Wellington, and a suitable money grant ; and with leisure to enjoy Broome in summer, and his sunny property in Kenya during the winter, quietly and without fuss until the end of his days. In the meantime he unwisely took the King's pledge to touch no alcohol until the war was won ; and he often dined alone with FitzGerald before working late into the night. He dined out also, whenever he could spare the time, sometimes with the King who said, laughingly, that on such occasions he found Kitchener so talkative that he had difficulty in getting a word in edgeways. He used also to dine with other friends, including Asquith, Grey, Haldane and Churchill. Occasionally he walked late into the Beefsteak Club which he had joined in 1899, and listened, with apparent enjoyment, to the talk and chaff ; but he had no use for any other club. He was annoyed when, through a misunderstanding, Randall Davidson, the Archbishop of Canterbury, proposed him for the Athenaeum, to which he was elected immediately under a special rule. He wrote at once firmly declining that election.

At the War Office on 6 August, after the Permanent Secretary had presented a few senior officials, Kitchener rang for his private secretary, and held out a broken pen with which he had been invited to sign his official stamp : " Dear me ! " he murmured sweetly, " What a place ! Not a scrap of army ! Not even a pen that will write ! " He then left for Buckingham Palace, where he received his seals of office ; and he made arrangements, later in the day, to move from Belgrave Square to a furnished house at 2, Carlton Gardens, which Lady

[1] *Experiences of a Dug-Out*, pp. 55–6.

Wantage offered to lend him until he could find a house of his own. As he made no attempt to look further, the King presently offered him York House, St. James's Palace, for the duration of the war, which he accepted. He moved there from Carlton Gardens in the middle of March, 1915, with Colonel FitzGerald, C.M.G., who became his personal military secretary and never left his side.

Kitchener assumed responsibility for three herculean tasks in addition to the ordinary routine of his Department. He undertook to raise, train and equip new armies of unprecedented size ; to mobilize the nation's industries for war ; and to supervise the conduct of British military strategy in every part of the globe. He took upon his shoulders that crushing burden for which no other support had been provided, because no thought had been directed before the war to the problem of devising effective machinery for the conduct of total war.

With characteristic detachment, Asquith [1] noted in his diary on 5 August that it would be 'amusing to see' how Kitchener 'gets on in the Cabinet' ; and it would be hard to exaggerate the impression which Kitchener made in those early days from the moment when he took his seat for the first time on 7 August on the Prime Minister's right. The vast but undefined responsibilities which he had shouldered temporarily undid the work of Gladstone, who had made the office of Chancellor of the Exchequer the second most important in the Government. None disputed Kitchener's title to rank second to the Prime Minister, and Asquith [2] noted that Kitchener was utterly unself-conscious and far too sure of himself to be vain : 'He did not pose for posterity ; he never laid himself out either for contemporary or posthumous applause'. He was genuinely indifferent to the lime-light which played upon him, and that indifference attracted it the more.

Winston Churchill recorded [3] the intense admiration with which he listened in Cabinet to Kitchener proclaiming 'in soldierly sentences . . . a series of inspiring and prophetic truths'. That was Kitchener's hour, and he proceeded to dissociate himself entirely from the view of the Government, the War Office, and the Defence Committee, that the war was likely to be brief. He declared, on the contrary, that it was likely to be long ; that it could not be won on the sea, nor by the traditional British weapon of sea-power. It could only

[1] *Memories and Reflections* II, p. 24.   [2] Ibid., p. 82.
[3] *The World Crisis, 1911–18* (abridged and revised edition, 1931), p. 140.

be won after many bloody battles fought on the European continent ; and Great Britain's contribution could not be limited to the miniature regular Army. It could not be limited in any way :

"We must be prepared to put armies of millions into the field, and to maintain them for several years."

Kitchener then announced that he intended, as a start, to base his calculations on a war lasting three years, and that he proposed at once to raise a new army of at least a million men.

After Kitchener had spoken, Churchill noted that that new and surprising doctrine was received by his colleagues ' in silent assent '. Sir Edward Grey's reaction was more typical. He noted [1] that Kitchener's estimate of the war's duration ' seemed to most of us unlikely, if not incredible '. Asked by a colleague, as he walked away, for his opinion of Kitchener's proposal to raise a new army of a million men, " I replied that I believed the war would be over before a million men could be trained or equipped, but that, if this expectation were wrong, the million men should of course be sent abroad to take part in the war."

After a lifetime devoted on the frontiers of empire to a study of the art of war, Kitchener spoke a different language from that of his colleagues. He had joined a Cabinet of high intellectual calibre, but the parliamentary and political atmosphere which was the breath of life to all his colleagues was so strange to Kitchener that it made him gasp. Unlike his colleagues, who all owed their positions to their parliamentary and political standings, Kitchener owed his position entirely to non-political and extra-parliamentary factors.

A stranger, a soldier, and a Conservative, introduced suddenly to second place on a closely-knit board of Liberal politicians, Kitchener wrestled with problems which he had been called in to solve, and which transcended all human experience. He longed to be allowed to get on with his job by methods to which he was wedded ; but he found twenty-two colleagues, one or two of whom he would have been happy to dispatch to Jericho if he had had the power, even though, as sometimes happened, he might fail for a moment to recall their names, who shared collective responsibility with him for every executive action which he took for the country's safety. He observed on one occasion that he found it repugnant and unnatural to have to discuss military secrets with a large number of gentlemen with some of whom he was but barely acquainted ; but his colleagues naturally expected

[1] *Twenty-Five Years, 1892-1916*, II, p. 68.

that he would cheerfully exert himself to convince them before they gave their consents to his proposals. They resented any show of abruptness, and Kitchener was not trained, as they were, to engage with refreshment and profit, after or during the course of a hard day's work, in the swift give and take of vivid verbal discussion.

Kitchener forgave his colleagues for what he regarded as collective sins of irresponsible omission before the war. But he grudged the time which they expected him to devote in Cabinet and in committee to the arts of persuasion and address which he found insuperably difficult and distasteful. He threatened on several occasions to resign if they persisted, and he could not always control his impatience. Lloyd George, who was Chancellor of the Exchequer in 1914, com- pared [1] Kitchener unkindly with ' one of those revolving lighthouses which radiate momentary gleams of revealing light far out into the surrounding gloom, and then suddenly relapse into complete darkness. There were no intermediate stages.'

Lloyd George [2] complained that Kitchener appeared to treat all his colleagues ' with the usual mixture of military contempt and apprehension. His main idea at the Council table was to tell the politicians as little as possible of what was going on, and get back to his desk at the War Office as quickly as he could decently escape '.

Lloyd George admitted [3] that all Kitchener's colleagues ' were frankly intimidated by his presence, because of his repute and enormous prestige amongst all classes of the people outside. A word from him was decisive, and no one dared to challenge it at a Cabinet meeting. I think I may say that I was the first to do so, on munitions . . . '

The masses of his countrymen were united behind Kitchener because they believed that he possessed plenary power to take decisions which would lead to victory. The Government encouraged that belief, and allowed Kitchener to act as supreme war lord for many months. No Secretary for War had ever borne such a weight of responsibility before, but the cloak of authority was missing, and the burden thrown on Kitchener was a measure of his country's unpreparedness. The vast undefined powers which Kitchener exercised were not derived officially from Parliament, but by informal delegation from the Cabinet ; and he possessed none of the essential constitutional and administrative aids which enabled Churchill in 1940 to discharge with incomparably greater effect the wartime dictatorship entrusted to him by Parliament.

Kitchener was neither Prime Minister nor Minister of Defence.

[1] *War Memoirs*, II, p. 751.   [2] Ibid., I, p. 83.   [3] Ibid., I, p. 499.

He lacked the vital machinery of the Chiefs of Staff Committee which co-ordinated the higher direction of the fighting services during the second World War, and provided Churchill in 1940 with a perfectly integrated instrument for directing the nation's war effort with the speed and consistency of a single will. Such an instrument was not provided by the War Council which, on 25 November, 1914, displaced the Committee of Imperial Defence.

The War Council, like its parent body, was a committee of the Cabinet with some experts added, including Arthur Balfour, an ex-Prime Minister and prominent Opposition leader. Its task was to assist the Cabinet in the higher direction of military and naval operations. Most Cabinet Ministers who were not members of the War Council were glad, in the interests of efficiency, to delegate to the smaller body their personal responsibility for the conduct of the war, but a few proved jealous of their rights. It was mainly due to complaints by Kitchener that he had not time to cover the same ground twice, that the War Council, unlike its parent body, the Defence Committee, began to give prompt executive effect to its most important decisions without awaiting or even requesting formal Cabinet approval.

Generals and Admirals, who were haphazardly summoned to advise the War Council, took a different view of their duties from that which was held by the ministerial members. Ministers assumed that the Service chiefs would speak their minds, but those experts did not consider that they had any duty to speak without being invited, or to express dissent if they disagreed with opinions which Ministers had expressed. Asquith, who always presided, never invited the attendant Service chiefs to speak, and he was wholly guided in technical matters by the Secretary for War and the First Lord of the Admiralty.

Kitchener, unlike Churchill, was an expert in his own right. In all strategic questions he dominated Asquith, and Churchill told the Dardanelles Commissioners : " I had not the same weight or authority as those two Ministers, nor the same power, and if they said ' This is to be done, or not to be done ', that settled it ." The position, therefore, was that Kitchener, acting as his own Chief of Staff, and overburdened by his other major responsibilities for recruiting and munitions, had to balance, by means of his almost unaided intuition, a fantastic variety of conflicting interests and opinions. He was faced, for example, by the Commander-in-Chief of the B.E.F., as well as by the French Government and High Command, who kept insisting that the war could only be won by large-scale offensive operations in France ; by Churchill, who argued with incomparable virtuosity that the quickest way to achieve victory was to force the Dardanelles and to capture Constantinople ; by Churchill's formidable First Sea Lord, Lord Fisher, who had his own plan for a military landing upon the German Baltic coast ; by Lloyd George, the dynamic and person- ally ambitious Chancellor of the Exchequer, who sought vehemently to convince everyone that the main British effort should be switched immediately from costly, useless and unimaginative attacks upon the Western Front, to the Balkans, Palestine and Syria ; by Lord Crewe, the Secretary for India, who was arranging the conquest of Mesopo- tamia (Iraq) by the Indian Army and Government, and who begged Kitchener, ' on constitutional grounds ', to forgo direct communica- tion with Indian Army headquarters ; by Sir Edward Grey who was concerned about the defence of Egypt and the Suez Canal, as well as about urgent Russian demands for supplies of British munitions ; and by Lewis Harcourt, the aesthetic Colonial Secretary, who was charmed with his novel rôle as director of military operations in different parts of Africa. Sir William Robertson, who took over Kitchener's responsibility for military strategy in December, 1915, recorded[1] his view that ' a more deplorable state of affairs can never have existed in the conduct of any war '.

Kitchener did his best from the outset to work in the closest unity with the Admiralty, and Churchill wrote to him (13 September, 1914) : ' It is a great pleasure to work with you, and the two Depart- ments work well together. As you say, they are only one Department really.' That precarious harmony, however, was not nearly enough to secure the effective co-ordination and direction of the entire field of war strategy. For that purpose the necessary constitutional and administrative machinery had not been invented, and confusion and misdirection were the inevitable result.

Kitchener's most urgent need in those circumstances was a strong and efficient General Staff ; and it is extraordinary to have to relate that he took no steps at any time towards providing himself with that indispensable assistance. It is true that in August, 1914, all the best staff officers rushed off to France with the B.E.F. ; but Kitchener had always stressed the importance of staff work, and his total neglect of his own doctrine when handling problems of global strategy proved

[1] Field-Marshal Sir William Robertson, Bt., *Soldiers and Statesmen*, I, p. 160.

disastrous. It is, for example, inconceivable that Sir Ian Hamilton would have been dispatched to Gallipoli without a full appreciation and recommendations for the conduct of his campaign, if Kitchener had been served by an adequate General Staff.

That neglect can be attributed only in a very minor degree to a generous unwillingness to handicap Sir John French by recalling valuable officers from France. The primary cause was Kitchener's strong instinctive desire to act as his own Chief of Staff, as he had done in South Africa and the Sudan. The qualities which had raised him so high became, in a global war, his undoing. His obsessional attributes of thoroughness and drive were rendered almost nugatory because they inhibited him from delegating responsibility at a time when such delegation had become an inescapable condition of success.

As his difficulties multiplied, Kitchener made no attempt to revive or reorganize his General Staff. He made no move even to replace the notoriously incompetent Chief of the Imperial General Staff, Sir James Wolfe-Murray, whom he had appointed and whom he never consulted, by someone of the calibre of Sir William Robertson or Sir John Cowans, the Quartermaster-General who possessed a genius for administration and who rendered immensely efficient service upon the supply side. Instead, Kitchener seriously contemplated answering his critics by inviting Parliament to add the office of Generalissimo, or supreme commander of British forces in all parts of the world, to the overwhelming burden which he already carried as Secretary for War, with responsibility for strategy, recruiting and munitions.

So great was the confidence which Kitchener inspired that Churchill considered that the Cabinet would have accepted conscription in August, 1914, 'to be applied as it might be required', if Kitchener had demanded it. Asquith, however, enjoyed the support of most of his colleagues in holding that any early move towards conscription would have been politically impossible. Kitchener, without a moment's hesitation, deferred to Asquith's judgment; and that decision was certainly wise.

On 7 August, 1914, Kitchener issued his first appeal for one hundred thousand volunteers; and the whole country was soon placarded with posters depicting Kitchener in the character of Big Brother, with a Field-Marshal's cap, hypnotic eyes, bristling moustache, pointing finger, and the legend, 'Your Country Needs YOU'. Volunteers thereafter flowed in at a rate which strained almost to breaking-point the hastily improvised machinery for accommodating, equipping and training them. Mrs. Asquith remarked indiscreetly that if Kitchener was not a great man, he was, at least, a great poster ; and Kitchener retorted by telling his personal staff that all his colleagues repeated military secrets to their wives, except Asquith, who repeated them to other people's wives.

During the first eighteen months of the war, 2,467,000 volunteers sprang forward in response to Kitchener's appeals, and in the mood to which Rupert Brooke gave touching expression :

> Now God be thanked who has matched us with His hour,
> And caught our youth, and waken'd us from sleeping. . .

In those circumstances, the most obvious advantage of conscription would have been an approach towards greater equality of sacrifice. As money wages rose, many laggards inevitably remained behind instead of volunteering to man the trenches. But Kitchener dreaded time-wasting political complications with which he was unfitted to deal. In view, therefore, of the conditions which he found, and of the contemporary climate of opinion, he cannot be blamed for having preferred liberty to equality until it had been clearly proved that the voluntary system was no longer adequate. He told the House of Lords (5 January, 1916) :

"We have been able to provide for the expansion of the Army, and its maintenance, on a purely voluntary system ; and I, personally, had always hoped that we should be able to finish the war successfully without changing that system which has given us such splendid material . . . I feel sure that everyone will agree when I say that the fullest and fairest trial has been given to the system which I found in existence, and of which I felt it my duty to make the fullest use. We are now asking Parliament to sanction a change . . ."

The prudence with which Kitchener handled the problem of conscription was not matched by his treatment of the Territorial Army. Haldane, who had created the system, complained [1] that he was unable to persuade Kitchener ' to adopt, or even to make much real use of the Territorial organization I had provided . . . He would not raise troops through the medium of the County Associations on whom,

[1] *Autobiography*, pp. 278–80.

under the existing arrangements, the duty of recruiting and supplying the troops would have devolved automatically. He insisted on raising, not Territorial line after Territorial line, each of which would have stepped into the place of the one in front as it moved away, but new "Kitchener Armies" through the medium of the Adjutant-General's Department of the War Office. The result was the confusion which arises from a sudden departure from settled principles . . . Kitchener and I remained on good terms. We used to dine with each other alone and have much talk. Still, move his mind on to modern lines I could not.'

Churchill and most others rightly agreed with Haldane in deploring Kitchener's decision to build his new armies upon fresh foundations which had to be specially improvised, and in condemning his neglect of the machinery of the local Territorial Associations. The two organizations continued to exist side by side, but the new Kitchener Armies enjoyed a monopoly of official favour. Of the 2,467,000 volunteers who enlisted during the first eighteen months of the war, 1,741,000 joined Kitchener's Armies and 726,000 joined the Territorials. A number of senior officers ventured at different times to call Kitchener's attention to the unnecessary waste and duplication of effort which his policy was causing, and those protests usually resulted in instant relegation to civilian status. Kitchener was extremely sensitive about that subject, and he invariably replaced officers, whom he suspected of disagreement with his policy, by others who were wholly amenable to his will.

Under strain, Kitchener could be extremely rude to senior officers. He had his off days, and no one in uniform, however senior, cared to approach him except through FitzGerald, who acted as a barometer, and who warned everyone that his chief was especially sensitive on the subject of the Territorial Army. Kitchener paid unqualified tribute to that Army's record in the field, and to the eagerness with which its members had volunteered for service overseas ; but his dislike of it was instinctive and inveterate, so that argument was useless.

There were two principal causes of that dislike. Kitchener took his profession so intensely seriously that he found it impossible to trust soldiers who were differently conditioned. He regarded the Territorials as playboys—amateurs conceived in a holiday spirit which they would never be able to live down. His brief experience during the Franco-Prussian War of 1870-1, and a much more extensive

tchener as Field-Marshal

Recruiting Poster, 1914, designed by Alfred Leete

experience during the Boer War of 1899–1902, had planted and confirmed in his mind an invincible prejudice against all non-professional soldiers ; and that prejudice had been reinforced by a close study of the American Civil War of 1861–5. Both sides in America had been compelled to undertake a rapid and unprecedented military expansion, and Kitchener had been profoundly shocked by its results. Desertions had occurred upon an unprecedented scale, and contemplation of the bare possibility of allowing well-trained professional armies, however small, to be contaminated again by the intrusion of uniformed but undisciplined mobs, made Kitchener physically ill. He was determined, therefore, that his new armies should spring out of the ground as regulars, enlisted for the duration of the war, cut to the standard professional pattern, and conditioned from the outset to the urgent needs of his personal military machine.

In the second place, because he owed his seat in the Cabinet to the mass enthusiasm and confidence which he inspired, and not to any political or parliamentary standing, Kitchener felt instinctively impelled to give some spectacular lead. Released miraculously like some Eastern jinn from a bottle, and charged with the duty of saving his country, he responded in the spirit of a tale out of the *Arabian Nights*. With a wave of his baton he started to conjure new ' Kitchener ' Armies out of the ground, formed in his own image instead of in that of Haldane, the clever lawyer, who had been bred in a different stable. The recruits who flocked in their hundreds of thousands to join the Kitchener Armies repaid the inspiration and leadership which Kitchener gave them by meeting a psychological need in his own nature.

By forming his new armies and placing them in the field, trained, equipped and on time, Kitchener performed a miracle of improvisation ; but that miracle was achieved at a much greater all-round cost in effort than would have been necessary if proper use had been made of the existing Territorial organization. That was a part of the price which the nation had to pay for the superb quality of the leadership which Kitchener gave it and for the radiant confidence which he inspired at a time when both those rare moral assets were of incalculable value.

Kitchener brought to his task a titanic energy and courage, and an autocratic resolve which, seasoned with a touch of inarticulate poetry, lifted his reputation to a height previously unparallelled in British annals. His word carried instant conviction, and individuals, dwarfed in the menacing gloom of huge and terrible events, were eager to merge their insignificant personalities in his commanding one which towered over the land, and which made him to the last, in the minds of the great mass of his countrymen, the legendary hero of the war, and the indispensable symbol of their will to victory.

The quality of Kitchener's leadership was tested within a month of the outbreak of war by the critical situation of the B.E.F. Kitchener had been unable, owing to the absence of any comprehensive war policy, to give Sir John French the kind of instructions to which a commander-in-chief is entitled. He had merely explained that French's mission was to co-operate with the French armies in repelling the German invaders ; that his command was ' entirely independent ' ; and that ' you will in no case come in any sense under the orders of any Allied General '. But French was given no information about the means which would be provided for the fulfilment of his mission. The only hint vouchsafed in Kitchener's laconic note of instructions was contained in a single sentence : ' The numerical strength of the British Force, and its contingent reinforcement, is strictly limited, and with this consideration kept steadily in view, it will be obvious that the greatest care must be exercised towards a minimum of losses and wastage.'

French was known as a man who had always been prepared to accept responsibility and to incur risks. He landed at Boulogne on 14 August, reached his headquarters at Le Cateau three days later, and started to advance on 21 August through Maubeuge on Mons. He was immediately outflanked by the Germans advancing in massive strength through Belgium on the widest possible front and on both sides of the Meuse as Kitchener had predicted ; and a powerful French counter-stroke in the Ardennes was bloodily repulsed on 22 August. The great fortress of Namur surrendered on the following day, and French telegraphed at about 2 a.m. on 24 August to inform Kitchener that Namur had fallen ; that he had ordered a general retreat of the B.E.F. ; and that ' immediate attention should be directed to the defence of Havre ', which was the British base.

That startling telegram was carried personally by Kitchener to Churchill at Admiralty House at seven o'clock on the morning of 24 August. Churchill was still in bed, but at work upon his papers, when Kitchener, with slightly unfocused eyes and looking positively gigantic, paused in the doorway and exclaimed in a hoarse voice, " Bad news ! " The Germans could easily at that moment have seized the Channel ports, but Kitchener remained imperturbable even when French, under very severe stress, was found wanting in the highest qualities of a commander.

Reeling under the double shock of the collapse of their general offensive in Lorraine and of the unexpected revelation of the scale of the German enveloping movement through Belgium into northern France, the French armies of the left and centre were plunged into full retreat. Sir John French, having been too headstrong and optimistic at the outset, became suddenly despondent and unreliable. He considered that he had been deceived by the French High Command, and he signalled to Kitchener that he intended to disengage his army, and to retire behind the Seine in a south-westerly direction. He followed up that telegram by a letter, written from Compiègne and dated 30 August :

'. . . My confidence in the ability of the leaders of the French Army to carry this campaign to a successful conclusion is fast waning, and this is my real reason for the decision I have taken to move the British Forces so far back . . .

' I feel most strongly the absolute necessity of retaining in my hands complete independence of action and power to retire on my base when circumstances render it necessary.

' I have been pressed very hard to remain, even in my shattered condition, in the fighting line ; but I have absolutely refused to do so, and I hope you will approve of the course I have taken. Not only is it in accordance with the spirit and letter of your instructions, but it is dictated by common sense . . .

' I have tried many times to persuade General Joffre to adopt a stronger and bolder line of action, but without avail . . .'

Kitchener regarded with the utmost gravity not merely French's declared intention to quit the line independently of his allies and to retire on Havre, but also the attitude of mind disclosed in that letter. French never regained his chief's confidence, and Kitchener telegraphed (31 August) :

' I am surprised at your decision to retire behind the Seine. Please let me know, if you can, all your reasons for this move. What will be the effect of this course upon your relations with the French Army, and on the general military situation ? Will your retirement leave a gap in the French line, or cause them discouragement of which the Germans could take advantage . . . ? Thirty-two trains of German troops were yesterday reported moving from the Western field to meet the Russians. Have all your requirements been supplied by the line of communications, and how has your reorganization progressed ? '

In Cabinet later that morning Kitchener demanded and obtained authority to order French to obey his original instructions ; and he accordingly telegraphed a second time :

' The government are exceedingly anxious lest your force, at this stage of the campaign in particular, should, owing to your proposed retirement so far from the line, not be able to co-operate closely with our allies and render them continual support. They expect that you will, as far as possible, conform to the plans of General Joffre for the conduct of the campaign. They . . . have all possible confidence in your troops and yourself.'

French's reply to both telegrams reached the War Office at midnight, and was repeated to Kitchener word by word, as it was deciphered :

' . . . If the French go on with their present tactics, which are practically to fall back right and left of me, usually without notice, and to abandon all idea of offensive operations, of course then the gap in the French line will remain, and the consequences will be borne by them.

' I can only state that it will be difficult for the force under my command to withstand successfully in its present condition a strong attack by even one German Army Corps ; and in the event of a pause in my retirement I must expect two Army Corps at least, if not three.

' If, owing to Russian pressure, the withdrawal of the Germans turns out to be true, it will be easy for me to arrest my retirement and refit north of Paris. But this I cannot do while my rearguards are still engaged . . .

' I do not think you understand the shattered condition of the second Army Corps, and how it paralyses my power of offence . . .

' My supply and l. of c. have been both excellent in every way.

' The difficulty of organization is not behind but in front.
' I think you had better trust me to watch the situation and act
according to circumstances . . .'

That telegram plainly showed that French intended to persist in
his intention of withdrawing independently from the line in order to
refit ; and Kitchener decided to cross to France immediately and to
make a personal intervention.   He thereby missed a further telegram
from French which, when he saw it, fully confirmed the urgent
necessity of that journey :
' I wish you to clearly understand ', French signalled during the
small hours of 1 September, ' that in my opinion the force under my
command is not in its present condition able to render effective support
to our allies, no matter what their positions may be '.

Shortly after midnight on the night of 31 August/1 September,
Kitchener hurried to Downing Street, where he saw Asquith, Churchill,
Lloyd George, Reginald McKenna (Home Secretary), and J. A.
Pease (President of the Board of Education).   On behalf of their
colleagues, they authorized Kitchener to cross the Channel immedi-
ately and to clear up the situation with French.

After ordering a special train to be ready at Charing Cross at 3 a.m.,
and a destroyer to take him from Dover to Havre, Kitchener asked
French by telegraph to leave at the British Embassy in Paris a message
to say where he would find it convenient to meet him that afternoon.
He reached Paris from Havre by special train before luncheon, and he
found, as he expected, that French had chosen the British Embassy as
their place of meeting.   French brought his Chief of Staff, Sir Archibald Murray ; and Viviani, the French Prime Minister ; Millerand,
the French War Minister ; a number of French senior officers ; and
the British Ambassador, Sir Francis Bertie, were also present.   With
questionable taste, French gave [1] in 1919, when Kitchener was dead,
a highly-coloured and ill-tempered account of that interview :
' I deeply resented being called away from my Headquarters at so
critical a time . . . Lord Kitchener arrived on this occasion in the
uniform of a Field-Marshal and from the outset of the conversation
assumed the air of a Commander-in-Chief, and announced the intention of taking the field and inspecting the troops.'
According to Sir John, the Ambassador ' at once emphatically
objected ', and ' after some discussion the Secretary of State decided

[1] Field-Marshal Viscount French of Ypres, *1914*, pp. 95–101.

to abandon his intention '. An acrimonious conversation was said to have followed, and to have been abruptly terminated by a curt order from Kitchener that the Commander-in-Chief ' should accompany him for a private interview in another room. When we were alone he commenced by entering a strong objection to the tone I assumed. I then told him all that was in my mind '.

French said that he informed Kitchener that he alone was responsible for the B.E.F., and that the presence in France of the Secretary of State ' in the character of a soldier could have no other effect than to weaken and prejudice my position in the eyes of the French and my own countrymen alike. I reminded him of our service in the field together some 13 years before, and told him that I valued highly his advice and assistance, which I would gladly accept as such, but that I would not tolerate any interference with my executive command and authority . . . I think he began to realize my difficulties and we finally came to an amicable understanding . . .

' It is very difficult for any but soldiers to understand the real bearing and significance of this Paris incident. If the confidence of troops in their commander is once shaken in the least degree . . . the effect reacts instantly throughout the whole Army . . .

' Then again there was the effect which might have been produced on the French. Ministers and Generals were present and witnessed Lord Kitchener's apparent assertion of his right to exercise the power and authority of a Commander-in-Chief in the field.

' Fortunately the incident terminated in a manner which led to no regrettable publicity. Lord Kitchener realized his mistake and left Paris that night.'

Kitchener left Paris at six o'clock on the following morning (2 September), and no second account exists of his private conversation with French behind closed doors. He had, however, summoned French to meet him in order to discuss French's declared intention of withdrawing the B.E.F. independently from the fighting line against the expressed wish of both the British and French Governments. French was silent in his book, which aroused widespread indignation when it was published, about an appeal to that effect which had been made to him by Joffre and repeated to Kitchener and to Sir Edward Grey through the French President and the French Ambassador in London. But it is clear that Kitchener received satisfactory assurances from French before he left Paris, and that French at once abandoned all thought of quitting the line.

Immediately after the interview Kitchener wrote French a note (1 September ; 7.30 p.m.) :

' After thinking over our conversation to-day, I think I am giving the sense of it in the following telegram to Govt. I have just sent—
' " French's troops are now engaged in the fighting line, where he will remain conforming to the movements of the French Army, though at the same time acting with caution to avoid being in any way unsupported on his flanks."
' I feel sure you will agree that the above represents the conclusions we came to ; but in any case, until I can communicate with you further in answer to anything you may wish to tell me, please consider it as an instruction.
' By being in the fighting line you, of course, understand I mean dispositions of your troops in contact with, though possibly behind, the French as they were to-day. Of course you will judge as regards their position in this respect.
' I was very pleased to meet you to-day . . . '

In acknowledging that letter (3 September), French wrote : ' I fully understand your instruction . . . I am enclosing a duplicate statement of casualties up to date. They reach a terrible total.'

Kitchener informed the Cabinet on 3 September that there had been friction and misunderstanding between French and Joffre ; and that owing to disorganization on the line of communication, French had not been receiving proper reinforcements or supplies. He said that he had done his best to straighten out both matters ; and the Cabinet resolved on that day to send French at once the sixth and last remaining original regular infantry division which had been detained in England as a defence against invasion. Kitchener informed French immediately, and the division embarked on 8 September.

At the time of the Paris interview the French Government had been in process of fleeing from Paris to Bordeaux. But as a result of a series of blunders committed by the weak and vacillating German Chief of Staff, Moltke, the tide of war changed suddenly in favour of the Allies. The turning-point occurred on 4 September, when Moltke finally threw on one side a plan which he had mishandled throughout, but which his predecessor, Schlieffen, had brilliantly elaborated for the destruction of France in a campaign lasting six weeks. Two German armies, leaving Paris, as well as the Channel ports, on their

297

right flank, struck south, across the Marne, in a muddled and premature attempt to finish the war by rolling up the French field armies, and by repeating in France the annihilating victory of Tannenberg which Hindenburg and Ludendorff had just won (25–31 August) against the Russian invaders of East Prussia.

Joffre seized that opportunity to strike east, out of Paris, at the exposed German flank ; and in the decisive Battle of the Marne which followed (4–9 September) the B.E.F. played a vigorous and successful part. The Germans retreated to the Aisne, and in the House of Lords, on 17 September, Kitchener went out of his way to praise French's ' leadership ', ' calm courage ' and ' consummate skill '. In a ' strictly private ' letter of thanks (18 September) French told Kitchener : ' I value your opinion and good word before anything . . . I thank you with all my heart. You have given me incalculable encouragement and help.'

CHAPTER 15

RIDING THE WHIRLWIND

1914–1915

KITCHENER told Asquith on 8 September, 1914, that he expected to have over a million trained troops organized in some fifty divisions within six months. Asquith remarked that the new recruits were badly overcrowded, but Kitchener smiled grimly, and made caustic references to 'the damned fools of doctors' who were always insisting upon 'ridiculous allowances of cubic space'. When real abuses were proved, however, and it became widely known that many recruits were without boots, clothing, accommodation and other necessaries, Asquith noted[1] that Kitchener presented himself 'in what he frankly termed a white sheet'. Kitchener said that he was furious to find that his orders had not been carried out; and he immediately dismissed the Chief Director of Contracts at the War Office.

Because he was grossly overburdened, Kitchener's orders often appeared arbitrary. He resisted all attempts which were made to lighten his load, but there was no element of pettiness in his nature, and he loved to operate on a big and dramatic scale. On 29 August, for example, he informed Sir Edward Grey that he expected the Foreign Office to provide immediately ten thousand live male he-goats every month in prime condition in order to meet the ritual dietary needs of Indian soldiers whom he had promised to send as reinforcements to Sir John French: 'It is impossible,' Grey wrote (30 August). 'France cannot provide them, and I don't think they can be purchased in Europe. I must refer it to you, because it raises the most serious and alarming difficulty.' Kitchener retorted that he did not understand the word impossible, and some acceptable equivalent to goat's meat was presently found.

Until the Ministry of Munitions was established in May, 1915, Kitchener was never overruled or even seriously challenged on any important issue in the War Council or in the Cabinet. His word was final, and on the rare occasions when his wishes were disregarded in small matters, he showed no malice. He had, for example, a tremendous dispute in Cabinet with Lloyd George at the end of October, 1914, about the religious needs of Nonconformist

[1] *Memories and Reflections*, II, pp. 32–4.

soldiers belonging to denominations unrecognized in the Army List.

During the small-scale wars of the past it had been impossible to make separate provision for the needs of fractional denominations, and Kitchener flatly declined to commission chaplains to minister to the needs of what he termed superfluous and eccentric sects. He said that their adherents would continue to be classified as ' Church of England ', and he thereby provoked uproar. When it died down, he gave way with a grace which charmed everyone, including Lloyd George ; and he found time to preside himself at a conference at the War Office which inaugurated a more acceptable system.

On another occasion Kitchener collided with the High Churchmen over the fact that the senior army chaplain—a colonel—was a Presbyterian. He solved that difficulty by commissioning his friend, L. H. G. Gwynne, the Bishop of Khartoum, as a major-general, with responsibility for all serving Anglicans. When the Presbyterians asked that their man should be promoted in order to redress the balance, Kitchener became really angry. He said, " I'll make him a General when you make him a Bishop," and the matter was allowed to drop.

On representations from Lloyd George, Kitchener cancelled a veto which he had unwisely imposed upon the formation of a Welsh division ; and he consented also to the formation of a northern Irish division with the red hand of Ulster as its emblem. He repulsed, however, an offer from John Redmond, the parliamentary leader of the Irish Nationalists, to raise a special force in southern Ireland to fight on England's side. Kitchener said that there was no place in his new armies for soldiers who did not conform in all respects to the standard pattern of British regulars. When Redmond, nevertheless, managed to raise a regular division of southern Irish Roman Catholic Volunteers, Kitchener unhappily refused to allow the Irish harp to be blazoned on its colours.

The enthusiastic way in which the Irish parliamentary leaders had responded to the outbreak of war had been extraordinary. They addressed recruiting meetings all over Ireland, and Redmond's brother, William, a popular member of the House of Commons, was killed in action in France. Kitchener's prejudiced refusal to allow the Irish harp to be used as a symbol on equal terms with the bloody hand of Ulster contributed its quota to the catalogue of historic discontents which caused the extremists to rise in armed revolt in April, 1916.

Kitchener's personal relationship with Sir John French, another

Irishman, collapsed finally in January, 1915. There were wide temperamental differences between the Secretary for War and the Commander-in-Chief, as well as important differences in outlook upon strategy. But the root of their bitter quarrel was inherent in the arrangement whereby Kitchener was at once a Cabinet Minister in control of war strategy, and a serving Field-Marshal with greater seniority than that of French.

French was in every way a much smaller man than Kitchener ; and he felt suffocated by that arrangement. He admitted[1] that his ' great and far-reaching ' differences with Kitchener ' may have been to some extent my own fault '. There were, however, faults on both sides, and it is apparent, on an impartial analysis, that a more subtle man than Kitchener might have been able to handle the touchy and excitable Commander-in-Chief with greater adroitness. Kitchener constantly told his friends that he was out to fight the Germans and not Sir John ; but he was almost as much relieved by the downfall of French in December, 1915, as he had been ten years earlier in India by the downfall of Curzon.

Sir John French felt that the primary responsibility for fighting the Germans was vested in him ; and Kitchener, working under intense pressure, was sometimes tempted to treat the Commander-in-Chief of the B.E.F. as a subordinate commander in the field. He discussed frequently with his friends the possibility of assuming the post of Captain-General, or Generalissimo, and of holding it in addition to his existing office of Secretary of State, in order to formalize the responsibility which he bore for the supreme direction of British military strategy.

French was well aware of that project, which Kitchener did not abandon until he was stripped of his responsibility for munitions when the first Coalition Government was formed in May, 1915. Even then, Kitchener's friends continued to advocate the change. Lord Esher for example, who published in 1921 a malicious and disparaging book[2] about Kitchener, wrote to FitzGerald on 7 July, 1915 : ' I go on harping on the *necessity* of his becoming C. in C. as well as S. of S., adding, if necessary, an Assistant S. of S. with a seat in the *Cabinet and the H. of C.* This is vital. It would free Lord K. a great deal and give him an *adequate* voice in Parliament.'

A passion for military glory reflects an instinct deeply implanted

---

[1] Viscount French of Ypres, *1914*, p. 333.
[2] *The Tragedy of Lord Kitchener.*

in mankind. It is normally sublimated without apparent frustration, but no one would expect or wish that it should be sublimated by commanding generals in time of war. Sir John French felt frustrated because he was overshadowed by Kitchener, who stole the glory which French coveted. Sir John became abnormally prickly and suspicious in consequence, and was even tempted at times to enfold himself within a cavalryman's pride of caste and to regard Kitchener as an outsider. Answering, for example, an inquiry from Kitchener about the state of his relations with the French General Staff, Sir John thought fit to write (15 November, 1914) : ' *au fond* they are a low lot, and one always has to remember the class these French generals mostly come from '. Having regard to the state of his relations with Kitchener at that particular moment, it seems not improbable that that barbed and irrelevant observation was aimed at Kitchener himself.

Sir Henry Wilson, French's Deputy Chief of Staff, proved a potent source of mischief. An excellent soldier, extremely popular with the French, Wilson was anxious to succeed his immediate chief, Sir Archibald Murray, whose stamina was precarious, as C.G.S. to the B.E.F. The arrangements made by Wilson while he was serving in the War Office before the war for transporting the B.E.F. across the Channel had worked without a hitch ; and his opinions carried more weight at G.H.Q. than those of any other officer. But he was intensely distrusted by Asquith on account of the clever way in which he had managed to exploit the Curragh incident in March, 1914 ; and he was disliked by Kitchener.

In July, 1909, Kitchener had visited the Staff College at Camberley at the end of Wilson's period of service as Commandant. Kitchener had then questioned some aspects of Wilson's teaching, and Wilson had not replied with becoming modesty. Relying upon the licence which his social popularity had earned in many quarters, he had displayed a casual breeziness which the Field-Marshal had deemed unsuitable. Five years later, on 7 August, 1914, Kitchener had occasion to summon Wilson to his room in the War Office in order to rebuke him for indiscreet discussion in Mayfair drawing-rooms of the transport arrangements of the B.E.F. Wilson hotly resented that rebuke, and thereafter did his best to poison the receptive mind of Sir John French against Kitchener.

Wilson told French that Kitchener was as great an enemy of the B.E.F. as Moltke or Falkenhayn. He complained constantly about Kitchener's policy of withholding from the B.E.F. a sufficient number of trained officers and N.C.O.s to serve as instructors of the new Kitchener Armies which were being formed. Wilson professed[1] to believe that Kitchener was mad; and he joked about Kitchener's 'shadow armies for shadow campaigns at unknown and distant dates'. Wilson told all his political friends, including Churchill and Bonar Law, that 'under no circumstances could these armies take the field for 2 years', and that it was 'scandalous' that the B.E.F. should be starved for the sake of Kitchener's 'ridiculous and preposterous army' which was 'the laughing-stock of every soldier in Europe'.

Those views were endorsed by Sir John French; and Wilson's wildest and most wounding remarks were carried to the ears of Kitchener, who strongly resented them. He was dismayed by the attitude of frantic optimism which gripped G.H.Q. after the Battle of the Marne. French was convinced that the Germans could be driven back across the Rhine in six weeks if Kitchener would treat the B.E.F. fairly, by giving it everything he had, without troubling about the future; and G.H.Q. considered that Kitchener's forecast of a long war would only be fulfilled if Kitchener himself prolonged it by starving the B.E.F.

Churchill, who was intimate with French, enjoyed flitting over to G.H.Q.; and he tried, without success, to bring the Commander-in-Chief to a reasonable frame of mind. He was asked by Wilson on 27 September, 1914, to stop talking nonsense, but Churchill noted[2] that he was wholly unable to share the universal optimism of the staff of G.H.Q.:

'I combated these views to the best of my ability, being fully convinced of Lord Kitchener's commanding foresight and wisdom . . . I consider now that this prudent withholding from the Army in the field, in the face of every appeal and demand, [of] the key men who alone could make the new armies, was the greatest of all the services which Lord Kitchener rendered to the nation at this time, and it was a service which no one of lesser authority than he could have performed.'

The First Battle of Ypres (19 October–22 November, 1914) destroyed the core of the original B.E.F., but French continued to press for massive and continuous attacks. Kitchener passed reinforcements as quickly as he could into France, but he wanted to postpone large-scale offensive operations until the spring, when he hoped that he would have adequate reserves of trained men and munitions.

[1] Sir C. E. Callwell, *Field-Marshal Sir Henry Wilson*, I, p. 178.
[2] *The World Crisis*, I, pp. 281–2.

Kitchener, who appreciated Churchill's efforts to improve his relations with French, gave unstinted support to Churchill, whom many of his colleagues tried unfairly to turn into a scapegoat after Antwerp surrendered on 10 October, 1914. Kitchener had sped Churchill on his way to Antwerp in order to put heart into the defence, at two o'clock on the morning of 3 October, after a midnight conference at 2, Carlton Gardens ; and a telegram from Churchill at Antwerp, containing an offer to turn the Admiralty over to Walter Runciman, the President of the Board of Trade, and to assume military command of the British forces inside the fortress, was read to the Cabinet on 4 October. That telegram provoked roars of incredulous laughter in which Kitchener alone refrained from joining. He waited until the mockery had died down, and then quietly offered to commission Churchill as a lieutenant-general immediately if Asquith would consent to release him from the Government.

Kitchener sent a special force to attempt the relief of Antwerp, and he placed that force, for sound tactical reasons, temporarily under the independent command of Sir Henry Rawlinson, who was one of his favourites. He explained his reasons in detail to French (10 October), who replied (13 October) that he fully understood and agreed ; but he made savage references [1] to it five years later ; and on 6 November, 1914, Asquith astounded Kitchener by informing him, in Cabinet, that French had sent an A.D.C. to London to complain personally to the Prime Minister that Kitchener was treacherously plotting to oust French from the command of the B.E.F.

Kitchener had conferred secretly on 1 November at Dunkirk about Anglo-French military co-operation with Poincaré, the French President, Joffre, the French Commander-in-Chief, and Foch, who was Joffre's deputy in Flanders. He had excused Sir John French from attending that conference because the First Battle of Ypres had then reached its most critical stage. Wilson noted [2] in his diary that on the morning of 5 November Foch informed him that Kitchener at Dunkirk had offered, if the French were dissatisfied, to replace Sir John French by Sir Ian Hamilton ; and that Poincaré and Joffre had both expressed their entire satisfaction with Sir John.

Encouraged by Foch, Wilson immediately repeated that story to

[1] 1914, p. 176.
[2] Cf. Sir C. E. Callwell, *Field-Marshal Sir Henry Wilson*, I, pp. 186–7 ; Earl of Oxford and Asquith, *Memories and Reflections*, II, p. 35 ; Lord Beaverbrook, *Politicians and the War*, II, p. 35.

Sir John, who was almost prostrated by grief and rage. He dispatched his friend and A.D.C., Captain the Hon. F. E. Guest, to London immediately to complain personally to Asquith ; and he ordered Wilson to accompany him to the French Headquarters at Cassel, where he shook Foch warmly by the hand and thanked him for his comradeship and loyalty.

Kitchener in Cabinet indignantly denied that story ; and Asquith was convinced that it had no shadow of foundation, and that Wilson had invented it to suit his own ends. The incident blew over after Asquith, Kitchener and Churchill had all written soothing letters to the Commander-in-Chief. Kitchener may have been a little unguarded at some point during his conversations at Dunkirk, but Wilson's action was malicious and wrong. The upshot was that when, at the end of January, 1915, Sir Archibald Murray relinquished the post of C.G.S. to the B.E.F., Asquith and Kitchener combined to veto Wilson's promotion. Murray was succeeded, accordingly, by Sir William Robertson, Quartermaster-General to the B.E.F., a magnificent soldier who had risen from the ranks.

As he turned over in his mind all possible causes of the continued deterioration of his relations with the Commander-in-Chief, Kitchener turned suddenly upon Churchill. The First Lord, in association with Sir John French, had been strongly advocating a large-scale amphibious operation aimed at turning the German flank in Belgium, and at recovering Ostend and Zeebrugge, which were being turned into bases for submarines.

Kitchener was as eager, in principle, as Churchill was to discover means of outflanking the enemy, and of breaking the deadlock which trench warfare had imposed. But the French were not satisfied with the form and scope of the proposed operation. It involved the taking over, by the British, of the extreme left of the line, where it reached the sea at Nieuport, in order to facilitate naval co-operation ; and Foch, at that moment, was pressing the British to relieve his 21 Corps on their right. After first supporting Churchill, Kitchener changed his mind because he was disgusted by Sir John French's attempt to use the proposed amphibious attack upon Ostend and Zeebrugge as a lever for extorting large additional quantities of heavy guns and high-explosive shells which were not yet available. Sir John also asked for fifty more Territorial or Kitchener Army battalions in addition to the reinforcements he had been promised in the normal way. When Kitchener explained that those battalions were required for the new armies which he was forming, French suggested that the new armies should be broken up before they took the field, and used, battalion by battalion, for strengthening the B.E.F.

Kitchener insisted upon husbanding his resources until a comprehensive plan had been worked out for the most effective employment in the field of the new armies during the spring. He told French that it was imperative to ship some munitions to Russia in order to avert the danger of a Russian military collapse ; and on 18 December he sent privately to French a copy of a secret telegram which the Foreign Office had received from the Ambassador in Petrograd :

' As far as I can calculate, Russian orders for shells will, when supplied, only provide 3·1/7 shells per gun per day and the estimate of time before they are ready may be months instead of weeks.'

The Russians were almost as short of guns as they were of shells ; and they were incapable of supplying the deficiency out of their own resources.

In those circumstances, Kitchener informed French (17 December) that he would not tolerate Churchill's ' wild cat ' scheme for a large-scale amphibious operation ; and he wrote on the same day to Churchill, who had asked if Kitchener would object to his going over on the following day to discuss the naval aspect of that operation with the Commander-in-Chief :

' I cannot, of course, object to your going over to discuss naval co-operation with Sir J. French ; but at the same time I think I ought to tell you frankly that your private arrangements with French as regards land forces is rapidly rendering my position as S. of S. impossible.

' I consider that if my relations with French are strained it will do away with any advantage there may be to the country in my holding my present position, and I foresee that, if the present system continues, it must result in creating grave difficulties between French and myself.

' I am suggesting to the P.M. that you should take the W.O. and let Fisher be 1st Lord ; then all would work smoothly, I hope.'

Kitchener showed that petulant letter to the Prime Minister who, as he had expected, asked that it should not be sent, and said that he would speak to Churchill himself. Kitchener spoke strongly to Asquith about the irregular formations which Churchill had assembled

306

at different times under Admiralty control for service on land in co-operation with the Army ; and in that way he helped, however unfairly, to shake Asquith's confidence in Churchill's judgement.[1] Churchill was justifiably annoyed by such underhand methods. He sent Kitchener a dignified letter of protest (18 December), suggesting that Kitchener should first have addressed him before troubling the Prime Minister unnecessarily ; and Kitchener retorted (19 December) :

'I wrote an answer to your letter asking me about visiting French, but before sending it to you I thought it advisable to show it to the P.M. He asked me not to send it, and said he would speak to you on the subject which is one that has caused me considerable anxiety. Perhaps you will bring it up in the Cabinet, or by any other means you please. Yours truly, Kitchener.'

Churchill again replied (19 December), with dignity and restraint : ' The statement that you seem to have made to the Prime Minister to the effect that I had been a cause of friction between you and French is not well-founded. The exact contrary is true. The causes of any friction which may exist are not difficult to see. They are inherent in the situation . . ,' That breeze blew over quickly, and Asquith noted[2] on 22 December that ' Winston and Kitchener had a meeting of reconciliation yesterday and fell on each other's necks '. Nevertheless that trifling incident had repercussions.

Churchill continued remorselessly to press the plan for an amphibious outflanking movement on the Belgian coast, which Kitchener continued to stonewall. Sir John French came over on 20 December to discuss it, and to confer with Asquith, Kitchener and the War Council about future strategy. Kitchener met French at Folkestone and motored him to Walmer Castle to lunch with Asquith ; he motored him on to London, and told him that in future he was to start his letters with ' My dear Kitchener ', instead of, as heretofore, with ' My dear Lord K.' But French noted[3] ' with deep sorrow ', that after that one last day of ' happy personal intercourse ', their old friendship finally collapsed.

French declined to accept Kitchener's gloomy appreciation of Russian prospects ; and Kitchener declined to sanction the full military part of the proposed amphibious operation on the Belgian coast. On

[1] Cf. Lord Beaverbrook, *Politicians and the War*, II, pp. 26–33.
[2] *Memories and Reflections*, II, p. 50.   [3] *1914*, p. 333.

the day when French recrossed the Channel (23 December), Kitchener
requested Churchill to hand over forthwith to the War Office the
armoured trains, buses, cars and other irregular units which he had
collected, and which were familiarly known in ministerial circles as
'the Dunkirk circus' :

> 'If these irregular units are only a means to enable certain officers,
> and gentlemen without military experience, to get to the front and
> take part in the war, then I think that it is even more important that
> they should form part of the Army, and not claim to be separate
> units under the Admiralty . . .
> 'I know how anxious you are to do all in your power to promote
> the success of our arms in France, and when I tell you that the
> morâle of the Army in the field is affected by these irregular addi-
> tions, and therefore its fighting power impaired, as well as that
> they cause discontent and give trouble to the staff entirely out of
> proportion to their utility, I think you will agree with me that
> something should be done to regularize the situation.'

In submitting to that somewhat heavy-handed rebuke, Churchill
wrote (23 December), 'It will be wrong to continue this discussion.'
He placed his irregulars, with their arms, at Kitchener's disposal ;
but his active mind and fertile imagination were frustrated by
Kitchener's opposition to the outflanking operation in Belgium which
he had so strongly advocated. He had protested bitterly to Kitchener
(21 December) about a futile local attack in France on the evening of
18 December which had gained five trenches, of which four were lost
the next day, at a cost of 1,500 casualties : 'These sporadic attacks,
at 40 officers a time, and 300 yards (lost again the next day) may keep
the enemy on the *qui vive* ; but this is a gloomy way of waging war.'

In those circumstances, Churchill switched his thoughts from the
Belgian coast to the ambitious and far-reaching project of outflanking the Central Empires by means of an attack upon Constantinople through the Dardanelles. That project at that time would have
offered much the best prospects in the entire field of war strategy, if it
had been embodied by the staffs of the Admiralty and War Office in a
combined, well-conceived and fully formulated operational plan, and
if that plan had been executed with the necessary degree of precision,
concentration and speed.

Those conditions were not fulfilled, and the resounding failure of the expedition to Gallipoli overshadowed Churchill's reputation for many years. It also destroyed Kitchener's credit with his colleagues and clouded the sunset of his great career. Kitchener was dead when, on 23 August, 1916, old Lord Cromer presided over the first meeting of the Commissioners who were appointed by Parliament to inquire into the 'origin, inception, and conduct' of the campaign in the Dardanelles. Unlike Churchill, therefore, Kitchener was not available to give evidence, and to state his case and opinions.

The fundamental need at the end of 1914 was to reconcile two conflicting approaches to the general strategy of the war. Sir John French, supported by all the leading British generals as well as by the French Government and High Command, held that the decisive theatre of operations lay in France, and that the war could only be won by breaking through the line of German fortified entrenchments upon the Western Front, and by killing as many Germans as possible in the process.

The alternative was to admit that a state of deadlock had gripped the Western Front, and to concentrate upon an attempt to finish the war speedily and triumphantly by attacking the hostile coalition at its weakest and most vulnerable points in south-eastern Europe or the Near East. Serbia, the port of Alexandretta (just north of Syria on the Turkish coast) and the Dardanelles were all considered by the War Council, which was eager to tempt Italy and the uncommitted Balkan States into the war upon the Allied side, and to secure a strong post-war diplomatic position. All the Ministers who normally attended the War Council—Asquith, Kitchener, Churchill, Lloyd George, Grey, Haldane and Crewe—as well as Balfour, who attended habitually as the unofficial representative of the Conservative Opposition, favoured in principle the latter alternative.

On 28 December, 1914, the exceptionally capable Secretary of the War Council, Sir Maurice (Lord) Hankey, circulated a minute which suggested that the unforeseen trench deadlock in the West could best be broken by means of an attack upon Turkey. Three days later Lloyd George circulated a memorandum which suggested that the new Kitchener Armies should be used in the spring for an attack, in support of Serbia, upon the Austro-Hungarian Empire through Salonica or on the Dalmatian coast, and upon the Turkish Empire in Syria through Alexandretta. He discussed those proposals with Kitchener, who was sympathetic and polite ; but Kitchener was, in fact, more strongly attracted to the project of a naval attack upon the

Dardanelles as a means of diverting Turkish attention from Egypt and from the Suez Canal, which advanced Turkish detachments actually succeeded in reaching, for a few hours, on 4–5 February, 1915.

On 2 January, 1915, Kitchener received from the Foreign Office a copy of a telegram from the Ambassador in Petrograd which caused him acute concern. It contained an urgent appeal from the Russian Commander-in-Chief, the Grand Duke Nicholas, for a naval or military demonstration against the Turks in order to relieve Turkish pressure in the Caucasus, where the Russians were being hard pressed. Kitchener dreaded a Russian collapse, and he immediately went into conference with Churchill about the possibility of doing something to meet the wishes of the Grand Duke. During the discussion he repeated several times that he had no troops to spare for a military attack in any new theatre of operations ; and later on that day (2 January) he confirmed, in a letter to Churchill, what he had said :

'I do not see that we can do anything that will very seriously help the Russians in the Caucasus . . .

'We have no troops to land anywhere. A demonstration at Smyrna would do no good, and probably cause the slaughter of Christians . . . The coast of Syria would have no effect. The only place that a demonstration might have some effect in stopping reinforcements going East would be the Dardanelles. Particularly if, as the Grand Duke says, reports could be spread at the same time that Constantinople was threatened.

'We shall not be ready for anything big for some months.'

Nevertheless, Kitchener could not wholly ignore that appeal from an ally who had advanced recklessly to our aid during the first month of the war at a cost of hundreds of thousands of casualties. On his own initiative, therefore, on the evening of that significant day, 2 January, 1915, Kitchener telegraphed to the Grand Duke Nicholas, and also wrote a letter to Sir John French. He promised the Grand Duke, through the Foreign Office, that 'steps will be taken to make a demonstration against the Turks. It is, however, feared that any action we can devise and carry out will be unlikely to seriously affect numbers of enemy in the Caucasus, or cause their withdrawal.'

To Sir John French, Kitchener wrote :

'The feeling here is gaining ground that although it is essential to defend the line, troops over and above what is necessary for that service could be better employed elsewhere.

' I suppose we must now recognize that the French Army cannot make a sufficient break through the German lines of defence to cause a complete change of the situation . . . If that is so, then the German lines in France may be looked upon as a fortress that cannot be carried by assault, and also cannot be completely invested, with the result that the lines can only be held by an investing force, while operations proceed elsewhere.

' The question, *where* anything effective can be accomplished, opens a large field and requires a good deal of study. What are the views of your staff?

' Russia is hard pressed in the Caucasus and can only just hold her own in Poland. Fresh forces are necessary to change the deadlock. Italy and Rumania seem the most likely providers ; therefore some action that would help to bring these out seems attractive, though full of difficulties.'

Kitchener must have known that the reaction of French's staff was bound to be extremely unfavourable to any proposal that the main British military effort should be diverted from the Western Front to some new theatre. He was, however, casting a fly, and French rose as he had expected. He replied to Kitchener's letter on 5 January.

Sir John stated that the German line could be broken by frontal attacks in France and Flanders ' provided a sufficiency of high-explosive shell, and of guns, is provided ' ; and he again advocated the employment of ' the maximum available forces ' in an amphibious operation on the Belgian coast, for which he again emphasized that he would need large extra reinforcements of troops, guns and high-explosive shells. French added that ' even if it were impossible to break the German line, so large a margin of safety is needed that troops could not be withdrawn from this theatre ', and that ' there are no theatres, other than those in which operations are now in progress, in which decisive results could be attained '.

In the course of elaborating those conclusions, French said that there were no circumstances in which the withdrawal of British troops from France could be justified ; that Joffre would strongly oppose such a move ; and that ' to attack Turkey would be to play the German game, and to bring about the end which Germany had in mind when she induced Turkey to enter the war, namely, to draw off troops from the decisive spot, which is Germany herself'.

Sir John French was so suspicious of Kitchener's methods and intentions that he sent his C.G.S. to London on 5 January, 1915, with orders to hand that document personally to the Prime Minister, and to give Kitchener a copy. Asquith caused the document to be printed immediately, and circulated to all members of the Cabinet, who were complaining at that time that Kitchener was keeping them too much in the dark. Kitchener, who was really angry, rebuked French in forthright terms on 6 January for writing direct to the Prime Minister and ignoring the Secretary for War ; and he added that such a secret document should not have been sent unsealed. French explained, equivocally, that his C.G.S. had made a mistake, and that the original document had been intended for Kitchener and the copy only for the Prime Minister : ' I had no idea that you could possibly object to such a course of proceeding, as the Prime Minister has throughout been so closely associated with our deliberations'. He concluded : ' As to your postcript about the letter being unsealed—of course it should have been, and I am sorry it was not. Such details are apt to be overlooked when one's mind is engaged with the command of a $\frac{1}{4}$ of a million men in war.'

Kitchener was by no means satisfied, and he wrote curtly to French on 7 January : ' I asked the Prime Minister to-day at the Cabinet whether he wished any change made in the rule that official communications from you to the Govt. should be made through me as S. of S. Mr. Asquith said he did not.'

Sir John's memorandum was considered by the War Council on 7 and 8 January, 1915. On the latter day, Kitchener stated that the Dardanelles was the most suitable objective in the field of war strategy ; that 150,000 troops would, theoretically, ensure the success of a combined operation aimed at forcing the Straits and capturing Constantinople ; and that he had no troops available for that purpose.

Kitchener's statement about the non-availability of troops was accepted without question by the War Council. The supreme war lord's views about strategy were never questioned at that time ; but it cannot be gainsaid that all the troops which were ordered later in the year to the Dardanelles in driblets under the pressure of untoward events could have been made available at the beginning of January for concentration in the eastern Mediterranean before the end of March. If Kitchener had, during January, countenanced a military descent in force upon the Gallipoli Peninsula during the spring, it would have been necessary to decide firmly and at once to postpone, until the autumn, further large-scale offensive operations upon the Western Front.

Lacking the authority as well as the administrative machinery which enabled Churchill to co-ordinate war strategy in 1940, Kitchener in 1915 was not prepared to go so far. He was in no position to ignore the views of Sir John French, the French Government and the French High Command, which were all strongly opposed to any suggestion that the growing military might of Great Britain should be diverted from the Western theatre, and from the direct effort to free the invaded industrial provinces of France. Kitchener may well have felt that the strained state of his relations with Sir John French involved a serious risk of permitting the best policy to become the enemy of the good.

Churchill believed that the Fleet was capable of forcing the Straits and capturing Constantinople on its own. He knew almost as much as Kitchener did about the new armies which were being formed, and he felt impelled to trust that troops would be made available to support the Fleet in case of need. Kitchener, who stated openly that no troops were available, accepted too uncritically the alluring proposition so eloquently expounded by Churchill that the Fleet alone would be strong enough to ensure the success of the operation. He cannot have excluded wholly from his mind the possibility that some troops might presently be made available ; but he thought it much more likely that they would be needed for a different operation. Serbia was threatened at that time by an overwhelming onrush of Austrians with a stiffening of Germans ; and Kitchener appreciated that an attempt to rescue Serbia, although militarily unsound, might become necessary upon political and diplomatic grounds.

At the same time, as an ardent imperialist, Kitchener had plans of his own for employing any spare force which might become available. He coveted the port of Alexandretta, which he wanted to link by a canal with the Euphrates after the conquest by the Indian Army of Mesopotamia. He became wedded to that project when his Cabinet colleagues had expressed their willingness to cede Cyprus to Greece in return for a Greek declaration of war upon Germany and Turkey. Kitchener, who had served in Cyprus, resisted its proposed cession ; but Grey remonstrated with him on 19 January, 1915 :

‘ It is true that the Cabinet hasn't yet come to a definite decision about Cyprus, though the discussions there in the Autumn were favourable to giving it to Greece at the proper time.

' I should not propose its cession unless a Balkan agreement were thereby achieved ; but surely Cyprus, of which the Admiralty have never been able to make a proper use, would be a cheap price to pay if we could get Greece and Rumania on such terms with Bulgaria as would secure their active participation.

' I also want the French and Russians to feel that we are prepared to play for the common cause, and not solely for our own hand in the East . . .'

Mankind, as General Smuts observed at the time, had struck its tents and was everywhere on the march. The 74-year-old Lord Fisher, whom Churchill had installed as First Sea Lord on 30 October, 1914, in succession to Prince Louis of Battenberg, who had been driven to resign by a vulgar outcry about his German origin, urged Kitchener not to worry about Cyprus : ' We don't want a barren island in the Mediterranean ', he wrote (11 March, 1915) : ' We want the waterway of the Euphrates valley up to Alexandretta ; and locks and dams will enable us to bring barges carrying the 170-ton guns of the future, with oil engines, by a short canal to Alexandretta from the Persian Gulf . . . Alexandretta can be made a harbour with less difficulty than Colombo or Cape Town ! Alexandria is not good enough for us . . .'

Asquith noted[1] on 26 March, 1915, that he and Grey were the only two members of the Cabinet who believed that Great Britain would be well advised to resist the temptation to expand the Empire in the peace settlement at the end of the war ; but Kitchener was less high-minded. He greatly wished to annex Alexandretta, and he was, with difficulty, persuaded by Grey to accept Haifa instead, and to agree to allow Alexandretta to be included with Syria, the Lebanon and a huge slice of Asia Minor in the spoil reserved for France under the terms of a secret Anglo-French agreement.

Kitchener personally supervised, through FitzGerald, every detail of that agreement, which was finally concluded on behalf of the British Government by Sir Mark Sykes, a well-known traveller and Oriental student who represented Hull as a Conservative, with Georges Picot, of the French Foreign Office, on 16 May, 1916. But Kitchener had not time to supervise equally carefully a series of letters which were

[1] *Memories and Reflections*, II, p. 69.

being exchanged between Sir Henry McMahon, the British High Commissioner in Egypt, and the Sherif Husein of Mecca. As a result, Sykes assigned Damascus and its hinterland in all good faith to France; while McMahon, in equally good faith, promised the Sherif of Mecca that that territory should form part of an independent Arab kingdom.

Responsibility for that maladroit diplomacy cannot fairly be laid upon Kitchener. His principal concern was to persuade the Moslem subjects of King George to remain loyal despite the holy war against the British infidel which the Sultan of Turkey, as the spiritual head of Islam, had proclaimed. For that reason Kitchener established contact with the Sherif of Mecca through Sir Henry McMahon, who was instructed to urge the Sherif to throw off the Turkish yoke and to facilitate, as in normal times, the annual pilgrimage to Mecca of Moslems from India, Egypt and the Sudan.

After a long series of complicated negotiations the Arab revolt was launched on 9 June, 1916, four days after Kitchener was drowned. The Sherif of Mecca proclaimed his independence upon that day, and Kitchener died in ignorance of the conflicting promises made by McMahon to the Arabs and by Sykes to the French. Before Sykes left for Russia in order to negotiate details of the Russian share of the spoils of Turkey-in-Asia, Kitchener instructed him to point out how extraordinarily modest the British claims were. They were restricted at that time to a small area around Haifa in Palestine, and to Meso-potamia, where an expeditionary force from India, which had been landed as early as 6 November, 1914, had begun its ill-starred march on Baghdad on 27 June, 1915.

At the beginning of 1915 Kitchener was in no position to spare troops to secure Haifa, or to forestall the French at Alexandretta if he could have persuaded the Cabinet to agree, or to assist the conquest by the Indian Army of Mesopotamia. He could do no more than privately earmark a modest number of troops for use in case of need to support Serbia, or, less probably, to support the Fleet if a serious check were encountered in the Dardanelles. He fervently hoped that neither call upon his resources would be made; and he did not, in those circumstances, see any need to incur the odium of ordering Sir John French to remain strictly upon the defensive. Accordingly, although both emergencies which he dreaded quickly arose in Serbia and in the Dardanelles, Kitchener sanctioned plans for the futile and costly offensives upon the Western Front in 1915 which are known

315

as the Battles of Neuve Chapelle (10-13 March), Second Ypres (22 April—25 May), Festubert (9 May—25 May) and Loos (25 September —8 October). All four battles were initiated in association with wider French offensive operations further south, which failed equally dismally at such an appalling cost in blood that Great Britain was compelled to institute conscription in order to keep the trenches fully manned.

Churchill, in the meantime, persuaded his staff to prepare a plan for forcing the Dardanelles by a purely naval operation because Kitchener had convinced him that no troops would be provided for a combined operation. The staff of the Admiralty would greatly have preferred a combined operation, and Churchill was censured by the Dardanelles Commissioners for not having brought their doubts more into the open : ' We hold,' the Commissioners stated,[1] ' that the possibility of making a surprise amphibious attack on the Gallipoli Peninsula offered such great military and political advantages, that it was mistaken and ill-advised to sacrifice this possibility by hastily deciding to undertake a purely naval attack, which from its nature, could not attain completely the objects set out in the decision.'

Kitchener and Churchill both made important admissions to the War Council on 14 May, 1915, and Kitchener preserved his statement among his papers :

' When the Admiralty proposed to force the passage of the Dardanelles by means of the Fleet alone, I doubted whether the attempt would succeed, but was led to believe it possible by the First Lord's statement about the power of the *Queen Elizabeth,* and by the Admiralty staff papers showing how the operations were to be conducted . . . I realized that, if the Fleet failed to achieve their object, the Army would have to be employed to help the Navy through. I regret that I was led to agree in the enterprise by the statements made, particularly as to the power of the *Queen Elizabeth,* of which I had no means of judging.'

Churchill retorted[2] that if he had known three months earlier that an army of between 80,000 and 100,000 men would be available in May for an attack upon the Dardanelles, the attack by the

[1] *First Report,* 12 February, 1917 (Cmd. 8490), p. 42.
[2] *Final Report,* 4 December, 1917 (Cmd. 371), p. 7.

Navy alone would never have been undertaken. He explained[1] subsequently :

> 'The Dardanelles Commissioners, studying the story from an entirely different angle, obviously felt that if there had been no naval plan in the field, there would later on have been a really well-conceived and well-concerted amphibious attack . . . But I think myself that nothing less than the ocular demonstration and practical proof of the strategic meaning of the Dardanelles . . . would have lighted up men's minds sufficiently to make a large abstraction of troops from the main theatre a possibility. I do not believe that anything less than those tremendous hopes, reinforced as they were by dire necessity, would have enabled Lord Kitchener to wrest an army from France and Flanders.'

The campaign in Gallipoli was crippled before and after it began because Kitchener had no means of controlling the fierce conflicting pressures to which he was continuously subjected. It must, however, be admitted, that Kitchener failed to make use of the delay imposed by his refusal to countenance a combined operation, to cause contingent military plans or appreciations to be prepared in the War Office. On 19 March, 1915, the day after the failure of the great naval attack, Kitchener was asked pointedly by the Prime Minister in the War Council whether any general plan had been worked out for landing troops. Kitchener replied[2] that it had not, and that the War Office had prepared no general plan of operations because it possessed insufficient information. He added that a detailed scheme of landing would have to be worked out on the spot by the military and naval commanders-in-chief.

That was a damning admission, for such preparations are among the most important duties laid by *King's Regulations* upon the shoulders of the C.I.G.S. The Dardanelles Commissioners commented[3] with good cause : 'We think that the conditions of a military attack on the Peninsula should have been studied, and a general plan prepared by the Chief of the Imperial General Staff, General Sir James Wolfe-Murray, special attention being paid to the probable effect of naval gunfire in support of troops ; and it was the duty of the Secretary of State for War to ensure that this was done.'

---

[1] *The World Crisis* (abridged and revised edition, 1931), p. 356.
[2] *Final Report*, p. 9.   [3] Ibid., p. 86.

Because he was grossly overworked and because also he liked to carry everything in his own head, Kitchener neglected that duty. Sir James Wolfe-Murray told[1] the Dardanelles Commissioners that that portion of the *Field Service Regulations* which dealt with the duties of the Chief of the General Staff were 'practically non-existent' under Kitchener. Kitchener had a poor opinion of Wolfe-Murray, but he had a high opinion of the Director of Military Operations, Sir Charles Callwell, who told[2] the Dardanelles Commissioners that 'the real reason why the General Staff practically ceased to exist was because it was not consulted', and that Kitchener never 'conferred with anyone very much'.

There were, on the staff of the War Office, many men of standing and intelligence ; but all appear to have been so petrified by Kitchener's personality and position that they were incapable of speaking to him as man to man, and of accepting, if necessary, the consequences. The Dardanelles Commissioners commented :[2]

'All the evidence laid before us points to the conclusion that Lord Kitchener was not in the habit of consulting his subordinates, that he frequently gave orders over the heads of the Chiefs of Departments, and sometimes without the knowledge of the Chief of the General Staff . . .

'There can, in fact, be no doubt that the principle of centralization was pushed to an extreme point by Lord Kitchener. It proved eminently successful during the minor operations in the Soudan which he conducted with conspicuous skill. But it was unsuitable to a stronger force than that which Lord Kitchener commanded in the Soudan, or to operations on so large a scale as those in which this country has recently been engaged. The result was to throw on the hands of one man an amount of work with which no individual, however capable, could hope to cope successfully.'

Kitchener resisted all attempts to lighten his load. He told French (9 January, 1915) that France would remain 'for the present the main theatre of operations for the British Army'. He added that the War Council had decided nevertheless that 'certain of the possible projects for pressing the war in other theatres should be carefully studied during the next few weeks so that, as soon as the new forces are fit

[1] *Final Report*, p. 13.   [2] *First Report*, p. 13.

318

for action, plans may be ready to meet any eventuality that may then be deemed expedient, or to enable our forces to act with the best advantage in concert with the troops of other nations throwing in their lot with the Allies '.

Diplomatic efforts to enlist neutrals on the Allied side appeared unavailing in the absence of military successes. But as Kitchener, without consulting his staff, had stated unequivocally that no troops were available for the Dardanelles, Churchill drove his staff against its will to prepare a plan for forcing the Straits by naval action alone, with the aid of old expendable battleships, as well as with that of the fast and superb new battleship, *Queen Elizabeth*, with her fabulously powerful 15-inch guns. Churchill's principal naval advisers, Admirals-of-the-Fleet Lord Fisher and Sir Arthur Wilson, were present but kept silence when Churchill presented that plan to the War Council on 13 January. Kitchener, who had taken the precaution of summoning Sir John French secretly from France to attend that meeting, said that Churchill's plan was worth trying, and that ' we can leave off the bombardment if it does not prove effective '. The War Council, accordingly, resolved unanimously on that day that the Admiralty should ' prepare for a naval expedition in February to bombard and take the Gallipoli Peninsula, with Constantinople as its objective '.

Between 13 and 28 January, Fisher began to regret bitterly his weakness in yielding to Churchill's importunity. He would have preferred a combined operation, but his altered attitude was due to a strong personal preference for a large-scale landing upon the German Baltic coast, in Schleswig-Holstein, to be followed by a march to Berlin ; and for the large-scale amphibious operation upon the Belgian coast which Kitchener had opposed. Churchill used his utmost efforts to keep the old sailor in line ; and he took him to see Asquith immediately before a vitally important meeting of the War Council on 28 January. Asquith then told Fisher that the Dardanelles operation would have to go forward, and Fisher appeared on the whole to be complaisant. Nevertheless, when the Council met at 11.30 a.m. to take its final decision, an untoward incident occurred.

Churchill asked if the Council attached importance to the Gallipoli expedition ' which undoubtedly involves risks '. Fisher said that he had understood that the question would not be raised at that meeting and that the Prime Minister knew his views. Asquith said that matters had reached a stage when the question could not be left in abeyance, and Fisher at once left the table and made for the the door. He explained subsequently that he had considered that it would be unseemly for him to enter into a dispute with Churchill, and that he had intended to seek out the Prime Minister's secretary, and to write a note resigning his office of First Sea Lord.

Kitchener, with some agility, succeeded in reaching the door before Fisher. Interposing his gigantic frame, he asked Fisher what he was about, and then drew him to a window, where he urged him as strongly as possible not to resign. He told Fisher that he was the sole dissentient, and that he owed a duty to his country to continue in office as First Sea Lord. Very reluctantly, Fisher allowed himself to be persuaded by Kitchener ; and he resumed his seat at the table with his colleagues. After the meeting had taken its final decision to proceed with the operation, Churchill had a long private talk with Fisher, who told the Dardanelles Commissioners : " When I finally decided to go in, I went the whole hog, *totus porcus*."

Thereafter, as Kitchener's Director of Military Operations told[1] the Dardanelles Commissioners, ' we drifted into the big military attack '. Churchill began, very cautiously, but with unanswerable arguments, to challenge Kitchener's pronouncement that no troops were available for the Dardanelles. He was strongly supported by his Admirals, and especially by Fisher ; and Kitchener went so far as to inform the War Council on 9 February that ' if the Navy requires the assistance of the land forces at a later stage, that assistance will be forthcoming '.

On 16 February, Ministers took what Lord Hankey termed[1] ' the all-important decision from which sprang the joint naval and military enterprise against the Gallipoli Peninsula '. Kitchener agreed to mass troops, in case they should be needed, on the Greek island of Lemnos, which had been occupied by British marines upon grounds of military necessity ; and he ordered that the crack 29th Division should be dispatched immediately from England, with ancillary horse-boats and landing-craft, and that the Australian and New Zealand Army Corps (Anzacs) should be warned to stand by in Egypt.

Sir John French, supported by his staff as well as by the French Government and military authorities, protested hotly and immediately against that decision ; and a battle raged for three weeks between the rival advocates of a Western and of an Eastern strategy. The 29th division was the cardinal issue in that dispute, and on 20

[1] *First Report*, p. 30.

February Kitchener cancelled its sailing orders, four days after they had been issued. He wrote, nevertheless (22 February), to Lord Esher, whom he used as a go-between :

'Millerand's complaints do not seem to me to be at all well-founded. I promised Sir John French to send a certain number of troops, and whether these consist of the 29th Division, or any other division, seems to me a detail that does not come into any agreement as regards troops to be sent to France.'

Churchill warned Kitchener on 20 February that 'at least 50,000 men should be within reach at 3 days' notice either to seize the Gallipoli Peninsula after it has been evacuated, or to occupy Constantinople if a revolution takes place'. But Kitchener felt unable to disregard the Westerners' argument that, as a consequence of recent Russian reverses, a large-scale German offensive was likely to be launched upon the Western Front during the early spring. While, therefore, continuing to withhold the 29th Division, he informed[1] the War Council on 24 February that 'if the Fleet cannot get through the Straits unaided, the Army will have to see the business through. The effect of a defeat in the Orient would be very serious. There can be no going back. The publicity of the announcement has committed us.'

The public announcement to which Kitchener referred was that the naval bombardment of the outer forts of the Dardanelles had been successfully begun on 19 February. The diplomatic repercussions were extremely favourable, and Churchill, supported by Asquith, proceeded at once to bring the strongest possible measure of continuous pressure to bear on Kitchener in order to induce him to agree to the immediate dispatch of the 29th Division to the Dardanelles. But Kitchener was adamant. He was under equally strong and continuous pressure from Sir John French and from Joffre not merely to send that division to France immediately, but to go himself to Paris in order to confer with Joffre and Millerand, who were afraid that Kitchener might be tempted to use his new armies, during the spring, in the East instead of in France. Joffre even professed to believe that French was concealing his plans from Kitchener upon security grounds. He said that he could not otherwise account for Kitchener's attitude of indecision ; and he complained that his staff would remain paralysed until Kitchener made his intentions clear. Kitchener did not help matters by announcing that he would be happy

[1] Ibid., p. 32.

to confer with Joffre at any time, but only on condition that the question of the future employment of the new British armies should be excluded from the agenda.

Vice-Admiral Sir Sackville Carden, commanding the Mediterranean Fleet, was confident that he could force the Straits by means of a piecemeal reduction of the forts by naval action. Kitchener, who was increasingly doubtful of that possibility, still wrote and spoke about the contingent need for minor military operations in support of the Fleet, aimed at the final destruction of batteries after they had been silenced, and at the reduction of concealed batteries of howitzers inland. His blood was up, however, and he was by that time resolved that the Army should see the operation through at any cost if the naval attack should fail. In the meantime he awaited news from Lieutenant-General Sir William Birdwood, Commander of the Australian and New Zealand Army Corps in Egypt, whom he had ordered (23 February) to reconnoitre the Dardanelles and to report to him about the prospects of military action.

Birdwood was one of Kitchener's dearest friends and favourites ; his reconnaissance was made necessary by the failure of the War Office staff to devote any attention to the Dardanelles. Kitchener continued to carry all available information—such as it was—in his head, and during the first week of March he began, without informing his staff, to communicate almost daily with Birdwood. Kitchener informed [1] Birdwood on 4 March, 1915, that 'unless Navy are convinced that they cannot silence guns in Straits without military co-operation on a large scale—in which case further orders will be issued—there is no intention of using troops to take Gallipoli Peninsula . . . The concentration of troops at the entrance to the Dardanelles is not so much for operations on Gallipoli Peninsula as for operation subsequently to be undertaken in neighbourhood of Constantinople'.

Birdwood at once warned Kitchener that Carden was 'very second-rate—no " go " in him, or ideas, or initiative '. On 5 and 6 March he reported formally to Kitchener that Carden was ' too sanguine ', and that ' I am very doubtful if the Navy can force the passage unassisted '. So Kitchener, on 10 March, informed the War Council that he had changed his mind again, and was now willing to despatch the 29th Division from England to the Dardanelles, together with other units which he had scraped together. He said that he was also ordering

[1] War Office Records.

the whole of Birdwood's Anzac Corps from Egypt. He added, without entering into details, that he had succeeded in arranging some French military co-operation, and that, after the fall of Constantinople, Russian forces would also be available.

The Russians, who had staged a remarkable recovery in the Caucasus, had just brought the pro-ally Greek Government down, and caused a pro-German Government to be installed in its place, by vetoing the employment of Greek troops in the Dardanelles campaign. Nevertheless, with the consent of the British Conservative Opposition, it was announced on 12 March that Great Britain and France would consent to the annexation of Constantinople and the Straits by Russia after the war.

On 10 March Birdwood wrote to Kitchener :

' My dear Chief, . . . If Carden cannot get through by himself —and I still think this very doubtful—and if it is decided that we are to help the Navy through—then I am still of opinion that our best way will be to land at Helles Point, and try to work up Northwards to help the Fleet through the Narrows. Once they are past that they should have no difficulty. I have worked out in detail the whole of my landing arrangements . . . I quite realize that I shall probably be vigorously opposed . . . Yours ever, Birdie.'

In a postscript, Birdwood thanked Kitchener for letting him know that the prospect of French and Russian help made it necessary for a senior General, Sir Ian Hamilton, to be given command : ' It would be useless to say it has not come as a bit of a disappointment. I know so well, though my dear old chief, no one but you would ever have contemplated my having command at all, in the first instance, of the 60,000 men of the original force . . .'

While Churchill ordered Carden (11 and 15 March) to take ' every well-conceived action for forcing a decision, even if regrettable losses are entailed ', Kitchener summoned the 62-year-old Sir Ian Hamilton to the War Office on the morning of 12 March. They were elderly men, but Kitchener was still the hero of Hamilton's life, and the Field-Marshal received the General with a dramatic casualness, and without at first looking up from the desk at which he was working. Then he remarked[1] : " We are sending a military force to support the Fleet now at the Dardanelles, and you are to have command."

[1] Sir Ian Hamilton, Gallipoli Diary, I, p. 2.

Kitchener then resumed his writing and Hamilton stood waiting respectfully until Kitchener again looked up and signified with a gesture that he was ready to enter into conversation.

Wolfe-Murray, the C.I.G.S., and Callwell, the D.M.O., were summoned to Kitchener's room, but Hamilton could obtain very little information. The C.I.G.S. appeared to be as ignorant as Hamilton was about Kitchener's intentions. Kitchener announced that Hamilton would have about 80,000 men, made up of Birdwood's Anzac Corps (30,000) ; the 29th division (19,000) ; a French division (19,000) ; and the Royal Naval division (11,000). Kitchener appeared a trifle arch when he spoke about the 29th Division, and he mentioned that Hamilton could only have it on loan. He added that Walter Braithwaite would be Hamilton's Chief of Staff, and that Braithwaite had already been ordered to collect a staff.

Callwell then gave Hamilton a number of old official handbooks on the Turkish Army, together with a map of the Peninsula which proved, later, to be inaccurate. Hamilton told the Dardanelles Commissioners that his first really good maps were obtained from Turkish prisoners. Callwell also gave Hamilton the outline of a plan which the Greek General Staff had prepared for landing 150,000 troops on the Peninsula. As he did so, Kitchener grimly observed that Hamilton would have to make do with half that number.

Hamilton asked how many troops the enemy had in Gallipoli, and for the names and backgrounds of the German and Turkish commanders. Kitchener said that he had no idea ; and neither he nor Wolfe-Murray vouchsafed any information about the enemy, the country, the political situation, or possible liaison with the Russians.

On the following morning (13 March) Hamilton called again on Kitchener to receive his written instructions. He found the war lord ' standing by his desk, splashing about with his pen at three different drafts ', all of which were entitled ' Constantinople Expeditionary Force '. Hamilton asked Kitchener to change that, for luck, to ' Mediterranean Expeditionary Force ' ; and Kitchener complied. After considerable labour Kitchener at last produced a document consisting of twelve laconic paragraphs, of which the vital sentences were :

' 1. The Fleet has undertaken to force the passage of the Dardanelles. The employment of military forces on any large scale for land operations, at this juncture, is only contemplated in the event

of the Fleet failing to get through after every effort has been exhausted.

' 2. Before any serious undertaking is carried out in the Gallipoli
Peninsula, all the British military forces detailed for the expedition
should be assembled so that their full weight can be thrown in.

' 3. Having entered on the project of forcing the Straits, there
can be no idea of abandoning the scheme. It will require time,
patience, and methodical plans of co-operation between the naval
and military commanders. The essential point is to avoid a check,
which will jeopardize our chances of strategical and political success.

' 4. This does not preclude the probability of minor operations
being engaged upon, to clear areas occupied by the Turks with
guns annoying the Fleet, or for the demolition of forts already
silenced by the Fleet . . .

' 5. Owing to the lack of any definite information we presume
that the Gallipoli Peninsula is held in strength . . .

.   .   .   .

' 7. . . . . The occupation of the Asiatic side by military forces is
to be strongly deprecated.

.   .   .   .

' 12. You will send all communications to the Secretary of
State for War . . .'

When he had completed that draft to his satisfaction, Kitchener
did not pause to wish Hamilton luck. He bid him good-bye and
observed quietly as the General left : " If the Fleet gets through,
Constantinople will fall of its own accord, and you will have won,
not a battle, but the war."

With those astonishingly inadequate orders, and with virtually
no information of any kind, Hamilton, accompanied by his staff, some
members of which he had never previously seen, left Charing Cross
station at five o'clock that afternoon, Friday, 13 March, for the
Dardanelles. Kitchener felt that he had stretched his resources and
duty to their extreme limit in undertaking what looked like developing
into a new campaign in order to enable the Navy to complete successfully a task which it had volunteered to accomplish on its own ; and
he was too busy to come to the station. The Churchills, however,
were at Charing Cross to wish good luck to Hamilton's party, which

arrived four days later at Mudros, on the island of Lemnos, off the Dardanelles, on the morning of 17 March, in the cruiser *Phaeton*, which had met it at Marseilles.

Churchill had ordered Carden on 13 March to concert immediately with Hamilton any large-scale military operations which might appear necessary. On 17 March, however, Carden suffered a nervous break-down, and the command of the detached Mediterranean Fleet devolved immediately upon Vice-Admiral Sir John de Robeck, whom Birdwood described to Kitchener (23 March) as 'a real fine fellow—worth a dozen of Carden'. Early on the following day, 18 March, the combined Fleet of fourteen British and four French battleships advanced in a supreme effort to force a passage through the Narrows. That attempt failed ; two old British battleships and one old French battle-ship were sunk by mines, and one British and one French battleship were severely damaged. At six o'clock on that afternoon Hamilton informed Kitchener : ' Certainly it looks at present as if the Fleet alone would not be able to carry on at this rate, and if so, the soldiers will have to do the trick.'

Five more battleships were immediately ordered to the Dardanelles to replace the ships lost and those temporarily out of action ; but on 19 March, Hamilton, after a close reconnaissance, again notified Kitchener : 'I am most reluctantly being driven to the conclusion that the Dardanelles are less likely to be forced by battleships than at one time seemed probable, and that, if the Army is to participate, its operations will not assume the subsidiary form anticipated.'

Kitchener replied the same day ; ' You know my view that the passage of the Dardanelles must be forced, and that, if large military operations by the Army are necessary to clear the way, they must be undertaken, after careful consideration of the local defences and must be carried through.'

Everyone's blood was tingling after the check suffered by the Fleet on 18 March. De Robeck signalled to Churchill on 20 March that after clearing the minefields he intended to renew the naval attack within three or four days. Twenty-four hours later he changed his mind. The Admirals were as sore about the naval units which had been lost as the Generals, straining at the leash, were sore about the prospect of standing by in comparative idleness. Above all, the naval Commander-in-Chief, who had been ordered to concert large-scale military action with Hamilton, learnt for the first time on 21 March that Hamilton's authority was unfettered ; that he enjoyed freedom of action ; and that at a word from the Admiral he was willing to fall with his full strength upon the southern tip of the Gallipoli Peninsula.

On 22 March Hamilton and de Robeck conferred on board the *Queen Elizabeth.* De Robeck maintained that Hamilton offered, at the start, on behalf of the Army, to undertake the task of forcing the Narrows ; but Hamilton was positive that de Robeck opened the conference by announcing categorically that he could no longer undertake to force a passage without the aid of Hamilton's entire force. Birdwood, who was present, recorded in a private memorandum that de Robeck had said that ' he was prepared to take a fair, sporting chance in which he included guns and mines, *but* he had heard there were submerged torpedo-tubes in the Narrows, and at such close range he could not regard those as such '. In those circumstances, the conference unanimously resolved that the naval attack should be discontinued in favour of a military landing ; and Hamilton announced that he would take the Army back to Alexandria in order to organize it for a landing in about three weeks' time.

There were, in fact, no torpedo-tubes in the Narrows ; and the enemy was desperately short of mines and shells. Enemy morale was extremely high, but it is almost intolerable to have to relate that had the naval attack been renewed, after allowing an interval of a couple of days for clearance of the few remaining mines, the defence must have collapsed for want of ammunition. Only twenty rounds apiece remained for the heavy guns which alone could harm the Fleet ; there were no reserves of shells or mines in Constantinople ; and as long as Bulgaria preserved her neutrality, months must have elapsed before fresh supplies of either could have reached the scene from German or Austrian sources.

That is the tragedy of Gallipoli. On 23 March Hamilton informed Kitchener, and de Robeck informed Churchill, that they had agreed to substitute a military attack for the Government's declared policy of forcing the Dardanelles by means of a naval operation. Birdwood reminded Kitchener (23 March) that he had, from the first, ' thought it impossible for the Navy to get through by themselves, but I didn't like to put it more positively, as not only were some of the Navy so very sanguine, but both Carden and de Robeck thought, and still think, they could push through with further heavy loss, but only to arrive with little ammunition, and no object attained as regards getting transport through . . .'

327

De Robeck explained to Churchill (26 March) : ' The check on 18 March is not, in my opinion, decisive ; but on 22 March I met General Hamilton and heard his views, and I now think that to obtain important results, and to gain the object of the campaign, a combined operation will be essential . . . For the Fleet to attack the Narrows now would jeopardize the success of a bigger and better scheme, and would, therefore, be a mistake.'

So the men on the spot took their fatal decision. Churchill fought desperately against it, but de Robeck's signal of 23 March inspired the Sea Lords to combine against Churchill. On the morning of 23 March high words passed in the Admiralty Board Room ; and Churchill was reminded that he could not afford another and greater Antwerp fiasco : ' If by resigning, I could have procured the decision, I would have done so without a moment's hesitation. It was clear, however, that this would only have made matters worse. Nothing that I could do could overcome the Admirals now that they had dug their toes in . . . I was therefore compelled, under extreme duress, to abandon the intention of sending direct orders to de Robeck to renew the attack.' [1]

In Cabinet that afternoon Churchill announced, ' with grief', that the naval attack must, for the present, be abandoned. He noted [2] : ' Lord Kitchener was always splendid when things went wrong. In a few brief sentences he assumed the burden, and declared that he would carry the operations through by military force . . . Three months before how safe, how sound, how sure this decision would have been. But now ! '

So the Fleet, after 18 March, remained idle ; and Hamilton, with his staff, sailed on 24 March from Mudros to Alexandria in order to organize the landing operation which did not finally take place until 25 April. The Turks, in the meantime, were working feverishly by day and night under German supervision to put the Gallipoli Peninsula into a state of defence. In an impatient signal to Hamilton on the evening of 23 March, Kitchener expressed his vexation at the prospect of further delays :

' I hear 14 April is considered by you as about the date for commencement of military operations, if the Dardanelles have not been forced by the Fleet before that date. I think you had better

[1] *The World Crisis* (abridged and revised edition, 1931), pp. 399-400.
[2] Ibid., p. 404.

328

know that I regard any such postponement as far too long. I should like to know how soon you could act on shore.'

Hamilton explained (25 March) the reasons which made delay unavoidable. He was not, of course, responsible for the muddle, and Kitchener, that evening, signified his acceptance of Hamilton's explanation and his assumption of all consequent responsibility. In Churchill's *The World Crisis*, and in the *Reports* of the Dardanelles Commissioners, Kitchener was criticized in chivalrous but severely forthright terms for that delay in the completion of military preparations, and in particular for the doubts and hesitations about the dispatch of the 29th Division to which he fell a prey between 20 February and 10 March.

Kitchener made up his mind too late, because he had accepted too blindly Churchill's undertaking that the Dardanelles would be forced by the Fleet on its own. The best course would have been to renew the naval attack, which would almost certainly have succeeded, even a month after the failure of 18 March, at the probable cost of a few more obsolete and expendable battleships. But the attack was not renewed because Churchill had lost his power to control the senior Admirals whose confidence he had shaken.

It is, of course, impossible to offer any defence of Kitchener's failure to cause a military appreciation and contingent plans of military operations to be prepared by his staff. But it is fair to emphasize that he wholly lacked anything resembling that machinery of strategic co-ordination which, born partly out of the agony of Gallipoli, was embodied in the Chiefs of Staff Committee during the second World War. In those circumstances his capacity for positive action was paralysed by an intolerable burden of conflicting pressures.

On the specific issue of the delay in dispatching the 29th Division from England, it is fair to quote the opinion of Lord Birdwood, who was of course, devoted to Kitchener's memory. In a private memorandum Birdwood affirmed his view that the matter was of no importance : ' What seems to be overlooked by everyone in this connection is—the *weather* when *landings have to be made on open beaches* . . . Had a dozen divisions been on the spot in February, it would have been impossible to use them, for they could not have been landed, and if they had got on shore with great difficulty on odd fine days, could not possibly have been kept going in food, water, ammunition, etc., by the Fleet. These conditions applied practically all through March and towards the end of April. 25 April was the earliest date on which combined operations could have been arranged for. The Navy should have had records of normal weather, and been able to advise accordingly.' It is worth adding that on 25 March, 1915, Kitchener warned [1] Birdwood by telegram not to tie himself to any definite date but to be ready to start landing operations upon the first fine day : ' as in my opinion weather will be much more a governing factor in determining date than our preparations.'

Birdwood may have been right ; but it has to be admitted that the responsibility resting upon the War Office for the collection of intelligence of that kind was at least as great as that which rested upon the Admiralty.

[1] War Office Records.

CHAPTER 16

LOOS AND THE DARDANELLES

1915

Lack of munitions of all kinds, and particularly of high-explosive shells, caused Kitchener acute concern within a month of the outbreak of war. No action on his part, however, could have availed for many months to overtake the pre-war blindness and indifference of the British people.

The German, French and Austrian General Staffs had learnt from the Balkan War of 1912 to appreciate the advantage which machine-guns possessed in defence, and which high-explosive shells enjoyed over shrapnel when entrenchments had to be made uninhabitable, parapets levelled and machine-gun emplacements destroyed. But at the outbreak of war the British establishment of machine-guns was only two per battalion, and British ordnance factories continued for some weeks to concentrate upon shrapnel instead of high explosives.

During the early months of the war Sir William Robertson, as Quartermaster-General to the B.E.F., was at times compelled to institute a heart-breaking and fantastic system of rationing ammunition. The allowance, for example, of 18-pounder ammunition was reduced from twenty to ten and, on the Second Army's front after the First Battle of Ypres, to two rounds per gun per day. The ration of 4·5 howitzer ammunition sank at one time to two rounds per gun per day along the entire front, and the ration for 6-inch howitzers was sometimes as low as six rounds.

Sir John French rightly protested in the strongest terms against those and similar shortages, and Kitchener exerted himself to overcome them. He did not, however, understand sufficiently the need to make those efforts apparent to the Army and to the public ; he tried to keep his troubles to himself ; and he did not trouble to take his colleagues in the Cabinet or War Council into his confidence.

In gearing British industry and commerce to meet the needs of total war Kitchener required all the help which he could wring from civilian sources and the Press. But he could not help blaming a Government which had been caught unprepared on account of its pre-war inability to outstrip public opinion. For that reason, he displayed too great a distrust of democratic methods, and he made no attempt to inform and educate public opinion.

Kitchener needed help in clearing obstacles out of his way. He often admitted that he knew nothing about the labour problem, but he fought nevertheless to keep the task of supplying the armies entirely under War Office control. He was horrified by the slackness and indifference of the factory workers, as well as by strikes, and by the delays which trade union rules about the dilution of skilled labour imposed upon the speedy delivery of contracts which he placed for the supply of arms and equipment. His mind, attuned to frugality, prompted him to complain, unhelpfully, that ammunition was being squandered at the front.

Kitchener told[1] the Prime Minister on 18 March, 1915, that Sir John French had been recklessly extravagant during the Battle of Neuve Chapelle. He said that, although the Commander-in-Chief possessed qualities of leadership, he was not ' a really scientific soldier '. He summoned French to Dover for a private talk on the evening of 23 March ; and he went himself to Chantilly to confer secretly on 29 March with French, Joffre and the French War Minister, Millerand. Sir Henry Wilson, who was present, noted[2] that Kitchener spoke freely and at length about his labour troubles, which startled the French.

Kitchener said at Chantilly that ' we had already increased our output three times over our peace output', and that the multiple would shortly be increased to the figure nine. He hoped soon to increase the output of 18-pounder shells from 45,000 to 370,000 a week, but ' the workmen would not work '. A recent speech which he had made at Liverpool had done no good ; and he remarked that a sensible system of industrial conscription would have avoided those troubles.

Kitchener gave no lead to the Cabinet, or to the country, on the subject of conscription, because he felt that he had lived too much abroad to be able to gauge its political implications. He was content, therefore, to be guided by Asquith, who told him that conscription would wreck the Government and shatter the Liberal Party. Accepting that advice, Kitchener addressed himself to the task of enlisting many hundreds of private firms at home, in Canada and in the United States in the task of producing munitions. At home he achieved many successes in persuading the unions to agree to necessary diversions and dilutions of skilled labour as well as to the employment of

[1] Earl of Oxford and Asquith, *Memories and Reflections*, II, p. 66.
[2] Sir Charles Callwell, *Field-Marshal Sir Henry Wilson*, I, pp. 218–19.

women ; and he turned an eminent scientist and judge, Lord Moulton, on to the development and production of high explosives.

Nevertheless, there were heart-breaking delays in deliveries, and the finished products often proved defective. Kitchener tried to conceal those misfortunes, and his lack of political experience caused him to treat the public, and even his colleagues, like children. He relied too much upon the secretive and autocratic methods which had served him well in the East, but which were out of place in an embattled democracy, and out of harmony with his new rôle as an idolized popular leader.

Because he unwisely resisted Lloyd George's necessary demand for the establishment of a Ministry of Munitions, the salutary public outcry which was led by Lord Northcliffe and Lloyd George was bitterly critical of Kitchener. A wiser statesman, or a more shrewd politician than Kitchener, would have taken that agitation under his wing. He would then have enlisted upon his side an indispensable Press campaign ; it would have been helpful instead of hostile ; and it could have been sustained and controlled as necessary by a rationed flow of official information and edited comment from the War Office.

Under pressure from Lloyd George, Kitchener consented to preside over a sub-committee of the Cabinet which met six times between 12 October, 1914, and 1 January, 1915, to examine the munitions problem ; but that Shells Committee fell into abeyance because Kitchener complained that he was too busy to attend its meetings. Lloyd George was so much exasperated that he told Asquith on 6 March that he might resign unless a new committee was appointed with someone other than Kitchener as its chairman. Lloyd George told Kitchener (25 March) that he was unable to conceive how he could hope to 'spare the time to attend the endless conferences of employers and employed which must be held if we are to increase, by an appreciable extent, the munitions of war produced in this country'.

Kitchener retorted that unnecessary committees were a hindrance and not a help. It is worth remarking that although Lloyd George and he were colleagues in Cabinet and War Council, all Lloyd George's letters began, 'My dear Lord Kitchener', whereas Kitchener invariably wrote, 'My dear Lloyd George'. Nevertheless, Lloyd George did not scruple to goad Kitchener to fury by accusing him in Cabinet of 'cooking' certain figures about munitions supply.

A small and easily explicable discrepancy had arisen between two sets of figures put forward at different times by Kitchener and by Kitchener's Master-General of Ordnance, Sir Stanley von Donop ; and Kitchener in turn became so angry that he told Asquith on 28 March that he would resign immediately if another Shells Committee were appointed. Lloyd George retorted that in that case he would appeal to public opinion, and Asquith, with difficulty, persuaded them to agree to a compromise.

In that compromise Kitchener conceded little ; but a Munitions of War Committee, with wide terms of reference, met for the first time on 12 April, 1915, under Lloyd George's chairmanship. Kitchener was represented on that committee, of which he was not a member, by von Donop and others, but he flatly refused to delegate to it, or to anyone, the responsibility which the War Office possessed for the production of munitions. He refused also, on security grounds, even to provide the committee with information about the number of men whom he proposed to put into the line by particular dates. Without that information Lloyd George was in no position to prepare accurate estimates of the quantities of munitions which would be required at specified times.

In those circumstances the committee was doomed to futility, and it met for the last time on 13 May, 1915. It paved the way, however, for Lloyd George's appointment as Minister of the newly-created Ministry of Munitions which emerged from the general reshuffle when a Coalition Government was formed at the end of that month.

In the meantime, Lloyd George invited Northcliffe to take up the question of munitions in order to compel Kitchener and the Government to act. Northcliffe, who considered that victory over Germany would be better assured if Kitchener were dispatched in some proconsular capacity to the Orient, was at that moment ready to launch a Press campaign against the war lord, because he had been provided with the necessary material by Sir John French.

Lloyd George, Northcliffe and French had a good case against Kitchener. The munitions problem was so vast and complex that a separate Ministry was essential ; but Kitchener's obtuseness on that subject cannot excuse the underhand methods of intrigue which Sir John French permitted himself to employ against his chief.

Kitchener openly proclaimed on 15 March his concern about the munitions situation. He departed so far from his habitual reticence as to inform the House of Lords that notwithstanding " all efforts to meet our requirements, we have unfortunately found that the output is not only not equal to our necessities, but does not fulfil our expectations, for a very large number of our orders have not been completed by the date on which they were promised. The progress in equipping our new Armies and also in supplying the necessary war material has been seriously hampered by the failure to obtain sufficient labour, and by delays in the production of the necessary plant."

That plain speaking encouraged Sir John French to attribute, wrongly, the defeat and the 13,000 casualties which he had just suffered in the Battle of Neuve Chapelle to shortage of ammunition at the moment when victory was within his grasp. In fact, however, there had been no shortage during that four days' battle, and the B.E.F. had fired off ammunition on an unlimited and unprecedented scale which Kitchener had described as irresponsible.

Shortages of ammunition undoubtedly hampered Sir John on other occasions ; and the Commander-in-Chief was as much worried by the diversion of munitions to the Dardanelles as he was by the dispatch of troops to that theatre. Nevertheless, on 14 April, nearly three weeks before Second Ypres began, Kitchener was able to inform Asquith :

' I have had a talk with French. He told me I could let you know that with the present supply of ammunition he will have as much as his troops will be able to use in the next forward movement.'

On the authority of that letter, Asquith rashly stated in a much-criticized speech at Newcastle on 20 April that a shortage of munitions was not crippling the Army, and that there had been no general slackness in the armaments industry on the part either of employers or employed.

One week before the start of the Battle of Festubert French wrote (2 May, 1915) to Kitchener : ' The ammunition will be all right '. But it was not all right ; and on the opening day (9 May) of the battle French received a warning message from Kitchener that 20,000 rounds of reserve ammunition would have to be earmarked for the Dardanelles.

That paper deficiency was remedied within twenty-four hours, but Kitchener's ill-timed message exhausted the prudence as well as the patience of Sir John French. The presence at the front of war correspondents had been vetoed by Kitchener upon security grounds ; but the military correspondent of *The Times*, Colonel C. à C. Repington, was at that time staying at Headquarters as French's personal guest. The Commander-in-Chief at once ordered that he should be shown the whole of the correspondence between the War Office and the B.E.F. on the subject of munitions supply.

French told Repington that all his efforts had been crippled by lack of high-explosive shells. At the same time, French sent his private secretary, Colonel Brinsley FitzGerald, and his A.D.C., Captain Frederick Guest, to London with copies of the correspondence which Repington had been shown. FitzGerald and Guest were ordered by French to show that correspondence personally to Lloyd George, as well as to the two Opposition leaders, Andrew Bonar Law and Arthur Balfour.

FitzGerald and Guest executed that disgraceful order, behind the backs of Kitchener and the Prime Minister, on 12 and 14 May, 1915 ; and on 14 May Northcliffe started his attack upon Kitchener, obliquely, in *The Times*. He printed a despatch from Repington under the comparatively mild headlines—' NEED FOR SHELLS. BRITISH ATTACKS CHECKED. LIMITED SUPPLY THE CAUSE.' A week later, in *The Daily Mail*, Northcliffe opened a fierce and direct attack, which was intended to hound Kitchener from office, with a banner headline—' THE SHELLS SCANDAL. LORD KITCHENER'S TRAGIC BLUNDER.'

That attack on the nation's idol caused widespread dismay and indignation. Copies of *The Daily Mail* were collected from offices in the city of London and burnt in a large bonfire outside the Stock Exchange by a mob of brokers and jobbers ; and for a few days the clubs of St. James's Street and Pall Mall discontinued their subscriptions to *The Daily Mail*. Kitchener, who was most deeply wounded and bewildered, tried to treat the matter with disdain ; but he ceased thereafter to speak of his own accord about the possibility of combining in his own person the offices of Generalissimo and Secretary for War.

On 14 May Kitchener had sent French a warning letter :

' A good many remarks are being made about *The Times* correspondent who is apparently staying with you and writing to his paper. At the War Council to-day I heard for the first time that this was a fact. Until war correspondents are allowed by the Government, I do not think it is right for you to allow Repington to be out with the Army '.

French replied (15 May) :

' Repington is an old friend of mine and has constantly stayed with me for the last 10 or 12 years.

' He was here for a day or two in an entirely private capacity.
' I really have no time to attend to these matters . . .'

Kitchener kept his temper with difficulty ; and the Press attacks
continued for some weeks. Northcliffe told[1] Lord Beaverbrook one
afternoon at the Ritz Hotel that he had thought that he was strong
enough to destroy Kitchener ; but that he had underestimated the
hold which the war lord had obtained on the love and loyalty of the
man in the street. Northcliffe was compelled, therefore, gradually
to call off the campaign which was affecting adversely the sales of his
newspapers. Douglas Haig, who commanded the First Army in
France, wrote to Oswald FitzGerald (24 May) to express his generous
indignation with the ' reptile press '. He said that Repington had
given away British gun positions by describing them in his
paper, and that in any well-governed country the editor of
The Times would have been placed against a wall and shot as a
traitor.

After consulting the King, who said that he would support Kitchener in any action which he took in dealing with French, Kitchener
sent Lord Esher to see French. He instructed Esher to say that the
Secretary for War was out to fight the Germans and not the Commander-in-Chief. Lord Stamfordham, the King's private secretary,
told Kitchener (22 May) that ' the King was delighted with your
message to French—short, and to the point '. At Kitchener's request,
Esher also informed French that Kitchener had no thought of taking
over command of the army in France ; that he was hampered by
want of ammunition for fresh troops, as well as by commitments in
other theatres of war ; but that he was resolved to continue to support
the Commander-in-Chief with all his power, and to send everything
which he could spare. Reporting on his mission, Esher wrote
(23 May) :

' Sir John has undoubtedly been hurt by messages delivered to him
from you by his Generals returning from home, as also by a certain
tone of coldness that he seems to detect in your telegrams and letters,
towards his operations and troops.'

Esher added that French had said ' that he commenced this war with
a feeling amounting to no less than personal affection for you, whom
he considered the greatest soldier he ever met,' and he concluded by
quoting a remark which French had made : ' " I quite allow that the
tensions through which I have gone, and trying times may have

[1] Lord Beaverbrook, *Politicians and the War*, I, pp. 95–6.

337

warped my perceptions. I hope it is so . . ." I have read this letter to Sir John.'

In a note written on the same day to Oswald FitzGerald, Esher reported that although ' the little F.-M.' was ' in a very fractious mood . . . I think there will be no recurrence ; but with people of that kind it is impossible to be sure. There is but one opinion here. The F.-M. has been simply " carted " by his intimate friends. He will never recover from the shock to his reputation.'

Sir John French claimed[1] that the disclosures about the shortage of shells which he had made to Northcliffe, through Repington, caused the fall, on 17 May, of the Liberal Government. That crisis, however, was precipitated solely by the Conservative Opposition, as a direct consequence of Lord Fisher's resignation of his office as First Sea Lord on 15 May. Fisher resigned, through excitement and strain, because he considered that a major disaster was impending in the Dardanelles.

The military landing which began on 25 April had encountered such formidable opposition that a deadlock rapidly developed. Kitchener felt that he was being tortured on the rack as he handled a continuous flow of urgent competing demands from Sir John French and from Sir Ian Hamilton, for massive reinforcements of men and munitions. On 13 May Kitchener sent Asquith a letter which fully indicates the intense strain to which he was being subjected :

' I went over to the Admiralty with the C.I.G.S. yesterday evening to discuss the, to my mind, very unsatisfactory distribution of the fleet for the defence of the East coast from invasion . . . and was to my great surprise confronted with a telegram that had been prepared recalling the *Queen Elizabeth* from the Dardanelles . . .

' I pointed out that the withdrawal of . . . the principal naval unit engaged on the operations would have a very serious and depressing effect on the army engaged in Gallipoli, at the same time greatly exhilarating our enemy . . .

' Lord Fisher said he would leave the Admiralty if the *Queen Elizabeth* was not at once withdrawn, as he could not stand the fear of losing the ship. I may say that I have had to face the loss of some 15,000 men in the operations to help the Navy . . .

' This desertion of the Army after coming to the assistance of the Navy when they failed to force the passage of the Dardanelles, will

[1] *1914*, p. 360.

undoubtedly have a very unpleasant effect on the confidence that ought to exist between the two Services.

' Late last night, Churchill sent me a telegram he was sending to the admiral at the Dardanelles, ordering the immediate withdrawal of the *Queen Elizabeth*.

' We may have to consider under these circumstances whether the troops [had] better not be taken back to Alexandria, as there may be a Moslem rising in Egypt, and I have denuded the garrison to help the operations.'

The Admiralty had been disturbed by the loss of another battleship in the Dardanelles. She had been torpedoed by a Turkish destroyer while anchored off shore on the morning of 12 May. Asquith wanted, if possible, to avert Fisher's resignation, and he therefore replied curtly to Kitchener that he was advised that the *Queen Elizabeth* could properly be replaced by monitors. Nevertheless Lord Fisher resigned, despite the recall of his favourite ship ; and, as a result of that resignation, Bonar Law informed Lloyd George privately that the Conservatives could no longer suppress their distrust of Churchill. He said that if Churchill were permitted to remain at the Admiralty after Fisher's departure, the unofficial party truce would end, and that, whatever the consequences, the Conservatives would initiate a debate attacking the Government's war policy.

Lloyd George took Bonar Law to see Asquith, who had himself begun to distrust Churchill, and who had for some time been convinced that a coalition government was necessary. Asquith, therefore, surrendered at once, and said that he would form a coalition administration. He asked all his colleagues, later that day, to place their resignations in his hands.

Churchill considered that Asquith should have resisted Bonar Law's demand and that he should have challenged a debate in both Houses in secret session. But although Asquith would probably have won majority votes in both Houses, it would have been difficult to prevent a leakage of secret information which might have had serious consequences. In a paper which he circulated (17 May) to the Cabinet, Asquith pointed out that Fisher's resignation, ' and the more than plausible parliamentary case in regard to the alleged deficiency of high-explosive shells, would, if duly exploited (as they would have been) in the House of Commons at this moment, have had the most disastrous effect on the general strategic and political situation : in particular such a discussion might have had the result of determining adversely to the Allies the attitude of Italy.'

Italy declared war upon Austria, after protracted bargaining, on 23 May, 1915 ; and the new Coalition Government assumed office three days later. Churchill's replacement by Arthur Balfour at the Admiralty was a part of the Conservatives' price, and that decision was as harsh and unjust as it was politically necessary. In his hour of distress, Churchill sent Kitchener a very generous and characteristic letter (21 May) :

' I must tell you how much I regret the odious tone of a section of the Press in their calculated attack upon your work. With great difficulties you have achieved incredible results. We have not always agreed, but having been under your displeasure as a subaltern, I shall always look back with satisfaction to having been your colleague.'

Churchill added, in a postscript, ' Fisher went mad ' ; and that madness took the form of a fit of megalomania. In an ultimatum addressed to Asquith on 19 May, Fisher undertook to win the war on six conditions, of which one was ' that I shall have complete professional charge of the war at sea, together with the absolute sole disposition of the Fleet, and the appointment of all officers of all rank whatsoever, and absolutely untrammelled sole command of all the sea forces whatsoever '.

Fisher also demanded ' that the First Lord of the Admiralty . . . should occupy the same position towards me as Mr. Tennant,[1] M.P., does to Lord Kitchener ' ; that Balfour should not be made First Lord ; that Churchill should be excluded from the Cabinet ; and ' that there shall be an entire new Board of Admiralty as regards Sea Lords and the Financial Secretary '. Fisher asked finally that his six conditions should be published verbatim to the Fleet.

Such was the volcano upon which Churchill had been sitting, while Kitchener sat, in a different sense, upon Fisher's opposite number at the War Office, the C.I.G.S., Sir James Wolfe-Murray, who stayed inconspicuously in Kitchener's shadow, frozen by terror into stone. Kitchener regretted the departure of Churchill, who noted[2] with gratitude that ' when I left the Admiralty . . . the first, and with one exception the only one of my colleagues who paid me a visit of ceremony was the overburdened Titan whose disapprobation had been one of the disconcerting experiences of my youth '.

[1] (The Rt. Hon.) H. J. Tennant, Under-Secretary for War.
[2] *The World Crisis* (abridged and revised edition, 1931), p. 140.

As a wise man and experienced politician, Asquith would have been prepared, if necessary, to sacrifice Kitchener, as well as Churchill, on the altar of the Dardanelles. He gave Churchill the sinecure office of Chancellor of the Duchy of Lancaster, with a seat in the Cabinet, and he told him, perhaps by way of consolation, on the evening of 17 May that Kitchener would have to quit the War Office. Asquith said that Kitchener would be transferred to some great position equivalent to that of Generalissimo, but Kitchener declined to consider that suggestion. He informed the King, who replied (22 May) through Lord Stamfordham :

'The King, to whom I showed your letter, thinks you have acted very rightly about the question of C.-in-C. It is imperative that whatever happens you remain S. of S., though personally I believe that our chances of beating the Germans would be vastly increased if you had absolute military control everywhere. Some people maintain you have it as S. of S.'

In fact it was almost immediately apparent that the new Coalition Government could not hope to inspire popular enthusiasm without Kitchener as Secretary for War. The King and, for a short time, the Conservative Party, supported him, and his hold upon the country was extraordinary. That hold upon the country was, if anything, strengthened by the campaign which was being waged against him vainly in the Northcliffe Press ; but Kitchener's position in the Cabinet and War Council was shaken. He was stripped immediately of his control over munitions, which was transferred to a new Ministry under Lloyd George.

On 29 May, Asquith informed Kitchener that he was to be made a Knight of the Garter in the Birthday Honours List. That was the Royal retort to Kitchener's detractors; and the war lord's banner was hung promptly in St. George's Chapel at Windsor, over the stall which had formerly belonged to the German Emperor. Asquith wrote : 'It is a great pleasure to me to couple with this announcement the assurance of my profound gratitude and unabated confidence.'

Owing to the political crisis no meeting of the War Council, which was renamed the 'Dardanelles Committee', was held between 14 May and 7 June ; and that interval caused an unfortunate delay in the dispatch of necessary reinforcements to Sir Ian Hamilton. On 14 May Kitchener asked[1] Hamilton what force would be needed to achieve victory, and added : 'You should base your estimate on

[1] War Office Records.

supposition that I have adequate forces to place at your disposal'. Hamilton replied (15 May) that he would need two additional army corps, and that he would be able to ' advance with half loss of life now being reckoned on, if I had a liberal supply of gun ammunition, especially high explosive'. Kitchener retorted (18 May) that that reply was ' not encouraging ' ; that ' a serious situation is created by present check ' ; and that Hamilton must realize ' my serious disappointment that preconceived views as to conquest of positions necessary to dominate forts on Straits with naval artillery to support our troops on land, and with active help of naval bombardment, were miscalculated'. Kitchener added : ' The question whether we can long support two fields of operations draining our resources requires grave consideration '. On 28 May, Kitchener circulated an important memorandum to his colleagues on the Dardanelles Committee, who were now H. H. Asquith, Prime Minister ; A. J. Balfour, First Lord of the Admiralty ; Lord Lansdowne, Minister without Portfolio ; Sir Edward Grey, Foreign Secretary ; Lord Curzon, Lord Privy Seal ; Lord Crewe, Lord President of the Council ; Lloyd George, Minister of Munitions ; Lord Selborne, President of the Board of Agriculture ; Reginald McKenna, Chancellor of the Exchequer ; Bonar Law, Secretary for the Colonies ; and Winston Churchill, Chancellor of the Duchy of Lancaster. That memorandum warned [1] his colleagues that withdrawal from Gallipoli would shake British prestige throughout the world, and particularly in the East ; that it would certainly involve ' much loss of life ' ; and that it could only be justified ' in order to avoid a great disaster '. He stated, however, that it was no longer possible to seek an immediate decision, because ' it has been shown that the military forces and, what is even more important, the necessary supplies of ammunition asked for by the G.O.C. on the spot, cannot be spared to bring the affair to a rapid conclusion.'

Kitchener pointed out that the difficulties of the enterprise had proved more formidable than was expected, and that a much greater effort was now required. But he warned the committee that in considering Hamilton's demands for reinforcements :

' I am somewhat in doubt, from the experience of trench warfare in Flanders, whether such increased forces would enable him to carry the position as he anticipates. Sir John French's forces have been increased very greatly, but no such advance as he had anticipated has occurred.'

Kitchener, therefore, recommended that Hamilton should be

---

[1] *Final Report*, pp. 25-6.

instructed ' to continue to push on and make such progress as is possible '. He argued that that course had ' much to recommend it. It avoids any immediate blow to our prestige. It keeps the door open to Balkan intervention. It ensures our hold on a position of great importance which rivets the attention of the Turks and, in all probability, limits active operations on their part against Egypt, or in Mesopotamia, or the Caucasus.'

In writing that memorandum, Kitchener was inhibited by the desire of Sir John French and of the French Government for further offensive operations in France. But decisive battles cannot be won in a spirit of half-hearted compromise. The Dardanelles Committee was not then disposed to sanction further futile offensives on the pattern of Neuve Chapelle and Festubert ; and on 7 June it pressed Kitchener for a more positive and energetic policy in the Dardanelles. Kitchener, instead of giving a lead, responded to his colleagues' mood. He agreed at once to dispatch three more Kitchener divisions to the Dardanelles, and exclaimed : " Do not let Sir Ian Hamilton throw away his strength in the interval. But let us send out ample reinforcements to see this thing through."

Kitchener's supine attitude alarmed his colleagues ; and his credit in the Cabinet and Dardanelles Committee began rapidly to evaporate, until by the end of the year it had fallen almost to zero. As his colleagues ceased to look to him for guidance, he was judged increasingly critically as a member of a team. It was not Kitchener but the Dardanelles Committee which decided at the end of June to give Hamilton's demands priority over those of French. That decision caused a crisis in Anglo-French relations, and the tortuous memoranda which Kitchener circulated to his colleagues in consequence, prove that, left to himself, he would have been unable to make up his mind on that vital issue of priorities.

On 6 and 7 July, nevertheless, Kitchener enjoyed an extraordinary personal success. He had gone on the previous day to Calais with Asquith, Balfour and Crewe to meet the French in order to settle allied differences. The French were represented by Viviani and Millerand, and by Delcassé, the Minister for Foreign Affairs. Sir John French also attended. Kitchener, who sat on Asquith's right, dominated the proceedings.

Everyone was astonished by the dominant part which Kitchener played. Grey, who was unwell and unable to attend, was represented by Crewe, and Kitchener was the only Englishman present who

343

spoke the French language with idiomatic fluency. He made a tremendous impression upon the French Ministers, and spoke, for once, with complete frankness and authority about his shortage of ammunition, and about the urgent need to send strong reinforcements to the Dardanelles. When the French raised the thorny question of unity of command, Kitchener delighted his colleagues by the resourcefulness which he showed. The French pointed out that their two divisions in the Dardanelles had been placed, as a matter of course, under Hamilton's command ; and they argued strongly for the principle of unity of command upon the Western Front.

Kitchener, by his own efforts, persuaded the French to agree that that subject should be indefinitely postponed. He was also mainly responsible for inducing the French to accept the British view that there should be no more large-scale offensives on the Western Front during 1915. That policy, which was defined as one of active defence, was not intended to preclude a few local surprise attacks in order to prevent the Germans from feeling too confident.

Asquith, Balfour and Crewe left the conference under the impression that Kitchener's bold diplomatic adroitness had gained every point which they had sought to secure. The Cabinet was gratified to learn that the French had agreed that the campaign in the Dardanelles was to enjoy priority over the Western Front. The full results of that conference, however, were not correctly reported to the Cabinet, because they were known only to Joffre, and to Kitchener who remained silent.

Joffre was extremely dissatisfied with the lukewarmness shown by the British on the question of unity of command in the West. He resented even more the British insistence upon a defensive policy on the Western Front throughout 1915. In the light of what happened six weeks later it is clear that Kitchener overcame Joffre's objections and steered that conference to a triumphant conclusion by using equivocal methods which were destined to prove embarrassing.

In the early morning of 7 July, Kitchener took a stroll with Joffre, followed by a long private conversation in the saloon of the special train which had drawn the French Ministers to Calais. Kitchener would never reveal any details about that conversation ; but the main conference, which was resumed later that morning, ended in complete agreement within a remarkably short time.

Joffre accepted, with apparent geniality, the decision to stand upon the defensive on the Western Front. But he took no notice of it whatever, and he continued to work secretly and uninterruptedly on his plans for a huge-scale autumn offensive in Champagne. He may have explained to Kitchener that the psychology of the French people made a defensive policy dangerous ; and it is certain that Kitchener knew what Joffre was planning. He probably hoped that Hamilton would break through the Dardanelles during August, and that the autumn offensive in France would then prove acceptable to both Governments. On that subject, at any rate, he reached a private understanding with Joffre which he did not reveal to his colleagues.

When the conference ended Kitchener ordered two more territorial divisions to be dispatched forthwith to the Dardanelles. He then accompanied Asquith on a visit to the troops. During that excursion an amusing incident occurred at Ypres, and it can best be told in Asquith's words : [1]

' We found ourselves, with a retinue of generals and staff officers, in the Grande Place, confronting the magnificent ruin of the famous Cloth Hall. Large parts of the fine arcades of statues were still intact and I observed that Kitchener was scanning them with an expert's gaze. A young staff officer came up to me, and, nudging my elbow, said : " Do you see that ? Those statues have been bombarded by the Germans for a hundred days, but they have never been in such danger as they are at this moment."

' " Do you mean ", I replied, " that we may some day hope to see one or more of them at Broome Park ? "

' The audacious youth nodded, and disappeared quickly into space, nor, to my regret, was I ever able to establish his identity.

' As we drove back I related the conversation to Kitchener who —far from showing any sign of resentment—was genuinely and immensely amused.'

*　　　　*　　　　*

Hamilton's army in the Dardanelles was established on two isolated beachheads in Gallipoli—at Cape Helles, on the tip of the Peninsula, and at Anzac Cove, some thirteen miles up the north coast. Both assaults had been brought to a standstill before the end of May by the Turks, whose quality had been badly underestimated and who fought as magnificently as their opponents. The extremely capable enemy commanders were the German, Liman von Sanders, and Mustafa Kemal who later took the name of Ataturk.

[1] *Memories and Reflections*, II, p. 83.

345

The Anzac front remained relatively quiet throughout June and July ; but on the Helles front a series of desperate battles were fought. By the end of July each side had sustained about 57,000 casualties ; the invaders were securely dug in on both fronts, and the Turks had failed to hurl them into the sea.

The five extra divisions which Kitchener dispatched, after the Government crisis, increased Hamilton's fighting strength to 120,000 men. He had under command nine British, two Anzac, and two French divisions ; but the last British division did not arrive until after the second great military attempt to break through to Constantinople was launched on 6 August, 1915. The division had, therefore, to go directly into action from an enervating three weeks' voyage.

Hamilton, on 6 August, launched three separate culminating assaults, of which the most vital was on the Anzac front. Sir William Birdwood was ordered to break out of his beachhead with 37,000 men, and to ' cut off the bulk of the Turkish Army from land communication with Constantinople '.

At the same time the Hon. Sir Frederick Stopford was ordered to make a fresh landing with 25,000 men at Suvla Bay, a mile or two north of Anzac Cove, in order to link up with and extend the Anzac front, and ' incidentally to secure Suvla Bay as a winter base for Anzac and all the troops operating in the northern theatre '. Finally, Sir Francis Davies, who had 35,000 men under command at Helles, was ordered to capture enough high ground ' to gain such a command for my artillery as to cut off the bulk of the Turkish Army from sea traffic, whether with Constantinople or with Asia '.

Such was the plan ; but by 21 August all three attacks had failed at a cost of 45,000 additional British casualties, apart from those suffered by the French. The main assault at Anzac came within an ace of success, for the second time during the campaign ; but the Turks were too strong, too well equipped and too well led. Such supine incompetence was displayed at Suvla by Stopford and by one or two of the divisional generals, that Hamilton, at Kitchener's suggestion, relieved them from their commands and posted them home while the struggle was in progress. The cardinal cause, nevertheless, of the British defeat was the failure to decide sufficiently soon to give priority to the Dardanelles as the only theatre of war which held out the prospect of quick and decisive victory in 1915.

Churchill, who saw that most clearly, arranged to go out to the

Dardanelles during July and to report to the Cabinet. Kitchener told Asquith, however (17 July), that he wished the Secretary of the Cabinet, Maurice Hankey, to accompany Churchill, and that he had informed Hamilton ' that Churchill will in no way interfere in military operations '. Asquith, accordingly, on 19 July instructed Hankey to accompany Churchill in a completely independent capacity. Hankey was given entire discretion and permission to communicate directly with the Prime Minister.

Those arrangements do not appear to have been agreeable to Churchill, for he did not go to the Dardanelles ; but after reading the first report from Hankey about the battle which had begun on 6 August, Asquith wrote (20 August) to Kitchener : ' I have read enough to satisfy me that the generals and staff engaged in the Suvla part of the business ought to be court-martialled and dismissed from the Army.' Kitchener had that gloomy reading-matter in his pocket, as well as a sheaf of equally depressing telegrams about a new and continuous series of heavy Russian reverses, when he crossed the Channel on 15 August to visit Joffre and French.

Kitchener first visited Joffre at Compiègne. He was received with all ceremony by the French Commander-in-Chief, as well as by Foch, Millerand and a glittering concourse of general officers. Kitchener had a number of private conversations with Millerand and one exceptionally protracted secret conference with Joffre which lasted for several hours. On 18 and 19 August he visited French and Haig.

Owing to the collapse of his relations with Sir John French, Kitchener had entered into a relationship of an unusual kind with Haig. Haig had visited Kitchener at the War Office, while on leave, on 14 July ; and Kitchener had instructed him to write to him secretly, personally and constantly, behind French's back, about any subjects affecting the Army. Haig noted[1] that Kitchener had said that ' he would not reply, but I would see my proposals given effect to, and must profess ignorance when that happened ! '

Haig would have been more startled at receiving that order if he had not, an hour or two earlier, had an audience at Buckingham Palace with the King, who had given him the same order, after explaining that he had lost confidence in Sir John French :

' The King quite realized the nature of such conduct on my part, because he told me he had said to Lord K., with reference to it, " If anyone acted like that, and told tales out of school, he would, at

[1] Robert Blake, *Private Papers of Sir Douglas Haig*, pp. 97–8.

school, be called a sneak." K's reply was that we are beyond the schoolboy's age ! '

In France, accordingly, Kitchener opened his mind more fully to Haig than he did to French. He told Haig that he wanted to talk privately, and then gravely observed that there was imminent danger of a complete Russian military collapse :

' Up to the present,' Kitchener continued, ' I have favoured a policy of active defence in France, until such time as all our forces are ready to strike. The situation which has arisen in Russia has caused me to modify those views. I now feel that the Allies must act vigorously in order to take some pressure off Russia, if possible.'

Kitchener said that Joffre had told him that Sir John French did not intend ' to co-operate to the utmost of his power ' when the French attacked in September, and he added :

' I have now decided that we must act with all our energy, and do our utmost to help the French, even though, by so doing, we suffer very heavy losses indeed.'

Haig, suppressing his doubts, said that the Army was ready to attack, and that all it needed was ammunition. Kitchener, ignoring the Dardanelles, said that he would send everything that he had, and he again begged Haig to continue their secret and direct personal correspondence.

So Kitchener honoured the private understanding which he had reached with Joffre at Calais in the early morning of 7 July. Hamilton had been given a second chance and had failed again ; and Joffre stated categorically that the French would attack in Champagne, whether the British co-operated or not. Joffre had explained his plan in detail to Kitchener, who had, as Joffre expected, been attracted by its vast scale. The failure in the Dardanelles had damaged Kitchener's credit, and he hoped, by changing his mind abruptly, to alter, suddenly and dramatically, the balance of advantage in the war, which had swung so heavily in the Germans' favour.

On 20 August Kitchener returned to London, bringing with him Sir John French ; and Churchill recorded[1] a curious scene which occurred in Kitchener's office on the following morning :

' To avoid unnecessary circulation of secret documents, it had been arranged that members of the War Committee wishing to read the daily War Office telegrams could do so each morning at the War Office in Lord Kitchener's ante-room . . . On the morning of August

[1] *The World Crisis*, pp. 502-3.

21 I was thus engaged when the private secretary informed me that Lord Kitchener . . . wished to see me . . . He looked at me sideways with a very odd expression on his face. I saw he had some disclosure of importance to make, and waited. After appreciable hesitation he told me that he had agreed with the French to a great offensive in France. I said at once that there was no chance of success. He said that the scale would be greater than anything before conceived ; if it succeeded, it would restore everything, including of course the Dardanelles. He had an air of suppressed excitement like a man who has taken a great decision of terrible uncertainty, and is about to put it into execution. He was of course bracing himself for the announcement that he had to make that morning to the War Committee and to the Cabinet.'

Kitchener took French with him to both meetings, and the Commander-in-Chief, who had no great confidence in the prospects of the proposed operation, was subjected to a close interrogation. But Kitchener took command for the last time. Where so much was uncertain, he declined to promise any decisive success ; but he insisted that Great Britain was bound to act in concert with the French, who were resolved, in any case, to take the offensive in September : " We must make war as we must ; not as we should like."

Right or wrong, Kitchener surprised his doubting colleagues by giving that forthright and dramatic lead at a time when they were beginning to think that he had lost altogether the power of making up his mind. He told his colleagues that a decision was required at once ; that the Western Front must be given priority over the Dardanelles ; and that, in view of Hamilton's resounding failure, he no longer felt justified in holding the French to the agreement reached at the Calais Conference of 6–7 July.

In that mood Kitchener was still acceptable as arbiter of British strategy ; and, despite strong opposition, the disastrous commitment which he had made to Joffre was endorsed by his colleagues on that day. Hamilton and his heroic army in Gallipoli were, in consequence, condemned to deadlock, attrition and heart-breaking uncertainty, while the Turks refurbished their defences and reorganized their shattered formations. The casualties which Hamilton had suffered during the August offensive had of course to some extent to be made good, in order to enable the Army to retain its footholds upon the Peninsula. But those footholds were useless without the strong reinforcements which Hamilton demanded in preparation for a third

349

great military assault which Kitchener declined to countenance. And yet, if he had come down upon the side of Hamilton instead of upon that of Joffre, Constantinople might still have been captured and the Russians effectively relieved at a third or even a quarter of the cost in life of the great futile autumn offensive in France.

That offensive, which failed everywhere completely, exacted the terrible forfeit of more than 300,000 Allied casualties. It is divided by military historians into three great battles which all began on 25 September, 1915. The British share, known as the Battle of Loos (25 September–8 October) was so badly mishandled by Sir John French that the Government braced itself to relieve him of his command. French tried, by falsifying details in his official account, to put the blame for his failure upon Haig, who thereafter declined to have any personal relations with his Commander-in-Chief.

Signs were not wanting that Kitchener, too, had exhausted the goodwill of his colleagues. An unhappy incident occurred on 21 August, on the day after Kitchener's fateful decision to attack in France had been endorsed. Lord Crewe, who had been made chairman of a Cabinet Committee on Manpower, summoned Kitchener to give oral evidence on 22 August about the strength of the armed forces, but Kitchener replied that he was too busy to attend. He said that he objected on principle to the system of oral interrogation, and he offered instead to supply, in writing, any information which Crewe might, in writing, demand. When Crewe insisted that Kitchener should submit himself to oral interrogation like Balfour, Lloyd George and everyone else, Kitchener wrote (22 August) to Asquith :

'I must leave the matter in your hands, but I think I ought to let you know that if this system is adopted during the war, I should be forced to resign.'

Asquith did not at that moment see fit to enforce his authority ; but a month later, on 22 September, when Kitchener happened to be absent from the Cabinet, a belated attempt was made to bring the war lord under control. It was resolved that Kitchener should be instructed to provide himself immediately with a competent General Staff ' to guide and advise the cabinet, and its committees, in matters of strategy '.

In notifying Kitchener of that decision, Asquith wrote (23 September) : ' With the enormous burden which lies upon your shoulders . . . it has become essential that both yourself and the

Government should have the best intelligence that the Army can supply for our common purpose '. The Prime Minister requested accordingly that Kitchener should arrange to appoint Sir Archibald Murray, the deputy C.I.G.S., to replace Sir James Wolfe-Murray immediately as C.I.G.S. ; that he should send for three or four of the best staff officers from the fighting fronts to assist the new C.I.G.S. ; and that ' there should be drawn up once in every week a considered appreciation by the General Staff here, of the military situation, actual and prospective.'

Kitchener hastened to give effect to those requests. Wolfe-Murray resigned on 25 September, and his namesake, Sir Archibald, was made C.I.G.S. on the following day. But the storm-clouds continued to gather around Kitchener's head. .Two powerful members of the Government, Bonar Law and Lloyd George, began to use every means at their disposal in an effort to persuade Asquith to dismiss Kitchener.

When the Coalition Government was formed, Asquith and Lloyd George had successfully intrigued to prevent Bonar Law from being made Chancellor of the Exchequer. As leader of the Conservative Party, Bonar Law would have been entitled to insist, but he listened to Lloyd George's appeals to his patriotism and modestly accepted the Colonial Office instead. When he now joined Lloyd George in an attempt to oust Kitchener, Bonar Law expected that Lloyd George would possess sufficient influence with Asquith to secure their object ; but Asquith supported Kitchener, and Bonar Law remarked laughingly to Lloyd George : " I only want to see you two on the same good terms you were when you combined to do me out of the Exchequer ! "

Kitchener would not have understood that joke. He often said that he was heartily sick of the atmosphere of continuous personal intrigue which existed around him ; and he did not understand the rules of the game. He was in many respects simple and straightforward, and Asquith found him personally congenial. But the Prime Minister would not, of course, on that account have hesitated to dismiss Kitchener if he had considered such action to be necessary or politically expedient. He required no convincing on the subject of Kitchener's defects.

Asquith supported Kitchener because he was dependent upon him for recruiting. In that field Kitchener's name was a talisman of incalculable potency. The voluntary system was breaking down rapidly during the autumn of 1915, but Asquith's Government was rent asunder on the subject of conscription. Most Conservatives and soldiers demanded, and most Liberals and factory workers opposed, conscription. But some Conservatives, like Lansdowne, also opposed conscription, while some Liberals, like Lloyd George, strongly advocated it.

The nation would have accepted conscription if Kitchener had pronounced it to be necessary. But it was apparent, after interminable discussions in the Cabinet, that the Government would be wrecked and that Asquith would feel compelled to resign if conscription were prematurely imposed. The Liberal Party would have been split, and a majority of Asquith's Liberal colleagues would have resigned, partly out of conviction and partly because they feared a revolt on the part of the Liberal rank and file in the constituencies.

The first coalition had been formed in response to a call for national unity. There was then a general expectation that conscription would be enforced at once, and the country had looked to Kitchener to give a lead. The Conservatives, who were straining at the leash, would not have shrunk from breaking up the Government if Kitchener had stated that conscription was necessary.

Kitchener, in those circumstances, held the fate of the Government, as well as that of Asquith and the Liberal Party, in his hand. He had told Haig as early as 19 August that although conscription would involve Asquith's resignation, he had not yet decided what was best and would act only for the good of the country. His sympathies were strongly Conservative; he appreciated the need for conscription to the full; and a group of nine dissident Ministers, who included Lloyd George, after a supper at Lord Curzon's house, approached Kitchener within a week of the Battle of Loos with a request that he would give a lead and force the issue.

Kitchener knew that his credit would sink still lower if he declined. The Conservatives naturally looked to the great soldier, who was also the Minister most closely concerned, to take action. But Kitchener rebuffed them, because he considered that a further period of delay would be less deleterious than the sacrifice of national unity.

While Kitchener was making up his mind Asquith wrote him an agonized letter of appeal (Sunday, 17 October, 1915), which was marked 'most secret':

'We are (as you realize) in a most critical situation. You and I have since the war began worked in daily intimacy and unbroken confidence. And you know well that, in every exigent crisis, I have given you—as you have given me—loyal and unstinting support.

' I should like you to know that what is now going on is being engineered by men (Curzon and Lloyd George, and some others) whose real object is to oust you. They know well that I give no countenance to their projects, and consequently they have conceived the idea of using you against me.

' God knows that we should both of us be glad to be set free. But we cannot and ought not. So long as you and I stand together, we carry the whole country with us. Otherwise, the Deluge !

' Cannot you say that, while you aim at and would like to obtain 70 divisions, the thing should be done gradually and with general consent . . . ?

' This would ease the way and, in my opinion, in view of our financial and other commitments, be the safe and statesmanlike course. There are, as you know well, grave difficulties to be faced in the way of equipment and officers, and in other respects.

' I do not appeal to personal considerations, but I am certain, in the interests of the Country, and of the effective prosecution of the war, that it is essential that you and I should stand together, and that the intrigue, which has for its main object both to divide and to discredit us both, should be frustrated.

' The matter is of such urgent importance that I am putting off the Cabinet to Monday afternoon and should be glad to see you at 10, Downing Street not later than 12.30.'

Kitchener saw Asquith and responded to his appeal. He sub-ordinated himself to Asquith, and stood at his side, while Lord Derby, who was called in to be Director-General of Recruiting, made a last forlorn attempt to save the voluntary system. Men of fighting age ' attested ' their willingness to enlist when wanted ; and one of the promises which Derby made constituted a virtual pledge that unmarried attested men would be called to the colours before married ones.

That absurd distinction caused hundreds of thousands of married men to attest in the confident belief that they would not be required for a long time, while at least a million unmarried men held back. After wearisome debates in Parliament and discussions in the Cabinet, an Act became operative at last on 10 February, 1916, which

353

compelled the attestation of all unmarried men between the ages of eighteen and forty-one.

Kitchener had become convinced, before the end of 1915, that a general measure of conscription was necessary in order to enable him to put into the field the seventy divisions which he had undertaken to provide; but he deliberately renounced a great opportunity by failing to give a clear decisive lead. The reason was his conviction that the only service which he could continue to render to his country, after his credit with his colleagues had evaporated, was to inspire national unity. Having forfeited the confidence of his colleagues, there could be no other reason for remaining in office.

So Kitchener kept in step with Asquith, who exaggerated the political disadvantages of conscription and sought to postpone a decision to the last. Many of those disadvantages would have dissolved into air if Kitchener had thought fit to give the nation a lead. Sir John Simon, the Home Secretary, was the only Minister who resigned from the Cabinet when the first Compulsory Service Act was passed in January, 1916 ; and the second Act, which conscripted all able-bodied men between the ages of eighteen and forty-one, made even less stir. It exempted conscientious objectors and came into effect on 8 June, 1916, three days after Kitchener was drowned.

War Lord

Kitchener in Gallipoli greeting French C.-in-C.

CHAPTER 17

ECLIPSE

1915–1916

KITCHENER'S power to give unity to the Government vanished when his colleagues lost confidence in his judgement. But he continued until the last to give unity to the country, and to provide a façade behind which soldiers and politicians, Liberals and Conservatives, and the rival advocates of an eastern and of a western strategy conducted their disputes and intrigues. A squalid French intrigue during the late summer of 1915 landed Kitchener finally in the mire.

The French Government, which had previously shown a strong distaste for the campaign in the Dardanelles, astonished Kitchener by suddenly offering to dispatch four French divisions from France, under General Sarrail, to form, with the two French divisions which Hamilton had under command already, and which he was asked to release, a French Army of the East. The French proposed that that army should attack the Asiatic shore of the Dardanelles, in association with a renewed British attack on the European shore after Hamilton had been reinforced.

Kitchener communicated that French offer to the Dardanelles Committee on 3 September and strongly commended it; and even those members who had begun to press most strongly for evacuation, and for acknowledgement of defeat, accepted it with gratitude. Kitchener urged that large reinforcements should be sent to Hamilton in order to ensure success; and the Committee agreed with enthusiasm. Churchill vainly begged Kitchener for a General's commission and the command of a corps in the Dardanelles.

Within a few days Kitchener became anxious because Joffre made no move to dispatch the divisions which he had promised. Sarrail lingered in Paris, and Kitchener, on 11 September, crossed to Calais in order to clear up the situation with Joffre and Millerand. It was then explained that political and not strategic considerations had prompted Millerand to make his dramatic offer to Kitchener.

Sarrail, who had been relieved of his command at Verdun by Joffre during July, was exceptionally capable. He was also the only officer in the highest ranks of the French Army who had consistently supported the unfortunate Captain Dreyfus through all his trials and tribulations. He was militantly agnostic and anti-clerical, and he therefore enjoyed the strong support of important radical-socialist elements which, in the interests of national unity, the French Government did not dare to offend. Those elements claimed that Sarrail had been victimized by the General Staff, and Millerand used his good understanding with Joffre to arrange a compromise. An Army of the East was created and Sarrail was given the command.

Sarrail's religious opinions were of no interest to Kitchener, who asked when he would leave for the Dardanelles with four divisions. To Kitchener's disgust, Joffre explained that he could not release the divisions until the results of the great offensive which was due to start on 26 September were known. He said that if the attack succeeded, the divisions would be needed in the pursuit ; but that, if it failed, they could probably start to embark between 8 and 10 October.

Before 8 October a grave emergency in the Balkans caused Sarrail's four divisions to be diverted to Salonica. The British defeat at Suvla brought Bulgaria into the war on the German side ; and the Bulgarian Army launched a flank attack against Serbia in association with an Austro-German invasion from the north which was launched in overwhelming strength on 7 October. Belgrade fell two days later, and within a few weeks Serbia and Montenegro were overrun.

In response to an invitation from the Greek Prime Minister, Veni-zelos, an Anglo-French force was landed at Salonica on 5 October. It advanced into Macedonia in a vain attempt to help the Serbs. But the Greek King, Constantine, who was the Kaiser's brother-in-law, repudiated the invitation which his Prime Minister had issued and Venizelos was dismissed a few hours before the Allies landed. The French Government was resolved, nevertheless, to reinforce strongly the Allied forces which had already violated Greek neutrality. They urged that something might yet be salvaged from the ruin of the Bal-kans if Hamilton's army were shipped from the Dardanelles to Salonica with orders to join Sarrail's Army of the East in Macedonia.

Kitchener considered that plan to be insane, but he failed to move Millerand when he went on 8 October to confer with him and Joffre at Chantilly. The British Cabinet, meanwhile, displayed an attitude of frantic indecision. Lloyd George, who had from the first opposed the Gallipoli campaign, strongly supported the new French plan. He had argued for months that an army should be sent to Salonica in order to forestall a German attack upon Serbia. That attack had long been foreseen, and Bonar Law joined Lloyd George in blaming

356

Kitchener for misleading the Cabinet, and for taking no timely action.

Asquith, on the other hand, supported by Balfour, Churchill and others, as well as by Kitchener's newly resuscitated General Staff, wanted to adhere to the decision of 3 September that Hamilton should be reinforced and that a last desperate effort should be made to break through to Constantinople. Asquith considered that it would be useless to send reinforcements to Salonica ; and that was also the advice of the General Staff, which added, nevertheless, that it was vital to maintain Anglo-French solidarity and to concentrate in the long run upon the Western Front.

Kitchener had no policy because he could not make up his mind. He was torn between a desire to maintain Anglo-French solidarity, and a conviction, which he wearied his colleagues by repeating un-helpfully and too often, that acknowledgement of defeat in Gallipoli would cause irreparable damage to British prestige in Egypt and throughout the Orient. During those critical October days his indecision disgusted his colleagues. His insistence upon the obvious, combined with an elaborate display of stolidity which he used as a defence mechanism in order to cover his ineffectiveness in verbal discussions, finally killed the admiration and even the affection which many of his colleagues had previously felt for him.

On 11 October a compromise decision was reached. Kitchener was instructed to dispatch six British and two Indian divisions from France to Egypt, to be used in Gallipoli or Macedonia as circumstances might dictate. On that day Kitchener telegraphed to Hamilton :

'What is your estimate of the probable losses which would be entailed if evacuation of the Gallipoli Peninsula was decided on and carried out . . . ?

'No decision has been arrived at yet . . . In your reply you need not consider possible future danger to the Empire that might thus be caused.'

Hamilton replied (12 October) : 'My opinion now is that it would not be wise to reckon on getting out of Gallipoli with less loss than that of half the total force, as well as guns which must be used to the last . . . Morale of those who got off would fall very low . . . We might be lucky and lose considerably less . . . On the other hand . . . we might have a veritable catastrophe.'

The French Government, which was at that time tottering towards its fall, resolved to jerk the British into making up their minds. Accompanied by Joffre, Millerand came to London to see Asquith and Kitchener on 17 October. Asquith, who had no relish for prolonged military discussions, retired to bed with a chill ; but the visitors conferred with the leading members of the Cabinet. Churchill was not present because he was not invited, but strong British opposition was expressed to the French plea for a large-scale reinforcement of the Allied Army in Macedonia. After everyone had spoken, Joffre amazed the British by breaking into an impassioned harangue. He said that the war would be lost if the British and French failed to co-operate ; he demanded a joint General Staff with a joint Anglo-French secretariat ; and he announced that he would resign his command at that instant, unless the British would undertake immediately to join the French in dispatching reinforcements to Salonica.

Churchill recorded : [1] ' In spite of the strenuous resistance of the British General Staff, and in defiance of their advice, the Cabinet yielded to this outrageous threat.' Kitchener threw over the advice of his General Staff, and agreed (14 October) to recall Hamilton on the ground that he was incapable of advising about evacuation with an open mind. Sir Charles Monro was sent from France to replace Hamilton, and to advise whether Gallipoli should be evacuated, or whether a fresh attempt to break through should be made. In the former case he was instructed to estimate the probable loss ; in the latter, to estimate the force which he would need.

On 31 October, after making his inspection, Monro recommended evacuation. He said that he was unable to estimate the forfeit which the enemy might exact. Kitchener at once informed Asquith that he found that recommendation unacceptable, and he asked Monro (1 November) for the opinions of his corps commanders.

Monro replied that Byng at Suvla and Davies at Helles recommended evacuation, but that Birdwood at Anzac was against it. Birdwood always considered that Monro had been primed before he left France by Robertson to recommend evacuation. Most of Kitchener's colleagues, including Asquith, regarded Monro's recommendation as decisive ; but Kitchener rose to his full height for the last time, and said in Cabinet on 3 November that he would never consent.

Everyone expected that a vote would be taken, and most hoped that Kitchener would subsequently carry out his threat to resign. The

[1] *The World Crisis*, p. 511.

evacuation of Gallipoli seemed the logical corollary of the decision to send reinforcements to Salonica. But Kitchener was provoked by his colleagues' unconcealed anxiety to be rid of him ; and on a hint from Asquith he offered to go out immediately to the Dardanelles in order to advise about eastern strategy and make a personal report to the Cabinet.

That offer was accepted with acclamation by a Cabinet which had become inured to evading difficult decisions whenever possible. The dispatch of Kitchener to the Dardanelles postponed the need to decide immediately about Gallipoli as well as about a drastic change which was known to be impending at the War Office. Asquith had, on the previous day, abolished the Dardanelles Committee and substituted a much smaller streamlined War Committee consisting only of himself, Kitchener, Balfour, Sir Edward Grey and Lloyd George. The moment seemed opportune for reviewing Kitchener's position.

The Cabinet was fully convinced that, in the national interest, the control of war strategy would have to be taken out of Kitchener's hands. Bonar Law and Lloyd George had been pressing Asquith hard to dismiss Kitchener ; and on 1 November Asquith suggested to Bonar Law that the offices of Prime Minister and Secretary for War might again be combined, as they had been after the Curragh incident. Bonar Law wrote (2 November) that he could not accept that proposal because Asquith would find himself too grossly over-worked.

Lloyd George begged Asquith (31 October) to dismiss Kitchener without delay : ' Unless ,' he wrote,[1] ' there is a complete change in the War Office, the new Council will be just as impotent as the Cabinet and old Council have proved themselves.' In a long and rancid letter of complaint about Kitchener, Lloyd George attributed the ruin of the Balkans to the wrong advice which Kitchener had given in Cabinet, and the great military failures upon the Western Front to Kitchener's neglect and mishandling of the munitions problem.

Lloyd George emphasized that Kitchener had received repeated warnings that a German invasion of Serbia was being planned ; yet he had failed to take steps to meet it, or to alert his colleagues, or to inform himself that the enemy had crossed the Danube until twenty hours after the first telegrams announcing the crossings had been received in the War Office. He did not bother to read telegrams himself or to cause them to be circulated. The War Council had

[1] *War Memoirs*, I, pp. 514-18.

decided six months earlier that a plan should be prepared for a landing at Salonica in case of need :

'Kitchener never took the slightest notice of that decision ; and not even a mule had been bought for transport when the German blow fell on Serbia.

'The public may have delusions now about Kitchener, but the moment these facts are told in the House of Commons, I have very little doubt what will be thought, and said, by all sections.'

Asquith toyed with the idea of making Kitchener Viceroy of the East, with a watching brief over the Governments of India and Egypt ; or of giving him command of all troops in Asia and Africa. But he appreciated how personally dependent he was upon Kitchener's immense popular prestige for recruiting ; and he was doubtful of his ability to remain Prime Minister for long if he were to consent to Kitchener's supersession. He grasped, therefore, with thankfulness the opportunity to dispatch Kitchener to the Dardanelles ; and he wrote that evening to inform his angry colleague, Lloyd George, that he would take over the War Office, temporarily, while Kitchener was away in the East :

'I am confident that in the course of the next month I can put things there on a better footing.

'We avoid by this method of procedure the immediate supersession of K. as War Minister, while attaining the same result.'

During the next twenty-four hours Kitchener was to give further proof of that growing infirmity of purpose which had alarmed his colleagues. On the evening of 3 November he cabled to Birdwood in Gallipoli :

'I absolutely refuse to sign orders for evacuation, which I think would be the greatest disaster, and would condemn a large number of our men to death, or imprisonment.'

He ordered Birdwood to take over the command from Monro, who was to consider himself superseded :

'I shall come out to you ; am leaving to-morrow night.'

Kitchener added that there would probably be a change in the naval command and that a renewed naval attempt would be made to force the Narrows. He ordered Birdwood accordingly to prepare a plan at once for a new landing on the Bulair isthmus : 'All the best fighting men that could be spared, including your boys from Anzac, and everyone I can sweep up in Egypt, might be concentrated at Mudros, ready for this enterprise . . . We must do it right this time.'

That was the true Kitchener, and the voice of an authentic war lord ; and it is lamentable to have to record that within twenty-four hours that mood of resolution had evaporated. A long and unsatisfactory conference at the Admiralty during the morning of 4 November, and a further telegram from Birdwood during the afternoon, sufficed to dispel it.

Sir John de Robeck, who commanded the Fleet in the Mediterranean, opposed any fresh naval attempt to force the Narrows. But his second-in-command, Sir Rosslyn Wemyss, was eager to put into operation a daring plan which had been prepared by his Chief of Staff, Roger Keyes. De Robeck, accordingly, gave Keyes permission to go to London and plead his case at the Admiralty ; and Keyes saw Kitchener, together with Balfour and the Sea Lords, on 4 November at the Admiralty. Keyes at that time was a comparatively junior officer, and Balfour and the Sea Lords were not impressed by his proposals. In those circumstances, Kitchener's incoherent arguments in support of a naval plan which he had not studied and about which he was not competent to pronounce, failed to achieve their object.

That afternoon, Birdwood respectfully informed Kitchener that his proposal for a fresh landing on the Bulair isthmus was unsound. With the freedom of an established favourite, he ventured to beg Kitchener to reconsider his action in superseding Monro for the offence of having given uncongenial advice, because it was calculated to destroy confidence. Monro had been profoundly mortified by the Cabinet's decision to send Kitchener to the Dardanelles ; and Birdwood begged Kitchener to hold his hand until he reached Mudros.

In reply, late that evening, Kitchener tamely agreed to do nothing until he had met Birdwood. He warned him that naval help might not, after all, be available, and he added :

'I am coming as arranged . . . The more I look at it, the less I see my way through. So you had better, very quietly and secretly, work out any scheme for getting the troops off the Peninsula.'

After dispatching that telegram, Kitchener went to say good-bye to the King and then left for the Dardanelles. He took the characteristic precaution of carrying his seals of office with him, in the mistaken belief that no new appointment to the office of Secretary of State for War could be made in their absence. The clubs buzzed with gossip

361

that he was under a cloud and that he had visited the King in order to resign.

Kitchener frequently strolled over to Buckingham Palace for a chat with the King and he was never refused an audience. He liked and understood the King and felt relaxed in his company ; and during the last months of his life he depended more than he cared to admit upon the King's friendship, kindness and encouragement, while he was receiving fresh wounding tokens almost every day of his colleagues' distrust and hostility. On 6 November a London evening newspaper, *The Globe*, announced that Kitchener had seen the King in order to resign owing to differences with his colleagues.

The Globe was suppressed at once under the Defence of the Realm Act ; and when it reappeared a fortnight later it was required to state that there were ' no grounds of dissension between Kitchener and his colleagues such as to affect their future ministerial co-operation '. That action, by F. E. Smith, the Attorney-General, was almost tantamount to an admission by the Government that Kitchener's dismissal or resignation would have been calculated to cause disaffection ; and Kitchener was grateful to F. E. Smith, whom he described to FitzGerald as more congenial than most of his colleagues.

On 5 November, accompanied by FitzGerald, Kitchener appeared at the British Embassy in Paris ; and on that day Bonar Law had second thoughts about the consent which he had given in Cabinet to Kitchener's mission. He wrote to Asquith that, as Monro had already recommended evacuation, Kitchener's mission was superfluous ; and he threatened to resign if Kitchener were not at once recalled.

The Cabinet would have looked very foolish if it had acceded to Bonar Law's demand ; and it was glad to be rid of Kitchener for a time upon any terms. Bonar Law therefore found himself in a minority of one, and, in order to avert his resignation, Asquith invited him to join the new War Committee and told him, privately, that he personally now favoured evacuation, whatever Kitchener might report. It was fortunate that Kitchener never knew about that understanding, which virtually prejudged the issue of his mission ; but standing with his back to the fire in his room at the Embassy, and wearing the look of a wounded animal, Kitchener spoke [1] bitterly to Lord Esher about his colleagues' open hostility. When Esher mentioned that Lloyd George frequently complained about the Field-

[1] Esher, *Journals and Letters* (6 November, 1915), III, p. 276.

Marshal's lack of candour and methods of oriental secrecy, Kitchener exclaimed quite humbly :

" Yes. I suppose it is so. But I am an old man, and I cannot change my habits now. It is too late."

The French Government had fallen on 28 October ; and Kitchener had long conversations with the new Prime Minister, Aristide Briand, as well as with General Gallieni, the new Minister for War, and with Joffre, who had once served under Gallieni in Madagascar. On 5 November, Kitchener informed Asquith that Briand and Gallieni were so set upon the campaign in Macedonia that it was ' very difficult to get in a word. They simply sweep all military dangers out of the way, and go on political lines.' He added : ' As regards Gallipoli, they both said it would be a disaster of the first magnitude if we were to abandon our positions there.' Gallieni explained to Kitchener that the French feared a rising in North Africa as much as the British feared trouble in Egypt, if defeat were acknowledged in Gallipoli.

After borrowing, as liaison officer from Gallieni, an exceptionally handsome colonel who had been wounded in Gallipoli, Kitchener reached Mudros via Marseilles in the *Dartmouth* on the morning of 10 November. He was met by de Robeck and Birdwood, and his first words to Birdwood were :

" I can't tell you how glad I am to have you with me again, Birdie, and to be away from all those bloody politicians."

Birdwood also noted, ' I always remember how he squeezed my arm and pressed it. He was normally so very undemonstrative.'

Birdwood told Kitchener at once that his opposition to evacuation had been based upon political and not upon military grounds. He said that there was no reasonable chance of launching a successful offensive at Suvla, and that Anzac could not be held if Suvla were abandoned. De Robeck told Kitchener that he was unable to recommend ' any naval action to clear up the situation '.

After that frank exchange of views, Kitchener was piped aboard de Robeck's flagship, the *Lord Nelson*, where he was met by Sir Henry McMahon and Sir John Maxwell, the High Commissioner and the Commander-in-Chief in Egypt, as well as by Sir Charles Monro. Throughout the rest of 10 November and the whole of the following day Kitchener conferred with de Robeck, Birdwood, Monro, McMahon and Maxwell.

Strongly supported by McMahon and Maxwell, Kitchener over-estimated the dangers to which Egypt would be exposed after Gallipoli had been evacuated. He telegraphed his provisional conclusions to Asquith on the evening of 11 November. Subject to a full inspection of the Peninsula which he proposed to start the next day, he recommended that Helles should be held ; that Anzac and Suvla should be abandoned ; and that the troops from Anzac and Suvla should be transported to make a fresh landing in Ayas Bay, near Alexandretta, in the extreme north of Syria, in order to divert Turkish and German attention from Egypt and to cut Turkish rail communications. He said that Egypt could not be defended by standing meekly on the defensive.

Asquith was much startled by that sudden and unexpected proposal. He replied at once that he had consulted the General Staff, which held that Egypt could best be defended along the line of the Suez Canal. Exasperated by that rebuff, Kitchener in turn exasperated the War Committee by retorting :

' McMahon, Maxwell, and myself must be admitted to know the difficulties of defence in Egypt, and we are unanimously of opinion that your plan for carrying this out on the Canal is doomed to failure.'

A series of discordant telegrams followed. They showed that the General Staff as well as the Cabinet and War Committee had risen in revolt against Kitchener, who seemed temporarily to have lost his sense of proportion. He adhered obstinately to the view that the war, as well as Egypt, would be lost unless the abandonment of Gallipoli were offset immediately by the seizure of Alexandretta. He telegraphed (16 November) to Asquith :

' The decision about to be come to appears to me to have such a momentous effect on the future of the war, that I should like to place my opinion on record, as it may, I think, be a turning-point leading to the loss of the war by the Allies.'

In the meantime, on 12 November, Kitchener made a thorough inspection of the British and French positions at Helles. On 13 and 14 November he conducted similar inspections of the British positions at Suvla and Anzac. A heavy, plethoric man with scarlet cheeks, Kitchener, aged sixty-six, puffed painfully as he plodded methodically forward and upward. He seemed almost eager to be exposed to fire ; and he was at times only twenty yards from the enemy trenches. He was received everywhere with extraordinary enthusiasm, and he repeatedly told the troops : " You have done excellently well. Better even than I expected. I am commanded by the King to tell you how splendidly he thinks that you have done." He told the officers that, whatever the result, they could feel that they had been engaged upon operations which had been as important for the war as any which were being undertaken in France.

Kitchener awaited, without much hope, Asquith's final reply to his proposal for a landing near Alexandretta. It came on 19 November in the form of a curt and outright rejection. Kitchener was instructed to dismiss Alexandretta from his mind, and to confine his considered advice to the question of ' the evacuation of the Peninsula, in whole or in part '.

Kitchener received that message at Mudros after returning from a brief visit (17 November) to General Sarrail at Salonica. He was much impressed by the tall, blue-eyed and independent French general ; and Sarrail was favourably impressed by Kitchener. Sarrail explained that the Allied forces in Macedonia were meeting great difficulties in their futile efforts to help the Serbs, and he warned Kitchener that if the Greek Army became actively hostile 300,000 troops would be needed to guarantee the security of the Allied base at Salonica.

In an attempt at diplomacy, and with the consent of the War Committee, Kitchener sailed from Mudros in the *Lord Nelson* on the night of 19-20 November in order to interview King Constantine in Athens. He reached the palace shortly before noon on 20 November and said that his business was too urgent to admit of any delay. He was received in audience at once and he assured the King, in the course of a conversation which lasted an hour and a half, that the Allies had no intention of coercing Greece to enter the war upon their side. He explained that their forces had violated Greek neutrality for the sole purpose of aiding the Greeks to fulfil, if they so wished, their treaty obligations towards the Serbs.

In voluble English, and with many gesticulations, King Constantine denied that Venizelos had possessed authority to invite the Allied troops to land. But Kitchener insisted that they had come in response to a lawful invitation extended by a constitutional government. When the King reminded Kitchener that he was threatened by an army of a million Germans, Kitchener observed that the British Army would number four millions during the course of 1916. He added that he had no wish to threaten the King, or to inconvenience him or his government, but he asked him to remember that Great Britain was

365

fighting for her life, and that any action taken by the Greek Army against Allied troops would be treated as an act of war.

When the conversation ended at 1.30 p.m., Kitchener was not invited to stay to lunch. He managed, however, before he left, to extract a promise from the King that Allied troops retreating from the front through Greece to Salonica would not be disarmed or interned.

On returning to Mudros, Kitchener grasped the nettle and telegraphed (22 November) a brief final recommendation to Asquith that Anzac and Suvla should be evacuated and that Helles should be retained ' for the present '. He added that he proposed to return to London at once, and added : ' I personally can do no good in Egypt.'

That telegram was considered on 23 November by the War Committee ; and its members spent more time in devising an excuse for preventing Kitchener's return to England and in drafting a telegram to convey that wish to Kitchener in suitable but unmistakable terms, than it did in reaching a decision about evacuation.[1] The question of evacuation was referred to the Cabinet with a unanimous recommendation that the entire Peninsula, including Helles, should be given up.

In conveying that provisional decision to Kitchener, Asquith begged the Field-Marshal to reconsider his decision to return to England. He said that the evacuation would have to be conducted by stages, in accordance with the judgement of the commander on the spot ; and that it was the unanimous hope of the War Council and Cabinet that Kitchener would feel inclined to visit Egypt, and to remain there, radiating confidence, while ' the moral effect ' of evacuation was being felt.

Kitchener knew well that his colleagues were anxious to relegate him permanently to the East. But he notified Asquith categorically (24 November) that he was returning at once :

' . . . I feel very strongly that I should be back in England, as time is passing and I can do no good here. I have arranged with McMahon to quieten the effect in Egypt as far as possible. If necessary I could go out again. My presence here calls attention to what is going on.'

After dispatching that telegram, Kitchener started for home immediately without allowing time for a possible reply. He travelled by way of Brindisi and Rome ; and he paid a brief visit on his way to the Italian front. He had talks with Italian Ministers ; he was decorated by King Victor Emmanuel ; and he found time to visit

[1] Cf. Sir William Robertson, *Soldiers and Statesmen*, I, p. 141.

366

shops in Rome and to make a number of purchases for Broome. He told the British Ambassador, Sir Rennel Rodd, whom he knew well, that he was at odds with most of his colleagues and that he might resign on reaching London.

Kitchener reached London on 30 November, after lunching with the French President in Paris on the previous day. He went straight to Downing Street and placed his resignation in the hands of Asquith, who firmly refused to accept it.

After telling Kitchener that a few sections of the War Office had been transferred, during his absence, to the Ministry of Munitions, Asquith asked Kitchener to allow the C.I.G.S. in future to replace the Secretary of State as the Government's principal adviser on military strategy. He made no attempt to deny that his colleagues had lost confidence in Kitchener's handling of strategic questions ; but he begged Kitchener to remember, nevertheless, that he alone stood between the armies and political chaos ; that he was the symbol of the nation's will to victory ; and that he would betray his duty to the armies, to the public and to the King, if he refused to return to his post.

That appeal to Kitchener's sense of duty was successful ; and Kitchener selflessly accepted the humiliating conditions which Asquith proposed. He resumed control only of War Office administration and of recruiting ; and his pride was constantly wounded by the knowledge that the colleagues who distrusted him and who sought to make him a scapegoat, were dependent upon his presence in their midst for much of the public confidence which sustained them in office.

Asquith informed Kitchener that on 25 November Sir John French had been notified that he was to be recalled and superseded by Sir Douglas Haig. He suggested that Kitchener should see Sir John's C.G.S., Sir William Robertson, who, he said, happened to be in London, in order to discuss the possibility of persuading Robertson to accept the post of C.I.G.S. at the War Office, with its greatly enhanced responsibilities, when French laid down his command. Kitchener accepted that hint also and he asked Robertson to dine with him at York House that evening.

When Kitchener returned home, the Cabinet had not yet taken its final decision about evacuating the Dardanelles. Curzon headed a die-hard section which was resolved to oppose that step until the last, on political and imperial grounds ; and breaking a silence of many years, Curzon wrote privately (12 December) to beg Kitchener to

reconsider, in the light of ' wider imperial interests ,' the recommendation to evacuate which he had made already upon military grounds.

The command of the Mediterranean Fleet had devolved upon Sir
Rosslyn Wemyss when de Robeck surrendered it on 25 November on
account of ill health. Wemyss had consistently favoured a renewal
of the naval attack, and, prodded by Roger Keyes, he now strongly
pressed that policy upon the Admiralty.

Kitchener, in those circumstances, confused the Cabinet by wobbling
again when he presented his final report on 2 December. He noted
that since his telegram recommending evacuation upon military
grounds had been dispatched on 22 November, the failure of the
British attack upon Baghdad had increased the danger of a catastrophic
collapse of British prestige throughout the Orient. He observed also
that as the Cabinet had been unable to make up its mind about sending
reinforcements to Salonica, he felt entitled to assume that Salonica
might be abandoned, and that troops might in consequence be available
for shipment to the Dardanelles from Macedonia. He concluded :

' I cannot go back on the military opinion I have stated . . . but
. . . should the Government decide to take this risk and remain on the
Peninsula, every soldier, and none more than myself, will do their
utmost to bring off the long odds that are now against us.'

That evening Kitchener gave far more striking proof of that crippling irresolution which had practically destroyed his usefulness in
council. Monro had pointed out to him by telegram on 1 December
that ' if evacuation is to be made possible, it is essential to take advantage
of every fine day from now. If decision cannot be reached very
shortly, it may be equivalent to deciding against evacuation.'
Kitchener replied (2 December) :

' Cabinet has been considering Gallipoli situation all to-day. Owing to the political consequences, there is a strong feeling against
evacuation, even of a partial character. It is the general opinion that
we should retain Cape Helles.

' If the Salonica troops are placed at your disposal up to four divisions for an offensive operation to improve the position at Suvla, could
such operations be carried out in time with a view to making Suvla
retainable by obtaining higher positions and greater depth ?

' The navy will also take the offensive in co-operation.'

Much of the blame for that lamentable display of indecision can
ultimately be attributed to the Government's failure to devise a
workable machinery of strategic control. But Kitchener's personal

attempt to control strategy reached its nadir when he dispatched that telegram. Everyone loathed the need to admit defeat in the Dardanelles ; and Kitchener's position would have been impregnable if he had resigned after refusing to countenance evacuation, or if he had adhered steadfastly to the considered advice to evacuate which he had tendered after making a personal inspection of the Peninsula. But the constant shilly-shallying which caused that last despairing appeal to Monro to reverse an opinion, which he had consistently maintained, tortured everyone who read it. It was the act of a passenger in a feeble team, rather than that of a leader of men in a critical situation ; and it proved its author's unfitness to remain the Government's principal adviser upon strategy. Kitchener's self-chosen motto of ' Thorough ' was applicable only when circumstances, in all their aspects, could be digested by a single mind. He seemed incapable of maintaining his poise when confronted for any length of time by imponderables.

On 3 December, Monro informed Kitchener that the proposal to employ fresh divisions at Suvla offered ' no reasonable chance of success ' ; that the divisions from Salonica could not be ready ' until storm weather sets in ' ; that the vital element of surprise could not be achieved ; and that the terrain at Suvla was unsuitable for naval co-operation. In those circumstances the Cabinet reached a typical compromise on 7 December, when it resolved that Suvla and Anzac should be evacuated and that Helles should be retained. Even then Sir Rosslyn Wemyss protested in strident terms to the Admiralty. He described the proposed evacuation in a telegram (8 December) to Balfour as ' disastrous, tactically and strategically . . . I am convinced that the time is ripe for a vigorous offensive, and I am confident of success.'

Suvla and Anzac were evacuated without loss on 18 and 19 December, 1915 ; and Sir William Robertson's first act on becoming C.I.G.S. was to insist upon the evacuation of Helles. The Cabinet agreed on 27 December, and that operation also was effected without loss on 8 January, 1916. All troops from Gallipoli were withdrawn to Egypt, whence they were shipped to France, after some months.

Loos and the Dardanelles had finally destroyed Kitchener's credit with his colleagues ; and on 23 December, four days after Haig replaced French in command of the army in France, Sir William Robertson assumed the post of C.I.G.S. in the War Office, with direct access to the Cabinet and War Committee. He took over from Kitchener the duty of acting as the Government's principal

369

adviser on military strategy, and he took the precaution of dictating his terms to Kitchener in a formal document.

Robertson, who had previously hardly known Kitchener, declined absolutely to become C.I.G.S. unless the General Staff were freed from subordination to a Secretary of State who happened also to be the senior serving Field-Marshal. Kitchener begged Robertson to discount current gossip about his autocratic methods, but Robertson asked for leave to set down on paper what, in his opinion, the duties of the C.I.G.S. ought, in future, to be. Kitchener assented, and one copy of that paper was sent to him, and another to the Prime Minister, on 5 December. The three vital paragraphs were :

' In order that the War Council may be able to reach timely decisions . . . it is essential that it should receive *all* advice on matters concerning military operations through one authoritative channel only. With us that channel must be the Chief of the Imperial General Staff . . .

' All orders for the military operations required to put into execution the approved policy should be signed and issued by the Chief of the Imperial General Staff, under the authority of the War Council, and *not* under that of the Army Council. Similarly, all communications from General Officers Commanding regarding military operations should be addressed to the Chief of the Imperial General Staff . . .

' The Secretary of State for War is responsible for the raising, maintenance and equipment of the forces which the policy of the War Council makes necessary. This is of itself a task of great magnitude in the circumstances in which we are placed, and the Secretary of State for War can therefore be connected with actual military operations only on the same footing as any other member of the War Council.'

In acknowledging (7 December) that ' frank letter ', Kitchener informed Robertson that he had advised the Prime Minister ' to accept your terms ' which nevertheless made it necessary for him to resign. He explained that he was unable ' to retain the responsibility of S. of S. without any executive work as regards the war, and with my functions curtailed to the feeding and clothing of the army. The Munitions Ministry now do all the rest '. Kitchener added :

' This change comes at a suitable time, as you know I told my

370

Kitchener with General Birdwood in Gallipoli and at Mudros, 1915

Kitchener leaving the War Office before his journey to Russia, June, 1916

colleagues I should be unable to remain responsible as S. of S. if the troops were kept at Salonica, and this is apparently what is to happen.

'I suggested to the P. M. that Derby might become S. of S. . . .'

The allied forces at Salonica were not withdrawn; they were, in fact, greatly augmented as time went on; but Asquith succeeded again in an appeal which he made to Kitchener's sense of duty. He persuaded Kitchener not to resign, on account either of disagreement with the Government's Salonica policy or with the terms which Robertson had dictated. The Prime Minister told Robertson that his first paragraph secured everything that was essential.

Kitchener objected to the second paragraph on the ground that it deprived the Secretary for War of a constitutional duty to answer to Parliament for the actions of the General Staff, and Robertson reluctantly altered it to read:

'All orders for the military operations required to put into execution the policy approved by the War Council should be issued and signed by the Chief of the Imperial General Staff, under the authority of the Secretary of State for War . . .'

The third paragraph, with its wounding references to Kitchener's curtailed authority, was deleted as unnecessary; and for the brief remainder of his life Kitchener ceased to interfere with strategy. He observed that compact which he had concluded with Robertson in the spirit as well as in the letter. He wrote to Asquith (10 December) from Paris, where, with Sir Edward Grey, he had attended a conference on the military situation in Macedonia:

'I met Robertson at Calais and brought him on here. We have had several long talks and have settled the difficulties raised by his letter, so it is all right about his being C.I.G.S . . . I feel he and I can work well together.'

He said that he had met French, who was feeling 'very bitter about Haig', but added that there was 'no unpleasant feeling' between French and himself.

Kitchener was extremely tired as he entered upon the last twilight months of his career. Defeats and disappointments had affected his health and spirits, and he began to wear the pinched look of an old man. One of the minor conditions which Robertson had thought fit to impose upon Kitchener in the agreement which governed their relationship, read: 'The Chief of the Imperial General Staff must . . . have sufficient leisure to think quietly out the many difficult problems which are continually arising, and also to keep himself thoroughly fit in mind and body.'

Exhausted as he was, Kitchener rallied magnificently, and confronted with an equal mind the colleagues who sought to make him a scapegoat for all failures, and the masses who acclaimed blindly his every act and word : ' Rightly or wrongly,' he told Haig (12 February, 1916), ' probably wrongly, the people believe in me. It is not, therefore, me that the politicians are afraid of, but of what the people would say to them if I were to go.' So Kitchener continued to inspire national unity, and the people had no inkling until many months after his death that a serious crisis had occurred in the central direction of the war.

Kitchener's relations with Haig were always as close and happy as his relations remained with the King. He paid many visits to G.H.Q., and was invariably received by a guard of honour—a courtesy which Sir John French had strictly forbidden. He sometimes confided to Haig his suspicions of French policy, and he told [1] him (29 March, 1916) that French enthusiasm for the Salonica expedition proved that they were pursuing private political ambitions in the eastern Mediterranean, and that they no longer intended to fight the Germans actively upon the Western Front. In the instructions which he issued to Haig (28 December, 1915), Kitchener wrote :

' The closest co-operation of French and British as a united army must be the governing policy ; but I wish you distinctly to understand that your command is an independent one, and that you will in no case come under the orders of any Allied General.'

The appointments of Haig and Robertson represented a triumph for the Westerners. It implied concentration upon the Western Front and dedication to a war of attrition ; and Asquith and Kitchener gave that policy their whole-hearted support. So preparations for the vast British offensive upon the Somme, which was launched after Kitchener's death, were pressed steadily forward. They were delayed only by the need to render some assistance to the French while the Germans hurled themselves against Verdun from 21 February to 31 August, 1916. Little attention was paid to the views of Lloyd George and his supporters, who demanded a more imaginative approach to strategy, until the last reverberating echoes of the great Battle of the Somme (1 July to 18 November, 1916) had died away into a third war winter of profound depression and discontent.

[1] Blake, *The Private Papers of Douglas Haig, 1914–1919*, p. 136.

Problems of man-power and finance preoccupied Kitchener during the last five months of his life. He wanted to put 70 divisions into the field during 1916, and to maintain a continuous offensive upon the Western Front in order to force the Germans to sue for peace before the end of the year. He warned his colleagues that the Allies would be unable to endure the strain if the war were prolonged into 1917, and that the war would probably be lost and the Empire dissolved unless the man-power and the money were found to hurl 70 divisions into offensive operations as soon as possible.

The man-power problem was solved, without either wrecking the Cabinet or splitting the Liberal Party, when Asquith, under the strongest pressure from Kitchener as well as from Lloyd George and Bonar Law, announced on 2 May, 1916, that he intended to conscript all able-bodied men between the ages of 18 and 41. That Bill, which passed rapidly through all its stages, received the royal assent on 25 May ; but those who most disliked the necessity for conscription had found, as early as January, a means by which, in Kitchener's opinion, they hoped either to prevent the Bill's introduction or at least to block its effects.

Reginald McKenna, Chancellor of the Exchequer, and Walter Runciman, President of the Board of Trade, declared early in January that the country could not afford to pay for an army of 70 divisions ; and that the Army must therefore be reduced in size by 13 divisions to save an annual expenditure of 60 million pounds. They argued that, if Kitchener's goal were realized, industry would be crippled and that it would be impossible for the Government to continue to pay subsidies to its allies.

Kitchener was careful until the last to keep in step with Asquith upon the subject of conscription. He frequently told his personal staff that he had lived too much abroad to be able to gauge the needs of industry or the mood of the trade unions. That was the business of the politicians ; but he was at no pains to conceal the disgust and contempt with which he regarded McKenna and Runciman, and he equated their arguments with low intrigue and sabotage.

On 14 January, 1916, Kitchener wrote to Haig :

' McKenna and Runciman are making a determined attack on the number of divisions I have formed for the field, because they say we cannot afford them in either men withdrawn from trade or money. When one looks at the streets full of loafers, and sees the extravagance going on in all Departments of Government, and in the Country, their statements are given the lie.

'There is no doubt a strong feeling against another offensive in France, owing to the failures hitherto. But, unless we can impose a peace by force of arms this year, we shall run a terrible risk of an unsatisfactory stalemate peace which will certainly necessitate hostilities again in about 5 years . . .

'Robertson is fighting splendidly, but has his work cut out for him by the politicians.'

Kitchener wrote equally strongly to Asquith (11 January). He said that 'the country as a whole is not yet feeling the pinch'; that there should be no difficulty in finding an extra sixty million pounds; and that 'unless we make every effort this year we may either lose the war, or drift into a dangerous peace'. He threatened more than once to resign, before he was given what he asked; and he flared up for the last time in April, 1916, when Asquith blamed him unfairly for certain shortages of men at the front. The Prime Minister suggested that they were 'due to the failure of the military authorities to carry out the directions given some months ago by the War Committee'.

The shortages were due, in fact, to the delay which had occurred in accepting Kitchener's demands. Esher had warned Kitchener in February that he was deceiving himself in trusting to Asquith's friendship; and Kitchener, whose patience was severely strained, wrote curtly (12 April) to the Prime Minister:

'I do not know of any directions of the War Committee that have not been carried out as far as possible by the military authorities.

'If, however, you are not satisfied with the manner in which military affairs for which I am responsible are conducted, I should be glad if you would allow me to resign.'

Only a burning sense of duty held Kitchener chained to his post during those last few months of bitter humiliation. The unparalleled dichotomy between the people's adoration of its idol and the contemptuous indifference which the Cabinet displayed towards its Secretary for War, haunted Kitchener's waking hours and caused him mental anguish. The war was everywhere going badly for the Allies, and Kitchener ached for Egypt and the desert peoples whom he understood. The world thought him insensitive, but there were times when he broke down and wept on receiving tidings of the deaths in battle of younger men whom he had known and loved. He wrote in August, 1915, to Lady Desborough after two of her sons had fallen in action in France : ' We all wish sometimes that the trumpet would sound for us, but we have to stick it out and do our very best until the release comes. I only wish that I could do more, or rather that what I do was better work.'

Kitchener wasted no time in speculative brooding about the outcome of the war ; but he never swerved from the broad view which he had formed privately at the outset, that victory was doubtful without the military intervention of the United States. He did not publish that view, and he believed that such aid would ultimately be forthcoming. For that reason he granted privileges to Americans, whenever he could, which he denied to all other neutrals. In November, 1914, for example, when neutral military attachés were rigorously barred from the battle zones, he dispatched secretly, without consulting the Foreign Office, Colonel G. O. Squier, the Military Attaché of the United States, to France. He gave Squier *carte blanche* to go wherever he pleased and to stay as long as he chose ; and he authorized him to draw English gold in unlimited quantities from any Army paymaster.

During the last weeks of his life Kitchener exerted himself to find suitable employment for the Prince of Wales. He had been attracted by the boy's intense eagerness to go into action with the Grenadier Guards at the start of the war, and by his plea that he had four brothers to take his place if he were killed. Kitchener told the Prince that he might allow him to take his chance of being killed, but that he would not accept the risk of his being taken prisoner before a settled line was established.

Kitchener allowed the Prince to serve in France as soon as a line was established, but he insisted that he should be employed on the Staff. The Prince complained that his employment was artificial, and it proved impossible to keep him out of the front line whenever he had the opportunity to go anywhere near it. In the spring of 1916 the Prince was sent to Egypt, and Kitchener instructed him to report personally about the situation in the Sudan.

That report (18 April) was, of course, a mere formal exercise ; but in Kitchener's mind it revived grateful memories of the Sudan which he had redeemed from barbarism, and of the culminating victory over the dervish host which he had planned and won. That was the warfare which he had understood and loved, and he began to long for a chance

375

to leave the country again for a time, in order to put himself temporarily out of reach of the renewed wave of hostile criticism of his War Office administration which reached its height during April and May, and which led to a formal motion in the House of Commons on 31 May, 1916, that his salary should be reduced by a token sum of £100.

On 13 May, Kitchener received through the Russian Embassy a personal invitation from the Czar to visit Russia. Kitchener had maintained a long correspondence with the Grand Duke Nicholas —a huge man, with an enormous, prominent tooth—who had been the Russian Commander-in-Chief until 5 September, 1915, when he was succeeded by the Czar himself. It was suggested that Kitchener should visit the Russian fronts; that he should offer such advice as he thought fit; and that he should report to his own Government about outstanding questions of military co-operation and supply.

Kitchener replied warmly to the Ambassador (15 May) that 'nothing would give me greater pleasure than to visit Russia'. He said, however, that he would first have to consult the King and the Prime Minister. Consultations took place, and it was found that, as at the time of his visit to the Dardanelles, Kitchener's colleagues were as happy to see him depart as he was to say good-bye to them for some weeks. On 26 May, accordingly, Kitchener informed the Ambassador that he accepted the Czar's invitation.

Before he left the country, Kitchener took a somewhat unusual step in an effort to meet his critics on the back benches of the House of Commons. Through the mouth of his Under-Secretary, H. J. Tennant, he offered (31 May) to vindicate his administration of the War Office personally to any Members of Parliament who cared to visit him at the War Office at 11.30 a.m. on Friday, 2 June. He said that he would give, in confidence, 'information on points of difficulty where it may properly be given'; and he asked that members wishing to take advantage of that offer should give their names to their Whips.

While he held office, Kitchener spoke in the House of Lords a bare dozen times in twenty-two months. That average of just over once in two months was uniquely low, and so many Members of Parliament announced their intention of hearing him speak on 2 June, that the meeting had to be transferred from the War Office to a large committee room at the House of Commons. It was held in the shadow cast by the great but disappointing Battle of Jutland.

Kitchener was accompanied by Sir William Robertson, who was unkindly described as his bear-leader by one of the junior Ministers.

But Kitchener was entirely at his ease and he took members into his confidence at once. He began by remarking that " My previous work in life has naturally not been of a kind to make me into a ready debater, nor to prepare me for the various turns and twists of argument . . . Members will overlook any of my shortcomings in this respect."

In the course of a plain factual defence of his administration of the War Office, Kitchener made a deft reference to Lloyd George :

" You will realize what a relief it was to me when the Ministry of Munitions was formed and put under the able hand of the then Chancellor of the Exchequer. He and I have ever been in loyal co-operation, and from the day he took charge there has not been a single cause of friction between us."

Kitchener said that he had refrained from giving a lead about conscription because :

" The question of a social change involving the whole country and running counter to the most ancient traditions of the British people, is not a matter for a department to decide. My task, and that of the War Office, was to find men, clothe them, arm them, and organize them. So long as sufficient men came in, it was not my duty to ask for special means of obtaining men."

He ended his speech with an appeal to members to stop asking foolish or unnecessary questions in the House ; and he concluded :

" Many questions which only take a moment to put down, and are not matters of first-class importance, mean the diversion of brains and energy from work which must be well done to be done at all."

That soldierly speech, and its confident delivery, straight from the shoulder by the remote and formidable monolith whom few members had ever met, evoked round upon round of applause ; and Kitchener, after answering a number of questions, enjoyed an immense and entirely unexpected personal triumph. Purring with satisfaction, he dropped Robertson at the War Office, and then motored first to Downing Street and afterwards to Buckingham Palace, where he related his story with the gusto of a schoolboy to Asquith and to the King. He had, in fact, carried his difficult audience the whole way with him, and Asquith noted [1] that Kitchener ' left the room, gay, alert, elastic, sanguine. I never saw him again '.

[1] *Memories and Reflections*, II, p. 84.

After lunching with the King on Saturday, 3 June, Kitchener went to Broome with FitzGerald for the night. He worked on Sunday morning in his sunken rose-garden where he had personally designed a special fountain embellished with nymphs and sea-monsters to be placed in a central grass square. He had arranged for four pairs of boys, designed by J. H. Bonner, to stand at the four corners of that square ; and in the modelling of those bronze figures Kitchener had taken a boyish delight. The first pair were running ; the second wrestling ; the third embracing ; and the fourth dancing. All four pairs of figures, which had already been cast, were shown after the war at *The Daily Mail* Ideal Home Exhibition.

On the afternoon of Sunday, 4 June, Kitchener motored from Broome to the War Office, where he signed a number of official papers, and also wrote to authorize his partner, Major Leggett, to turn their property in Kenya into a private company. He then took the night train from King's Cross to Thurso, on his way to Scapa Flow. The official party consisted of Field-Marshal Earl Kitchener of Khartoum, K.G., K.P., P.C., G.C.B., O.M., G.C.S.I., G.C.M.G., G.C.I.E., Secretary of State for War ; Colonel O. A. G. FitzGerald, C.M.G., Personal Military Secretary to Lord Kitchener ; Sir Frederick Donaldson, K.C.B., Technical Adviser to the Ministry of Munitions ; L. S. Robertson, assistant to Sir F. Donaldson ; H. J. O'Beirne, C.B., Counsellor at the British Embassy in Petrograd ; Brigadier-General W. Ellershaw ; Second-Lieutenant R. D. Macpherson ; a cipher clerk ; three servants ; and Kitchener's personal detective.

On the morning of 5 June Kitchener was conveyed with his staff on the destroyer *Oak* to the *Iron Duke*, the flagship of Sir John Jellicoe. After lunching with Jellicoe and touring the ship, Kitchener left at 4.15 p.m. and went at once with his party on board the *Hampshire* (Captain H. J. Savill, R.N.), which had been detailed to convey him to Archangel. The weather was extremely bad and a heavy north-easterly gale was worsening ; but Kitchener, who was an excellent sailor, rejected Jellicoe's suggestion that his departure should be delayed.

The *Hampshire* sailed, accordingly, at a few minutes before 5 p.m. On Jellicoe's orders she took the route westward of the Pentland Firth and close to the western coast of the Orkneys. She was escorted by the destroyers *Unity* and *Victor* until about 7 p.m., when the Captain of the *Hampshire* detached the escort on account of the very heavy seas which had already caused the cruiser to be partially bat-

tened down. At approximately 7.40 p.m., when about a mile and
a half off Marwick Head, the *Hampshire* struck a mine which had been
laid by the German submarine U.75 (Lieut.-Commander Kurt
Beitzen) on the night of 28–29 May, when the German High Seas
Fleet had been preparing to come out in order to challenge the British
Grand Fleet in the battle which is known to the Germans as Skaggerak
and to the British as Jutland. The German object had been to hamper
the British concentration by mining the exits from Scapa Flow.

The *Hampshire* heeled over to starboard, settled down by the head,
and sank within a quarter of an hour. Some dozen survivors only
reached a wild and inhospitable coast with cliffs rising sheer out of
the sea ; and they gave no coherent account of Kitchener's movements
during the few moments which elapsed between the explosion and
the sinking of the cruiser. Kitchener, who was seen by one survivor
in the gunroom flat immediately after the explosion, was extremely
sensitive to cold ; he probably kept on his heavy greatcoat and choked
to death among the first in the angry waters. FitzGerald's body was
washed ashore, but Kitchener's was devoured by the Atlantic.

The news reached London on the morning of 6 June and was published at about midday. The journey to Russia had been a closely-
guarded secret ; and a sense of awed numbness gripped the land.
Messages of grief and condolence poured into London from every
corner of the allied and neutral worlds.

Strange rumours at once began to circulate that Kitchener was not
really dead. They were foolishly encouraged by his sister, Mrs.
Parker, and it was said that Kitchener had been betrayed to the Germans ; that he was a prisoner ; or that he had been spirited away to
a cave in some remote island of the Hebrides where he lay plunged,
like King Arthur or Barbarossa, into an enchanted sleep from which
he would presently awake. The subconscious minds of a surprisingly
large section of the semi-educated masses recoiled, irrationally, from
the need to accept the fact that their deified hero could share the
common lot of death without jeopardizing the cause which he sym-
bolically embodied.

The masses acclaimed Kitchener as a man of action ; but he possessed
few of the attributes of a Kipling hero. Between the Battle of the
Atbara in 1898 and the landing on Gallipoli in 1915, on both of which
occasions he was painfully and exceptionally hesitant, he was only
once required to display that faculty of instant decision which is the
signature of a man of action ; and on that unique occasion, at the

379

Battle of Paardeberg, he charged bull-headed, and suffered a humiliating defeat.

The professional middle class acclaimed Kitchener's alleged genius for administration ; but he was useless for teamwork, upon which all administration is founded. He was an individualist of great conceptions, whose hard and selfish nature was capable, at times, of kindness, sympathy and even affection. His two basic attributes were an unparalleled thoroughness, and an unparalleled drive.

Kitchener's thoroughness constrained him to swing his boot into any system of administration and to rend in pieces any established chain of command. His system was, in reality, the negation of any system ; and his drive prompted him inexorably to centralize every species of authority in himself. After he had done so, he performed miracles of improvisation, and extracted from subordinates whom he trusted and occasionally loved much more than they or anyone else believed that they had to give.

Kitchener developed his twin authoritarian attributes to an unique pitch of obsessional intensity. They combined to form an imposing personality which lifted him high above his fellows ; but they were stultified in conditions which made it impossible for Kitchener personally to subdue the minds of those with whom he worked, and to weigh accurately all the facts with which he was confronted. For that reason he hated teamwork as much as he feared imponderable factors ; and his proportions were drastically reduced as soon as he was confronted with the divergent opinions of a number of independent colleagues, or with the incalculable intentions of an equal enemy, or with a problem of transcendent complexity such as that of munitions.

Within a few months of Kitchener's death his executors approached the Chancellor of the Exchequer, Bonar Law, about a parliamentary grant towards the cost of completing the alterations at Broome Park in accordance with the plans of the fallen Field-Marshal. Bonar Law advised them that the proposal was inopportune and that it would excite opposition and controversy. The executors, therefore, decided to await the end of the war, when it was hoped that Parliament and the nation would be in a more appreciative mood. After the victory, however, when the services of many of the nation's leaders on sea and land were generously rewarded, Kitchener was ignored ; and his name and achievements seemed already to have receded into some remote perspective of history.

Egypt, which Kitchener ruled with such relish, and the Sudan which he conquered have thrown off the reins which he handled so confidently. South Africa, which he also conquered, has forgotten his appeal to Boer and Briton. In India and Pakistan the echo of dead controversy about dual control falls upon the ear like something out of Homer or the Old Testament. Few people trouble to-day to visit the memorial chapel which was dedicated in his memory, at the heart of the Empire which he served, in St. Paul's Cathedral on 10 December, 1925 ; and his beloved Broome has become an hotel, in which the coroneted ceilings and entwined ' K.K.' monograms on the walls appear to mock the honourable ambition of the man who gutted its interior, laid out its gardens, and planned to fill it with masterpieces of western and eastern art before handing it down through his eldest brother's son as a seat which should enshrine his name for centuries.

Nevertheless, Kitchener was fortunate in life and in death. The mould which produced him was not broken until his place in history was assured. His strenuous life of service on the frontiers of Empire provided the puritanical conscience of a rich but increasingly rootless and unsatisfied bourgeoisie at the centre with a species of vicarious atonement for a subconscious sense of guilt as it plunged ever more deeply into material pursuits and pleasures which helped to precipitate the catastrophe of 1914.

In that way Kitchener became a legend during his lifetime. He subdued the hearts and minds of uncounted millions of men and women as he worked out the vivid pattern of a military proconsular career during the years of Great Britain's imperial apogee. At the moment when that pattern became too complex to be extended or unravelled, the signature of a soldier's death crowned the work and brought release.

INDEX

INDEX

Ababda Frontier Force, 43, 53
Ababda Tribe, 43, 46
Abadai, 132
Abbas Hilmi II, *see* Khedive
Abdullahi, Khalifa, *see* Khalifa
Abu Hamed, 43, 51, 55, 101, 103, 104, 105, 106, 111, 116
Abu Klea, 60, 62
Abyssinia, 90, 101-2
Acre, 17, 19
Addis Ababa, 90, 101
Adelaide, 244
Adowa, Battle of, 90
Adrianople, 20, 21
Afghanistan, 64-5, 197, 199, 200, 220
Africa, 42, 64, 287, 360; colonial scramble for, 69, 81
Africa, British East, *see* Kenya
Africa, South, 152-8, 182-96, 198, 201, 231, 245, 288, 381
Ahmed, Mohammed, *see* Mahdi
Aisne, R., 298
Akasha, 95, 96
Alanbrooke, F.-M. Viscount, 235
Albany, H.R.H. Duchess of, 69
Alcester, Lord, *see* Seymour, Admiral Sir Beauchamp
Aldershot, Kitchener's dislike of, 11; Kitchener increases Anglo-Catholic congregation at, 11; Kitchener revisits, 144. Mentioned, 160, 199
Aldworth, Lieut.-Col. W. A., 167-8
Alexandretta, 309, 313, 314, 315, 364, 365
Alexandria, riot in, 32; bombardment of, 34. Mentioned, 32, 33, 36, 254, 270, 277, 314, 327, 328, 338
Algeria, 32
Aliab, 119
Amara, 46
Ambukol, 49, 55, 56
America, opening up by railroads of, 3; American intervention in First World War, 375; American imperialism, 26; American Civil War, 291. Mentioned, 156
Amery, L. S., 170

Amiens, 280, 281
Ampthill, Lord, Governor of Madras, 214
Anatolia, 28, 29, 30, 43
Anglo-French Middle East Agreement (1915), 314
Anglo-Turkish Convention, 27
Antwerp, 304, 328
Anzac Cove, 345-6, 358, 360, 363, 364, 366, 369
Anzacs, 320, 322; in Gallipoli, 323, 324, 345-6
Aqaba, 38
Arabah Valley, 38, 39, 40
Arabi, Colonel, 31-2, 33, 34, 35
Archangel, 378
Ardennes, 280, 292
Army (*see also* British Expeditionary Force), unpopularity of, 2; new importance of, 3; composition of forces in South Africa, 158; lack of trained staff officers in, 160, 170; Kitchener reports on, 195; Kitchener's views on reorganization of, 198; army reform, 174-6, 196, 198-203, 206, 233; creation of Territorials, *see* Territorial Army; Kitchener undertakes to build new army, 283-4; call for volunteers, 288-9; 'Kitchener Armies', 290, 303, 305-6, 309, 365; conditions in, 299; provision for religious denominations in, 299-300; in Dardanelles campaign, 324; problems of supply, 331-2; voluntary recruiting begins to fail in, 352-3; Compulsory Service Act, *see* Conscription; difficulties of financing, 373-4
Arnold-Forster, H. O., 215, 228
Ashanti, 11
Ashridge, 195
Asia Minor, 23, 24, 26, 29, 314
Aspall Hall, 1; part of Kitchener title, 137, 191
Asquith, H. H., 1st Earl of Oxford and Asquith, on cession of Cyprus to Greece, 313-14; on imperialism,

385

314 ; on Dardanelles, 319, 342 ; fall of his government, 339 ; declares confidence in Kitchener, 341 ; visits troops with Kitchener, 345 ; supports Kitchener against Bonar Law and Lloyd George, 351 ; finds Kitchener congenial, 351 ; views on conscription, 352-4 ; rejects Kitchener's plans for Gallipoli, 365. Mentioned, 239, 246-7, 250, 253, 277, 278, 280, 281, 282, 283, 286, 288, 289, 295, 299, 302, 304, 305, 307, 309, 312, 317, 321, 333, 334, 335, 338, 340, 341, 343, 344, 347, 350, 358, 359, 360, 371, 372, 374, 377
Asquith, Mrs. (afterwards Countess of Oxford), lionizes Kitchener, 258 ; 289
Assyria, 31
Aswan, 43, 76, 84, 116 ; Aswan Dam, 83, 196, 268
Ataturk, see Kemal, Mustafa
Atbara, River, 118, 119, 379 ; Battle of, 120-3, 165, 379
Athenæum Club, 282
Athens, 365
Auckland, 245
Australia, 247 ; Kitchener's tour of, 240, 244 ; Kitchener reports on defence of, 244-5
Austria-Hungary, Kitchener's visit to, 11 ; and Egyptian finance, 64 ; war with Italy, 340 ; in First World War, 356. Mentioned, 275, 309, 313

Babylonia, 31
Baden-Powell, Lieut.-Gen. Sir Robert (afterwards Lord), 157, 178
Bahgdad, 315, 368
Baker, (Mary) Hermione, 66
Baker, Sir Samuel, friendship with Kitchener, 30 ; high opinion of Kitchener, 49, 58. Mentioned, 63, 66
Baker, Valentine (Pasha), 21, 66
Baker, Mrs. Valentine, 66
Balfour, Arthur (afterwards Earl of), opinion of Kitchener, 142 ; Kitchener stays with, 195 ; on War Council, 286, 309 ; First Lord, 340 ; on Dardanelles

Committee, 342 ; on War Committee, 359. Mentioned, 143, 197, 207, 209, 213, 215, 220, 227, 230, 240, 336, 343, 344, 350, 357, 361, 369
Balkans, 287, 309, 343, 356, 359 ; Balkan War, 331
Ballygoghlan, 4-5
Balmoral, 142, 195, 252, 260, 271
Baltic, 287, 319
Baring, Sir Evelyn, see Cromer, 1st Earl of
Barrington, Hon. Sir Edward, private secretary to Lord Salisbury, 95
Barrow, Maj.-Gen. Sir Edmund, 221
Basingstoke, 192
Battenberg, Prince Louis of (afterwards Marquess of Milford Haven), 314
Bayuda Steppe, 49, 59, 61
Bazaine, Marshal, 8
Beaconsfield, Earl of, see Disraeli, Benjamin
Beatrice, H.R.H. Princess, 172
Beatty, David (afterwards Earl), 101
Beaverbrook, Lord, 337
Beefsteak Club, 282
Beersheba, 12, 19
Beit Jibrin, 13
Beitzen, Lieut. Cmdr. Kurt, 379
Belgians, Leopold II, King of the, 63
Belgium, 280, 281, 307, 308, 311 ; German advance through, 292-3, 305
Belgrade, 356
Bengal, 197, 234
Bennett, Rev. J., 7
Berber, road to Suakin reopened, 106 ; Kitchener prepares to attack, 118 ; triumphal march through, 122. Mentioned, 42, 43, 47, 48, 54, 55, 56, 61, 101, 106, 108, 109, 112, 116, 119
Berlin, 236, 319 ; Congress of, 23, 26, 142
Bertie, Sir Francis (Viscount Bertie of Thame), 295
Besant, Sir Walter, 12, 16, 17, 29, 37, 38, 40, 41, 43
Beyrout, 16, 18, 19
Biddulph, Maj.-Gen. Sir Robert, succeeds Wolseley as High Commissioner for Cyprus, 28 ; persuades Salisbury to consent to

renewal of Cyprus survey, 29 ; appoints Kitchener Director of Survey for Cyprus, 29 ; forbids Kitchener to go on archaeological expedition, 31 ; refuses Kitchener extension of leave, 33 ; reactions to Kitchener's absence without leave, 34–5. Mentioned, 37
Birdwood, Lieut.-Gen. Sir William (afterwards F.M. Lord), in command of Anzacs in Dardanelles, 322, 324, 327, 346, 358, 360, 361, 363 ; intimacy with Kitchener, 322–3. Mentioned, 191–2, 196, 204, 205, 230, 234, 235, 247, 248, 323, 326, 329–30
Birkenhead, Earl of, see Smith, F. E.
Blackwood's Magazine, Kitchener contributes to, 21, 23
Bloemfontein, 156, 162, 163, 165, 166, 170 ; capture of, 171 ; 191
Bluff, The (New Zealand), 245
Boers, independence granted to, 32 ; Kitchener advocates cruel treatment of, 184–6 ; Kitchener's respect for, 187–8, 190
Boer War, 153–90 ; causes, 154–6 ; hostilities begin, 157 ; Battles of Colenso, Magersfontein, and Stormberg, 157 ; disposition of British forces, 158, 162 ; disposition of Boer forces, 158 ; Battle of Paardeberg, 164–9 (see Paardeberg) ; relief of Ladysmith, 170 ; surrender of Cronje, 170 ; relief of Mafeking, 171 ; capture of Johannesburg and Pretoria, 171 ; Battle of Tweebosch, 173 ; blockhouse system, 177 ; drives and scorched earth policy, 177 ; concentration camps, 178–81 ; losses, 178 ; discussion of terms, 183–4, 188–90 ; peace signed, 190. Mentioned, 196, 215, 216, 291
Bombay, 194, 196, 201, 243
Bonar Law, Andrew, on Dardanelles Committee, 342 ; tries to get Kitchener dismissed, 351, 359 ; blames Kitchener for Dardanelles, 356–7 ; joins War Committee, 362. Mentioned, 303, 336, 339, 362, 373, 380
Bonner, J. H., 378

Boscawen, Lieut.-Col. the Hon. E. E. T., 60
Botha, Louis, 162, 171, 173, 178, 183 ; Kitchener's opinion of, 184, 189, 190, 194
Boulogne, 292
Boy Scouts Association, Kitchener's interest in, 259–60
Braithwaite, Maj.-Gen. Sir Walter, 324
Brebner, W. J. C., 190
Briand, Aristide, 363
Brindisi, 366
Brisbane, 244
British Association for the Advancement of Science, addressed by Kitchener, 22
British East Africa, see Kenya
British East Africa Corporation, 255, 257, 259
British Expeditionary Force, 279, 280, 281, 286, 287, 292, 293–7, 301, 302, 305, 306, 335, 336
British Museum, invitation to Kitchener to take charge of archaeological expedition, 31
Broadwood, Col. R. G., 124
Brodrick, St. John (Earl of Midleton), Secretary of State for India, relations with Kitchener, 174–8, 181, 183, 184–9, 197–8, 212, 214, 216–19, 221, 223, 231–2 ; succeeded by John Morley, 230
Brooke, Rupert, 289
Brooke, Victor, A.D.C. to Kitchener, 204–5, 235
Broome, Viscount, see Kitchener, Lord
Broome, Viscount (nephew), 255
Broome Park, 254, 256, 257, 259, 270, 277, 282, 345, 361, 377–8, 381 ; alterations to, 260, 271, 380
Bryce, Viscount, 180
Bulair Isthmus, 360–1
Bulawayo, 160
Bulgaria, Kitchener visits, 20–1 ; atrocities, 21 ; enters First World War, 356
Buller, Gen. Sir Redvers, V.C., complains about Kitchener, 57 ; sent to succeed Wilson in command desert column, 61 ; bloated incompetence of, 157 ; superseded

K—CC

by Roberts, 157-8. Mentioned, 56, 62, 69
Burger, Schalk, 188, 190
Burnaby, Col. F. G., 60
Butler, Sgt.-Maj., 98
Butler, Sir William, 141
Butros Pasha, Prime Minister of Egypt, 264
Byng, General (afterwards Viscount Byng of Vimy), 358

Cairo, society, 77 ; Kitchener's house in, 95, 270. Mentioned, 35, 39, 40, 42, 56, 147, 196, 252, 254, 271, 274
Calais, 277, 343, 348, 355 ; Conference at, 204, 211
Calcutta, 204, 211
Cambridge, Field Marshal H.R.H. the Duke of, Kitchener rebuked by, 9 ; Kitchener's merits brought to the notice of, 22 ; congratulates Kitchener on Handub exploit, 72 ; appoints Kitchener as Sirdar, 80 ; opinion of Kitchener, 80 ; succeeded by Wolseley, 91 ; backs Kitchener's request for money in River War, 102. Mentioned, 143, 192
Cambridge, Kitchener's honorary degree at, 144
Campbell-Bannerman, Sir Henry, 137 ; denounces Kitchener's methods, 179-80 ; 230, 232
Canada, 231
Canterbury, 254, 257, 259
Canterbury, 254, 257, 259
Canterbury, Archbishop of, see Davidson, Randall
Cape Colony, 155, 156, 157, 171, 183, 184, 185, 187
Cape of Good Hope, 154
Cape Town, 159, 160, 190, 314
Capernaum, 22
Carden, Vice-Admiral Sir Sackville, 322-3, 326-7
Carmel, Mount, 16
Cassel, Sir Ernest, 146
Castle Stewart, 195
Caucasus, 310-11, 343
Cecil, Lord Edward, opinion of Kitchener, 10 ; Kitchener's friendship with, 78 ; A.D.C. to

Kitchener, 95 ; Financial Adviser to Egyptian Government, 267. Mentioned, 99, 100, 101, 142, 197, 277
Chamberlain, Joseph, 155, 180, 194
Champagne, 345, 348
Chantilly, Conferences at, 332, 356
Chanzy, General, 8
Chatham : School of Military Engineering, 9, 11, 144
Chesterfield, Earl of, 77
Chevallier, Rev. John, 1
Chicago, 246
China, 42, 235
Christie, Miss Ella, 205
Churchill, Lord Randolph, 118
Churchill, Sir Winston ; with Khartoum espedition, 118 ; Kitchener's prejudice against, 118, 125 ; at Omdurman, 125, 128 ; First Lord, 277, 280 ; admiration for Kitchener, 283 ; relations with Kitchener, 304, 307, 310 ; ' Dunkirk Circus ', 308 ; Dardanelles strategy, 313, 316-17, 319-21, 323, 326-30 ; Conservatives' distrust of, 339 ; replaced by Balfour in Coalition Government, 340 ; feelings for Kitchener, 340 ; Chancellor of Duchy of Lancaster, 341 ; on Dardanelles Committee, 342 ; vainly begs Kitchener for commission in Dardanelles, 355. Mentioned, 82, 282, 284, 285, 286, 287, 288, 290, 292, 295, 303, 305, 306, 309, 325, 326, 329, 346-7, 348, 358
Cigal, Marcus, 15
Clermont-Ganneau, C., 13
Coalition Government, 301, 334, 339
Cobbold, Thomas, 23
Colenso, 157
Collinson, Lieut.-Col. J., in command 4th Egyptian Brigade at Omdurman, 124, 126
Colombo, 314
Colvile, Lieut.-Gen. Sir Henry, 162 ; at Paardeberg, 164-9
Colville, Commander Hon. S. C. G., R.N., 98-9, 100
Compiègne, 293, 347
Compulsory Service Act, see Conscription

Concentration camps in South Africa, Kitchener's responsibility for, 178-181

Conder, Lieut. Claude, friendship with Kitchener, 7 ; studies Hebrew with Kitchener, 8 ; lent to Palestine Exploration Fund, 12 ; clash with Arabs, 14-16 ; wounded, 15 ; returned to England sick, 17 ; succeeded by Kitchener, 18 ; continues work on map of Palestine, 22 ; breach with Kitchener, 38-9. Mentioned, 11, 13, 20

Congo, R., 143

Connaught, H.R.H. Prince Arthur of, 192

Connaught, H.R.H. the Duke of, 151, 192 ; resigns from Mediterranean Command, 239, 240-2

Conscription, 3 ; industrial, 332 ; major political issue, 352-4 ; Kitchener convinced of necessity for, 354 ; Kitchener's reasons for not advocating, 288-9, 332, 352-4, 377 ; Asquith decides to bring in conscription, 373 ; Compulsory Service Act, 354. Mentioned, 228, 280, 316.

Constantine, King of the Hellenes, 356, 365

Constantinople, 19, 21, 28, 230, 236, 252, 254, 255, 274, 287, 308, 310, 312, 313, 319, 323, 325, 327, 346, 350, 357

Cookson, Sir Charles, 32

Coronation (Edward VII), 67 ; (George V), 257-8, 260

Cowans, Gen. Sir John, 288

Cowper, Countess, 151

Cowper, Earl, 78

Cranborne, Viscountess, see Salisbury, Lady

Cranborne, Viscount, see Salisbury, 4th Marquess of

Creagh, Gen. Sir O'Moore, 242, 243

Crewe, Marquess of, on Dardanelles Committee, 342 ; dispute with Kitchener, 350. Mentioned, 247, 287, 309, 343

Crimean War, 2-3

Cromer, 1st Earl of (Sir Evelyn Baring) ; disagreement with Kitchener's trade policy in Sudan, 71 ; admits wisdom of Kitchener's policy, 73 ; opinion of Kitchener, 74, 75, 78, 80-1, 96, 116 ; lifts ban on trade at Suakin, 75 ; opinion of Grenfell, 75 ; peerage, 80 ; suggests Kitchener should be appointed Sirdar, 80 ; not convinced of wisdom of liberating Sudan, 82 ; opinion of Khedive Abbas Hilmi II, 83 ; serious view of Khedive's behaviour, 87-8 ; supports Kitchener against Khedive, 88-9 ; Kitchener's opinion of, 89, 113 ; Khedive's attitude towards, 89 ; startled by Cabinet's decision to invade Sudan, 90 ; high opinion of Kitchener, 90, 93, 96, 133-4 ; supports Kitchener as C.-in-C. Egyptian Army, 91 ; rejects Kitchener's plea to advance to Khartoum, 106 ; changes Sudan policy, 106 ; warns War Office not to interfere in Sudan, 107 ; acrimonious correspondence with Kitchener, 108-9 ; puts finance before military security, 109 ; attitude to war and estimate of Kitchener, 110 ; considers recapture of Khartoum unjustified, 110 ; fears a soldiers' conspiracy, 111-12 ; opinion of Kitchener and attitude to his resignation, 109-12 ; concern about Kitchener's treatment of civilians, 115 ; gives Kitchener free hand to advance to Khartoum, 116 ; advice requested by Kitchener, 119 ; congratulates Kitchener on victory of the Atbara, 121 ; close supervision detrimental to Kitchener's powers of decision, 123 ; supports Kitchener in affair of the Mahdi's skull, 136 ; frugality, 136 ; terms for government of Sudan rejected by Kitchener, 147 ; wife's illness and death, 147-8 ; assures Kitchener of friendship, 148 ; advice to Kitchener, 148, 272-3 ; critical of Kitchener, 149-51 ; autocratic rule of Egypt, 261 ; views on Egypt, 263-4, 266 ; presides over

Dardanelles inquiry, 309. Mentioned, 42, 53–4, 65, 70, 72, 73, 79, 81, 86, 87, 101, 102, 103, 118, 120, 132, 133, 135, 136, 139, 140, 141, 146, 150, 152, 153, 158, 209, 230, 259, 271

Cromer, Lady, illness and death of, 147–8

Cronje, General, 162, 163, 165–70, 171

Crotta House, 4–5

Curragh, Mutiny at the, 278, 302, 359

Curzon, Lady, 198, 205, illness of, 213, 224

Curzon, Lord (afterwards Marquess), as Viceroy of India, 196–7 ; character of, 197 ; friction with Kitchener, 200, 201, 203 ; opinion of Kitchener, 202 ; quarrel with Kitchener, 204–26 ; term of office (Viceroyalty) extended, 209, 211 ; on leave in England, 212–213 ; ill-health, 213 ; suffers moral defeat by decision of Cabinet about dual control of Indian Army, 218–19 ; resigns, 222 ; on Dardanelles Committee, 342. Mentioned, 152, 173, 176, 194, 198, 200, 203, 227, 230, 231, 243, 258, 301, 352, 353, 367

Cyprus, survey of, 22–9, 34, 36, 37 ; ' key of the East ', 24 ; reorganization of land registry, 30 ; elective self-government and its effects, 30 ; difficult to survey, 30 ; map published, 37 ; proposed cession to Greece, 313–14. Mentioned, 33, 35. Museum, 31, 36

Czar Nicholas II of Russia, invites Kitchener to visit Russia, 376

Daily Mail, 94, 134, 336

Dalmatia, 309

Damascus, 18, 315

Danube, R., Kitchener inspects bridging equipment, 11 ; Germans cross the, 359

Dardanelles, campaign, 286–369 ; inquiry into, 286, 309, 316–18, 324, 329 ; plan of attack on, 316–17, 319, 320, 322 ; bombardment begun, 321 ; enemy forces in, 324 ; allied forces in, 346 ;

naval attack, 326 ; naval attack fails, 328 ; munitions for, 335 ; military landings in, 338, 345–6 ; allied military defeat, 346 ; French plan for, 355–6 ; Suvla, Anzac and Helles evacuated, 369 ; disastrous effect of, on Kitchener's reputation, 369. Mentioned, 287, 308, 309, 312, 315, 323, 325, 338, 339, 341, 344, 347, 348, 355–6, 367, 368. Gallipoli, 101, 123, 288, 308, 313, 316–17, 319, 320, 321, 323, 324–30, 338, 342, 349, 379 ; consequences of allied defeat in, 357–69 ; evacuation of, 369

Dardanelles Committee, 341–3, 355 ; abolished, replaced by War Committee, q.v., 359

Dartmouth, H.M.S., 363

Davidson, Randall, Archbishop of Canterbury, 282

Davies, Gen. Sir Francis, 346, 358

Dawkins, Sir Clinton, 110–11

Dawson, Henry, 8

De Aar, 160

Dead Sea, 38–9

Deakin, Alfred, Prime Minister of Australia, 244

Debbeh, see Ed Debba

De Beers Combine, 157

Defence of the Realm Act, 362

De Kiel's Drift, 162

De La Rey, Jacobus H., 173, 187, 190, 194

Delcassé, Théophile, French Minister, 343

Delhi, 275

Derby, 15th Earl (Lord Stanley), 222, 353, 371

Desborough, Lady, 375

Desborough, Lord (William Grenfell), Kitchener meets, 67 ; impression of Kitchener, 67 ; Kitchener's friendship with, 68 ; death of sons, 375. Mentioned, 171

De Wet, Christian, 162–3, 168–9, 171, 173, 178, 182, 190, 194

Diamond Jubilee, 103

Disraeli, Benjamin (Earl of Beaconsfield), and imperialism, 2, 19 ; comes into power 1874, 12 ; achieves ' peace with honour ' at Congress of Berlin, 23 ; plan for

INDEX

forming protectorate over Asia
Minor, 28 ; fall from power in
1880, 29 ; Suez Canal coup, 31.
Mentioned, 27, 64, 142, 154
Donaldson, Sir Frederick, 378
Dongola, reached by Kitchener, 46 ;
captured, 101 ; effect of expedition
on Britain, 103 ; Kitchener's
harsh rule of, 115. Mentioned,
43, 48, 49, 51, 54, 55, 56, 94, 97,
100, 101, 102, 103
Donop, Sir Stanley von, 334
Dover, 257, 275, 277, 295, 332
Dreyfus, Captain, 355-6
Dublin, Kitchener visits, 22
Duff, Sir Beauchamp, 231, 241, 243
Dufferin, Marquess of, 78, 82
Dulgo, 98
Dundee, 195
Dunedin, 245
Dunkirk, 304, 305, 308
Dunottar Castle, 159
Durban, 157
Dutch East Indies, 186, 244

East London, 160
East Prussia, 298
Ed Debba (Debbeh), 48, 49, 52, 53, 55,
56, 58
Edward VII, King of England, as
Prince of Wales, 66, 144 ;
Coronation, 67 ; Kitchener stays
with, 195 ; requests Kitchener to
accept Mediterranean Command,
241 ; supports Kitchener's claim to
Indian Viceroyalty, 242, 246 ;
Kitchener has audience with, 246 ;
death, 250. Mentioned, 189, 192,
194, 224, 239, 240
Edward (VIII), Prince of Wales, 375
Egeiga, 125, 126
Egypt, conditions in, 31, 64, 77, (in
1890's) 83; conquest of, 30–52 ;
finance, 31, 64, 94, 102–3, 273 ;
Khalifa prepares to invade, 76 ;
views on continued occupation
of, 76 ; G. W. Steevens on, 94 ;
Kitchener ambitious to rule,
230 ; Kitchener revisits, 254–5 ;
Kitchener governs, 259–75 ;
Kitchener tears up constitution,
262–6 ; outstanding success of

Kitchener's economic policy, 262,
266–8 ; Kitchener establishes
Ministry of Agriculture, 271 ;
Turkish suzerainty, 255, 270, 273,
274 ; question of annexing to
Britain, 273 ; British protectorate over, 174 ; danger of Moslem,
rising in, 339. Mentioned, 11, 26,
29, 148, 240, 277, 287, 310, 315,
343, 357, 360, 363, 364, 366, 369,
374, 375, 380
Egyptian Army, mutiny of, 31 ; old
army disbanded, 35 ; new army
formed, 36 ; Kitchener commissioned in, 36 ; laughing-stock of
Europe, 38 ; Kitchener resigns
commission, 67 ; proves itself,
77 ; disgust of, at Kitchener's
appointment as Sirdar, 80 ;
Kitchener prepares army for
battle, 82 ; inspection of by
Khedive, and consequent crisis,
83–9 ; invades Sudan, 89 ; distrusted by Wolseley, 91 ; outbreak of cholera in, 97 ; ' death
march ', 98 ; finance, 94–5, 102,
105, 106, 108 ; unrest in, due to
Kitchener's brutal methods, 153–4.
Mentioned, 94, 201, 209
Egyptian Police, 66 ; corrupt, 79 ;
Kitchener made Inspector-
General of, 79
Elcho, Lady, 142
El Dhoheriyeh, 12
Elections, General, April 1880, 29 ;
June 1885, 65 ; October 1900
(Khaki Election), 173 ; July 1892,
81 ; March 1894, 82 ; December
1905, 197
Ellershaw, Brig.-Gen. W., 378
Elles, Maj.-Gen. Sir Edmund, 201, 203,
208, 211 ; Kitchener's patho-
logical hatred of, 214 ; 215, 216,
217, 218, 221
Elliot, Sir Henry, 16
El Obeid, 41, 132
Elphinstone, Lieut.-Col. K. E., 11
Enchantress (Admiralty yacht), 247
Encounter, H.M.S., 244
England in Egypt (pub. 1893), 82
Entebbe, 255
Entente Cordiale, 143
Eritrea, 90, 115

INDEX

Esher, 2nd Viscount, opinion of Kitchener, 152 ; 170, 227-9, 232, 240, 241, 250, 279, 301, 321, 337, 338, 362, 374
Euphrates, R., 313, 314

Falkenhayn, General von, 302
Fashoda (Kodok), 112, 135, 138-41,143
Fawcett, Millicent, 180
Ferguson, Lieut.-Col. Charles, 137
Festubert, 316, 335, 343
Firket, 96-7, 99, 101
First World War, see Great War
Fisher, Lord, First Sea Lord, views on Cyprus, 314 ; views on Dardanelles, 319-20 ; resignation, 338-9. Mentioned, 287, 306, 340
FitzGerald, Col. Brinsley, 336
FitzGerald, Col. Oswald A. G., A.D.C. to, and intimate friendship with Kitchener, 235, 245 ; personal military secretary to Kitchener, 283 ; drowned, 379. Mentioned, 238, 243, 254, 255, 256, 257, 258, 260, 274, 277, 282, 290, 301, 314, 337, 338, 362, 377, 378
Flanders, 304, 311, 317, 342
Foch, Marshal, 304-5, 347
France, Kitchener's part in Franco-Prussian War of 1870, 8-9 ; interest in Egypt, 31-2, 64 ; imperialist policy of, 32 ; interest in Sudan, 81, 112, 138-41, 143 ; interest in Equatorial Africa, 102 ; Fashoda crisis, 112, 138-41, 143 ; in First World War, 276-381 passim ; Government moves to Bordeaux, 297 ; interest in Asia Minor, 314 ; Anglo-French Agreement, 314 ; Damascus assigned to, 315 ; strain in Anglo-French relations, 343-4 ; desire for unity of command, 344 ; fall of government, 363
Francis Joseph, Emperor of Austria, 11
Franco-Prussian War, 8-9, 290
Freeman, Rev. Allen, 6
Fremantle, 244
French, Field Marshal Sir John (afterwards Earl of Ypres), in command of cavalry division at Paardeberg, 162-3, 164-9 ; C.-in-C. British Expeditionary Force in 1914 War, 280-1, 288, 292-8 ; relations with Kitchener, 300-7 ; strategy of, 309, 311 ; offends Kitchener, 312 ; protests at decision to send troops to Dardanelles, 320-1 ; protests at shortage of munitions, 331, 335-7 ; loss of confidence in, 347-8 ; relieved of command after mishandling of Battle of Loos, 350 ; superseded by Haig, 367, 369, 371. Mentioned, 306, 307, 310, 313, 315, 318, 319, 332, 334-5, 342-3, 344, 372
Frost, Rev. George, 7

Gadkul, 60-1
Galilee, 14, 18, 19, 22 ; Lake, 20
Galliéni, General, 363
Gallipoli, see Dardanelles
Gambetta, Léon, 8, 32
Garstin, Sir William, 83
Gatacre, Maj.-Gen. Sir William, in command British contingent in Sudan, 118 ; Churchill's description of, 118 ; liked by Kitchener, 118 ; advice of, at Atbara, 120 ; at Omdurman, 124, 128 ; defeated at Stormberg, 157 ; Kitchener's harshness to, 171. Mentioned, 119, 120
George, David Lloyd, see Lloyd George, David
George V, King of England (also Prince of Wales and Duke of York), Kitchener's friendship with, 152, 277, 361-2, 377 ; coronation of, 260 ; supports Kitchener in dispute with Sir John French, 337 ; strong support for Kitchener as Secretary of State for War, 341 ; loses faith in Sir John French, 347-8. Mentioned, 192, 274, 282, 283, 361, 362, 367, 372, 376
German East African Company, 69
Germany, and Egypt, 64 ; supports Italy on appeal for help in Sudan, 90 ; influence in Turkey, 254 ; in First World War, 276-381 passim
Gezira Sporting Club, 269
Gibraltar, 159, 247
Girouard, Col. Sir Percy, friendship with Kitchener, 104-5, 171 ;

grants land to Kitchener in Kenya, 256

Gladstone, William Ewart, declares policy in Russo-Turkish War, 19 ; ousts Disraeli in 1880, 29 ; policy in Cyprus, 30 ; loathing of imperialism, 32 ; concedes independence to Boers, 32 ; reluctantly supports Khartoum relief expedition, 47 ; attitude to Gordon, 48 ; unpopularity due to fall of Khartoum, 61 ; condemnation of, by Wolseley, 62 ; declares new policy for Sudan, 63 ; refusal to praise Gordon, 63 ; seeks means of withdrawing from Sudan, 64 ; sees 'divine retribution' for invading Egypt, 64 ; firm stand against Russian activities in Afghanistan, 65 ; decides against further operations in Sudan, 65 ; fall of government of, June 1885, 65 ; Prime Minister for last time, 81 ; retires from office, 82. Mentioned, 21, 41, 103, 111, 122, 154, 283

Godley, Sir Arthur, see Kilbracken, Lord

Gold Coast, 11

Gordon, Maj.-Gen. Charles George, sent to Khartoum, 42 ; Governor-General of Sudan, 42 ; character of, 42 ; attitude to relief expedition, 48 ; high opinion of Kitchener, 48–9 ; sends Stewart out of Khartoum, 55 ; writes 'can hold out 40 days', 59 ; writes 'can hold out a few days', 60 ; death of, 61 ; bitter letter to Kitchener about Gladstone, 62 ; suggests Kitchener as Governor-General, 49, 63 ; effect of death of, on Kitchener, 65 ; popular desire to avenge, 72 ; Kitchener's desire to avenge, 78, 117 ; memorial service for, 132–3 ; inspiration to Kitchener, 270. Mentioned, 19, 43, 46, 47, 48, 49, 54, 56, 62, 65, 70, 111, 120

Gordon, Maj. W. S., 133

Gordon Memorial College, Kitchener appeals for funds for, 144–6 ; Kitchener's lack of interest in,

146 ; foundation stone laid, 148 ; Kitchener revisits, 196

Gorringe, Lieut.-Gen. Sir George, 109

Gorst, Sir Eldon, critical of Kitchener, 106 ; Kitchener's dislike of, 149 ; succeeds Cromer as Consul-General in Egypt, 230 ; illness of, 252, 258–9 ; death of, 260 ; character and policy of, 261–2, 263–4, 268. Mentioned, 148, 237, 252, 255, 270, 271

Graham, Surgeon-Major, 84

Grant, Lieut. S. C. N., 35, 37

Granville, Earl, 40

Greaves, Brig.-Gen. George, 11

Great War, 276 et seq. ; Kitchener's forecast for duration of, 283–4, 375 ; outbreak of, 277–8 ; Battle of Tannenberg, 298 ; Battle of Marne, 298, 303 ; Antwerp surrenders, 304 ; Battle of Ypres (I), 303–4 ; Battle of Neuve Chapelle, 316 ; Battles of Ypres (II) and Festubert, 316 ; bombardment of Dardanelles begun, 321 ; Navy tries to force Dardanelles, 326 ; Army tries to force Dardanelles, 338 ; autumn offensive on Western Front, 350 ; Battle of Loos, 316, 350, 369 ; Battle of Jutland, 376, 379 ; Battle of Somme, 372 ; Haig C.-in-C. B.E.F., 367 ; Robertson C.I.G.S., 367, 369–72 ; evacuation of Dardanelles, 369 ; American intervention in, 375

Greece, change of government in, 323 ; allied landing in, 356 ; neutrality of, 356, 365–6. Mentioned, 156, 313–14

Green, Emma, see Kitchener, Emma

Grenfell, Field Marshal Lord, Sirdar of Egyptian Army, 71 ; estimate of Kitchener, 72 ; sent to defend Suakin with Kitchener, 75 ; Baring's opinion of, 75 ; wins Battle of Toski, 76 ; succeeded by Kitchener as Sirdar, 80 ; in command British Army of Occupation in Egypt, 107 ; meets Kitchener in Cairo, 112 ; Kitchener fears encroachment by, 107, 112, 116

Grenfell, Maj. H. M., 67, 78

Grenfell, Hon. Imogen, 68
Grenfell, Hon. Julian, Kitchener's liking for, 67 ; description of Kitchener, 67–8 ; Kitchener's page at Coronation, 67 ; Kitchener writes to, 171 ; death of, 67, 375
Grenfell, Hon. William (Billy), Kitchener's liking for, 67 ; Kitchener writes to, 171 ; death of, 67, 375
Grenfell, William, see Desborough, Lord
Grey, Sir Edward (afterwards Viscount), views on imperialism, 314 ; on Dardanelles Committee, 342 ; on War Committee, 359. Mentioned, 138, 231, 254, 255, 259, 260, 263, 264, 265, 266, 273, 280, 282, 284, 287, 299, 309, 313, 343, 371
Groves, Sir George, 13
Guest, Hon. Frederick, 305, 336
Gwynne, L. H. G., Bishop of Khartoum, 300

Habibullah, ruler of Afghanistan, 200
Hafir, 100–1
Haifa, 16, 18, 314, 315
Haig, Field Marshal Earl, relationship with Kitchener, 347–8, 372 ; breakdown of relations with Sir John French, 350, 371 ; succeeds French, 367. Mentioned, 337, 352, 373
Haldane, R. B. (afterwards Viscount), faith in Kitchener, 195 ; Kitchener's disapproval of, 233 ; Mediterranean Command proposal, 239–42 ; premature announcement of Kitchener's acceptance and results, 248–50, 252, 253 ; Kitchener's opinions of Territorial Army, 279, 280, controversy over Kitchener's Armies and Territorials, 289–91 ; supports proposed Dardanelles campaign, 309. Mentioned, 258, 262, 282
Hamilton, Lord George, 194, 202, 205, 212
Hamilton, Hubert, 197, 200, 207, 211, 214, 219

Hamilton, Gen. Sir Ian, chief of staff to Kitchener in South Africa, 182 ; at Gallipoli, 288, 323–9, 338–46, 348, 349–50, 355, 356, 357 ; recalled, 358. Mentioned, 203, 206, 304
Hampshire, H.M.S., 258, 378–9
Handub, 71
Hankey, Sir Maurice (afterwards Lord), Secretary of War Council, 309, 320, 347
Hannay, Col. O.C., in command mounted infantry at Paardeberg, 162, 163, 165–8
Harcourt, Lewis (afterwards Viscount), 287
Harcourt, Sir William, 180
Hartington, Marquess of, 47
Harvey, Sir Paul, 267
Hatfield House, 73, 142, 151, 195
Havre, 292, 293, 295
Hebron, 13
Hedjaz, 73
Helles Point, 323, 345–6, 364, 366, 368, 369
Hepworth Dixon, W., 20
Hertzog, General J. M. B., 189–90
Hicks, Colonel, 41
Hicks-Beach, Sir Michael (afterwards Earl St Aldwyn), Chancellor of the Exchequer, grants Kitchener's request for money for River War, 102–3 ; close-fisted, 103 ; praises Kitchener, 103. Mentioned, 102, 111, 115, 190
Hillingdon, Lord, 146
Hindenberg, Field Marshal von, 298
Hobart, 244
Hobhouse, Emily, 180
Howard, Hon. Hubert, 131, 134
Hull, Prof. Edward, 38, 39, 40
Hungary, 156
Hunter, Gen. Sir Archibald, in command Egyptian division at Omdurman, 124, 128, 129, 131. Mentioned, 105, 116, 119, 120, 132
Husein, Sherif of Mecca, 315
Hussein, Sultan of Egypt, 274

Imperial Defence, Committee of, 209, 240, 250 ; Kitchener, says he has been dismissed from, 251–3 ; 279,

283. Kitchener accepts seat on, 254; Committee displaced by War Council, 286
Imperialism, American, 26; British, 2–3, 12, 19, 23–6, 314; French, 32, 314; Russian, 25
India, alarmed at Russian activities in Afghanistan, 64; Kitchener visits (1899), 79; Walter Kitchener recalled from, 95; Kitchener's interest in, 152, 173, 175, 176; frontier problem, 176; danger from Russia, 196; defence, 207–209; Kitchener Commander-in-Chief in, 196–243; Kitchener's *A Note on the Military Policy of India*, 229–30. Mentioned, 42, 151, 152, 196–201, 269, 275, 315, 360, 381
India Councils Act, 247
Indian Army, state of, 196, 198, 199; Kitchener's reforms, 199–201; dual control of, 200, 201, 206, 207, 208, 210, 212, 213, 216, 217, 231; decision of Cabinet about dual control, 218–19, 273; estimate of merits of dual control controversy, 225–6; expedition to Mesopotamia, 287, 313; march on Bagdad, 315
Indian Mutiny, 2, 3, 32, 198
Iraq, *see* Mesopotamia
Ireland, Kitchener's birthplace, 1; conditions in, 1–2; potato famine, 1; Kitchener visits the Curragh, 151; Kitchener visits Northern, 195; drift towards civil war, 227; Kitchener visits Southern, 251; Home Rule, 253; Kitchener's attitude towards, 300–1
Iron Duke, H.M.S., 378
Isis, H.M.S., 159
Islam, in First World War, 315
Ismail (Khedive), *see* Khedive
Ismailia, 35, 39
Italy, and Egypt, 64; occupies Kassala, 90; defeated at Adowa by Abyssinians, 90; appeals to Britain for help in Sudan, 90; evacuation of Kassala, 103, 108; strategic importance of Kassala, 111; war with Turkey, 261; declares war on Austria, 340;

Kitchener visits, 366. Mentioned; 156, 309, 311

Jacobsdal, 162, 164, 170
Jaffa, 21
Jameson, Dr. (afterwards Sir Leander), 156
Japan, war with Russia, 213, 217; Kitchener plans to visit, 235, 240, 242; Kitchener visits, 243–4; Emperor of, 244
Jebel Surgam, 125, 127–9
Jellicoe, Admiral of the Fleet Sir John (afterwards Earl), 378
Jerusalem, 12
Joffre, Marshal, Kitchener reaches private understanding with, 343–345; persuades Kitchener to accept plan for great offensive operation in France, 347–50; offers reinforcements for Dardanelles, 355–6; demands joint Anglo-French General Staff, 358. Mentioned, 281, 293–4, 297, 298, 304, 311, 321, 322, 332, 363
Jordan, R., 12
Junior United Service Club, 81
Jutland, 376, 379

Kababish tribe, 46, 49
Kaiser Wilhelm II, 257, 258, 279
Kassala, held by Italians, 90; possibility of evacuation of, 103; strategic importance of, 108, 111; Cromer undecided about, 109; Kitchener gets funds to move troops to, 112; Kitchener confers with governor of Eritrea about, 115
Kastamanu, 28
Kekewich, R. G., 162
Kelly-Kenny, Lieut.-Gen. Thomas, at Paardeberg, 162–9
Kemal, Mustafa (Ataturk), 345
Kennedy, Lord John, 30
Kenya, 254, 255, 256–7, 258, 282, 378
Keppel, Commander Colin, 124
Kerma, 99
Kerreri, 125, 126, 127, 130
Keyes, Roger (afterwards Admiral Lord), 361, 368
Khalifa Abdullahi, ready to invade Egypt, 76; loyalty of Sudanese to, 94; character of, 94; asks

Abyssinia for help, 102 ; prepares assault on Berber, 112, 116 ; hampered by internal feuds, 119 ; at Omdurman, 124–31 ; brother Yakub killed, 129 ; escape from Omdurman, 132 ; death of, 132, 153. Mentioned, 70, 71, 106, 117, 119, 124, 135, 138, 139, 141, 151, 152

Khartoum (see also Omdurman), siege of, 47–65, 138, 139, 143, 144, 148, 151–3, 158 ; fall of, 61 ; effects of the news, 61 ; Kitchener writes full report on, 65 ; rebuilding of, 148–9 ; Kitchener leaves, for South Africa, 158 ; Kitchener revisits, 196, 255 ; becomes fashionable, 271. Mentioned, 41, 42, 81, 94

Khartoum, Bishop of, see Gwynne, L. H. G.

Khedive, the : 1867–79 Ismail, 32, 35. 1879–92 Tewfiq, makes Kitchener a Pasha, 72 ; mentioned, 83. 1892–1914 Abbas Hilmi II, succeeds his father, 83 ; Cromer's opinion of, 83 ; quarrel with Kitchener, 83–8 ; ultimatum to, 88 ; surrender of, 88–9 ; hatred of Kitchener, 89 ; anti-British feeling affects Anglo-Egyptian relations, 89 ; Kitchener lunches with, 255 ; visits Gorst, 260 ; affection for Gorst, 261 ; character of, 272 ; deliberately humiliated by Kitchener, 272–3 ; George V declines to see, 274 ; deposed, 274. Mentioned, 140, 154, 268, 269, 270, 271, 272

Kilbracken, Lord (Sir Arthur Godley), 218

Kimberley, 155, 157, 160, 162, 163

Kipling, Rudyard, 25, 146

Kirk, Sir James, 69

Kitchener Armies, see Army

Kitchener, Arthur (brother), birth, 5 ; education, 7 ; Kitchener's attitude to, 191–2

Kitchener, Mrs. Emma (stepmother), marriage, 7 ; separation, 23

Kitchener of Khartoum, Field-Marshal Earl (Horatio Herbert) :
Appearance—as child, 5 ; as adult,

8, 9, 11, 13, 26, 67–8, 78, 102, 115, 125, 152, 276 ; beard, 17, 23; moustache, 30, 266
Career :
(1850–64) birth and parentage, 1–3 ; boyhood, 4–5 ; early ambitions, 5 ; education, 6–8.
(1864–7) moved to Switzerland, 7 ; death of mother, 7 ; at school in Switzerland, 7.
(1867) returns to London and crams for Woolwich, 7.
(1868–70) at R.M.A., Woolwich, 8.
(1871–3) takes part in Franco-Prussian War, 8–9 ; goes up in balloon, 9 ; illness, 9 ; returns to England, rebuked, 9 ; commission, and posted to Chatham, 9.
(1873) A.D.C. to Brig.-Gen. Greaves in Austria, 11 ; inspects bridging equipment on Danube, 11 ; posted to mounted troop of R.E. at Aldershot, 11.
(1874) spends leave in Hanover, 11 ; seconded for special duty in Palestine, 11–12 ; archaeological and survey work, 12–13 ; praised for work in Palestine, 13.
(1875) wounded in Safed riot, 14–16 ; returns to England on sick leave, 17 ; spends Christmas in Dinan, 17.
(1876) works in London on Palestine map, 17–18.
(1877) succeeds Conder in command of survey of Palestine, 18 ; completes survey of Galilee, 19 ; rests in Lebanon, 19 ; visits Constantinople, 20 ; attaches himself to Turkish army, 21.
(1878) returns to England, visits Dublin, 22 ; tries to reconcile father and stepmother, 23 ; posted to Cyprus, 22 ; lands in Cyprus, 23 ; views on importance of Cyprus, 24 ; incurs Wolseley's wrath, 26–8.
(1879) posted as Military Vice-Consul at Kastamanu, 28 ; condemns Turkish oppression, but likes Turks, 28.
(1880) appointed Director of

Survey for Cyprus, 28 ; anxious to see active service, 30 ; shares house with Lord John Kennedy and keeps bear-cub, 30.

(1881) fired at by escaped convict at Pissouri, 30 ; perfects horsemanship, 31 ; curator and hon. sec. to Cyprus Museum, 31 ; applies to Wolseley for secondment to South Africa, 31.

(1882) takes sick leave and goes to Alexandria, 33 ; goes disguised on reconnaisance into Egyptian territory, 33 ; overstays leave, 33.

(1883) selected to help train new Egyptian Army, 36 ; Acting Major (Egyptian Army), 36 ; Captain (British Army), 36 ; designs uniform for Egyptian cavalry regiment, 37 ; helps to survey Arabah valley, 38.

(1884) rides 200 miles across desert, 39 ; refused Egyptian medal of 1882 by Wolseley, 34 ; ordered to Sudan for survey work, 39 ; suggests ways of raising Arab force, 40 ; ordered to Berber, but held up at Aswan, 43 ; moves to Korosko, 43 ; moves to Dongola, 46 ; anxious to help Gordon, 47, 56-7 ; reconnoitres routes to Khartoum, 49 ; promoted Brevet Major (British Army), local unpaid rank of Lieut.-Col., 49 ; confidence in ability to relieve Khartoum, 54 ; D.A.A.G. on Khartoum relief expedition, 56 ; special permission to wear Arab headdress, 58 ; formally seconded to expeditionary force, 58 ; public acknowledgement in Press, 58 ; intelligence officer to desert column, 59.

(1885) with Buller as intelligence officer, 61 ; reaches Gadkul and hears news of fall of Khartoum, 61 ; fills in wells on retreat, 62 ; promoted Brevet Lieut.-Col., 62 ; commended by Wolseley, 62 ; sickened by inaction in Sudan, 65 ; organizes chain of desert intelligence posts, 65 ; writes full report on Khartoum, 65 ; resigns

commission in Egyptian Army and returns to England, 67 ; appointed British member of Zanzibar Boundary Commission, 69.

(1886) criticized by German Ambassador for partiality to the French, 69; C.M.G., 70; appointed Governor of East Sudan and Red Sea Littoral, with acting rank as Colonel, 70 ; policy for Sudan, 70-1.

(1887) disagreement with Lord Cromer over ban on trade, 71.

(1888) wounded at Handub, 72 ; made a Pasha, appointed A.D.C. to Queen, promoted to Brevet Colonel, 72 ; returns to Suakin, 72-3 ; returns to England, stays at Hatfield, 73 ; Adjutant-General of Egyptian Army, 73 ; defeats Osman Digna at Suakin, 75.

(1889-92) returns to new house in Cairo, 75 ; in command cavalry at Battle of Toski, 76 ; awarded C.B., 76 ; spends leave in India, 79 ; made temporary Inspector-General of Egyptian Police, 79 ; improves working of police, 79-80.

(1892) appointed Sirdar with rank of Maj.-Gen., 80.

(1894-5) continues to agitate for war, 82-3 ; criticized as unfit for high command, 83 ; quarrel with Khedive, 83-9 ; K.C.M.G., 89 ; self-confidence shaken by Khedive incident, 89 ; Radical press attacks Kitchener, 89-91.

(1896) Cromer and Salisbury support Kitchener, 91 ; Kitchener placed under absolute control of Cromer, 92 ; hampered by need for economy (River War), 94 ; stringent economies, 94-5 ; wins Battle of Firket, 96-7 ; designs *Zafir* class gunboat, 97 ; setbacks : cholera, freak storms, and failure of gunboat, 97-9 ; Battle of Hafir, 100 ; captures Dongola, 101 ; K.C.B., 101 ; promoted Brevet Maj.-Gen., 101 ; arrives in London to see Prime Minister and

Kitchener of Khartoum:
Career (*contd.*):
asks Chancellor for funds, 102 ; lunches with Queen, 102 ; authorized to advance beyond Dongola, 103.
(1897) praised in House by Chancellor, 103 ; starts building Sudan Military Railway, 104 ; moves up to Abu Hamed, 105 ; occupies Berber, 106 ; further plans meet with hostility at home, 106 ; anxious and frustrated, 107 ; acrimonious correspondence with Cromer and Palmer about finance, 108-9 ; tenders resignation, 109 ; near nervous breakdown, 109-11 ; visits Cromer and Grenfell in Cairo, 112 ; fears of being replaced by Grenfell, 107, 112 ; employs brutal methods, 115 ; given free hand by Cromer, 116 ; supreme command of all forces, 116.
(1898) Battle of Atbara, 120-1 ; leave in Cairo, 123 ; begins advance up the Nile, 124 ; Battle of Omdurman, 126-30 ; memorial service for Gordon, 132 ; Mahdi's tomb razed, 133 ; controversy over Mahdi's skull, 133-6 ; in charge of Fashoda expedition, 138-41 ; civic reception in England, 141-2 ; made Governor-General of Sudan, 142 ; stays at Hatfield and Balmoral, 142 ; Freedom of City of London, 142 ; honorary degrees at Cambridge and Edinburgh, 144 ; appeals for funds for Gordon Memorial College, 144-6 ; visits Queen at Windsor, 147 ; Freedom of Cardiff, 147 ; rejects Cromer's conditions for governorship of Sudan, 147 ; leaves England, stays with Cromer in Cairo, 147.
(1899) rough and ready methods in government of Sudan, 148-9 ; policy in Government of Sudan, 149-50 ; denies charges of inhumanity, 136 ; White Paper in his support, 136 ; peerage, thanks of Parliament and money grant,

136-7 ; leave in England, 151-2 ; inquiries about posts in India and South Africa, 152 ; honorary degree at Oxford, 152 ; friendship with Duke of York, 152 ; expedition to hunt down Khalifa, 152 ; appointed Chief of Staff to Lord Roberts in South Africa, 157.
(1900) arrives Cape Town, 159 ; rebuked for changing transport organization, 160 ; Battle of Paardeberg, 164-9 ; succeeds Roberts as C.-in-C. South Africa, 172 ; seeks to become C.-in-C. India, 174, 176 ; refuses War Office appointment, 175 ; organizes blockhouse system in South Africa, 177.
(1901) concentration camps and effects on Kitchener's reputation, 178-81 ; discusses peace terms with Botha, 183-5 ; advocates permanent deportation of all combatant Boers, 185-6.
(1902) further discussion of terms with Boers, 188-90 ; signs peace treaty, 190 ; leaves for England, 190-1 ; O.M., 191-2 ; created viscount and promoted to Brevet rank of General, 191 ; Parliamentary money grant, 191 ; Freedom of Southampton, and of Basingstoke, 192 ; receives thanks of City of London, 195 ; stays with King and Prime Minister, 195 ; leaves for India as C.-in-C., visits Cairo and Khartoum, 196 ; reorganizes Indian Army, 198-201, 233 ; friction with Curzon 200, 201, 203.
(1903) bitter quarrel with Curzon, over dual control, 204-26 ; appeals to Roberts, rebuked by Curzon, 206 ; plans for defence of India, 207, 209 ; brief truce with Curzon, 208 ; riding accident, 209.
(1904) composes new paper condemning dual control, 211 ; asks for full Commission of Inquiry, 212 ; threatens resignation, 213 ; quarrel with Governor of Madras, 214.

(1905) overthrow of Curzon, 219–224 ; success and limitations of new system, 225–6 ; refuses post of C.I.G.S., 228 ; *A Note on the Military Policy of India*, 229–30 ; excellent relations with new Viceroy, 231–2.

(1906) worried by growth of sedition in Indian Army, 233, 236.

(1907) given two years' extension of command, 234 ; G.C.I.E., 236.

(1909) G.C.S.I., 240 ; offered Mediterranean Command, 239–240 ; accepts under pressure, 241 ; promoted Field Marshal, 240 ; hands over India Command, 243 ; arrives Peking on leave, 243 ; great reception in Japan, 243 ; tour of Dutch East Indies, 244.

(1910) tour of Australia, 244 ; report on Australian defence, 244 ; tour of New Zealand, 245 ; arrives in U.S.A., 245 ; cuts short tour and returns to England, 246 ; audience with King about Mediterranean Command, 248 ; passed over for Viceroyalty, 251 ; refuses Mediterranean Command, 251 ; visits Ireland, 251 ; wants Egypt, 252 ; accepts seat on Defence Committee, 254 ; takes shooting holiday in Middle East, 254 ; visits Turkey, Cairo and Khartoum, 254–5 ; in danger of assassination, 255.

(1911) enters into Songhir Estates partnership, 256–7 ; returns to England for Coronation, 257 ; attends House of Lords, 258 ; ruler of Egypt, 259 ; K.P., 260 ; acclaimed in Egypt, 260.

(1911–14) reorganizes Egyptian constitution, 262–6 ; reorganizes Egyptian economy, 262, 265–9 ; bad relations with Khedive, 272.

(1913) receives commemorative medal for Franco-Prussian War, 9 ; assassination attempt, 274.

(1914) plan to annex Egypt, 274 ; leaves Egypt for last time, on leave, 274 ; receives earldom, 275 ; Secretary for War, 277–8 ; attitude to regular army, and to territorials, 279 ; clash over placing of B.E.F., 280–1 ; his effect on War Office, 282 ; pledge to touch no alcohol, 282 ; undertakes to build up new army, mobilize industries, supervise all military strategy, 283 ; out of element in political atmosphere, 284 ; conflicting opinions facing him, 287 ; failure to use or develop general staff, 287 ; appeals for volunteers—the Poster, 288–9 ; 'Kitchener's Armies' policy criticized, 290 ; crosses to France to see Sir John French, 295 ; reports on military situation, 297 ; failure to delegate, 299–300 ; tactlessness with Irish, 300 ; friction in and out of War Council, and between Kitchener and Sir John French, 301–8.

(1915) resists plan to cede Cyprus to Greece, 313 ; conflicting negotiations in Middle East, 315 ; consents to 1915 offensives on Western Front, 316 ; agrees to the Dardanelles naval operation, 315–319 ; agrees to provide troops for Dardanelles, 320 ; undecided whether to send 29th Division to France or Dardanelles, 320–2 ; criticized, 329 ; decides to send troops to Dardanelles, 322–3 ; inadequate orders and information to Constantinople Expeditionary Force, 324–5 ; dispute about munitions supply, 333–7 ; Press campaign against, 335–7, 340 ; campaign defeated by his popularity, 337 ; Royal support and public opinion keep him as Secretary for War in new Coalition Government, 341 ; control of munitions taken from him, 341 ; K.G., 341 ; stresses importance of Gallipoli, 342 ; unable to decide between demands of Dardanelles and Western Front, 343 ; supine attitude alarms colleagues, 343 ; displays bold diplomacy with the French, 343–4 ; sends five more divisions to Dardanelles, 346 ; visits Joffre, 347 ;

Kitchener of Khartoum:
  Career (*contd.*):
    decides to give Western Front priority, 348–9 ; told to provide himself with a General Staff, 350–1 ; Bonar Law and Lloyd George try to oust him over conscription issue, 351 ; Asquith appeals to, and warns him, 353 ; his indecision kills esteem of colleagues, 355, 357 ; refuses to consent to evacuation of Dardanelles, 358 ; Lloyd George's criticisms of, 359–60 ; suggests new landing in Gallipoli, 360 ; leaves for Dardanelles, 361 ; Press rumours of his resignation, 362 ; recommends seizure of Alexandretta, 364 ; visits King of Greece, 365–6 ; recommends partial evacuation of Gallipoli, 366 ; War Committee tries to keep him in the East, 366 ; returns via Italy and Paris, 366–7 ; Asquith rejects his resignation, 367 ; accepts Asquith's conditions, 367 ; accepts Robertson's conditions but again hands in resignation, 370 ; overruled by Asquith, 371 ; relinquishes control of military strategy, 371.
    (1916) maintains army strength against Government opposition, 373–4 ; continued criticism of his War Office administration, 376 ; accepts Czar's invitation to visit Russia, 376 ; successfully vindicates policy to meeting of M.P.s, 376–7 ; visits King, 377 ; sails in H.M.S. *Hampshire* for Archangel, 378 ; drowned, 379.
  Character as a boy, 5–8
  Characteristics :
    Aloofness, 10, 78, 158, 237
    Ambition, 32, 37, 38, 40, 67, 70, 75, 76, 77, 78, 107, 113, 152, 230, 245–52
    Autocratic behaviour, 113, 201, 226, 229, 288, 291–2, 318
    Brusqueness, 113, 133, 183
    Brutality, 81, 114–15, 148–9, 154
    Conscientiousness, 10, 11, 75, 123, 238

  Criticism, sensitiveness to, 150
  Cynicism, 108, 114
  Determination, 38, 123
  Economy, 13, 20, 78–9, 81, 95, 121, 136–7, 178, 332
  Finesse, lack of, 13, 31, 77, 87, 174
  Friendship, 237
  Generosity, 114
  Habits, personal, 78, 113–14, 182, 200, 205, 236–8, 270–1, 282, 290
  High spirits, 13
  Honesty, 239
  Horsemanship, 5, 50
  Humility, 10, 237
  Idleness, 236, 242
  Impulsiveness, 13
  Indecision, 119, 120, 123, 320–2, 329, 343, 355–7, 359, 360, 368–9
  Indifference to others' feelings, 78, 81, 98, 113, 121–2
  Inexperience as a speaker, 143, 216
  Intuition, reliance on, 25
  Lavish tastes, 204–5
  Leadership, 30, 38
  Linguistic ability, 7, 8, 11, 13, 33, 50, 77, 183, 344
  Loneliness, 67, 141
  Moodiness, 110, 113
  Patriotism, 117
  Petulance, 269
  Romance, 66
  Ruthlessness, 121–2, 132, 136, 157–8
  Self-confidence, 78, 113, 147, 283
  Self-discipline, 10, 239
  Shyness, 141
  Superstition, 105, 120
  Tactlessness, 77
  Understanding of foreigners, 74, 77, 78
  Unsociability, 68, 78
  Wit, 269, 270, 271
  Dislikes :
    Ceremonial occasions, 68, 78, 83, 237
    Criticism, 150
    Delegation of authority, 113, 288, 318
    Display of emotion, 10, 114, 239
    Filing systems, 75, 113, 203–4, 223

Photographers, 68
Political intrigue, 351
Public dinners, 68, 78
War Office, 230
Health: early overwork and strain,
7–8 ; illnesses, 9, 13, 234–6 ; eye-
sight permanently impaired, 39,
113, 119 ; wounded, 72 ; indi-
gestion, 113 ; nervous strain and
breakdown, 109–11, 119, 187,
213 ; riding accident, 209–10
Incidental views:
Army, 198, 202, 228, 229
Imperialism, 23–5, 314
Looting, 121, 148, 191
Marriage, 81
Music, 73
Politics, 197, 232, 351
Press, 98, 133
Sport, 8, 195, 238
Women, 37, 66, 77, 194, 246
Opinions of Kitchener, other
people's :
Arthur Balfour, 142
Lord Cromer, 74, 112, 116
Winston Churchill, 125
Lord Curzon, 202, 203
Lord Esher, 152
Sir Francis Grenfell, 72, 77
Julian Grenfell, 67–8
Hubert Hamilton, 214
Frank Maxwell, 183
Lord Minto, 231
Lord Roberts, 170
Lord Salisbury, 72
Osbert Sitwell, 276–7
Sir Frederick Stephenson, 50–1
Lieut.-Col. Taylor, 50
Queen Victoria, 102
Sir Evelyn Wood, 50
Personal relationships :
Hermione Baker, 66
Sir Samuel Baker, 30
Sir Robert Biddulph, 34–5
Sir William Birdwood, 322–3
Lord Edward Cecil, 78
Winston Churchill, 118, 125, 304,
307, 310, 340
Claude Conder, 7–8, 38–9
Lord Cromer, 123, 148
Lord Curzon, 202, 204–26
Sir Clinton Dawkins, 110–11
Lord Desborough, 67–8

Oswald FitzGerald, 235
Sir John French, 163, 300–7, 337–8
King George V, 152, 282, 372
Sir Eldon Gorst, 149
Earl Haig, 347–8, 372
Sir Ian Hamilton, 182, 323
Prof. Edward Hull, 39
Pandeli Ralli, 30, 68
Lord Roberts, 158, 170
Lord Salisbury, 270
Lady Salisbury, 197
Sir Herbert Stewart, 42, 56
R. H. Williams, 9–10
Sir Charles Wilson, 28
Sir Garnet Wolseley, 36, 50, 62
Popularity, 103, 115, 136, 141, 227
Unpopularity, 37, 75–6, 77, 78, 80,
98, 116, 152, 175 ; due to jealousy,
73, 77, 81, 107, 116, 119, 158, 164
Kitchener, Frances (Millie), birth, 1 ;
see also Parker, Mrs.
Kitchener, Mrs Frances Ann, née
Chevallier (mother), birth and
ancestry, 1, 137 ; bad health, 1,
6 ; worried about Herbert's sensitiveness, 5 ; adored by husband
and children, 7 ; death, 7
Kitchener, Francis Elliot (cousin), 6, 7
Kitchener, Henry Chevallier (brother),
1, 129, afterwards 2nd Earl
Kitchener, Lieut.-Col. Henry Horatio
(father), birth and marriage, 1 ;
career, 1, 4 ; stationed India, 1 ;
returns to England on half-pay,
1 ; sells commission and settles in
Ireland, 1 ; love for his family, 2,
7 ; dislike of Ireland, 2 ; frustration, 4 ; foul language of, 4 ;
eccentricities of, 4, 6, 10 ; martinet, 4, 5 ; character, 4 ; habits,
4 ; management of estates and
activities, 4 ; views on education,
6 ; moved to Switzerland, 7 ;
dependence on wife, and wife's
death, 7 ; second marriage, 7 ;
moves to New Zealand, 7 ;
settles in Brittany, 7 ; respect for
son's hobbies, 10–11; opposes
Kitchener, 11 ; separation from
second wife, 23 ; letter to Besant,
37 ; helps with publicity for
Kitchener, 58 ; death of, 58.
Mentioned, 8, 22.

Kitchener, Kawara (half-sister), 7
Kitchener, Toby (nephew), see Broome, Viscount
Kitchener, Walter (brother), birth, 5 ; education, 7 ; Kitchener's favourite brother, 22 ; in India, 79 ; recalled from India and posted to Sudan, 95 ; description of Kitchener at Omdurman, 129, 131 ; in command of expedition to hunt down and kill Khalifa, 152 ; Kitchener asks for, 234 ; wife, 22, 95, 121, 141 ; letters, 22, 23, 95, 121, 129, 131, 141
Kitchener, William (grandfather), 1
Kitchener's Kopje, 169
Klip Drift, 162
Knightsbridge Barracks, 276
Knowsley Hall, 195
Knox, Brig. C. E., 168
Kodok, see Fashoda
Koodoo's Drift, 163
Kordofan, 41, 132
Korosko, 43, 46, 51, 53
Korti, 55, 59, 60, 61, 62, 65
Kruger, President Paul, 154, 155, 156, 172, 191
Krugerism, 153–6, 160–81
Kurow, 245

Ladysmith, 157, 162, 170
Lansdowne, 5th Marquess of, Secretary for War, 107, 111–12, 157 ; succeeded by Brodrick, 157 ; Foreign Secretary, 218, 219 ; on Dardanelles Committee, 342
Larnaca, 36
Layard, Lady, 257
Layard, Sir Henry, 28
Lebanon, 19, 314
Le Cateau, 292
Leggett, Maj. E. H. M., 255, 256, 257, 378
Le Mans, Battle of, 8
Lemnos, 320, 326
Lewis, Lieut.-Col. D. F., in command 3rd Egyptian brigade at Omdurman, 124, 126, 128, 129, 130
Libya, 261
Limassol, 33, 34
Liverpool, Kitchener's speech at, 332
Lloyd George, David (afterwards Earl), compares Kitchener to a revolving lighthouse, 285 ; dispute with Kitchener, 299–300 ; critical of Kitchener, 333–4 ; on Dardanelles Committee, 342 ; tries to get Kitchener dismissed, 351, 359 ; asks Kitchener to give lead on conscription, 352 ; backs French plan for Dardanelles, 356 ; on War Committee, 359 ; criticisms of Kitchener, 359–60, 362–3. Mentioned, 173, 180, 287, 295, 309, 336, 339, 350, 353, 372, 373, 377
Lockhart, Gen. Sir William, 173, 182
Londonderry, Marquess of, 78, 195
Long, Col. C. J., 124
Loos, 316, 350, 352, 369
Lord Nelson, H.M.S., 363, 365
Lorraine, 281, 293
Losses in battle : Tel-el-Kebir, 35 ; El Obeid, 41 ; Toski, 76 ; Firket, 96 ; Hafir, 100 ; Abu Hamed, 105 ; Atbara, 120 ; Omdurman, 131–2 ; Paardeberg, 169 ; Boer War, 178 ; 18–19 December 1914, France, 308 ; (French) at Lorraine, 281 ; Gallipoli, 346 ; Loos, 350
Lucknow, 199
Ludendorff, Gen. von, 298
Luxor, 84
Lyttelton, Lieut.-Col. the Hon. (afterwards General Sir Neville), at Omdurman, 124, 126, 129, 131
Lyttelton, N.Z., 245

Macdonald, Lieut.-Col. Hector, at Omdurman, 124, 126, 128, 129, 130. Mentioned, 105, 167
Macedonia, 356, 357, 358, 363, 365, 368, 371
McKenna, Reginald, Chancellor of the Exchequer, 247, 295, 372 ; on Dardanelles Committee, 342
McMahon, Sir Henry, 315, 363, 364, 366
McMurdo, Maj. A., 254, 255, 256, 257
Macpherson, Sub.-Lieut. R. D., 378
Madagascar, 186, 363
Madras, 214
Mafeking, 157, 160, 178 ; relief of, 171, 172

Magersfontein, 157
Mahdi, and Khartoum, 43, 59 ; dies
    of smallpox, 65 ; tomb, 125, 131 ;
    tomb razed to the ground, 133 ;
    Kitchener plays with skull of,
    133-6, 150
Mahdism, 53-74, 78, 94, 134-5, 153,
    255
Maher Pasha, 83, 88, 89
Mahmoud, Emir, 106, 109, 119, 120 ;
    captured   at   Atbara,   122 ;
    Kitchener's harsh treatment of,
    122
Majuba, Battle of, 32, 154
Malta, 27, 239, 241, 242, 248, 250
Marchand, Major, 138-41, 143
Marker, Maj. R. J., 215, 224
Marlborough, 1st Duke of, Kitchener
    compared with, 77
Marne, Battle of, 298, 303
Marseilles, 277, 326, 363
Martin, Col. R. M., 124
Massawa, 115
Maubeuge, 280, 281, 292
Maxwell, Brig. Gen. Frank, V.C.,
    A.D.C. to Kitchener, 182-3, 187,
    204, 210, 211, 235
Maxwell, Lieut.-Col. J. G. (afterwards
    General Sir John, in command
    2nd Egyptian brigade at Omdur-
    man, 124, 126, 128, 129 ; Military
    Governor of Omdurman, 130.
    Mentioned, 363, 364
Mecca, 315
Mediterranean   Command,   239-42,
    248-50, 253, 254
Mediterranean Fleet, 322-3, 326-7,
    328, 361, 368
Mehemet Ali Pasha, 21
Melbourne, 244
Menelik, Emperor of Abyssinia, de-
    feats Italian army at Adowa, 90 ;
    Khalifa appeals for help to, 102
Merowe, 54, 55, 101, 104, 105
Mesopotamia, 226, 287, 313, 315, 343
Metemma, 59, 60, 62, 106, 119
Methuen, Lord, defeated at Magers-
    fontein, 157 ; in command 1st
    Division at Paardeberg, 162 ;
    defeated at Tweebosch, 178, 183
Metz, surrender of, 8
Meuse, R., 280, 292
Meyer, L. J., 190

Middelburg, 183
Midlothian, 64
Millerand, Alexandre, French War
    Minister, 295, 321, 332, 343, 347,
    355-7
Milner, Sir Alfred (afterwards Vis-
    count), 82, 156, 179, 183, 189,
    190, 258
Minto, Earl of, Viceroy of India, 222,
    230 ;   understands   and   likes
    Kitchener, 231-2 ; Kitchener am-
    bitious to succeed, 237, 240, 241,
    242, 246-50.   Mentioned, 225,
    233, 234, 235, 236, 243
Modder, R., 157, 162-9
Moltke, Gen. von, German Chief of
    Staff, 297, 302
Mombasa, 70, 257
Monro, Sir Charles, replaces Hamilton
    in Dardanelles, 358.   Mentioned,
    360, 361, 362, 363, 368, 369
Montagu-Stuart-Wortley,   Maj.   the
    Hon. E. J., 124
Montenegro, 356
Moreton, Hon. Lady (Janie Ralli),
    68-9
Moreton, Hon. Sir Richard, 68
Morley, John (afterwards Viscount),
    Secretary of State for India, 230 ;
    opinion   of   Kitchener,   232 ;
    Kitchener's dislike of, 232 ; anti-
    military attitude of, 233 ; opposes
    Kitchener's claim to Indian Vice-
    royalty, 243, 246, 258.   Men-
    tioned, 137, 200, 225, 231, 234,
    235, 236, 240, 242, 243, 246,
    258
Morning Post, 125
Mosul, 31
Mottistone, Lord (J. E. B. Seely), 278
Moulton, Lord, 333
Mudir of Dongola, questionable loy-
    alty of, 51, 59 ; K.C.M.G., 59.
    Mentioned, 46, 54, 55, 57, 65
Mudros, 326, 328, 361, 363, 365, 366
Muhoroni, 256
Mukden, 243
Munitions in Great War, lack of, 331-5,
    342 ; increased production, 332-
    333 ; Shells Committee, 333-
    334 ; Munitions of War Com-
    mittee, 334 ; demand for Min-
    istry of, unwisely opposed by

Kitchener, 333, 367 ; established, 334, 341. Mentioned, 370, 377
Murray, Gen. Sir Archibald, 295, 301, 305, 351

Nablus, 13, 20
Nairobi, 256
Nakheila, 119
Namur, 292
Nandi tribe, 256
Napier, N.Z., 245
Naples, 257
Napoleon I, 2, 133
Napoleon III, 8
Natal, 155, 157, 162, 183, 184
Navy, 2-3 ; reliance on, in first World War, 279, 283 ; in Dardanelles campaign, 313, 316, 319, 322, 325-30, 360, 361, 368 (see also Mediterranean Fleet)
Nazareth, 13
Nelson, Admiral Lord, 2
Neuve Chapelle, Battle of, 316, 332, 335, 343
Newspaper correspondents, Kitchener's unwise treatment of, 118, 133-4, 335
New York, 246
New York Herald, 131, 246
New Zealand, Kitchener plans to visit, 242 ; Kitchener tours, 245 ; Kitchener criticizes forces, 245. Mentioned, 247
Nicholas, Grand Duke, 310, 376
Nicholas II, Czar of Russia, see Czar
Nicosia, 26, 30
Nieuport, 305
Nile, R., 40, 41, 42, 43, 49, 53, 55, 60, 61, 62, 70, 76, 81, 95, 96, 97, 99-132, 138, 139, 140, 141, 143, 144, 146, 255, 268, 271
Nile Expedition, 53, 55, 60, 82, 92, 111
Northcliffe, Viscount, The Times controlled by, 278 ; critical of Kitchener, 333 ; launches Press campaign against Kitchener, 334-338, 341
Nubian Desert, 46, 104

Oak, H.M.S., 378
O'Beirne, H. J., 378
Oceanic, 246

Oliver, C. A., 190
Omdurman, 65, 90, 111, 119, 151, 153 ; Battle of, composition of forces, 124 ; Kitchener advises removal of women and children from, 124 ; bombardment of, 125 ; enemy's attack, 126-7 ; second phase, 128-9 ; charge of 21st Lancers, 128 ; Khalifa's ambush, 129 ; third phase, 129-30 ; Kitchener enters city, 130 ; great slaughter of dervishes, 131-2. Mentioned, 134, 138, 141, 147, 227
Orange, R., 157
Orange Free State, 154, 155, 156, 157, 171, 173, 188, 190
Oriental Club, 58
Osman Azrak, 127
Osman Digna, 71, 75
Osman Sheikh-Ed-Din, 127, 130
Ostend, 305
Otago, 245
Oxenden family, 254, 257
Oxford, 144, 152

Paardeberg, Battle of, description of battleground, 164 ; relations of Kitchener with other commanders, 164, 166 ; inadequate reconnaissance, 165 ; Kitchener's tactical plan, 165 ; confusion caused by Kitchener's methods, 166, 167, 168 ; Boer laager surrounded, 166 ; intervention of Boer commandos, 166-7 ; British main attack held, 167, 168 ; intervention of De Wet's column, 168-9 ; British withdrawal, 169 ; losses, 169. Mentioned, 123, 379
Pakistan, 381
Palestine, 11, 26, 270, 287, 315 ; Survey, 12, 13-29, 30 ; cholera in, 16
Palestine Exploration Fund, 11-13, 16, 22, 38, 40
Pall Mall Gazette, attacks Kitchener's Sudan policy, 71
Palmer, Prof. E. H., 39
Palmer, E. N., 12
Palmer, Sir Elwin, critical of Kitchener, 106 ; loathed by Kitchener, 109 ; correspondence about finance, 108-9. Mentioned, 149

Palmer, Gen. Sir William Power, 173, 175, 196, 237

Paris, 274, 277, 294, 295, 297, 298, 355, 362, 371 ; Siege of, 8

Parker, Mrs. (Millie), Kitchener's sister, nurses Kitchener, 72 ; returns with him to Suakin, 73 ; in New Zealand, 245 ; foolishly encourages rumours that Kitchener is not dead, 379

Pease, J. A., President of the Board of Education, 295

Peking, 243

Pendjeh, 64, 65

Persian Gulf, 314

Peshawar, 199

Petra, 39

Petrograd, 306, 310

Phaeton, H.M.S., 326

Philistia, 12

Picot, Georges, 314

Pissouri, 30

Plymouth, 246

Poincare, President Raymond, 304

Poland, 311

Ponsonby family, 4

Poona, 79, 243

Port Arthur, 243

Port Darwin, 244

Port Elizabeth, 160

Port Said, 196

Portland, Duke of, 78, 151

Powis, Earl of, 78

Powis (House), 195, 252

Pretoria, 157, 171, 172, 173, 182, 191

Promotion, limited opportunities for, in Army, 32 ; Kitchener's, *see* Kitchener, Lord

Prussia, East, 298

Prussia, war with France, 290

Punjab, 197, 234

Queen Elizabeth, H.M.S., 316, 327, 338

Quetta, 199, 233

Quseir, 40

Railways : Wadi Halfa to Akasha, 95, 97 ; extended to Sukkot, 97 ; damage by floods, 98 ; financing of, 102, 105 ; Sudan Military Railway, 104, 105 ; locomotives borrowed from Cecil Rhodes, 105 ; gauge, 105 ; extended to Fort Atbara, 123 ; Kitchener's plans for strategic railways, 200; rejected by Liberal Government, 232–3 ; Kitchener joins Board of London, Chatham and Dover Railway, 259

Ralli, Janie, *see* Moreton, Lady

Ralli, Pandeli, intimate friendship with Kitchener, 30, 68 ; his house used as Kitchener's social headquarters in London, 68, 142, 192, 246, 276. Mentioned, 160, 194, 196

Ramdam, 162

Ramleh, 270

Rand Goldfields, 190

Ras-el-Hudi, 119

Rawlinson, Gen. Sir Henry (afterwards Lord), 304

Redmond, John, 300

Redmond, William, 300

Red Sea, 38, 42, 43, 51, 63, 70, 72

Regiments, in order of appearance : 13th Light Dragoons, 1 ; 9th Foot, 1 ; 29th Foot, 1 ; Royal Engineers, 11 ; Royal Scots, 30 ; 19th Hussars, 38, 50 ; 11th Hussars, 42 ; Coldstream Guards, 60 ; Royal Fusiliers, 105 ; 21st Lancers, 118, 128, 261 ; 1st Lincolns, 130 ; Cameron Highlanders, 138 ; Kitchener's Horse, 169 ; 9th Lancers, 196 ; (Indian) Guides, 198 ; 18th Bengal Lancers, 235 ; Household Cavalry, 276 ; Grenadier Guards, 375

Reitz, F. W., 190

Renshaw, Arthur, 230, 232, 243, 259, 260

Repington, Col. C. à C., Military Correspondent of *The Times*, 335–8

Revelstoke, Lord, 146

Rhine, R., 303

Rhodes, Cecil, 105, 155, 156, 157, 162

Rhodesia, 156

Riaz Pasha, Prime Minister of Egypt, 88

Riet, R., 162

River War, the, finance of, 94–5, 102, 105, 108–10, 112, 117, 121, 136 ; psychological effect of cholera and freak storms, 97–8 ; Kitchener

crosses Nile, 100 ; Berber occupied, 106 ; change of attitude
because of finance, 106 ; Khalifa's
threat to Berber, 117 ; Kitchener
prepares to advance, 117. Battles :
Firket, 96–7 ; Hafir, 100 ; Dongola, 101 ; Abu Hamed, 105 ;
Atbara, 120–1 ; Omdurman
(q.v.), 124–30. Mentioned, 82,
92, 94–117
Robeck, Vice-Admiral Sir John de,
326–8, 361, 363, 368
Roberts, Field Marshal Earl, succeeds
Sir Redvers Buller in South
Africa, 157, 159 ; death of son,
157–8 ; high opinion of Kitchener,
170 ; succeeds Wolseley as C.-in-
C. at Horse Guards, 172 ; receives
thanks of City of London, 195 ;
in favour of conscription, 280.
Mentioned, 137, 142, 151–2, 160,
162, 164, 166, 169, 171, 175, 177,
178, 180, 183, 185, 187, 191, 192,
203, 206, 207, 209, 212, 218, 219,
225, 229, 237
Robertson, L. S., 378
Robertson, Field Marshal Sir William,
C.I.G.S., 367 ; delicate relations
with Kitchener, 369–72. Men-
tioned, 287, 288, 305, 331, 358,
374, 376–7
Rodd, Sir Rennel (afterwards Lord
Rennel), 367
Rome, 254, 366
Rosebery, 5th Earl of, supports
Kitchener in Khedive dispute, 89 ;
Kitchener stays with, 144. Men-
tioned, 69, 83, 88, 143, 229
Rothschild, Lord, 146, 196
Royal College of Surgeons, 133, 134,
135
Rumania, 311, 313
Runciman, Walter (afterwards Vis-
count), President of the Board of
Trade, 304, 373
Rundle, Gen. Sir Leslie, jealousy of
Kitchener, 53 ; threatens resigna-
tion, 118. Mentioned, 43, 82, 86,
95, 113
Rushdi Bey, Colonel, 17
Russia, war with Turkey, 18–19, 21 ;
interest in Egypt, 64 ; interest in
Afghanistan, 64, 196, 200, 209 ;

war with Japan, 213 ; crisis with
Britain, 217 ; requests British
munitions, 287 ; in danger of
collapse, 348 ; Kitchener invited
to visit, 376. Mentioned, 42, 143,
232, 235, 294, 298, 306, 307,
310–11, 314, 315, 321, 323, 324,
347, 350, 376, 379
Russo-Japanese War, 213, 217 ;
Kitchener tours battlefields of, 243

Safed, 14, 18, 39 ; riot, 15–17
St. Helena, 133
St. Paul's Cathedral, memorial chapel
to Kitchener, 381
St. Petersburg, 196
Saleh, Sheikh of the Kababish, 46, 49
Salisbury, 3rd Marquess of, Kitchener
stays with, 73, 142, 151, 195 ; re-
commends Kitchener for appointment as Sirdar, 80 ; ousted by
Gladstone, 1892, 81 ; back in
office, 82 ; supports Kitchener as
Sirdar, 91 ; personal control of
Sudan campaign, 95 ; supports
Cromer's Sudan policy, 107 ;
alarmed at Kitchener's depression,
111 ; congratulates Kitchener on
victory at Atbara, 121 ; speech
in praise of Kitchener, 143 ; views
on centralization, 147 ; succeeded
by Balfour, 195 ; death of, 197 ;
Kitchener's warm feeling for, 270.
Mentioned, 23, 27, 28, 70, 75, 76,
78, 94, 96, 100, 101, 102, 103,
112, 116, 118, 119, 120, 123, 133,
136, 137, 141, 142, 144, 146, 149,
150, 151, 153, 157, 173
Salisbury, 4th Marquess of (Viscount
Cranborne), invited to stay with
Kitchener at Cairo, 76 ; succeeds to title, 197. Mentioned,
152, 153, 207
Salisbury, Marchioness of (Lady Cranborne), wife of 4th Marquess,
confidante of Kitchener and channel of unofficial communication
with Government, 197 ; correspondence, 170, 171, 174, 175, 198,
200, 202, 203, 206, 207, 208, 209,
210, 211, 212, 214, 215, 216, 219,
220, 221, 222, 223, 224, 225, 228,
231, 232, 233, 235, 236, 242, 244,

252, 253, 260, 272, 274, 277.
  Mentioned, 76, 152, 153, 258
Salonica, 309, 356, 357, 358, 359, 360,
  365, 366, 368, 369, 371, 372
Sanders, Liman von, 345
Sanderson, Sir Thomas (afterwards
  Lord), 111
Sandringham, 144
San Francisco, 245
Sarrail, General, 355-6, 365
Savill, Capt. H. J., R.N., 378
Sayol, 124
Scapa Flow, 378, 379
Schleswig-Holstein, 319
Schleswig-Holstein, Prince Christian
  of, 141
Schlieffen, Gen. von, previously Ger-
  man Chief of Staff, 297
Scott, Maj.-Gen., 225
Scouts, see Boy Scouts Association
Sedan, Battle of, 8
Seely, J. E. B., see Mottistone, Lord
Seine, R., 293
Selborne, Earl of, 342
Serbia, 275, 309, 313, 315, 356, 359, 360
Seymour, Admiral Sir Beauchamp
  (Lord Alcester), 33-4
Shanghai, 243
Sharpe, Mrs., 5
Shendi, 49
Simla, 204, 205, 209, 224, 234, 238, 243
Simon, Sir John (afterwards Viscount),
  354
Sinai, Mt., 39
Singapore, 235
Sitwell, Sir Osbert, 276-7
Slatin, Gen. Sir Rudolph, Pasha,
  269-70
Smith, F. E., 362
Smith, Hugh Colne, 146
Smith-Dorrien, Gen. Sir Horace, 167,
  168, 216, 225
Smuts, Gen. Jan Christian, 173, 189,
  190, 314
Smyrna, 310
Sofia, 20, 21
Solomon, Sir Richard, 189
Somme, R., 372
Songhor Estates, Kitchener' sacquisi-
  tion of, 256-8 ; 378
South-African War, see Boer War
Spion Kop, 162
Spring-Rice, Sir Cecil, 196

Squier, Col. G. O., American Military
  Attaché, 375
Stamfordham, Lord, Private Secretary
  to King George V, 337, 341
Stanford, Edward, 37
Stanley, Eddy, see Lord Derby
Stedman, Sir Edward, 219
Steevens, G. W., With Kitchener to
  Khartoum (1899), 94 ; Kitchener's
  liking for, 134
Stephenson, Sir Frederick, 47 ; opinion
  of Kitchener, 50-1
Stephenson, T. E., 167
Stewart, Brig.-Gen. Sir Herbert, com-
  plains about Kitchener, 57 ; in
  command desert column in relief
  of Khartoum, 59 ; victory at
  Abu Klea, 60 ; death of, 60.
  Mentioned, 57, 62
Stewart, Lieut.-Col. Herbert, with
  Gordon to Khartoum, 42 ; close
  friendship with Kitchener, 42 ;
  murdered 55-6 ; Kitchener's
  opinion of, 56. Mentioned, 47,
  48, 68
Steyn, Marcus, President of Orange
  Free State, 171, 173, 188, 190
Stopford, Gen. the Hon. Sir Frederick,
  supine incompetence of, 346
Stormberg, 157
Suakin, 42, 43, 61, 63, 70, 71, 73, 106,
  108, 109, 112, 255 ; siege, 75
Sudan, conditions in, 39, 41 ; instructions to evacuate, 42 ; Gladstone's
  policy for, 63 ; Kitchener's views
  on, 63-4 ; rumour that Gladstone
  would withdraw from, 64 ; growing public demand for re-conquest of, 76 ; Kitchener's desire
  to re-conquer, 78 ; setback caused
  by change of government, 81 ;
  France's interests in, 81 ; arguments for and against invasion of,
  82 ; British Cabinet orders invasion to start, 89 ; Italian interests in, 90 ; war started by Britain
  as deliberate act of policy, 92 ;
  war, 94-117 (see River War) ;
  Sudan's fierce nationalist resistance, 94 ; enemy morale higher
  than that of Egyptian Army, 94 ;
  Kitchener's rule of, 147-59 ;
  Anglo-Egyptian condominium

INDEX

over, 148 ; unrest in army, 150–1 ;
mutiny in army, 153–4 ; hardship
caused by Kitchener's trade policy,
151 ; Kitchener's hope for creation of Viceroyalty of Sudan and
Egypt, 275. Mentioned, 43, 59,
62, 65, 67, 70, 80, 139, 143, 174,
196, 209, 231, 253, 254, 255, 273,
288, 375, 380
Suez, 39 ; Canal, 31, 264, 287, 310,
364
Suffragette Movement, 227
Sukkot, 97
Suvla Bay, 346–7, 356, 364, 366, 368,
369
Sydney, 244
Sykes, Sir Mark, 314–15
Syria, 17, 24, 287, 309–10, 314,
364

Tahiti, 245
Tannenberg, 298
Taplow Court, 67
Tatar Bazardjik, 21
Taylor, Lieut.-Col., 38, 50
Teck, Prince Adolphus of (afterwards
Marquess of Cambridge), 141
Teck, Prince Francis of, 141
Tel-abu-Hareirah, 39
Tel-el-Kebir, Battle of, 35
Temple Moore, Noel, 17
Tennant, H. J., Under-secretary for
War, 340, 376
Territorial Army, Kitchener's con-
tempt for, 233, 253, 279, 289–91 ;
formation of, 279
Thursday Island, 244
Tibet, 197, 220
Times, The, 58, 89, 118, 131, 134, 142,
146, 156, 170, 223, 242, 248, 277,
335–7
Tokyo, 243
Toski, Battle of, 76
Trade Unions, production of muni-
tions hampered by, 332 ;
Kitchener's attitude to, 373
Transvaal, 154, 171, 173, 188, 189,
190 ; gold-mining, 155
Tucker, Gen. Charles, 162, 170
Tudway, Maj. R. J., 124
Tugela, R., 157
Tullock, Lieut.-Col. A. B., 33
Tunisia, 32

Turkey, Sultan of, 28, 35, 270, 274, 315
Turkey, war with Russia, 18–19, 21 ;
influence in Sudan, 46 ; Hedjaz
tribes urged to rise against, 73 ;
Kitchener's liking for Turks, 230 ;
conditions in, 254 ; war with
Italy, 261 ; suzerainty over Egypt,
255, 270, 273 ; war with England,
274. Mentioned, 14, 23, 26, 28,
309, 328, 343, 345, 364
Turkish Army, Kitchener attaches
himself to, 21 ; mentioned, 66,
324, 346
Turkish Empire, 31, 255
Tweebosch, 173, 187
Tyrwhitt Drake, Charles, 12

Uganda, 254, 255
Ulster, 300
U.S.A., see America
Unity, H.M.S., 378

Vaal, 191
Vaal Kranz, 162
Vendutie Drift, 163, 164
Venice, 254, 257
Venizelos, Eleutherios, Prime Minister
of Greece, 356, 365
Verdun, 372
Vereeniging, Peace Conference at,
189–90
Viceroy of India (see Curzon, Har-
dinge, and Minto), Kitchener
ambitious for post, 230, 241, 242,
246–50, 277
Victor, H.M.S., 378
Victor Emmanuel, King of Italy, 366
Victoria, Queen of England, protests
against Gladstone's decision to do
nothing in Sudan, 65 ; congratulates Kitchener on Handub
exploit, 72 ; Kitchener lunches
with, 102 ; description of
Kitchener, 102, 142 ; Diamond
Jubilee of, 103 ; congratulates
Kitchener on victory at Atbara,
121 ; moved by account of
Gordon's memorial service, 133 ;
shocked by Kitchener's treatment
of Mahdi's remains, 133 ; correspondence about Mahdi's skull,
134–5 ; congratulates Kitchener
on Mansion House speech, 143 ;

408

death of, 172. Mentioned, 19, 82, 94, 132, 156, 175
Vienna, 254
Viviani, René, Prime Minister of France, 295, 343
Vredefort, 172

Wad Bishara, Emir, 99–100, 101
Wad el Negumi, Emir, 76
Wad Hamed, 124
Wadi Halfa, 56, 59, 76, 83, 84, 87, 88, 95, 99, 104, 105, 113, 115, 136
Wales, Prince of, see Edward VII, Edward VIII, and George V
Walmer Castle, 307
Walter, John, of The Times, 118
Wantage, Lady, 283
War Committee, 359, 362, 364, 366, 369, 374
War Council, 286, 307, 309, 316, 317, 318, 319, 320, 321, 322, 370 ; re-named Dardanelles Committee q.v., 341
Ward, Sir Joseph, Prime Minister of New Zealand, 245
Waterford, Marchioness of, 82
Waterford, Marquess of, 78
Wauchope, Lieut.-Col. A. G., 124, 126, 128, 129, 130
Welbeck House, 195, 252
Wellington, Duke of, 228, 276
Wellington, N.Z., 245
Wemyss, Sir Rosslyn (Lord Wester-Wemyss), 361, 368, 369
West Point, 246
Western Morning News, 58
White, Gen. Sir George, 157
Whittingehame, 195
Williams, Col. R. H., Kitchener's friendship with, 9–11 ; High Churchmanship of, 10–11
Wilson, Admiral of the Fleet Sir Arthur, 319
Wilson, Col. Sir Charles, Consul-General in Anatolia, 28 ; praises Kitchener, 22 ; started Palestine survey, 28 ; posts Kitchener as Military Vice-Consul at Kastamanu, 28 ; suggests Kitchener for survey of Arabah valley, 38 ; in command intelligence branch of Nile expedition, 56 ; loyalty to Kitchener, 57 ; blamed for

bad transport arrangements, 59 ; in command desert column in relief expedition, 60 ; not used to action, 60 ; fatal indecision, 60 ; military opinion unanimously condemns, 60 ; reaches Khartoum, 60 ; reputation partially redeemed by skilful withdrawal, 61 ; succeeded by Buller in command of desert column, 61 ; bitterness of, 62. Mentioned, 35, 40, 59, 65
Wilson, Field Marshal Sir Henry, dislike of Kitchener, 302–3, 305, 332
Windsor Castle, 102, 144, 147, 195
Wingate, Gen. Sir Reginald, makes summary of quarrel between Khedive and Kitchener, 83–8 ; at Omdurman, 131 ; hunts down Khalifa, 153 ; Governor-General of Sudan, 153, 159. Mentioned, 81, 82, 83, 101, 102, 112, 116, 138, 147, 148, 252, 255
With Kitchener to Khartoum, G. W. Steevens (1899), 94
Witwatersrand, 155
Wodehouse, Col. Josceline, 80, 85
Wolfe-Murray, Sir James, 288, 317–18, 324, 340, 351
Wolseley, Viscount (Sir Garnet), clash with Kitchener over Cyprus survey, 26–8 ; accepts command in South Africa, 28 ; refuses Kitchener Egyptian medal of 1882, 34 ; goes to Egypt to restore order, 35 ; peerage and money grant for victory at Tel-el-Kebir, 36 ; Adjutant-General at War Office, 36, 70 ; views Kitchener with disfavour, 36–7 ; in command of Nile expedition, 47–8 ; warms to Kitchener, 50, 62 ; plan for relief of Khartoum, 59 ; bitterness about retreat from Sudan, 62 ; condemnation of Gladstone, 62 ; asks Kitchener to write full report on fall of Khartoum, 65 ; resumes post as Adjutant-General, 70 ; backs Kitchener's Sudan policy, 71 ; succeeds Duke of Cambridge as C.-in-C. British Army, 91 ; no faith in Egyptian Army, 91 ;

fears Kitchener is too headstrong, 91–2 ; supports Kitchener in River War dispute, 106–7 ; urges advance to Khartoum, 112 ; congratulates Kitchener on victory at Atbara, 122. Mentioned 11, 53, 56, 58, 60, 62, 65, 67, 70, 142

Wood, F.-M. Sir Evelyn, V.C., first Sirdar of Egyptian Army, 36, 66 ; opinion of Kitchener, 50 ; Chief of Staff to Wolseley, 62 ; overrules Kitchener on subject of Winston Churchill, 118. Mentioned, 38, 39, 43, 46, 49, 53, 55, 57, 107, 142

Woolwich : Royal Military Academy, 7–8, 144

World War I, see Great War

World War II, 286

Wyndham, George, 141

Wynyard, 195

Yakub, brother of Khalifa, 129

York, Duke of, see George V

Yosemite Valley, 246

Zafir (gunboat), 97–101

Zagazig, 33

Zanzibar Boundary Commission, 69, 70

Zeebrugge, 305

Zulus, 154